THE COLLECTED WORKS
OF ABBOT VONIER

THIS first volume comprises the following
books in the revised edition:

THE CHRISTIAN MIND
THE PERSONALITY OF CHRIST
THE VICTORY OF CHRIST
THE DIVINE MOTHERHOOD

THE COLLECTED WORKS

OF

ABBOT VONIER

Volume One

THE INCARNATION AND REDEMPTION

With a Foreword by

THE RIGHT REV. DOM BRUNO FEHRENBACHER, O.S.B.
ABBOT OF BUCKFAST

THE NEWMAN PRESS
WESTMINSTER, MARYLAND

PRINTED AND MADE IN GREAT BRITAIN BY
FLETCHER AND SON LTD NORWICH AND
THE LEIGHTON-STRAKER BOOKBINDING CO LTD LONDON

FOREWORD

BUCKFAST has become one of the most familiar place names in this country, its fame has even spread abroad, and inseparably linked with it is the name of Abbot Vonier, who is undoubtedly best known as the restorer of its Abbey Church, beneath whose sanctuary floor lie buried his mortal remains. The great building is a glorious monument to his memory, but it is not his only legacy to posterity. As a distinguished layman aptly expressed it: 'pari passu with the aedificatio of the Abbey there went forward another edifying. It was the upbuilding of a temple "not made with hands", wherein the loveliness was not of marble and mosaic, of carven wood and painted glass, but of souls attuned by this true Father to the will of God and vibrant even in this life with His glory.' No doubt the Editor of the Tablet, Mr Ernest Oldmeadow, then paying tribute to a deceased friend, had chiefly in mind the Community of monks whom the Abbot had governed so wisely during the thirty-two years past; but he also wished to include the many men and women outside the cloister who had profited by his spiritual instruction, whether as hearers of his spoken word or readers of his many books. The remarkable career of Dom Anscar Vonier was indeed many-sided: any one of its aspects—as Abbot, administrator, builder, writer, preacher, priest or monk—would need one to take account of all the others if it were to be fairly appraised. An adequate life-story still remains to be written, but the few biographical notes which follow will enable this literary monument—the collection of his principal writings—to be seen in due proportion to his other activities.

Martin Vonier was born on the feast of his patron-saint, November 11, 1875, at Ringschnait in the former Kingdom of Württemberg, South Germany. His parents were Theodulf and Agatha Vonier, both from families that for centuries had known no other faith than that of the Holy Catholic Church. The family shortly afterwards moved to Rissegg, another village in the valley of the Riss, a tributary of the great Danube. Here young Vonier spent his early boyhood, and it was from the curate of its parish church that he first learned of the recent foundation by an exiled community of French Benedictines of a monastery at Buckfast, on the actual site of an ancient Abbey in the valley of the Dart.

In September 1888, being then thirteen years old, Martin and six other lads went to the College of the Holy Ghost Fathers at Beauvais; but he had been there less than a year when with two companions he entered the alumnate at Buckfast to continue his study of the humanities. Even at this early stage he showed signs of unusual proficiency, so that during his fourth year he was allowed to read philosophy with some of the junior monks. It was at this time too that he developed that passionate love of scriptural studies which never left him. On May 12, 1893, he was clothed with the holy habit and given the religious name of Anscar. His year of canonical noviciate being ended, he made his profession of simple (then perpetual) vows on the feast of Our Lady's Visitation, 1894. These were confirmed on July 11, 1897, by his making solemn vows; and on December 17, 1898, being just turned twenty-three, he was ordained to the sacred Priesthood.

Shortly after his Ordination Father Anscar was sent to Rome to study for a degree in philosophy. His scholastic career at the Benedictine College of Sant' Anselmo was so brilliant that in one year he had attained his doctorate. The thesis which gained for him the well-merited diploma was characteristic of the temper of his searching mind; it dealt with the problem of *The Infinite*. In 1900 the young priest was back in his own monastery, where he successively held the offices of Master of the Alumnate and Procurator. At that time Buckfast was not yet an Abbey: it was only in 1902 that from being a Priory dependent upon the Mother-house of La Pierre-qui-Vire it was raised to an independent status under its first Abbot, Dom Boniface Natter. It was he who conceived a plan for the restoration of the Abbey Church, whose ancient foundations were accordingly laid bare and strengthened, while he sent away Brother Peter to learn the mason's craft. In the meantime Fr. Anscar was fulfilling his appointed tasks; but the impression he had made upon the higher Superiors in Rome had not been forgotten, and in October, 1905, he was recalled to the College on the Aventine Hill to join the staff as professor of philosophy.

At the end of his first year of teaching Abbot Natter requested

Fr. Anscar to meet him in Spain and accompany him on a canonical visitation of one of our monasteries in South America. Accordingly the two travellers met in Barcelona on August 2, 1906, and on the following day they embarked on that ill-fated vessel, an Italian steamship—the *Sirio*. Early in the morning of the 4th the ship was well under way. In the glorious sunshine all was a picture of peace, but tragedy was waiting for them. Between two and three in the afternoon as they were passing between the small group of Hormigas Islands eighteen miles east of Cartagena the ship struck a rock and very quickly foundered. Nearly three hundred people lost their lives in the wreck, and Dom Boniface Natter was among them. Providence was kind to Fr. Anscar who, with many others, was rescued by a Spanish boat—the *Joven Miguel*; but he had not the consolation of discovering the body of his beloved Abbot among those recovered from the sea.

On September 14 the bereaved Community at Buckfast voted for a successor to their lost Father; the result of the election was that his companion and survivor was chosen to be their second Abbot; and on October 18, 1906, Dom Anscar Vonier was solemnly blessed and enthroned by the Bishop of Plymouth, Dr. Graham. He was not yet thirty-one, and actually the youngest Abbot in the Order; yet all were confident that the work begun by the first Abbot of Buckfast would be worthily carried on by his successor; the mantle of Elias had fallen on the shoulders of Eliseus. These high expectations were not long left unfulfilled, for the new Abbot had held the reins of office only a few days when he announced his intention of starting to rebuild the Abbey Church immediately. Before the close of the year the first cart-load of stone was brought through the gates, and soon benefactors were coming forward to add their generous gifts or promises of future help. On July 2, 1907, the foundation stone was solemnly laid by Bishop Graham.

After this came the years of comparative obscurity, and the monks had to toil with little else besides high ideals to support their labour of love. Before another decade had passed the Great War had broken out, and this brought further difficulties and anxieties. Had it not been for the prudence and loyalty of their head, the very existence as a community of a body of men made the butt of misguided hostility might have speedily come to an end. But the periodical alarms of war-time conditions only became further evidence of the merciful Providence blessing and guiding Abbot Anscar in his rule. After the war came a period of renewed interest and support; the work of restoration made unimpeded progress, and in 1922 the church was far enough advanced to be opened for public worship. The solemn blessing was performed on August 2 by the Bishop of Plymouth, Dr Keily, who on the following morning sang Pontifical High Mass in the presence of H. E. Cardinal Bourne and many other members of the English Hierarchy. Since that inauguration of the new church Buckfast has been thrust into the light of unavoidable publicity. An ever-increasing influx of visitors has added its quota of encouragement to the support of old friends. In consequence not only the extension and completion of the building, but also its worthy furnishing, has been made easier. Some of the treasures which now adorn the Abbey, such as the 'Golden Altar', were actually intended as gifts in honour of Dom Anscar's Silver Jubilee of Abbacy in 1931. But the crowning of his life's work undoubtedly came in 1932, when on August 25 the church was consecrated by the late Dr Barrett, Bishop of Plymouth, in the presence of H. E. Cardinal Bourne acting as Legate of Pope Pius XI. It was on that occasion that His Holiness conferred the honour of the use of the *Cappa magna* upon Abbot Vonier, in recognition of his signal services to the Church.

During the few remaining years of his life the Abbot continued to superintend the completion of the building and its embellishment. Added to his administrative duties was the increasing burden of public engagements—retreats, sermons, lectures—in England and on the Continent. It is amazing how he also found time for an extensive correspondence and the writing of his books, and of course he never neglected the spiritual guidance of his own monastic family or the instruction of the faithful layfolk who lived around or visited Buckfast. Besides his regular conferences to the Community in the Chapter Room, it was his custom to occupy the pulpit in the Abbey Church almost every Sunday evening when he was at home. It is no wonder then that in his later fifties his health was obviously declining, for he seldom gave himself enough rest. Early in November, 1938, he left Buckfast to fulfil two or three preaching engagements in the North and London; then he crossed over to France where he had two retreats, and afterwards continued his journey to Rome where he read a paper on Saint Augustine of Canterbury before the great Missionary Conference then taking place. On his return journey he caught a chill, and arrived home on December 6 a very sick man. As he approached the Abbey on that day he saw for the first time its beautiful completed tower at last unencumbered of scaffolding. On Saint Thomas's Day he insisted on presiding at the solemn profession of one of the young monks, but the strain of that long function proved too much, and the next day he collapsed. He spent the next three days in bed, although no immediate danger was feared. He deeply regretted being unable to take an active part in the Christmas Liturgy. Early on the morning of Saint Stephen's Day he received Holy Communion, and some two hours later it was found that he had passed away peacefully in the Lord. The cause of his death was a coronary thrombosis. Thus went to his reward a great monk and churchman. The funeral obsequies took place four days later in the presence of many eminent ecclesiastics, clergy, religious, and a large concourse of the laity. As was fitting, the Abbot's body was laid to rest beneath the floor of the sanctuary which he had raised and adorned so magnificently.

Such is the outline of Abbot Vonier's sixty-three years. His was a life unselfishly dedicated to the service of God and his fellow-men. It is hoped that our brief sketch will enable the reader to see his writings in true perspective. With so many other demands upon his time and ennrgy literary work could hardly be his chief pre-occupation; indeed the Abbot was well in his middle years when his first book, *The Human Soul*, was published (1931). This was followed by fourteen more volumes of varying size and importance, not to mention many lesser treatises and articles of a theological character. Unfortunately, partly owing to the normal depletion of stocks, but chiefly on account of destruction by fire during the late war, practically all these are now unobtainable. A new edition of his works therefore has long been overdue. The present restrictions of book-production make it impracticable to re-issue all these books separately, so it has been decided to reprint ten of the more important in three volumes.

The arrangement of these writings has presented no little difficulty, for while they deal with most of the contents of the Faith, their author never attempted to develop them into a systematic body of doctrine. Hence a certain amount of overlapping is inevitable. On the other hand it was felt very desirable that the late Abbot's own compositions should be interfered with as little as possible, so the actual revision has been confined to a slight abridgement of the text—this being achieved by the elimination of needless repetitions —and a few verbal corrections and clarifications where these were obviously necessary or advantageous. (It must be remembered that the English language was not the Abbot's native tongue, so that its idiom was not always a ready instrument to his brilliant thought. It is generally admitted however that, in spite of this handicap, he achieved in his later years a literary style of fine distinction and maturity.) In effect therefore each book remains a complete and self-contained unit. The projected edition will be no mere synthesis or anthology, but a truly representative collection. It is planned as follows:

Vol. I.   (The Incarnation and Redemption):

      THE CHRISTIAN MIND
      THE PERSONALITY OF CHRIST
      THE VICTORY OF CHRIST
      THE DIVINE MOTHERHOOD

Vol. II.   (The Church and the Sacraments):

      THE SPIRIT AND THE BRIDE
      THE PEOPLE OF GOD
      A KEY TO THE DOCTRINE OF THE EUCHARIST

Vol. III.   (The Soul and the Spiritual Life):

      THE HUMAN SOUL
      CHRISTIANUS
      THE LIFE OF THE WORLD TO COME

The above table should be sufficient to indicate the scope of the three volumes. It may be useful to preface a few general remarks on the ideals which the late Abbot set himself in writing. In spite of the great value he placed on sound theology his literary aims were not academic; he wrote principally for the instruction and edification of the ordinary Catholic. It is true that two or three of his books demand more than the average intelligence on the part of their readers, nay they even assume some measure of training in philosophy and theology for their just appreciation; nevertheless the common purpose of all is the encouragement of those whose heritage is the Faith and Sacraments of the Catholic Church. There is a clarion call of legitimate pride and unbounded enthusiasm in his teaching. He has sought to strengthen devotion, not by appealing to sentiment, but by adapting to modern needs the classical exposition of the Fathers and Scholastics, especially those of his great Master in Divinity—St Thomas Aquinas. It is not surprising that Abbot Vonier's books came to be eagerly awaited by an expectant multitude of readers; and were especially welcomed and appreciated by priests, religious and the educated laity.

There were not wanting some who criticised the undisguised note of enthusiasm in the Abbot's books as excessive. Even the human tragedy of the First World War and the disillusionments of the twenty years that followed failed to dispel from his clear mind that personal conviction of the triumph of Christ's cause. We may wonder whether the cataclysm of the Second World War and its grim aftermath of ruin, famine and fear, would have altered his almost light-hearted judgements of the power of evil in this world had he lived. We think not; indeed that very optimism which found such unrestrained expression in *The Victory of Christ* (1934) has found a striking vindication in these words of Pope Pius XII addressed to the Convention of Catholic Young Men in Rome in the Autumn of 1948: 'You know the mysterious riders mentioned in the Apocalypse. The second, the third and the fourth, are war, hunger and death. But who is the first rider on the white horse? "He that sat on him had a bow, and there was a crown given Him, and He went forth conquering that He might conquer!" He is Jesus Christ. The prophetic Evangelist did not only see the ruin caused by war, hunger and death. He also saw, in the first place, the victory of Christ. The way of the Church through the centuries is certainly a Way of the Cross, but it is also at all times a march of triumph. The Church of Christ, the men of faith and of Christian life, are always those who bring light, redemption and peace to a mankind without hope.'

BRUNO FEHRENBACHER, O.S.B.
Abbot of Buckfast

St Mary's Abbey,
Buckfast, S. Devon

CONTENTS

Foreword. By The Right Rev. Dom Bruno Fehrenbacher, o.s.b., Abbot of Buckfast *page* v

BOOK ONE

The Christian Mind

BOOK TWO

The Personality of Christ

THE CHRISTIAN MIND

Written during the First World War, and published (1920) after its con-
clusion, this is the third of Abbot Vonier's books in order of time. Its pur-
pose is to remind Christians that their Faith in the Son of God should be a
practical life philosophy, rooted in the transforming power of the Incarna-
tion, ever operative in the Church and in the souls of His elect. By its very
nature this conspectus of Catholic life and doctrine provides a fitting
introduction and summary of all the Abbot's writings, whether strictly
theological or devotional. Its place here has the additional usefulness of
emphasising the author's characteristic line of approach to every aspect of
Christian life and thought.—Editor.

CHAPTER I

Christian Theology and the Christian Mind

THE doctrines concerning Christ's sacred Person stand out as a clearly defined and fullgrown body of dogmas, which has reached maturity long ago; and, unlike man's bodily frame, it keeps its freshness, health, vigour and youthfulness, unimpaired as the world grows older. These doctrines are commonly designated by the term 'Christology'.

It may be said that Christology reached its perfection at the end of the eighth century. By that time the Universal Councils of the Church had made it clear for all times what are the true elements that enter into that wonderful Personality, Jesus Christ. Later Councils, for instance the Council of Trent, have defined many doctrines concerning Christ's rôle in the work of man's salvation, but they did not add anything to our knowledge of the mystery of Christ's Person, considered in Himself.

The great Doctors of the Church, and foremost amongst them St. Augustine of Hippo and St. Thomas Aquinas, have made it their task to explain to the Christian intellect the meaning and the far reaching bearing of the conciliar definitions concerning the God Incarnate. Taken together with the pronouncements of the Church their explanations form a body of thought of the highest intellectual order, independently of their value as Christian dogmas. No intellect could busy itself with the supreme truths of Christology without reaching a high mental perfection, besides having the merit of the obedience of faith.

The God Incarnate, however, is essentially and intrinsically the *life* of individual souls. It is His most constant and solemn assertion that He is Life, man's Life. The life of the Christian therefore has a function that is all its own, namely to express and translate into actuality Christ, the Son of God; for Jesus could not be man's life unless that life had as one of its organic functions to give expression to the Son of God.

To be the Son of God, and to be the life of man, is the most adequate definition of Our Lord's rôle. Christology, or the theology of the Incarnation, is primarily concerned with the wondrous fact that Christ is the Son of God. It is chiefly theoretical in nature. But Christ's other rôle, that of being the life of man, is still to a great extent an unexplored field of immense spiritual possibilities, at least for individual souls. It is simply impossible to tell to what extent individual souls may find Christ to be their life. The past exhibits some very glorious patterns of Christ as the life of man. The future may have in store other and no less surprising manifestations of the same life.

When I say that Christ's rôle as the life of man is in great part an unexplored field, I owe my reader a word of explanation. There are, of course, the clearly defined doctrines of the influence and action of mankind's Redeemer on mankind. The Church has pronounced on all matters that are pertinent to the general question of man's salvation and sanctification through Christ. But when all such doctrines of general Christology have been enumerated, there still remains another realm of supernatural realities that invites exploration.

The question is this: how does a man behave, to whom the Incarnation and all that it implies has become a living fact, and in whom the Son of God is an actual and pulsating life? How does such a man feel, how does he act, what does he dare, what view does he take of man in life and death? What sort of mind has he, what sort of heart, what sort of character? And more generally, how far is the Incarnation capable of producing a specific character, a specific mentality, in the people who believe it all literally, without any reservations? Is there, or can there be, here on earth, a race of men and women whose characters, whose minds, are not only modified, but are actually created by sincere and living belief in the Son of God, so that a great dramatist could place them in some heroic play, being quite certain of the behaviour of such characters? Is there, or can there be, a psychology of the Incarnation in men and women as truly as there is a psychology of nationality and race and heredity and environment, and what are its essential elements?

Put in this way the matter becomes clearly distinguished from the more generic question as to Christ's rôle in man's redemption. It is the distinction between principles and character. The great truths of Christology are the principles. What we are trying to find out now, is the sort of character such principles are able to produce, and do in fact produce. Or again it is a distinction between theory and life. To hold the doctrines of the Incarnation in their entirety may still be considered as theory, but to live out such principles is evidently quite a different matter. It constitutes a new spiritual phenomenon of endless freshness and variability, of which a man who otherwise admits every one of the articles of the Christian creed may be devoid.

The present book is an analytical study of the specific spiritual character produced in man by the principles of traditional Christology. It is a study of Christian character, as opposed to Christian theology. By Christian I mean here the Christ-thing, in its own specific nature. (It is a pity that there is no adjective derived from the word Christ, so as to enable us to express easily and promptly the ideas that contain attributes which are meant for the Son of God in Person. The word 'Christian' is hardly equivalent to 'Christ' in adjective form.) When I speak of character, psychology, and life as opposed to doctrine, dogma, and theology, the opposition is, of course, not an opposition of contrariety, as character is caused by doctrine, and though it be something distinct, yet it bears the stamp of doctrine.

I think that the expression 'Christian Mind' is an appropriate enough title for a book whose object it is to analyse and to describe the kind of mentality bred in man through a practical assimilation of the wondrous truths of the Incarnation. Mind is something between mere intellect and conduct. It is both an attitude, and a behaviour. It is something more than character, as it implies a relish and a keenness for wide views, qualities not necessarily contained in character. Mind again has a practical side which does not belong to mere intellect, or to speculative thought, and is more intimately part of our individual life than abstract truths, or doctrines held by our faith.

The matter of the book suggests its division. On the one hand we may consider the Christian mind as a possibility, insofar as from the study of the truths of the Incarnation we may deduce the sort of mind that could be bred in man if he made such doctrine his own, following them up in his life logically and fearlessly. On the other hand we may take a Christian mind from the realm of actuality, that of a man who has lived Christ thoroughly and boldly, and which thus transformed has been revealed to his fellow Christians. We have such an example in the person of St. Paul. So a considerable portion of this book really amounts to a character-study of that great Apostle. For a long time I had thought of calling my book 'The Christ of St. Paul', but the more general title under which the book now goes forth enables me to give my studies a wider scope, for even St. Paul did not express in his life the totality of Christ.

It is not my intention, however, to divide the book ostensibly into two sections, though its matter be twofold, potential and actual. But the book will be a blending of spiritual possibilities, such as the Incarnation may produce, and spiritual actualities, such as it did produce in Paul of Tarsus.

CHAPTER II

Two Views of the Son of God

THE Catholic doctrines concerning Christ's Divine Personality, however lofty and speculative they may seem at first sight, are found, sooner or later, to be the sources of living waters for the humblest soul, and to give life and growth to the tiniest spiritual plant.

There is hardly a more impressive spectacle in nature than that to be seen in some of the great mountainous districts of Europe. A great mountain rises straight up to the sky, its flanks forming a sheer precipice, a rugged wall of rocks; and from the rock there leaps a fully formed stream, born as it were in full manhood, beginning its career with a great volume of water, there being none of that silent oozing out from the ground of waters that meet gently, and gradually form themselves into a rivulet. No, the dry hard rock itself lets loose a fully formed stream. It is, of course, the overflow of the ever active lakes inside the mountain fastness.

What strikes the observer when he comes upon a phenomenon of that kind, is the contrast between the apparent lifelessness of the huge mass, and this glorious manifestation of energy, the living stream coming out of the mountain's side. Yet a moment's reflexion will tell the traveller that the stern rigidity of the mountain is the direct physical cause of that entrancing spectacle of movement. The lofty and unyielding rock gathers the waters inside itself, and sends them out a very marvel of light and life.

The loftiness and unchangeable finality of our Christology are the total if remote cause of all the higher life in Christ that is to be found in souls. But the rigidity is merely apparent. There are in the doctrines of the Incarnation many aspects that proclaim the fundamental fact that God in becoming man meant it to be a transformation of man, soul and body. We all believe, in a general and vague way, that God became man for man's sake, for his spiritual profit. But very few amongst us grasp the deeper truth, that the Incarnation is in itself, in its innermost nature, the highest possible uplifting of human nature and of mankind.

We may consider the Incarnation, then, in a twofold light. Assuming the common principle that God becomes man for the sake of man, our first line of approach will be somewhat as follows: The God-Man, possessing infinite personal dignity, worth and power, does something for the human race that uplifts and saves it. His mission on earth is essentially to accomplish that great act, in the way, and under the circumstances He knows best. It would be essentially a transient act, an act that might be dated and described by the historian as the act of man's redemption. We are orthodox Christians the moment we believe that God made Man redeemed mankind by an act of His that took place here on earth.

But there is a second aspect of this divine truth, higher and more comprehensive, which includes that first point of view, but goes a good deal beyond. The Redemption, says the man who is wiser in the mystery of Christ, is more than a transient act on the part of the Son of God made Man. The rôle of the Son of God Incarnate is Redemption, is the uplifting of human nature.

The various acts and phases of Christ's career on earth have but one object, to consummate Christ's fitness to be the Redemption, the uplifting of mankind. 'Of him (God) are you in Christ Jesus, who of God is made unto us wisdom and justice and sanctification and redemption.'[1]

This deeper understanding of the mystery of Christ lays great stress on what the Son of God is, both in the divine and in the human elements of Himself. In this view the acts and facts of His life here on earth are infinitely precious because they reveal His permanent character. It might even be said that they are so precious, because they have permanently shaped Christ's human character. We have the *Epistle to the Hebrews* as an authority for this: 'Whereas indeed He was the Son of God, He learned obedience by the things which He suffered. And being consummated, He became, to all that obey Him, the cause of eternal salvation.'[2]

I might describe the two views as the verb view and the substantive view. The first says, Christ *gives* life; the second says, Christ *is* life. The two views, as already remarked, do not exclude each other, but they complete each other. It is, of course, a much greater thing to be life substantively, than merely to cause life, and when I say that Christ is life substantively, I mean this literally, for He *is* the life of man, not only life in Himself. No one questions the expression that the Son of God is life in Himself. But what is so consoling, is the ever recurring phraseology of the Scriptures, that the Son of God not only produces life in man, but *is* the life of man.

I select for the moment this one attribute of life, for the sake of simplicity in my argument. Any other of Christ's rôles and attributes might be instanced with the same degree of appropriateness. The circumstance that the New Testament so constantly states Christ's relation to man in terms of substantives can never receive enough attention. Were such phraseology used even once it ought to rouse the keenest interest. Yet it is not once, but hundreds of times, that the inspired writers express themselves in such fashion when speaking of man's share in the mystery of the Incarnation. No one can fail to see the immense spiritual significance of such a turn of mind and speech in the sacred writers.

Although the less educated Christian says a true thing when he professes his faith that Christ did redeem him, the better informed

[1] 1 Cor. i. 30.   [2] Heb. v. 8, 9.

speaks much more wisely and correctly when he says: Christ *is* my redemption. For the first, redemption is a result, most gracious indeed, but something that came out of Christ; for the other, redemption is something inside Christ. He, too, feels redeemed, but his feelings are on a much higher plane, of a much diviner fibre. And it is evident that the Incarnation becomes a much more glorious thing if the God Incarnate, instead of merely redeeming, is Redemption itself. For once granted that God became Man, that there is infinite power and sanctity in the God-Man, the actual work of redemption is no new marvel; it might be said to be child's play for the divine giant. But to *be* Redemption, intrinsically, through His human nature, as well as through the divine element in Himself, enlarges the scope of the One 'who was predestinated the Son of God in power, according to the Spirit of sanctification'.[1] To do the great work, for one who is Omnipotence, is no new mystery. To be Himself life, light, food, happiness eternal, is a development of the initial mystery of the Hypostatic Union absolutely worthy of it.

The Son of God calls Himself the Resurrection and the Life, the Way, the Truth, the Light, the Beginning and the End. He is every thing that renders man happy and holy, substantially and substantively. The only mode of being man's Saviour that is really worthy of the Hypostatic Union is that the Incarnate God should be Salvation itself. The aim and goal of the whole drama of the Incarnation, from the conception through the Holy Ghost in the Virgin's womb to the glories of the risen Jesus on the Easter morning is this, that the God-Man, Christ Jesus, Son of God and Son of Mary, true God and true Man, should be, both through His human as well as through His divine element, man's eternal life; and all the parts of that divine drama, with such a wonderful chief Actor in the centre of it, are indispensable to that crowning achievement, that He, Jesus of Nazareth, is man's life substantively, and not only life-giver to man. To be life-giver needed no such life-drama as is described in the Gospel: it needed only God's eternal omnipotence. But to be life to man necessitated a Christ, who is the Son of God born of a Virgin, who suffered under Pontius Pilate, who died, was buried and rose again from the dead.

The Incarnation of Christian theology is indeed the personal

[1] Rom. i. 4.

union of Divinity with humanity. But let us always bear in mind that Incarnation, or Hypostatic Union, is still a general mystery, a mystery that could take place under other forms. Thus any of the three Divine Persons could become incarnate. The personal union could have an Angel for its object, or any other human being, or even many other beings at the same time, either human or angelic. In fact, no man knows under how many different conditions Hypostatic Union could take place. Thus Hypostatic Union need not at all include 'the form of slave', the abasement of the Christian Gospels; it could be all a mystery of glory and happiness. But the mystery that is the ground work of Christian spirituality is a Hypostatic Union of a well defined mode, deeply characterised and modified through its special purposes. Through it the Son of God, the second Person of the Trinity, becomes man, assuming one individual human nature into the partnership of the Divine Personality with the specific purpose of becoming the higher life of that fallen man whose fall culminates in death. To study the doctrines of the Incarnation without taking into account that very deep characterisation is to miss the whole point. It would be like introducing some great personage into a dramatic play, without giving him a rôle or a character. That God should become man is the first marvel; that God made man should be man's life, is another marvel, as great as the first, in the sense in which a man's character is as great a thing as a man's being.

CHAPTER III

The Rôle of Christ's Humanity

BEFORE proceeding with my description of the Christian mind, I think it worth while to give the reader an opportunity of understanding more clearly the rôle of Christ's humanity, in being to man life, and resurrection, and all other things substantively. It is the human nature in the Word Incarnate that gives to the

Hypostatic Union its proper character, its traditional and wonderful individuality. To explain all things that make up the riches of our redemption in Christ only through the infinitude of the divine element in Jesus is a great practical error; Christ's humanity is as indispensable to His rôle as the Life of the world as is His divinity. It is therefore of the utmost importance for the Christian mind to have such views of the rôle of our Lord's humanity as to make it the delight of our mental contemplation, and to enable us to grasp at one glance the composite perfection of our new life in God, it being an indissoluble blending of the divine and the human.

A not uncommon phrase used with regard to the Incarnation is this: Christ's humanity is totally absorbed by His Divinity. What pious people generally mean when using such an expression is that Christ's human nature has been brought so completely into conformity with the Divinity, has been made so absolutely subject to it, and has been sanctified by it so entirely, that it could never be to man an obstacle, when man wants to go directly to God through Christ. According to this view the Godhead in our Lord is so predominant, that practically His humanity is nowhere, and when you are in presence of the Lord, you are in presence of Divinity, pure and simple, for the practice of Christian contemplation. Christ's humanity is thus considered as being in a state of divine passiveness. It is a way of looking at our Lord frequently found with beginners in the spiritual life, whose mind is for the first time overpowered by the thought of the all-sufficiency of God. Of course they hold more or less theoretically the Christian doctrine that all life, grace and redemption come through Christ's humanity as through a divinely appointed mediumship; but such knowledge does not render the humanity a living part of their minds. It is really a mental awkwardness, resembling in some way the difficulties the Protestant mind has to find joy and rest in the thought that the Saints intercede for us with God. The Protestant sees in the Catholic doctrine of the Intercession of Saints an obstacle between man's soul and God.

Now mature Christian sanctity suffers from no such awkwardness. On the contrary, it exults in all things that come from God, and it never feels itself nearer to the fountain head of all goodness than when it contemplates some wonderful manifestation of God's creative love. Far from considering Christ's humanity as having been absorbed by the Divinity, it rejoices at the thought that the humanity in Jesus is the highest and most potent expression of the Divinity. The Godhead, instead of absorbing it, brings it out, so to speak, with infinite effect. Divinity communicates to humanity such potentialities, such vitalities, that no distinction need be made by our mind, as to what is the share of the one or the other in our redemption. It is an undivided result, and an undivided life, the divinised humanity, and the humanised Divinity, being the total life.

The Incarnation is adequately appreciated by those only to whom Christ's humanity is the marvel of marvels, a superb creation, in which they have their being, in which they live, work, die, and in which they hope to rise again, in which they find the fulness of the Godhead, as Moses found the fire in the bush. The astonishing frailty of human nature being made to blaze forth the glory of eternal Godhead, and yet remain unconsumed and keeping its native greenness, is the ever amazing paradox of Christ's humanity. 'And the Lord appeared to him [Moses] in a flame of fire out of the midst of a bush: and he saw that the bush was on fire and was not burnt. And Moses said: I will go and see this great sight, why the bush is not burnt.'[1]

The Hypostatic Union is God's most astonishing production, it is the effect of what I may call super-creation, of an incomprehensibly high scale of perfection, a creation through which, instead of an ordinary finite mode of existence, Divine personality is given to an individual nature. And although the saint knows that Christ's human nature is something inferior to the Divine nature in Him, he realises that this inferiority has been practically bridged over, that there are in the mystery of the Hypostatic Union such resources of life and power that at no point are we in contact with anything which does not bear the stamp of infinity; there are no banks to that stream of life, which is Christ Jesus.

In sacred theology are contained the metaphysical principles that explain how, with the relative superiority of the divine element in our Lord over His humanity, this same humanity is yet a full and total cause of our higher life with God. In our practical thinking we need not make any such distinction, just as we do not distinguish between a man's soul and a man's body when we think of some beloved person. We walk up bravely to that Person, Jesus, just as

[1] Ex. iii. 2, 3.

He stands before us, and we find Him to be infinite truth and infinite grace. In all His manifestations, in the phases of His career, He is the one great wonder of heaven and earth, and our mind rejoices in Him exceedingly and endlessly. 'And evidently great is the mystery of godliness, which was manifested in the flesh, was justified in the spirit, appeared unto Angels, hath been preached unto the Gentiles, is believed in the world, is taken up in glory.'[1]

CHAPTER IV

The Necessity of Possessing the Christian Mind

IT was to be expected that a great philosophy of life would be built up on the fundamental facts of the Incarnation. Yet being apprehended intuitively by the Christian intellect, it is stated by the Christian writers more as an obvious truth than as a theory of life. St. Paul especially takes it all for granted, and on that very account he is our best authority on the subject. He sees at a glance how every practical problem of life finds its solution in this main fact, that Christ, the Son of God, lived, died, and rose again from the dead. According to him, the work of building up a practical Christian life on the great foundation of the Incarnation belongs to every Christian teacher; but it is a work in which one man is more successful than another: 'According to the grace of God that is given to me, as a wise architect, I have laid the foundation: and another buildeth thereon. But let every man take heed how he buildeth thereupon. For other foundation no man can lay, but that which is laid: which is Christ Jesus. Now, if any man build upon this foundation, gold, silver, precious stones, wood, hay, stubble: every man's work shall be manifest. For the day of the Lord shall declare it, because it shall be revealed in fire.'[2]

If anything can be expected of the belief in the Incarnation, it is a philosophy of life, an attitude of the mind entirely and exclusively

[1] 1 Tim. iii. 16.   [2] 1 Cor. iii. 10-14.

based on it. Both from its intrinsic principles, and from the utterances of those that have best experienced the powerful vitalities of the Incarnation, we ought to be able to construct a rule of life and thought so high, so comprehensive, and at the same time so workable, as to throw into the shade all other human philosophies. God was made man for the sake of man: such are our wonderful premises. 'And I live, now not I: but Christ liveth in me',[1] is one of the many *a posteriori* axioms of the same truth. Who does not see at a glance what a magnificent theory of life could be built on such principles?

In our own days thinking men have soared high in their efforts to out-distance the soul killing miasmas of materialism. They have elaborated all kinds of ethereal philosophies: philosophies of the Mind, of the Infinite, of the Absolute, the Divine in Man, and so on. They are pathetic efforts indeed, signs of the times in which we live; yet one of their most interesting features is this, that many of them are ready to receive Christ, are houses that seem built for such a guest as the Incarnate Son of God. What they call Mind, the Infinite, the Absolute, the Divine in Man, is an empty thing by itself, a house without an inhabitant, without any life in it. They are mere expressions of vague, undefined longings. But let Jesus of Nazareth be called Mind, for He is the Word of God; let Him be called Infinite, in whom all fulness dwells; let Him be the Divine in man, being the Word made flesh; let Him be the Absolute, as He is the Alpha and the Omega; and you have a perfect, a heavenly philosophy, yet one as true, as practical, as real, as a living person can be.

It would be a great disadvantage for Christianity, if it were barren of all philosophy, if it were not such as to enable man to read life, the world, and the world's history, in the light of the Incarnation; if the Christian doctrines had to be deposited as precious family heirlooms in the very top storey of the human mind; whilst all our practical life and activity were under the influence of systems of thought not begotten of Christ's Revelation. Such a state of mind would be a most dangerous limitation of the Kingdom of Christ. Christianity without a Christ-philosophy of life, with the Son of God relegated to an upper chamber, while intellectual feasts and adventures are going on below, is clearly an impoverished and perilous state for the baptised. A Christian mind that could not move with

[1] Gal. ii. 20.

the greatest ease 'in Christ', finding in Him a world of infinite interests and boundless perspectives, is indeed in a sorry plight. Whatever may be such a mind's reverence for the God Incarnate, it never knows exactly where to place Him, and what to make of Him, in the universal scheme of things.

Now it might be objected that a living and practical philosophy of the Incarnation, as here postulated, could hardly be the achievement of the mind, even of a sincere Christian, without a special illumination, or private revelation, which is the privilege of very few. All our mind could possibly aspire to, it might be said, is a reverent acceptance of the mystery of the Incarnation, bowing before it in blind obedience. Is it not presumption to hope that one could train one's mind to think in terms of the Incarnation? My answer is, that the acquisition of so glorious a mental attitude is a comparatively easy thing, and that it is an achievement possible with the ordinary graces given by God to His faithful. There is first of all the Christian Mind *au fait* in St Paul, who is known and read in all the churches. To conform our minds to his, is not so much a process of mental deduction, as a direct influence, a direct contact of mind upon mind, as when we receive the warm effulgence of a great fire. It is not a reasoning, but a living participation of our minds in St. Paul's mind.

No doubt, in the case of St. Paul the mental illumination was entirely the direct gift of the Holy Ghost. But like all other productions of grace and genius, once they are expressed, it becomes the natural dwelling place of all men's minds. Who could write a Shakespearian tragedy? Yet how many millions of minds have been trained to assimilate the thoughts and use the language of the great poet!

I do not admit that it is beyond our mental range to acquire the attitude here described, by an unceasing exercise of the mind and a constant contemplation of the principles of the Incarnation. Granted our faith in the Incarnation, and our knowledge of the more obvious axioms of theology, why should it be beyond us to think habitually in terms of the Incarnation? God's grace is as ready to help our thinking as it is prompt to support our acting. And if it ought to be every Christian's effort to do all things in Christ, why should we be debarred from thinking all our thoughts in Christ? Surely so great a phenomenon as the Incarnation is meant to modify deeply all human thinking under every possible aspect. Christ is the Logos, the Word of God, the Wisdom of God. Through His very nature He is meant to be the source of a mentality that is all His own.

CHAPTER V

Special Christian Mind versus General Christian Mind

WE may now consider more fully what is really meant by the Christian Mind.

There are only two complete mental systems in the history of human thought, diametrically opposed and exhaustive of their subject. On the one hand we have Christian thought, and on the other we have monistic thought. All the other systems find their place within those two universal forms, as incomplete things are over-shadowed by those which are complete. Monism, as its name implies, makes it its fundamental principle that there is no distinction between Creator and creature. The world with all its phenomena is the evolution of one force. Even then, when Christian conclusions and monistic conclusions seem to coincide, the similarity is merely apparent. Monism is radically and hopelessly the opposite of Christian thought. Christianity starts with the assumption of the real distinction between God and the world, between the Creator and creature; and the relations between the two, the Infinite Maker and the finite creature, enter everywhere into Christian thought. This is why Christian philosophy may be also called dualism, in direct opposition to monism, as it is an upholding of the distinction between the Creator and the created. St. Thomas Aquinas may be considered as the most comprehensive exponent of the Christian dualism, though dualism is much less the work of a few well-known thinkers than is monism. Dualism is really the common inheritance of mankind. Monism is a freak of darkness.

This philosophical digression will be helpful in our effort to define the scope of the Christian mind in the more restricted sense of this book. In a very true sense, every sort of thinking that is not monism is Christian thinking, however much it may be overlaid by error and confusion. The heathen who worships false gods is at bottom following out the principle of duality. He is certainly nearer to the kingdom of truth than the German monist. On the other hand, Christian mind in its general aspect is every truth that is based ultimately on dualism; while antichristian mind is everything that rests on monism. Christian mind, as the philosophical opposite of monism, is exceedingly vast and comprehensive. It implies certain views on religion, on politics, on economics, on science, on sociology, on eugenics, etc. Such views are simply called Christian, because they imply that the laws of the world, spiritual, moral, social, natural, are the property, so to speak, of an infinitely wise Creator, who is not only the world's origin, but also the world's last court of appeal.

In this very general sense Christian thought differs in no wise from Jewish thought. Monism is its only real enemy. But the specific Christian Mind of which we are treating in this book may be said to be the opposite of Jewish thought in its post-messianic phase; for the Jew, whilst worshipping God, and whilst having the zeal of God, refuses to surrender his mind and his will to the higher manifestations of God found in the Incarnation. With all his faith in God, he suffers from a lamentable ignorance of God, because he fails to understand the infinitely sweet mystery of His love in the Incarnation. 'Jesus answered: If I glorify Myself, My glory is nothing. It is My Father that glorifieth Me, of whom you say that He is your God. And you have not known Him: but I know Him.'[1]

Christian Mind, in our restricted sense, is not so much a special view of the world and its laws, as of God and His free favours. It presupposes the general Christian thought, but rises infinitely higher. Christian Mind, therefore, may be defined as the attitude of man's mind caused directly and totally by the Incarnation. It is to the general Christian view, to dualism, what Paul the Apostle is to Saul the Pharisee. Saul saw the world in God. Paul sees both God and the world in Christ Jesus. Such enlightenment is an immense uplifting of the mind; so great an uplifting indeed that to many it seems an

[1] John viii. 54-55.

entire upheaval, to be dreaded and hated. It is the lot of the Christian Mind to be so totally misunderstood by the ordinary religious mind of mere believers in God and His works, as to make its extermination an apparent service rendered unto God. 'They will put you out of the synagogues: yea, the hour cometh, that whosoever killeth you will think that he doth a service to God.'[1]

The question will be asked, how does the general Christian mind range itself under the special Christian Mind, for it is unnatural that our mental perspective should be subdivided into regions? We must see all things as lying within one plane, bounded by one horizon. Our plane is Christ; the horizon is Christ's human nature. For the Christian Mind, all things must be seen in Christ. The great doctrine of the Word made Flesh gives us the true focus: 'All things were made by Him: and without Him was made nothing that was made.'[2] The Word Incarnate is universal power, universal harmony, universal wisdom made flesh. We cannot dissociate Christ from the truth and beauty to be found in nature. Christ is truly the 'heir of the world'.[3]

This comprehension of all things in God made Man will be more fully developed as the book goes on; but I thought it appropriate to say these few words on the relationship of what I have called the general Christian mind, and the noble thing that will now claim all our attention: the Special Christian Mind.

CHAPTER VI

A Criticism of Certain Attitudes of Mind Among Christians

AS Christianity implies everything that is good and true, a man may be a sincere professor of the Christian faith without actually giving evidence in his life of that special mental attitude, the Christian Mind, which is the subject of this book. It is, of course, obvious that no one has a right to call himself a Christian

[1] John xvi. 2.   [2] John i. 3.   [3] Rom. iv. 13.

unless he sincerely believes that all his spiritual hopes are based on the Incarnation. But it is quite possible for one to hold such a faith, to lead a godly life, and yet to remain unconscious of the mystery of the living Christ: to go through life without ever having experienced the truth of St. Paul's maxim: 'For to me, to live is Christ: and to die is gain.'[1]

It is so very easy even for the faithful Christian to order his life merely according to the rules of that general Christian mentality which is the opposition of materialism and infidelity, including always at least a theoretical acceptance of the Redemption in Christ. It is perhaps more difficult for the Catholic not to enter at least a few steps into the mystery of the Incarnation, as he is bound to make use of the Sacraments, which are the most palpable means of contact with the Risen Son of God. It seems strange that a man who receives with faith and devotion the Bread of Life, should not go beyond a merely theoretical acceptance of his life in Christ. Yet it must be confessed that even for a Catholic, with the habitual use of the Sacraments, the Christian Mind is often conspicuous by its absence. For such a one the Sacraments are received chiefly as helps to moral goodness. They are this, of course, but they are something vastly greater.

Again, a great deal of spiritual literature is based, not on the specific, but on the general Christian mind. Let us take for instance its treatment of the virtue of temperance, in its classical meaning of purity of life. From Tertullian, through Cassian, St. Thomas Aquinas and Rodriguez, down to Father Maturin in our own days, the virtue is described in terms mostly philosophical; terms which any man who is not a Nietzschean, must accept. Now and then Christ's example is pressed into service. But the exhortations to temperance are such that no sensible pagan can jeer at them. Every possible philosophic system, with any claim to intellectual respectability, is ransacked and quoted in support of the virtue. Indeed we are given a most complete synthesis of *nova et vetera*. But going beyond this very general view of the virtue of temperance we have St. Paul's own experience and statement: 'Let us walk honestly, as in the day: not in rioting and drunkenness, not in chambering and impurities, not in contention and envy. But put ye on the Lord

[1] Phil. i. 21.

Jesus Christ; and make not provision for the flesh in its concupiscences.'[1] The Christian temperance in opposition to pagan profligacy
is made clear in one magnificent phrase: 'Put ye on the Lord Jesus
Christ.' Far be it from me to say that our teachers have ignored such
a view of Christian temperance, or that they never made allusion to
it. The preacher and writer, through the very nature of their profession, tend to diffuseness of expression; but the prophet who speaks
God's own words avoids such prolixity, and utters truth in its
highest and most concentrated form. Every other aspect of Christian life could be made the object of similar study. The whole of
Catholic morality has been cast into the mould of Aristotelian philosophy by the great friar and thinker St. Thomas Aquinas. The Greek
genius and the mediaeval Doctor meet and make friends. It is only
men who have never taken the trouble to study his great *Summa*, in
the *Prima Secundae* and *Secunda Secundae*, who could dare accuse
St. Thomas of having fettered the principles of Christian ethics, of
having curtailed the liberties of the children of God. The ethics of
St. Thomas are the most liberal, the most generous, the most practical ethics in the world. Yet with all their beauty and generosity,
they are no more than an adumbration of the heavenly born morality of the Incarnation, thus described by St. Paul in his own person:
'According to the justice that is in the Law, (I was) conversing without blame. But the things that were gain to me, the same I have
counted loss for Christ. Furthermore, I count all things to be but
loss for the excellent knowledge of Jesus Christ, my Lord: for
whom I have suffered the loss of all things and count them but as
dung, that I may gain Christ: And may be found in Him, not having
my justice, which is of the Law, but that which is of the faith of
Christ Jesus, which is of God; justice in faith. That I may know
Him and the power of His resurrection and the fellowship of His
sufferings: being made conformable to His death. If by any means I
may attain to the resurrection which is from the dead.'[2]

The services of the general Christian mind are incalculable. They
give satisfaction to man's reasoning powers. They produce that kind
of mental wellbeing which comes from the fulness of truth. To
neglect the general Christian mind would be the greatest mistake;
it would imply a kind of contempt of one of the laws of spiritual

[1] Rom. xiii. 13, 14.   [2] Phil. iii. 6-11.

life, the law of the liberty of the children of God. At the same time there could be no greater danger for the Christian cause than an attempt to express Christian life only in philosophical or legal terms, and to consider such expressions as exhaustive of the subject. The fellowship of Christ's passion and resurrection will always defy definition. It is something higher than philosophy and law. The general Christian mind and the special Christian Mind are not two opposites; they complete each other. 'Do not think that I come to destroy the law, or the prophets. I am not come to destroy, but to fulfil.'[1]

No man since the days of St. Paul saw the things of Christ more clearly than did St. Francis of Assisi. In the possession of the Son of God all other gifts of mind were as nothing to him. In that great love of the Son of God he gathered together his disciples. But even Francis very soon learned that he could not dispense with the less inspiring elements of ecclesiastical authority. The stern Roman canonists did him great service in restraining the fervour which he had brought into the world from becoming unruly. At a later period St. Teresa of Avila, whose mind was full of the Son of God, if ever human mind was, professed her indebtedness and admiration for the unemotional scholastics who gave her the assurance that her intuitions of divine things were in perfect conformity with the reasoned theories of Catholic philosophy and theology.

On the other hand, to live merely by rationalised systems of spirituality, however perfect, would be the greatest disaster to the Church. It would mean law without love, power without meekness, authority without the gentle influence of paternity, intellectual keenness without humility, zeal for God without knowledge of God's true character. A spiritual life that is not a reproduction of the life of Christ will sooner or later become a dangerous adventure, all the more hazardous as it is so fascinating.

Happy are we, if we live at a period of Christian history when the mystical knowledge and love of the Son of God go hand in hand with sound thought and wise government.

[1] Matt. v. 17.

CHAPTER VII

St. Paul's Mind

THE specific Christian Mind is essentially mystical, in the modern sense of the word: that is to say, it is the possession and intuition of a great spiritual fact, whose reality is greater than anything the mind can acquire by its own reasoning powers. It is a reality that is overwhelmingly present; it transcends classifications and definitions, though containing them implicitly.

St. Paul is the greatest mystic of all times, because he apprehended Christ's personality so mightily, and read all things in Him so clearly and directly. All the minor realities of human life are to him law. But when Christ comes as the newly found reality of life, law disappears; He alone remains, and all life, big and small, the Apostle reads now in terms of Christ.

Before expounding the more positive elements of the Christian Mind, I intend stating its more critical aspect by following St. Paul in his wonderful analysis of the respective values of the law and the living Christ. We are all familiar with the well worn antithesis that opposes the Old Law to the New. We hear it constantly said that the Old Law was a state of servitude, whilst the New Law is a state of superabundant grace. The antithesis is a true rendering of spiritual facts, and above all, it has the consecration of ecclesiastical tradition. But I doubt whether St. Paul would have liked it as a theological phrase. Certainly it does not come from him. It is against St. Paul's genius to think of the new era that came with Christ as a law, however pure and lofty, and nowhere do we find him stating this opposition. For him the law is simply abrogated, it is dead, as Christ died on the cross; with this difference however, that Our Saviour rose again, whilst the law is not meant to rise. It is dead and buried and condemned, for ever. The new state of things is not a law, not a system, it is the living God Himself, it is the risen Christ. The antithesis of St. Paul is not between the Old Law and the New Law, but between law and grace, between law and Christ. 'You are not under the law, but under grace.'[1] 'You also are become dead to the law,

[1] Rom. vi. 14.

by the body of Christ: that you may belong to another, who is risen again from the dead.'[1]

It is true that once or twice the Apostle uses the term 'law' in connexion with the new dispensation. 'The law of the spirit of life, in Christ Jesus, hath delivered me from the law of sin and death.'[2] 'Bear ye one another's burdens: and so you shall fulfil the law of Christ.'[3]

In both these instances the term 'law' has an almost ironical meaning, as it denotes things that are essentially not matters for a law. So it may be asserted safely that the common antithesis between the Old Law and the New Law is by no means a Pauline idea, as for him the Incarnation and its grace could never be encompassed within legal concepts, even of the loftiest order.

Christ the Son of the living God stands before Paul as the essence of Christian sanctity. The concept of Christ Himself being all law and all religion, may be rightly called St. Paul's central spiritual fact. In order to establish it firmly, the Apostle wrote more on this subject than on any other. He lays a regular siege to the Jewish, as well as to the heathen mind, that he may convince it of the all important truth that the Son of God made man, and crucified for man, has become man's spiritual life. The Epistle to the Romans, the one to the Galatians, large sections of the Epistles to the Corinthians, the Colossians, and the Philippians, would be incomprehensible if we did not read them in the light of that great Pauline idea, that Christ Himself is spiritual life.

Before proceeding, let me put more clearly the practical distinction embodied in St. Paul's view of Christ's rôle in man's higher life. One might consider spiritual life as a thing perfect in itself, for whose realisation and attainment every sort of supernatural help is given us, the greatest help being the Incarnation, and all that it involves. On the other hand one might consider the Incarnate God as possessing all finality, and spiritual life as a road to Him. The first view makes of spiritual life the end, and the Incarnation a means towards that end. The second view, on the contrary, makes the Incarnate God the aim, and spiritual life, or the practice of all justice, the means towards finding Him. It is evident that the two views differ profoundly, and must in practice affect deeply the soul's movements.

[1] Rom. vii. 4.   [2] Rom. viii. 2.   [3] Gal. vi. 2.

St. Paul will not rest content until he has destroyed in our minds the last vestige that gives any finality to anything, however holy, outside Christ. He has the impatience of a man of generous disposition, who has had his soul cramped for a long time by a spiritual system of inferior merit, that had been given to him as the highest perfection, and whose defects he had cherished in his former enthusiasm as much as its good points. He has now found out his mistake: he sees how crushed he had been, and there are no bounds to his indignation. The former system that had enslaved his soul was the Law, the Old Law of Moses. It had kept him and his people from Christ. His denunciations of that Law now are as strong as they are varied in character. His mind finds endless stratagems to break down the obstacles which kept men from immediate and personal contact with the Son of the living God.

The objection might be made, at this stage, that St. Paul's rancour was aroused by the law of Moses, with its material burdens, and that we are not justified in reading into his utterances that higher and much more subtle distinction between Christ's Person and general spiritual life, as described above. But let me give at once the assurance that this substitution of the living Son of God for a mere system of spirituality is essential to St. Paul's teaching. The law of Moses represented to the mind of St. Paul the limited system of justice and spirituality known to man up to the glorious advent of Life itself.

CHAPTER VIII

St. Paul's Arguments

TO St. Paul the great truth that Christ is our higher life had come like a flash of lightning: in an instant it transformed him into a being of light and joy. But he takes both Jew and Gentile over the picturesque and rugged ground of his theological arguments to leave them, panting with the effort, at Christ's feet. 'Here,' he tells them, 'is the source of the living waters.'

I think it worth while to go over St. Paul's reasonings, for I am afraid that many a student of the Scriptures has an unconscious prejudice against those very passages in his writings; thinking them too exclusively rabbinical in their content and style, or as having no longer any practical value, since the controversies which gave rise to them did not survive the first Christian ages. No mistake could be more fatal. Those rugged efforts of St. Paul's intellect are the hard rock and the wild tree where we find the purest spiritual honey; the sweetest of all truths: that Christ Himself is our Life.

I take the various arguments in the order in which they are found in the Epistles, beginning with that to the Romans. The fourth chapter takes us back to the heroic age of the Jewish nation, to the calm and simple days when God made a compact of friendship with Abraham. The great Patriarch was without a son. It was the one shadow in a life full of sunshine. Even when God came near to him in a vision, and spoke to him words of comfort, the humble old man turned round to the Lord and boldly told Him that without a son kind words were no full consolation. 'Now when these things were done, the word of the Lord came to Abram by a vision, saying: Fear not, Abram, I am thy protector, and thy reward exceeding great. And Abram said: Lord God, what wilt thou give me? I shall go without children: and the son of the steward of my house is this Damascus Eliezer. And Abram added: But to me thou hast not given seed: and lo, my servant, born in my house, shall be my heir. And immediately the word of the Lord came to him, saying: He shall not be thy heir; but he that shall come out of thy bowels, him shalt thou have for thy heir. And he brought him forth abroad, and said to him: Look up to heaven and number the stars, if thou canst. And he said to him: So shall thy seed be. Abram believed God, and it was reputed to him unto justice.'[1]

This glorious promise, that includes the future Messiah amongst the seed of Abraham, is a most gratuitous advance on the part of God, a token of personal friendship and unexpected liberality. Abraham, on his side, rose to the height of those divine advances. He believed in the promise without a moment's hesitation. 'Who against hope believed in hope; that he might be made the father of

[1] Gen. xv. 1-6

many nations, according to that which was said to him: *So shall thy
seed be*. And he was not weak in faith. Neither did he consider his
own body, now dead (whereas he was almost an hundred years old),
nor the dead womb of Sara. In the promise also of God he staggered
not by distrust; but was strengthened in faith, giving glory to God:
most fully knowing that whatsoever He has promised, He is able
also to perform. And therefore it was reputed to him unto justice.'[1]

St. Paul keeps on reiterating the gratuitousness of Abraham's
privilege. Abraham's spiritual elevation comes from his meeting
God's loving advances so wholeheartedly. God, on the other hand,
makes those advances freely, not as a reward of any special works on
the part of the Patriarch: above all, true and faithful observance of
the law could not be credited with such recognition at God's hands.
The law of Moses did not exist yet, and circumcision itself, the
primary article of the law, had not yet been imposed on Abraham.
The whole of that manifestation of divine friendship is not only
superior to the law, it took place long before the law was established. 'For not through the law was the promise to Abraham or to
his seed, that he should be heir of the world, but through the justice
of faith.'[2]

But all this subtle analysis of Abraham's privilege is meant to lead
to the following conclusion, which states the Christ spirituality in
such uncompromising language: 'Now it is not written only for him
that it was reputed to him unto justice. But also for us, to whom it
shall be reputed, if we believe in Him, that raised up Jesus Christ,
our Lord, from the dead. Who was delivered up for our sins, and
rose again for our justification.'[3] From the uncovenanted and un-
systematised privileges and graces and virtues of Abraham, St. Paul
leaps to the still higher liberties of the Christian. Christ's resurrection, and our practical faith in that resurrection, bring us nearer to
the living God, 'who calleth those things that are not, as those that
are,'[4] than Abraham's unwavering trust in God's promise that a son
would be granted to him, though 'he was almost a hundred years
old.' It is the same spirit of the liberty of the children of God, and
the risen Christ, more than Abraham's joyful fatherhood, that is the
real sign of God's love for the elect. No law however perfect, no
covenant however sacred, can come up to the spiritual perfection

---

[1] Rom. iv. 18-22.   [2] Rom. iv. 13.   [3] Rom. iv. 23-26.   [4] Rom. iv. 17.

of that most personal token of divine friendship, the risen Christ. It is the Christian's matchless advantage that life with the risen Christ sums up, or rather takes the place of, all God's covenants, just as with Abraham the honours of a glorious fatherhood represent all that the Lord God is to him.

The thought occurred very soon to St. Paul, as it must, of course, to every thinking man, that this absolute superiority to law, in virtue of Christ's personal friendship enjoyed by the Christian, would lead to a kind of contempt of the law, and that the liberty of the Incarnation would be turned into a disregard of the ordinary moral precepts. In his effort to rebut the objection he plunges into a new consideration, which on the one hand saves him from a dangerous antinomianism, and on the other hand is a still more brilliant exposition of his absorbing theme, the all-sufficiency of Christ, as a principle of sanctity. This second argument, instead of being borrowed from Jewish history, is taken from the beginnings of Christian life, baptism. 'What shall we say, then? Shall we continue in sin, that grace may abound? God forbid! For we that are dead to sin, how shall we live any longer therein? Know you not that all we who are baptized in Christ Jesus are baptized in his death? For we are buried together with Him by baptism into death: that, as Christ is risen from the dead by the glory of the Father, so we also may walk in newness of life. For if we have been planted together in the likeness of His death, we shall be also in the likeness of His resurrection. Knowing this, that our old man is crucified with Him, that the body of sin may be destroyed, to the end that we may serve sin no longer. For he that is dead is justified from sin. Now if we be dead with Christ, we believe that we shall live also together with Christ. Knowing that Christ, rising again from the dead, dieth now no more. Death shall no more have dominion over Him. For in that He died to sin, He died once; but in that He liveth, He liveth unto God: So do you also reckon that you are dead to sin, but alive unto God in Christ Jesus our Lord. Let not sin therefore reign in your mortal body, so as to obey the lusts thereof. Neither yield ye your members as instruments of iniquity unto sin; but present yourselves to God, as those that are alive from the dead; and your members as instruments of justice unto God.'[1]

[1] Rom. vi. 1-13.

The death of Christ and baptism, then, are the same spiritual reality. Our own higher life and Christ's resurrection are also the same spiritual reality. The Christian detests sin, is dead to sin, not in virtue of a law that says: 'Thou shalt not', but in virtue of his keen realisation of Christ's death, who died on the cross to destroy sin. Through the innermost fibres of his regenerated being the death of Christ makes him have a horror of sin. Does he want a law to forbid sin, when he sees that Christ died from the evil of man's sin? Such a sight, the sight of the crucified Son of God, is warning enough for the Christian: it is more than warning, it is a permanent state of conscience that makes sin appear in its full hideousness. And how does he ever want to go back to sin, when it is his very condition to walk with the risen Christ in newness of life? It is possible, of course, for the Christian to commit grievous sin. But his whole spiritual being, built up on Christ's death and Christ's resurrection, simply cries out against that deed in a way that law never can do. His sin is against his own regenerated soul, much more than against a law. Could there be a better description of the Christ psychology, of the all-sufficiency of Christ, as the principle of spiritual life?

The general idea of the substitution of Christ for the system of law, and the more specific idea that such a substitution, far from being an open door to antinomianism, is a quickening of the moral sense, are illustrated by one and the same example, at the beginning of the seventh chapter of the Epistle to the Romans. It is taken from the law of matrimony. 'Know you not, brethren (for I speak to them that know the law) that the law hath dominion over a man, as long as he liveth? For the woman that hath an husband, whilst her husband liveth is bound to the law. But if her husband be dead, she is loosed from the law of her husband. Therefore, whilst her husband liveth, she shall be called an adulteress, if she be with another man; but if her husband be dead, she is delivered from the law of her husband; so that she is not an adulteress, if she be with another man. Therefore, my brethren, you also are become dead to the law, by the body of Christ: that you may belong to another, who is risen again from the dead that we may bring forth fruit to God. For when we were in the flesh, the passions of sins, which were by the law, did work in our members to bring forth fruit unto death. But now we are loosed from the law of death wherein we were detained; so that we should serve in the newness of spirit, not in the oldness of the letter.'[1]

Two main ideas come out very clearly from this seemingly involved, but very telling, argument.

The soul leaves the law, now dead, and is wedded to the risen Christ, and the natural fruit of this happy and loving alliance is spiritual fecundity. This liberty to go away from the law, to be with another, is not a forgetfulness of duty, it is not a barrenness in spirit, but it is fruitfulness in God Himself. It is the higher matrimony of the soul with God, and if it is a service, it is 'in the newness of spirit, not in the oldness of the letter'.

I must remind the reader that I do not profess to be writing a commentary on the Epistles of St. Paul, but am concerned with the study of his Christ-psychology. Were I to write such a commentary, I would give very special attention to St. Paul's way of using metaphors and similes. The Apostle never uses a parable in the logical sequence of a Gospel parable; for him, an example is not a thing of rigid logic, but of broad analogy. Between the great truth that overwhelms his mind, and a given example from history, law or nature, he perceives points of contact, and his mind jumps from one to another irrespective of reasoned connections. So in this instance; death of the husband means liberty for the wife. Christ also is another man in His risen state from what He was in death. And those things which follow, concerning the new fruitfulness in God, are so many scintillating sparks of light struck from St. Paul's mind as it works upon his simile of the wedding with the risen Christ, and as it meets new points of contact. It would be futile to press St. Paul's comparison beyond what it really is, a brilliant assemblage of analogies. No amount of subtlety could ever make of Christ's death the logical parallel of a husband's death, for the simple reason that the soul was not wedded to Christ before His death. But the great fact remains, that Christ's death has set man free from sin, and servitude, even from spiritual servitude, and through the merit of that death we are entitled to the unspeakably high grace of the spiritual nuptials of the soul with the risen Christ, we are called to serve in the newness of spirit, not in the oldness of the letter.

The living spirit, as opposed to the dead letter, is one of St.

[1] Rom. vii. 1-6.

Paul's ever-recurring ideas, and the relation of this idea to what I might call Christ-spirituality is obvious. Christ is the living spirit, everything else is a dead letter. Paul has drunk so deep from the cup of Christ's love, that the wisest and the best thing, when not informed by Christ's presence, is dull and dead to him. In the second Epistle to the Corinthians we find him quite unexpectedly giving utterance to this obsessing thought; the occasion seeming hardly adequate to provoke so noble an utterance. His enemies had been trying to undermine his position at Corinth; he appeals to their old affection and to his own well-known affection for them. With contempt he spurns away the idea that he is trying to commend himself to their favour, after so many years of loyal love. He is not the man who is in need of an epistle of commendation to them, a letter of introduction!

But the word 'epistle of commendation' coming here as a natural development of his eager effort to show his real footing with the Corinthians, is an idea too full of bright facets to be neglected: 'Do we begin again to commend ourselves? Or do we need (as some do) epistles of commendation to you, or from you? You are our epistle, written in our hearts, which is known and read by all men: being manifested, that you are the epistle of Christ, ministered by us, and written: not with ink but with the Spirit of the living God: not in tables of stone but in the fleshly tables of the heart. And such confidence we have, through Christ, towards God. Not that we are sufficient to think anything of ourselves, as of ourselves: but our sufficiency is from God. Who also hath made us fit ministers of the new testament, not in the letter but in the spirit. For the letter killeth, but the spirit quickeneth.'[1]

It would be impossible to find anywhere a more vivacious use of a metaphor, where there is such an absolute disregard of the logical parallelism combined with so effective a working up to the final statement. The underlying simile is a letter of commendation, the metaphor reaches its climax when the writer makes the assertion that the Corinthians themselves are a letter written by Christ 'with the Spirit of the Living God ... in the fleshly tables of the heart'.

It would be difficult to express in a more telling way that the psychology of the Christian is something quite unique, something

[1] 2 Cor. iii. 1-6.

very personal to Christ. 'Being manifested, that you are the epistle of Christ.' The regenerated soul bears Christ's private signature. We know, when we have read the passage, that St. Paul has once more spoken his great conviction, that Christ is the living spirit.

In his metaphor of the commendatory letter, St. Paul, quite unexpectedly again, introduces the allusion to the tables of stone on which the Law had been written, in opposition to 'the fleshly tables of the heart'. He rises easily to the parallel of Moses, who carried the tables, and to the countenance of Moses, which was so transformed in glory that the children of Israel did not dare to look upon it. This new thought, of the veiled face of Moses, is one more welcome illustration, by way of contrast, of the excellency of the Christian ministry (which ministry is merely another aspect of the Christian's relations with Christ). It leads up to one of the most striking pronouncements, even from St. Paul, on the immediateness of our relations with our Lord. 'Now the Lord is a Spirit, and where the Spirit of the Lord is, there is liberty. But we all, beholding the glory of the Lord with open face, are transformed into the same image from glory to glory, as by the Spirit of the Lord.'[1] These beautiful words are frequently quoted as a description of the blessed vision of God in Heaven. Such interpretation can be read into them, by way of extension, but there is no doubt that the words refer to the process of spiritual identification between Christ and man, here on earth. The whole context demands that we should apply the doctrine to our present life. It is in the present life we enjoy the privileges, the glories of that higher ministry, which has finality, in opposition to the Mosaic dispensation which is made void in Christ.

As the minister of a God who speaks with us directly, the Apostle disdains to put a veil over his face in his daily intercourse with the faithful. Let every Christian gaze constantly and boldly on the face of Christ. Nothing can stand between the Son of God and the soul for 'the Lord is a Spirit' who is not tied down to any circumstance of time and place, of laws and ceremonies. 'Now if the ministration of death, engraven with letters upon stones, was glorious (so that the children of Israel could not steadfastly behold the face of Moses, for the glory of his countenance), which is made void: how

[1] 2 Cor. iii. 17-18.

shall not the ministration of the Spirit be rather in glory? For if the
ministration of condemnation be glory, much more the ministration
of justice aboundeth in glory. For even that which was glorious in
this part was not glorified by reason of the glory that excelleth. For
if that which is done away was glorious, much more that which
remaineth is in glory. Having therefore such hope, we use much
confidence: and not as Moses put a veil upon his face, that the
children of Israel might not steadfastly look on the face of that
which is made void. But their senses were made dull. For, until this
present day, the selfsame veil, in the reading of the old testament,
remaineth not taken away (because in Christ it is made void). But
even until this day when Moses is read, the veil is upon their heart.
But when they shall be converted to the Lord, the veil shall be taken
away. Now the Lord is a Spirit. And where the Spirit of the Lord
is, there is liberty. But we all, beholding the glory of the Lord with
open face, are transformed into the same image from glory to glory,
as by the Spirit of the Lord.'[1]

The Epistle to the Galatians, more than any other epistle, is of set
purpose the defence of the doctrine that 'as many of you as have
been baptized in Christ, have put on Christ.'[2] The Galatians, instructed and baptized by St. Paul, directly from Paganism, had lent
their ear to false teachers, who made them believe that the law of
Moses was indispensable to salvation. St. Paul rebukes their credul-
ity with the masterfulness of a loving and watchful father. His theme
once more is about the law versus the living Christ: directly and
primarily he means the law of Moses, but, as in many other places,
he extends his doctrines, and he applies his arguments to the moral
law in general, and he contrasts it with the advantage of having one's
higher hopes anchored in the living Christ. There are three distinct
arguments establishing that truth in this epistle. First, the Apostle
gives a new and abridged version of the argument we have already
seen in the Epistle to the Romans. It deals with the promise made to
Abraham. The essential point is the nature of that promise. It was
not a bilateral compact, but an unilateral one; God alone making the
promise. 'Now a mediator is not of one; but God is one.'[3] The Law
was a bilateral arrangement between God and man, and Moses had
been the mediator between God and the people. The covenant that

---

[1] 2 Cor. iii. 7-18.   [2] Gal. iii. 27.   [3] Gal. iii. 20.

came more than four hundred years after could not weaken that great promise. The Law cannot give life, if it did the great promise of God concerning the seed, which is Christ, would have become superfluous. 'That the promise by faith of Jesus Christ might be given to them that believe,' is just the Christian's hope. He stands and falls by the reliability of that personal, unilateral act of God, a promise. 'To Abraham were the promises made and to his seed. He saith not, *And to his seeds*, as of many: but as of one, *And to thy seed*, which is Christ. Now this I say: that the testament which was con-firmed by God, the law which was made after four hundred and thirty years doth not dis-annul, to make the promise of no effect. For if the inheritance be of the law, it is no more of promise. But God gave it to Abraham by promise. Why then was the law? It was set because of transgressions, until the seed should come to whom he made the promise, being ordained by angels in the hand of a mediator. Now a mediator is not of one: but God is one. Was the law then against the promises of God? God forbid! For if there had been a law given which could give life, verily justice should have been by the law. But the scripture hath concluded all under sin, that the promise, by the faith of Jesus Christ, might be given to them that believe. But before the faith came, we were kept under the law shut up, unto that faith which was to be revealed.'[1]

The last sentence, containing the metaphor of children shut up under tutorship, gives rise to a new comparison, the beautiful simile of the pedagogue. The Law is a mere pedagogue, our peda-gogue in Christ: faith sets us free from the pedagogue's tutorship, and makes us children of God. All men are equally privileged through baptism, they are all one in Christ Jesus. The spiritual con-dition of the Christian is absolutely superior to any other state of morality, and the soul of the Christian enjoys an endless measure of spiritual liberty. The metaphor is worked out more consecutively than most others, and the climax is reached quite naturally in the familiar words: 'And because you are sons, God hath sent the Spirit of His Son into your hearts, crying: Abba, Father.'[2]

But here is the whole of that glorious text: 'Before the faith came, we were kept under the law shut up, unto that faith which

[1] Gal. iii. 16-23.   [2] Gal. iv. 6.

was to be revealed. Wherefore the law was our pedagogue in Christ; that we might be justified by faith. But after the faith is come, we are no longer under a pedagogue. For you are all the children of God, by faith in Christ Jesus. For as many of you as have been baptized in Christ have put on Christ. There is neither Jew nor Greek: there is neither bond nor free: there is neither male nor female. For you are all one in Christ Jesus. And if you be Christ's, then are you the seed of Abraham, heirs according to the promise. Now I say, As long as the heir is a child, he differeth nothing from a servant, though he be lord of all, but is under tutors and governors until the time appointed by the father. So we also, when we were children, were serving under the elements of the world. But when the fulness of the time was come, God sent His Son, made of a woman, made under the law: that He might redeem them who were under the law: that we might receive the adoption of sons. And because you are sons, God hath sent the Spirit of His Son into your hearts, crying: Abba, Father. Therefore, now He is not a servant, but a son. And if a son, an heir also through God. But then indeed, not knowing God, you served them who, by nature, are not gods.'[1]

The third argument from the Galatians embodies once more the idea of the gratuitous promise made to Abraham. St. Paul, for once, stops to give the allegory a connecting link, when in the twenty-fifth verse of the fourth chapter he makes Sina, the Mount in Arabia, the parallel of the earthly Jerusalem, by reason of the geographical affinity. His argument differs from the preceding ones in this, that instead of the individual soul, it is the whole new Jerusalem, the Church, that is the free-woman. 'Tell me, you that desire to be under the law, have you not read the law? For it is written that Abraham had two sons; the one by a bond-woman and the other by a free-woman. But he who was of the bond-woman was born according to the flesh; but he of the free-woman was by promise. Which things are said by an allegory. For these are the two testaments. The one from mount Sina, engendering unto bondage, which is Agar. For Sina is a mountain in Arabia, which hath affinity to that Jerusalem which now is: and is in bondage with her children. But that Jerusalem which is above is free: which is our mother. For it is written: *Rejoice, thou barren, that bearest not; break forth and cry, thou*

---

[1] Gal. iii, 23-iv. 8,

that travailest not: for many are the children of the desolate, more than of
her that hath a husband. Now we, brethren, as Isaac was, are the
children of promise. But as then he that was born according to the
flesh persecuted him that was after the spirit: so also it is now. But
what saith the scripture? Cast out the bond-woman and her son: for
the son of the bond-woman shall not be heir with the son of the free-
woman. So then, brethren, we are not the children of the bond-
woman, but of the free: by the freedom wherewith Christ has made
us free.'[1]

The last argument in favour of Christ's spirituality occurs in the
Epistle to the Colossians. In the passage to be quoted we again find
St. Paul at his best. Here is metaphor within metaphor, it is a playing with light and shade of which only a very poetical mind is capable. I shall first give the whole section appertaining to my subject,
though I must confess that it would be necessary to transcribe the
whole epistle if one were to give the argument its proper setting;
but nothing is easier for my reader than to take up his New Testament, and go through this beautiful epistle himself. What St. Paul
says of Christ's super-eminent spiritual glories in the first chapter,
and in the earlier parts of the second chapter, is all meant to lead
up to his practical appeal, to save his converts from relapsing into
lower and false forms of spirituality.

But the argument proper, where the Apostle begins to come to
close grips with the enemy, may be said to start at the eighth verse
of chapter two. 'Beware lest any man cheat you by philosophy and
vain deceit; according to the tradition of men, according to the
elements of the world and not according to Christ. For in Him
dwelleth all fulness of the Godhead corporeally: and you are filled
in Him, who is the head of all principality and power. In whom also
you are circumcised with circumcision not made by hand in despoiling of the body of the flesh: but in the circumcision of Christ.
Buried with Him in baptism: in whom also you are risen again by
the faith of the operation of God who hath raised Him up from the
dead. And you, when you were dead in your sins and the uncircumcision of your flesh: He hath quickened together with Him, forgiving you all offences: blotting out the handwriting of the decree that
was against us, which was contrary to us. And He hath taken the

[1] Gal. iv. 21-31.

same out of the way, fastening it to the cross: And despoiling the principalities and powers, he hath exposed them confidently in open shew, triumphing over them in Himself. Let no man therefore judge you in meat or in drink or in respect of a festival day or of the new moon, or of the sabbaths, which are a shadow of things to come: but the body is of Christ. Let no man seduce you, willing in humility and religion of angels, walking in the things which he hath not seen, in vain puffed up by the sense of his flesh. And not holding the head, from which the whole body, by joints and bands, being supplied with nourishment and compacted, groweth into the increase of God. If then you be dead with Christ from the elements of this world, why do you yet decree as though living in the world? Touch not: taste not: handle not. Which all are unto destruction by the very use, according to the precepts and doctrines of men. Which things have indeed a shew of wisdom in superstition and humility, and not sparing the body: not in any honour to the filling of the flesh. Therefore, if you be risen with Christ, seek the things that are above, where Christ is sitting at the right hand of God. Mind the things that are above, not the things that are upon the earth. For you are dead: and your life is hid with Christ in God. When Christ shall appear, who is your life, then you also shall appear with Him in glory.'[1]

The great liberation from the 'elements of the world', as St. Paul so aptly calls everything that is lower than Christ Himself, is here expressed in five different metaphors, amongst which there is only one he has already made use of. The old circumcision itself, his *bête noire*, is turned into a thing of beauty: 'You are circumcised ... in the circumcision of Christ.' Then there is the sacrament of baptism, that glorious successor of the old carnal rite. 'You are buried with Him in Baptism.' It is the idea we already found in the Epistle to the Romans. The third and fourth metaphors are new, and deeply original, and found nowhere else in St. Paul's writings. They speak of Christ's absolute triumph over the old order of things, and over the power that swayed the old order. First the metaphor of the bill that is fixed on the cross. 'Blotting out the handwriting of the decree that was against us, which was contrary to us. And He hath taken the same out of the way, fastening it to the cross.' Then the

[1] Col. ii. 8-iii. 4.

triumphal procession; Christ leading all vanquished powers, as their captor, to the Capitol: 'And despoiling the principalities and powers, He hath led them confidently in open shew, triumphing over them, in Himself.' Finally there is the metaphor of the body versus the shadow, which is strengthened by the doctrine that Christ is the Head. 'The body is of Christ ... the head, from which the whole body, by joints and bands, being supplied with nourishment, and compacted, groweth into the increase of God.'

With such a presentment of Christ's care, and of the soul's nearness to Him, who would still mould his mind by ancient and low standards? 'Why do you yet decree as living in the world?' Let it all depart before the glory of the Easter sun; life in Christ is the only thing worth cherishing. 'Therefore if you be risen with Christ, seek the things that are above: where Christ is sitting at the right hand of God: mind the things that are above, not the things that are upon the earth. For you are dead: and your life is hid with Christ in God. When Christ shall appear, who is your life, then you also shall appear with Him in glory.'

It might be said without fear of exaggeration that the whole concept of the Christian Mind is contained in the arguments of St. Paul here set forth. St. Paul's great contention is that Christ is a heavenly substitute for all law, containing the virtue of all law in Himself, *per modum eminentiae*. All other considerations concerning the nature of the Christian Mind flow from this central thought. The Son of God, Jesus Christ, is such as to embody in Himself all the needs, and laws, and hopes, and destinies of man. The remaining chapters of my book will be nothing more than an expansion of this root fact of the Incarnation. They will endeavour to cover practically the whole subject of the Christian Mind; I mean those elements of our higher life which are derived specifically from the Incarnation, though I do not profess to set them forth in a strictly logical order. It is impossible logically to dissect a personality; and it must always be borne in mind that the Christian Mind is a religious philosophy based on a divine Personality.

CHAPTER IX

The New Creature in Christ

ST. PAUL'S concept of man's transformation through the life that comes from the Incarnation, is as radical as possible. The Incarnation is simply a new creation, and through Christ and in Christ we are new creatures: 'For we are his workmanship, created in Christ Jesus in good works, which God hath prepared that we should walk in them.'[1] 'Put on the new man, who according to God is created in justice and holiness of truth.'[2] 'If then any be in Christ a new creature, the old things are passed away. Behold all things are made new.'[3]

The Greek term χτίσις has a very definite meaning in St. Paul's writings. It stands for creation in its specific significance as the act of God, or the product of God, implying omnipotence. All things that are, are God's creation. When therefore St. Paul repeats with such insistence that in Christ a new creation has taken place, he is writing in his own way something as great and original as the first chapter of Genesis. Man is re-made, re-created in the Son of God, not by an inferior sort of χτίσις, but by one that is the proper act of God, such as He exercised when He made all things in the beginning. And the new creature that is in Christ lives and thrives on that creative act of God, just as the created universe rests on the divine *fiat* that brought it out of nothingness.

Here, as in many other instances, it is only our mental timidity that makes us attach to the words of the inspired writer a meaning different and inferior to their direct and native significance. But why should we take in a diminished and lower sense the word χτίσις, creation, when St. Paul utters it in connection with the great supernatural reality, our life in Christ? Why should we qualify its bearing, or modify its literalness? Surely the Incarnation and its results are not such as to give rise to hyperbole, as their reality will always be greater than any words contrived by man to express them. It is therefore both my right and my privilege to give the term χτίσις in connection with the life in Christ as literal an interpretation

[1] Eph. ii. 10.   [2] Eph. iv. 24.   [3] 2 Cor. v. 17.

as I do when the same word states the great fact that God made all things out of nothing.

The 'new creation', taken in this direct and literal sense, leads us at once to one most precious result for our spiritual estate: through Christ we are lifted bodily above the ordinary human conditions. We are transplanted into a new world, whose laws and conditions have finality and completeness in themselves. This new world is not necessarily in opposition to the first, the natural world created by God; it is above it, it has higher and more permanent rights and obligations. To conceive Christ, and ourselves in Him, as a totally new creation, with all the universal laws inherent to a creation, settles once for all a subtle perplexity of the Christian Mind; the Christian's relation with the merely natural order of things, and its legitimate interests and aspirations. How is the Christian, who is part of a new creation, to make use of the first, the old creation?

As I said, the same term χτίσις expresses the making of the world, and the making of the Christ and His graces. It is the incommunicable act of God. Both creative acts, though resulting in a lower and a higher order of things, come from the same source; they could not be at enmity. The Christian, therefore, ought to be completely at home in every aspect of creation, precisely because as Christian he is God's creation, and as man again he is God's creation. There is indeed in him a duality of life, the life of nature, and the life of grace. But this duality is not an opposition, as it comes from one and the same fountain head, God's causative omnipotence.

'Every creature (χτίσμα) of God is good, and nothing to be rejected that is received with thanksgiving: for it is sanctified by the word of God and prayer.'[1] Such is the general principle laid down by St. Paul writing to Timothy, as to the worth and moral status of the natural creation. Already at that early period there were signs of a false, unchristian dualism. There were 'spirits of error, and doctrines of devils, speaking lies in hypocrisy and having their conscience seared, forbidding to marry, and (wanting people) to abstain from meats, which God hath created to be received with thanksgiving by the faithful, and by them that have known the truth.'[2] A hypocritical reluctance to enter into communion with the things of the natural

---

[1] 1 Tim. iv. 4-5.   [2] 1 Tim. iv. 1-3.

order, besides leading to a most disastrous spiritual pride, assumes
that nature is not God's creation, that there is a chasm between
Christ and the natural universe. But if this error is corrected through
knowledge that both nature and grace in man are the creation of
God, there is the more important healing of his mind, through the
fact that the grace of the Incarnation, being a true creation, has a
status superior to and independent of nature.

The claims of the Incarnation on man are infinite, because the
Incarnation is an infinite mystery of life. Nature however vast, is
finite, with finite claims on man's allegiance. When therefore man
is at any time tempted to give too much to nature, he is brought
back to the golden mean through the infinitely vaster, and more
persistent claims of the Incarnation. Now St. Paul has this aspect in
view when speaking of the grace of Christ compared with the
natural claims of race and nationality. Without under-estimating the
value of such claims, he simply states that in virtue of the new
creation in Christ, such a perfect brotherhood, such a complete
community of blood exists between Christians, that racial differences, however legitimate, are in no danger of becoming excessive,
if Christian grace be given a chance. 'For in Christ Jesus neither
circumcision availeth any thing, nor uncircumcision, but a new
creature.'[1] 'Putting on the new (man), him who is renewed unto
knowledge, according to the image of Him that created him.
Where there is neither Gentile nor Jew, circumcision nor uncircumcision, Barbarian nor Scythian, bond nor free. But Christ
is all and in all.'[2]

This divine supra-nationalism of St. Paul, the consequence of his
clear vision of the New Creation in Christ, was as bold and difficult
then as it is to-day, when racial passions are so sorely on edge. Yet
this attitude of the Christian Mind is the only thing that can rescue
the nations from the absurd and appalling results of racialism out of
bounds. For a good many centuries Christian thought and national
thought were happily wedded together. The most unworldly follower of Christ is a lover of his country. But periodically the question is put to Catholics, whether their religion or their allegiance to
their country holds the first place. Non-Catholics seem to think
that in the minds of the perfect Christian there is such a dualism,

[1] Gal. vi. 15.   [2] Col. iii. 10-11.

when in fact it is nowhere to be found. It would be just as absurd to ask any citizen what holds the first place in his mind, personal honesty, or loyalty to his country. He would be puzzled no doubt by such a division of his duties; for him honesty and loyalty are inseparable things. But, on reflection, he might realise that loyalty to the state is contained in personal honesty, as a smaller thing may be contained in a bigger thing. Personal honesty is something more universal, as all men may possess personal honesty, whilst loyalty to a definite community of men and interests is only possible if such a community exists. After all it is at least theoretically possible for men to live without such sharply defined communities, whilst honesty is at the base of all human life that is superior to animal instincts. Personal honesty can never be truly in opposition to any legitimate loyalty, as no worthy cause can be served by anything that is dishonest. Therefore it is as idle as it is irritating to ask a man such questions. Enough for him to know that patriotism is a virtue, though it be not the whole of righteousness.

So likewise with that new creation, the Christian Mind. The all embracing charity of Christ is the greater reality. Any other love, as love of one's country, is a smaller thing, contained in the universal charity of Christ. All things are the creation of God, but 'Christ holds in all things the primacy.'[1] All things are in Him and under Him and therefore all things are lovable. Nothing that is true and good need ever be sacrificed on the altar of Christ, it merely needs to be brought into subjection to Him, into harmony with His own lovableness.

This universality of charity that recognises no difference of races in the higher sphere where Christ dwells, is perfectly compatible with difference of special claims on the part of the one nation to which we belong. But it is not compatible with any kind of hatred, except the hatred of iniquity. Patriotism is no more served by racial hatred than it is by dishonesty, for racial hatred, not patriotism, simply renders man unfit for that immense human advantage of entering into communion with the wealth, spiritual and material, of other nations. The charity of Christ therefore is the finest mental attitude for all genuine diplomacy. No men are more fit to handle the great international problems than the men who love all races in

[1] Col. i. 18.

Christ, and before whose mind the infinitely great factor of universal Redemption through the Incarnation stands out as the one unchanging institution. A thousand wars, lost or won, cannot do away with the claims of the new Creation in Christ. We Christians simply must love all men in Christ. If we refuse to do so, we can have no share in the new Creation.

Nationalism in religion makes of nationalism itself a most unreasonable thing, a thing charged with most dangerous potentialities. The boldest statement of this spiritual superiority over racial exclusiveness is found in St. Paul's Second Epistle to the Corinthians: 'Wherefore henceforth, we know no man according to the flesh. And if we have known Christ according to the flesh: but now we know Him so no longer.'[1] The Messiah to come was more than anything else the boast of the Jewish nation. The Christ to their minds was essentially Jewish. His mission according to their belief would be a great racial triumph. Such had been the dream of Saul of Tarsus. He too, before being struck down by the light from Heaven, was all aglow with hope and fervour for a national Messiah.

It was an enthusiasm all according to the flesh. But when Christ, the Son of David, manifested Himself finally to the mental eyes of Saul, in His own transcending glory, then he understood the mystery of Christ's glorious universalism. At once he felt lifted up to a new world, the boundaries of which are infinite, and this new world is Christ's. Paul can move freely in it, his mind travels over it without check or hindrance. In an ecstasy of joy he cries out: 'If then any be in Christ a new creature, the old things are passed away. Behold all things are made new.'[2]

CHAPTER X

The Central Position of the Christian Mind

SPIRITUAL tendencies are often represented as being either centripetal or centrifugal. This division, taken from natural science, is an easily understood simile. Centripetal tendencies

---

[1] 2 Cor. v. 16.   [2] 2 Cor. v. 17.

are movements of the mind towards the centre of all things, God; centrifugal tendencies are the opposite: they are destructive of harmony and unity in things spiritual. The Christian Mind is radically centripetal: all its tendencies and aspirations are towards God, and they make for harmony and unity. The obedience of the Christian Mind is at bottom nothing else than this blissful convergence of all its powers towards the eternal centre of all light and truth, God.

But there is something more in the Christian Mind than this centripetal tendency; for it not only tends towards the great centre, God, but it is itself *central*. It occupies a central position from the very start. Being in Christ in a most excellent way, and from that point of vantage, Christ, it looks at all things. 'The peace of God, which surpasseth all understanding, keep your hearts and minds in Christ Jesus.'[1] As God is in Christ, reconciling the world unto Himself, so, in a finite but analogous way, the mind perfectly educated in the things of the Incarnation is in Christ, as in its natural centre; looking at the world from that sublime height, and bringing all things into harmony.

It is quite evident that the early Christian Mind was thus centred in Christ. To the faithful of the first Christian period there was only one great object of contemplation: the Son of God in His power and glory. They looked at the world in general, and at mankind in particular, through the Son of God; from the height of Christ's glory. I might almost say, that by comparison mankind was practically an indifferent thing, incapable of arousing interest. Their enthusiasm was centred on Christ, and His grace, the propagation of that grace, and the preaching of the name of Christ for its own sake, because it is the greatest of all names. Their missionary zeal was more love of Christ, than love of mankind. They knew little about mankind, they only dreaded its dark enmities. But they knew much about Christ, and they basked in the sunshine of His love. They were sure of Him. In fact He was their only security, their true harbour of refuge. In Him alone they dared to approach the world. If their preaching was successful, it was Christ's power operating through them. If their mission failed, it was Christ's judgment on an unworthy world. As for themselves, neither failure nor success could alter their sense of

[1] Phil. iv. 7.

^spiritual possession. They possessed Christ, and in Him they possessed Heaven and earth, whatever the beliefs and conduct of their fellow-men.

That such was the attitude of the primitive Christian, and above all of St. Paul, can be proved by innumerable references. In order to understand it more clearly, let us compare it with another attitude of mind, extremely common in our days amongst those who have the missionary spirit. Most of these people look at mankind first. Their fellow-men are their paramount interest. They love them, and pity them for their own sake, and in consequence they are anxious to see as many men and women converted to Christ as possible. If believers be few, they feel as if they belonged spiritually to a small world only; there is a general sentiment of disappointment in their life. If, on the contrary, believers be many, their heart is dilated with the satisfaction of being the children of a great Kingdom. Their first and leading thought is the conversion of mankind, not the coming of Christ.

Humanity, its evolution and its progress are the fetishes of modern non-Christian thought. Everywhere we find the religion of humanity pushing back the worship of the Son of God. It is the sort of religion that easily becomes popular, as it has all the external signs of love and philanthropy. In a certain way, this idea of the predominant value of humanity has affected Christian thought; and the conditions of salvation for mankind as a whole are more absorbing and perplexing problems to many present-day believers than they were to other generations of Christians.

As in many other instances of subordinate principles, the minor truth may engender a helpful and salutary attitude of the mind, so long as it be regulated by the major truth. Taken away from the control of the higher principle, the lesser may easily become an aberration, a mental disturbance. So in this matter of the relative importance of mankind and Christ. To love mankind is a good thing; to love it outside Christ gives it at once a disproportionate place in the mind. To give to mankind any other but a subordinate place would be a great mental disorder in those who believe in the Son of God; for the one Son of God made man is an infinitely vaster thing than the whole aggregate of men, past, present, and future. The great questions for the Christian Mind all have the Son of God directly for their object. What is He in Himself, and what are His dealings with the children of men? This is what I call the central position of the Christian Mind.

Nowhere in the Gospels do we hear Christ giving utterance to an expectation that mankind as such, i.e. the human race, will ever be entirely conquered by His grace in this world. On the contrary, He solemnly describes Himself as being accessible only to certain pre-ordained classes of people: 'I confess to Thee, O Father, Lord of Heaven and earth, because Thou hast hid these things from the wise and prudent, and hast revealed them to little ones. Yea, Father: for so hath it seemed good in Thy sight. All things are delivered to Me by My Father. And no one knoweth the Son, but the Father: neither doth any one know the Father, but the Son and he to whom it shall please the Son to reveal Him.'[1] Of universal and uncontested conquest of mankind to the obedience of His faith, there is never any assurance in the mind or on the lips of Christ. With constant utterance as to the universality of His power, our Lord couples assertions not less emphatic as to the limited number of His followers, and the restricted success of the Gospel: 'Will not God revenge His elect who cry to Him day and night? And will He have patience in their regard? I say to you that He will quickly revenge them. But yet the Son of man, when He cometh, shall He find, think you, faith on earth?'[2]

His disciples are bidden to look upon mankind generally as upon a hostile, savage power: 'Behold I send you as sheep in the midst of wolves. Be ye therefore wise as serpents and simple as doves. But beware of men.'[3] On the other hand, they are bidden to meet the world protected by their faith in the Son of God, as by armour. To go out to the world in their own name, and in their own wisdom, would be suicidal to them. 'But when they shall deliver you up, take no thought how or what to speak: for it shall be given you in that hour what to speak. For it is not you that speak, but the Spirit of your Father that speaketh in you.'[4]

Nothing would be easier than to collect quotations from St. Paul showing how he possessed that central attitude of mind, how to him apostolic activity was essentially a glorification of Christ, and how he practically ignored all things outside Christ. 'What have I to do

[1] Matt. xi. 25-27.   [2] Luke xviii. 7, 8.   [3] Matt. x. 16, 17.   [4] Matt. x. 19, 20.

to judge them that are without?...For them that are without, God wil
judge.'¹ There is in St. Paul's attitude a marked love of predestination, in its orthodox sense. He knows Christ and those that are in
Christ; he is full of activity, travelling all over the world to convert
to Christ those that are predestined to His grace, whose election has
made them already potentially Christ's. Outside that circle he has
no real interest. Whatever is beyond the radius of Christ he leaves
to the judgment of God, it is no concern of his. The spiritual
destinies of 'those without' are not even a problem to his mind.
They are no part of his world. That such is the attitude of St. Paul's
mind is beyond doubt. Christ and the things of Christ are essentially
life, a practical activity of the heart and the mind. Outside Christ
nothing is practical or possible in the spiritual order. So for St.
Paul's mind there is practically only one sphere of thought and
activity, that of which Christ is the centre.

Now and then it would seem as if the great Apostle, in a less re-
strictive frame of mind, were concerned with questions of more
universal salvation. In the Epistle to the Romans he alludes to the
possibility of spiritual justification for the Gentiles to whom no
Revelation has been granted, 'who shew the work of the law written
in their hearts, their conscience bearing witness to them.'² In
1 Tim. ii, 4, he says of 'God our Saviour' that 'He will have all men
to be saved and to come to the knowledge of the truth.' Again in
1 Tim. iv, 10, God is said to be 'the Saviour of all men, especially
of the faithful.' Better known still are St. Paul's pathetic utterances
concerning the salvation of the Jewish people who had not believed
in Christ: 'Brethren, the will of my heart, indeed, and my prayer to
God is for them unto salvation.'³ But in all these utterances St.
Paul's mind never leaves its centre. The salvation which God has in
store for us all, the prayer of St. Paul, the judgment over the
heathen who has not known the Law, it is all in Christ. The
heathen's conscience will be his accuser or defender 'in the day
when God shall judge the secrets of men by Jesus Christ, according
to my Gospel.'⁴

In the Gospel of St. John this Christ-centredness is most evident:
'All things were made by Him: and without Him was made nothing
that was made. In Him was life, and the life was the light of

¹ 1 Cor. v. 12, 13.   ² Rom. ii. 15.   ³ Rom. x. 1.   ⁴ Rom. ii. 16.

men.'[1] All through St. John's Gospel we find the exclusiveness of the infinite stated most emphatically. Christ is infinite life, yet it is an infinity to which only a few have access, which practically touches only a chosen number. The failure of Christ's mission with regard to individuals is one of the facts most insisted upon in St. John's Gospel. 'Remember my word that I said to you: The servant is not greater than his master. If they have persecuted Me, they will also persecute you. If they have kept my word, they will keep yours also.'[2] But with all this failure, the great life, the great kingdom of God is in no way damaged or circumscribed. It is all fulness from the very beginning, and those that believe are beyond the reach of disappointment. 'That which My Father hath given Me, is greater than all: and no one can snatch them out of the hand of My Father.'[3]

Even when St. Paul uses expressions that at first sight seem to denote more universal application, his aspirations never go outside Christ. It is St. Paul's dream to present every man perfect; but not without this qualification—in Christ Jesus; in whom also he labours, as if He were the proper field of his activities, and as if all his movements were contained within His universality of grace: 'To whom (i.e. the Saints) God would make known the riches of the glory of this mystery among the Gentiles, which is Christ, in you the hope of glory. Whom we preach, admonishing every man and teaching every man in all wisdom, that we may present every man perfect in Christ Jesus. Wherein also I labour, striving according to His working which He worketh in me in power.'[4]

CHAPTER XI

Our Equality in Christ

THE inequalities of human life and human conditions have always been a trial to man's patience. Certain generations have felt them more than others; but no age has been without the angry rumblings of resentment at the inequalities

[1] John i. 3-4. [2] John xv. 20. [3] John x. 29. [4] Col. i. 27-30.

of human destinies. From the revolt of slaves and plebeians in the Roman world to the idolisation of equality in the French revolution may be a far cry in point of time; but as a matter of psychology it is the same threatening voice of offended humanity. To the practical theories of human equality which are at the root of social reforms throughout the ages, there corresponds in the realm of religious thought a distinct socialism of outlook. Many philosophical and even religious systems are to a great extent the outcome of rebellion, albeit unconscious, against privilege and preference, either in the order of nature or even in the Christian dispensation.

It was to be expected that the problem of human inequalities should be brought into contact with the grace of the Incarnation, and if a solution were possible, that it should be solved in Christ. It is very gratifying, then, to see this problem constantly brought up by St. Paul, and as consistently solved in the same manner. The mind of the Apostle had grasped the principle of equality in Christ from the very beginning, and he applies it with perfect appropriateness and success to the most diverse cases. This idea of Christian equality is one of the most precious elements of the Christian Mind, and it is as original as the Eucharist, or the Pleroma, with which in fact the principle is intimately associated. It comes to this: Christ is substantive fulness. As such, He fills up all inequalities, so that he who is less, or has less, provided he be in Christ, is not really unequal to him that is greater, or has more.

Such is, to my thinking, the general enunciation of the principle of equality in Christ. Whilst safeguarding the difference of attributes and gifts, it does away with inequality of condition. 'He that had much, had nothing over: and he that had little, had no want.'[1] We must make a distinction between difference of gifts, nay, even inequalities of gifts, and inequalities of condition. Gifts in the natural and spiritual order may differ; there may be more or fewer of them; they may even be called unequal gifts, but such differences, so long as they do not produce inequalities of condition, are not resented by man. But the moment the greater endowment isolates its possessor from the man less endowed, makes of him a being apart, the difference is resented; the inequality is no longer in the gift, but in the mode of existence. Wealth is the main object of

[1] Exod. xvi. 18; 2 Cor. viii. 15.

human jealousies, not so much on account of the greater material enjoyments it brings, as on account of the social gulf it creates between the wealthy and the poor. Yet wherever Christian charity bridges over the gulf, when the true fraternity between rich and poor is a practical fact of life, it is wonderful how little resentment there is on the part of the more destitute classes against the rich.

The Son of God in His own person has abolished all inequalities of condition, in things spiritual and natural, in Heaven and on earth, though there be in Him diversity of gifts and grace and ministries, though there be in Him the more excellent and the less excellent way: and it is one of the greatest privileges of the Christian Mind to have grasped this divine fact. This wonderful achievement of the Son of God is tersely put by St. Paul in his Epistle to the Ephesians: 'But to every one of us is given grace, according to the measure of the giving of Christ. Wherefore He saith: *Ascending on high, He led captivity captive; He gave gifts to men.* Now that He ascended, what is it, but because He also descended first into the lower parts of the earth? He that descended is the same also that ascended above all the heavens, that He might fill all things.'[1]

There is no region in the Father's creation which the Incarnate Son does not fill with the presence of His power. And this all pervading presence of the Son of God, this prior occupation by Him of all things, makes it impossible for any other power to bring about a real inequality of conditions in those that possess Him. There may be more power in some, less in others: but there can be no real inequality in the condition of existence amongst creatures that live and move and have their being in a world whose most distant regions and sections are filled with the presence of the Son of God. And what is true of the gifts, is likewise true of the more static element, sanctity, in its specific meaning. There is the greater sanctity, and the lesser sanctity, amongst the elect: there are the higher spirits, and there are the lower spirits. But as Christ is the Head of all, as His grace is in them all, the element of union in Him infinitely outweighs the element of variety in the degrees of grace and glory. 'And He [God] hath subjected all things under His feet, and hath made Him Head over all the Church, which is His body, and the fulness of Him who is filled all in all.'[2]

[1] Eph. iv. 7-10.   [2] Eph. i. 22-23.

The practical conclusions of this great principle are not far to seek, and St. Paul points them out most clearly. There is in fact hardly anything more completely worked out by the great Apostle, if we except his teaching about law and grace, than this principle of Christ's unifying rôle as the God-Man. It is the thought that underlies his metaphor of the Body of Christ, and the mutual services and sympathies of its members. The full recital of the Pauline text requires no further commentary. 'For as the body is one and hath many members; and all the members of the body, whereas they are many, yet are one body: so also is Christ. For in one Spirit were we all baptized into one body, whether Jews or Gentiles, whether bond or free; and in one Spirit we have all been made to drink. For the body also is not one member, but many. If the foot should say: Because I am not the hand, I am not of the body: is it therefore not of the body? And if the ear should say: Because I am not the eye, I am not of the body: is it therefore not of the body? If the whole body were the eye, where would be the hearing? If the whole were hearing, where would be the smelling? But now God hath set the members, every one of them, in the body as it hath pleased Him. And if they all were one member, where would be the body? But now there are many members indeed, yet one body. And the eye cannot say to the hand: I need not thy help. Nor again the head to the feet: I have no need of you. Yea, much more those that seem to be the more feeble members of the body are more necessary. And such as we think to be the less honourable members of the body, about these we put more abundant honour; and those that are our uncomely parts have more abundant comeliness. But our comely parts have no need: but God hath tempered the body together, giving to that which wanted the more abundant honour. That there might be no schism in the body; but the members might be mutually careful one for another. And if one member suffer anything, all the members suffer with it; or if one member glory, all the members rejoice with it. Now you are the Body of Christ and members of member. And God indeed hath set some in the Church: first apostles, secondly prophets, thirdly doctors; after that miracles; then the graces of healings, helps, governments, kinds of tongues, interpretations of speeches.'[1]

[1] 1 Cor. xii. 12-28.

CHAPTER XII

The Christian Mind and Eternal Life

TO expect eternal life for the just, and as a reward of sanctity, belongs to the general Christian mind. Religious men of all ages have hoped for a happy and everlasting life beyond the grave. Their efforts at representing the nature of that life have met with varying success. Some have seen more clearly than others what immortality of soul means for the just; but all good men have believed in the fundamental fact of immortality. The Catholic doctrine of Beatific Vision is certainly the loftiest, as well as the truest expression of the state of the elect in the world to come. It has been worked out as completely as possible by the theologians. Yet glorious and sublime as it is, and though it was never grasped clearly except amongst Christians, I should not class it amongst the doctrines that are specifically Christian, as depending intrinsically on the doctrine of Incarnation. For there could be Beatific Vision even if God had not taken to Himself a human nature. The grounds on which the holy men of all times have based their hopes for a blessed immortality also belong to the general Christian mind. Such arguments and motives of belief are partly inherent in our reasoning natures, and partly they are God's revelation. But they have no direct connection with the fact that God became Incarnate.

Yet nothing could be more false than the idea that the Incarnation has not brought us an entirely new set of doctrines and arguments with regard to the great question of the fate of the just who live and die in the grace of Christ. As there is the general Christian belief in eternal life, the specific Christian Mind moves in spheres unknown to the general Christian mind, when it thinks of man's hereafter. Christ's resurrection and ascension into Heaven constitute for the Christian Mind a ground of hope quite different from all other arguments; for the eternal life of the faithful Christian is a necessary concomitant of the glorious estate of the risen Christ. Eternal life for the specific Christian Mind is essentially life in Christ, and life with Christ, a condition of existence that includes all other facts known to man about his personal survival. When he wants to have an irrefragable proof of the reality of eternal life, the Christian turns for arguments, not to philosophy, nor to the traditions of mankind, but he goes directly to Christ's sepulchre. Christ is risen, and He will not die again; this glorious fact settles forever all his hesitations and perplexities. He is now convinced that there is such a thing as eternal life. Such a man may be well instructed in philosophy; he may be capable of reasoning out the logical necessity of immortality for man's spirit; he may be deeply impressed by the fact that human goodness has always thrived on the conviction that there is the great hereafter; he may live on the generic Christian faith of reward for the good in heaven. But he is hardly conscious of such supports and props. His mind is suffused with the glory of Christ's resurrection; and the eternal life of the just is the radiance of the risen Son of God.

Christians ought to dread nothing more than a diminution of their faith in Christ's bodily resurrection, for as Christians, and in virtue of our mystical incorporation with the Incarnate God, all our hopes of personal immortality are based on Christ's resurrection. We do not ignore other motives; nowhere are such motives searched into, and probed, and held with greater reverence than in Catholic schools of theology; yet when all has been said, the mental satisfaction derived from such speculations is as nothing when compared with the overpowering conviction that comes to us from the constant contemplation of the sweet mystery of Easter. To speak and think lightly of the mystery of Christ's bodily rising from the dead, and to rely merely on the philosophical grounds of belief in our soul's immortality, is indeed to sell our birthright for a pottage of lentils. I will not enter here into the question whether it is possible for the human reason, in the long run, to hold as a deliberate conviction any doctrine as to man's personal immortality, and at the same time reject the dogma of Christ's resurrection. I do not believe that faith in survival after death could have deep roots in a mind that recoils from the faith in Christ's resurrection. All I need say here is that the doctrine of Christ's resurrection, being a specifically Christian doctrine, is of such a nature as to give us an unshakable assurance of our personal immortality; so that for us temptations of doubt and despair are best overcome, not so much by investigations into the philosophical grounds of the soul's survival, as by meditating humbly on the Paschal mystery.

Such is evidently St. Paul's attitude with regard to the motives why we all should look forward to a happy immortality. The resurrection of Christ establishes for ever the fact that the dead, at least those that die in Christ, will also rise. A happy eternity is identical with fellowship in Christ's resurrection. 'For if we believe that Jesus died and rose again; even so them who have slept through Jesus, will God bring with Him.'[1]

The powerful reasoning of St. Paul in the fifteenth chapter of his First Epistle to the Corinthians bases the general truth, that there is a resurrection awaiting Christ's disciples, on the fact that He rose from the dead, who is 'the first fruits of them that sleep.' The Apostle's mind seems at first sight to move in a way that is the reverse of the movements of an ordinary logical mind. It is quite logical to deduce the fact of one individual's resurrection from the universal principle that there is a resurrection for all; but St. Paul establishes the general truth of universal resurrection from the particular fact that Christ is risen. The inversion is merely apparent. As Christ's resurrection is the cause of all other resurrections, it is really something vaster, something more universal than the general truth of the resurrection of all the just. 'For by a man came death; and by a Man the resurrection of the dead. And as in Adam all die, so also in Christ all shall be made alive.'[2] There is no doubt as to St. Paul's outlook. For him eternal life and eternal happiness simply mean participation in Christ's resurrection. 'That I may know Him, and the power of His resurrection.'[3]

Several doubts might occur to the reader when he is told that, for the specific Christian Mind, the whole problem of the world to come is solved by this keen realisation of the mystery of Christ's resurrection. It might be argued that the doctrine of our Lord's resurrection, with its effects on our own happy immortality, leaves entirely untouched the general question whether the souls of all men, good or bad, are immortal. Christ's resurrection, in the mind of St. Paul, seems to have a direct bearing only on the fate of the elect. To this I answer, that the Christian Mind is not just a speculative turn of thought, but essentially a practical view of each one's

[1] 1 Thess. iv. 13.   [2] 1 Cor. xv. 21-22.   [3] Phil. iii. 10.

spiritual interests. As the eternal loss of the reprobate has nothing to do with me practically, I am fully justified in reading the great question of my own eternal future in the light of Christ's resurrection, as my own future is entirely decided, and shaped by it, and by nothing else. Whether the doctrine of Christ's resurrection settles the eschatological questions of all mankind is a point that need not be discussed here. It certainly can solve all such questions as far as they have reference to me.

Again, it might be said that the doctrine of Christ's resurrection is more a doctrine for the body, than for the soul. It does not directly confirm the belief that man's soul is immortal through its own innate elements. To this I reply, that Christ's resurrection implies all the conclusions of philosophy and the consensus of mankind, as well as the facts of the broader Revelation to man with regard to the nature of our immortal souls. Resurrection means the survival of the soul after death, as well as the quickening of the body. The power, the life, and the self-consciousness of Christ's soul, after His death on the cross, constituted one of the great Christian dogmas: the descent into the lower world of the just spirits, with its illuminating and saving power for the souls awaiting the Redemption. 'Because Christ also died once for our sins, the just for the unjust: that He might offer us to God, being put to death indeed in the flesh, but enlivened in the spirit. In which also coming He preached to those spirits that were in prison: which had been some time incredulous, when they waited for the patience of God in the days of Noe, when the ark was a-building: wherein a few, that is, eight souls, were saved by water.'[1] The departure of Christ's soul from the body, its self-conscious existence, its power of enlightenment, its return to the body, are all part of the Paschal mystery. No man could believe in Christ's resurrection without his apprehending more clearly the natural immortality of the human soul.

It would seem, lastly, that faith in Christ's resurrection does not of necessity imply a revelation of the more spiritual factors of eternal life, such as the clear vision of God; it would seem, indeed, as if the resurrection were of the secondary order of spiritual realities, being directly the glorification of the body, not of the soul. So Christ's resurrection could not be to us the glorious sum-

[1] 1 Pet. iii. 18-20.

mary of all our hopes. Such is the objection, and common as it is, it reveals a very great ignorance of the conditions and glories of our new life in Christ. If anything is clear, it is the fact that the bodily resurrection of Christ, and our bodily resurrection in Him, is eternal life to the mind of St. Paul. It means the totality of our hopes, not only the possession of a secondary happiness. Resurrection, in Apostolic language, is everything: glory of the soul, and glory of the body, triumph over the world, and vision of God. The above quotation from St. Peter's Epistle is followed by a very clear statement on this very point: 'Whereunto baptism, being of the like form, now saveth you also: not the putting away of the filth of the flesh, but the examination of a good conscience towards God by the resurrection of Jesus Christ. Who is on the right hand of God, swallowing down death that we might be made heirs of life everlasting: being gone into Heaven, the angels and powers and virtues being made subject to Him.'[1]

Christ Himself quite plainly identifies the mystery of man's resurrection on the last day with the mystery of man's adoption as God's child. 'And Jesus said to them: The children of this world marry and are given in marriage: but they that shall be accounted worthy of that world and of the resurrection from the dead shall neither be married nor take wives. Neither can they die any more: for they are equal to the angels and are the children of God, being the children of the resurrection.'[2] If anything is certain, it is the fact that in the New Testament language the idea of resurrection as applied to Christ and to His elect, though it be primarily the mystery of the quickening of the body, is not a secondary spiritual factor, but is the main factor, of our glorious hereafter. Eternal life is simply stated as being the resurrection from the dead. It is sometimes said that through the resurrection, both in the case of Christ and His elect, a merely accidental joy and glory accrues to human nature. Such language is hardly scriptural. Everywhere the mystery of the resurrection is spoken of as the great crowning of God's works in the natural and supernatural order, an act of God that brings with itself every other glory, all the fulness of divine life. 'Now, if we be dead with Christ, we believe that we shall live also together with Christ. Knowing that Christ, rising again from the

---

[1] 1 Pet. iii. 21, 22.   [2] Luke xx. 34-36.

dead, dieth now no more. Death shall no more have dominion over Him. For in that He died to sin, He died once; but in that He liveth, He liveth unto God.'[1]

This then is the essentially Christian attitude of mind with regard to our future life: a keen love, and a profound grasp of the great dogma of Christ's resurrection. It gives wonderful definiteness to all our hopes and aspirations. It makes of the Son of God the end of all our longings, and never the means towards something else, however lofty, outside Him. Our eternity is entirely a participation in Christ's risen life.

The doctrine of Christ's bodily resurrection, and consequently the doctrine of our own bodily resurrection, means infinitely more than we commonly imagine. It means the complete glorification of human nature, in soul and body. Catholic theology knows well how to distinguish between final glorification and other states of sanctity and happiness. Thus our Lord on earth had Beatific Vision, and yet, before the hour of His resurrection, He was not a glorified being, and did not enjoy the supereminent happiness of a glorified being. On the other hand, the Saints whose souls are in Heaven now, before the great awakening of the last resurrection comes, have Beatific Vision and happiness; but it could not be said that they are in a state of glorification. Such a state will become theirs on that great day, and what they possess now is but a partial anticipation of it.

No words could be a better conclusion to these considerations than Christ's own confident and unequivocal assertion, in His last prayer: 'Father, I will that where I am, they also whom Thou hast given Me may be with Me: that they may see My glory which Thou hast given Me, because Thou hast loved Me before the creation of the world.'[2]

[1] Rom. vi. 8-10.   [2] John xvii. 24.

CHAPTER XIII

The Christian Mind and Death

NO occurrence in this world is more capable of giving rise to a greater variety of philosophies than the ever recurring and unavoidable event of man's death.

Death has been envisaged from the most various angles. It has provided both optimist and pessimist with plenty of food for thought. Both the spiritualist and the materialist have made of death the corner-stone of their theories as to the real worth of human things.

But coming at once to the strictly religious attitude of men towards death, we find that the dire reality of man's ending has impressed them in ways most varied, though seldom, if ever, contradictory. The physical terrors of death, the sudden snapping asunder of all the interests of life, the uncertainty of one's individual fate in the Great Beyond, the fear of God's judgments, and many similar considerations, have made of death a source of sadness even for Christians, though it be a salutary sadness. Death makes us 'sorrowful according to God'. Such considerations of course belong to the general Christian mentality; the Incarnation presupposes them, and our Lord Himself made use of them in His Gospel, as in the parable of the foolish rich man, whose fields had yielded a plentiful harvest, and who had said to his soul: 'Soul, thou hast much goods laid up for many years. Take thy rest; eat, drink, make good cheer.'[1] Christ's description of that foolish man's fate is extremely striking: 'But God said to him: Thou fool, this night do they require thy soul of thee, and whose shall those things be which thou hast provided?'[2]

Yet who would dare to think that the Incarnation has not lifted the philosophy of death to a much higher plane? St. Paul in the Epistle to the Hebrews asserts that a new attitude of man towards death is one of the primary results of the Incarnation. 'Therefore because the children are partakers of flesh and blood, He also Himself in like manner hath been partaker of the same: that, through

[1] Luke xii. 19.   [2] Luke xii. 20.

death, He might destroy him who had the empire of death, that is to say, the devil: and might deliver them who through the fear of death were all their life-time subject to servitude.'[1]

It may be stated as a broad proposition that the Incarnation has heightened the reality of all the spiritual factors of the general Christian mind, whilst in the case of death it softens its dreaded character. It lessens the terror of death, physical and spiritual; it lessens its uncertainties, its consequences. For as the doctrine of the resurrection of all flesh is a specifically Christian doctrine, death loses its sting through the Incarnation. 'Death is swallowed up in victory.—O death, where is thy victory? O death, where is thy sting?'[2] The fact that Christ died ought to reconcile all of us to the prospect of death. A preacher who would put death before the eyes of the faithful merely as a naked reality of terror, bodily and spiritual, without softening his presentment with the sweet lights that come from the Son of God, who tasted death in His own body, instead of building up, would merely destroy souls. His terrors would be of the lowest order, with nothing essentially Christian.

But the Incarnation has done more than merely soften the horrors of death. Not only has it overcome death, and robbed it of its sting, but it has actually abolished the difference between life and death. It has given to death the same spiritual value as to life. For those who actively share the grace of the Incarnation, it has made life and death to be one continuous, uninterrupted function of Christ's life in man.

It is St. Paul who gives us this lofty and specifically Christian view of death. In his Epistle to the Romans, referring to an apparently small matter, he soars all at once to that wonderful height of Christian thinking where life and death become fused in the higher reality of our membership with Christ. The occasion for so glorious a pronouncement was the settlement of a practical difficulty amongst the early Christians. To what extent were the faithful allowed to eat of the meat that had been sacrificed to the idols in the pagan temples, and was being retailed in the shops of the city butchers? St. Paul wants absolute freedom for everyone, as the meat could not be considered to have been made sacrilegious through the circumstance of having been offered to the idols. For

---

[1] Heb. ii. 14, 15.   [2] Osee xiii. 14; 1 Cor. xv. 54; Heb. ii. 14.

idols are nothing, and therefore could not be said to leave a curse on the meat. Let every Christian use his own discretion, and consult his own conscience, and act in a way he thinks best calculated to give glory to the Lord: 'And he that eateth eateth to the Lord: for he giveth thanks to God. And he that eateth not, to the Lord he eateth not and giveth thanks to God.'[1] But in St. Paul's mind there was present then a much larger principle, which no doubt was a constant preoccupation with him. For nothing shows better to what an extent a man has assimilated a comprehensive truth than the spontaneous ease with which he applies it to the circumstances and problems of every-day life. 'For none of us liveth to himself: and no man dieth to himself. For whether we live, we live unto the Lord: or whether we die, we die unto the Lord. Therefore, whether we live, or whether we die, we are the Lord's. For to this end Christ died and rose again: that He might be Lord both of the dead and of the living.'[2]

I feel confident that my reader will easily perceive the wonderful novelty, as well as the deep significance of this view of St. Paul about life and death and their respective values. Nothing of the kind had been said by man before. In fact, how could man view life and death as mere functions of a higher life, as St. Paul does here, unless he believed that the Son of God had died and had risen from the dead, that He might be Lord both of the dead and of the living? It might be said that St. Paul's doctrine about life and death is already included in that other gracious consequence of the Incarnation: the radical identity of human conditions in Christ, of which I have spoken already. In Christ the rich are poor and the poor are rich, or, more truly, both rich and poor of this world are rich in Him. Christ is all things in all. So with life and death. To be dead is not a disadvantage, because we are dead in order to live for Him: and if we are still alive, our life is not ours, but His. Yet there is a peculiar originality of thought in St. Paul's expression that no Christian dies to himself, and that we who die, die unto the Lord, which invites further meditation.

It is comparatively easy to understand that a Christian is not meant to live to himself, but unto the Lord. A Christian's life ought to be entirely dedicated to Christ: life's activities ought to have that

[1] Rom. xiv. 6.   [2] Rom. xiv. 7-9.

peculiar unselfishness which comes from our having been bought at a great price, the Blood of the Son of God. We are not our own, but His, and all we are and do ought to be impregnated with the purpose of glorifying Him. But it is not so obvious a thought that is expressed in the second half of St. Paul's aphorism, 'no man dieth to himself' and 'we die unto the Lord'. The phrases would be more than clear, if it were a question of laying down one's life for Christ through martyrdom. But evidently St. Paul spoke his great words irrespective of the glory of being Christ's witness in one's blood. He speaks of the ordinary natural death of the Christian. If death then were the total cessation of man's higher life, the Apostle's assurance would be meaningless. For a cessation of all activity could not be something good, that is unto the Lord; St. Paul's words essentially imply that death as well as life is a gift of man to Christ his Redeemer. Now a mere cessation and negation could never be a gift. We have to conclude therefore that the Apostle's words imply a continuation of activity, a survival of something very positive.

The state of death is only another phase of our spiritual incorporation in Christ. His death was the most positive, the most spiritual thing. The Christian's death is a membership in that most adorable mystery, Christ's death. Therefore life and death for the Christian are merely two phases of the same glorious event, our life in Christ, embracing both the state of the living and the state of death. St. Paul corroborates his view with the statement: 'for this end Christ died and rose again, that He might be Lord both of the dead and the living.' This clearly supports my contention that the Apostle considers the state of death as another phase of life. Christ's dominion over the dead is a dominion of graciousness over positive, living, conscious beings, as much as His dominion over the living; not a power over vague shadows, or distant memories, or unconscious personalities.

The Son of God in St. John's Revelation gives, so to speak, the phases of His own existence: 'I am the First and the Last, and alive, and was dead. And behold I am living for ever and ever and have the keys of death and of hell.'[1] Yet there is no more undivided, no more simplified existence than the existence of the Son of God, as He exists through the unchanging duration of the Word. The successive

[1] Apoc. i. 17, 18.

phases He describes are but one life. So for the Christian life and death are one life, through the unchanging oneness of Christ's personality. 'Therefore whether we live, or whether we die, we are the Lord's.' Our Christian Minds then find, in the grace of Christ's total proprietorship over us, that wonderful philosophy which has been man's dream from the beginning, but which has proved a mere illusion outside the grace of the Incarnation; I mean a practical and workable conviction that life and death are at bottom one and the same thing.

The preceding considerations may serve as a commentary on another passage in St. Paul's Epistles, as beautiful and significant as the one in the letter to the Romans. It is in the Epistle to the Philippians: 'According to my expectation and hope: that in nothing I shall be confounded, but with all confidence, as always, so now also, shall Christ be magnified in my body, whether it be by life or by death. For to me, to live is Christ: and to die is gain. And if to live in the flesh, this is to me the fruit of labour. And what I shall choose I know not. But I am straitened between two: having a desire to be dissolved and to be with Christ, a thing by far the better. But to abide still in the flesh is needful for you. And having this confidence, I know that I shall abide and continue with you all, for your furtherance and joy of faith.'[1] The occasion for Paul to pour out his innermost feeling in this manner is different from the circumstance that brought about that great mental flight of his when writing to the Romans. With the Philippians it is the anticipation of a possible separation from his dear friends through death. But the leading idea is the same: death or no death, it is all one in Christ. Life is profitableness in Christ, death is nearerness unto Christ. No wonder it is difficult to choose between two such excellent states: 'And what to choose, I know not.'

Another passage with the same ultimate meaning is to be found in the Second Epistle to the Corinthians. Life is there described as a bodily absence from the Lord, whilst death, which implies an absence from the body, results in a presence with the Lord. But the practical mental attitude is the same for life and death: 'And therefore we labour, whether absent or present, to please Him.'[2]

The frightful gulf between life and death is one of the things that

[1] Phil. i. 20-25.   [2] 2 Cor. v. 9.

seem most repulsive to the modern mind. The modern mind wants continuity in all things. One of the commonest efforts to bridge this gulf is the exhortation to feel happy at the thought that after death man's personality passes into the great Universe as a new force. In order to preserve continuity of life, men are willing to sacrifice personality. Yet man will not go to Christ for the very thing he yearns for. 'And you will not come to Me that you may have life.'³ As a philosophy the continuance is of course a deeper concept than the hiatus. But it is only the Christian Mind that reconciles continuity of life with survival of personality.

CHAPTER XIV

The Attitude of the Christian Mind towards those who sleep in the Lord

THE Catholic doctrine implied in the rather vague term 'Purgatory' is certainly the one in which man's imagination has the greatest chance of crowding out the solid and definite facts of the Church's teaching. There is the constant danger with pious people of giving too great a preponderance to what I might call the spiritistic side of this doctrine, with a tendency of laying too much stress on the disembodiment of the human soul, a state which results in new conditions of existence, mysterious and painful, for the faithful departed. The predominant idea, however, that ought to shape our whole mental outlook in this matter is that death for the Christian is essentially a falling asleep in the Lord. No greater error could be committed than to suppose that the Christian soul from the moment of its baptismal regeneration up to the moment of being introduced to the Blessed Vision of God in Heaven is ever to pass through a phase of existence in which its membership with Christ would be less accentuated, or almost suspended. This vital force of membership with the living Son of God is the

¹ John v. 40.

one certain spiritual fact in the history of the Christian's soul about which there can be no doubts, and all other doctrines are essentially subservient to that dominating factor. To assert that in the purgatorial state the life of redeemed man is less entirely a life in Christ than it is here on earth, would be as gratuitous as it is dangerous. Nowhere in the Scriptures, in theology or tradition, is there any trace of such a diminution of the soul's membership with Christ. On the contrary, everywhere we find that the life of man in Christ and Christ's life in man are, from their very nature, not only continuous, but progressive. Mortal sin is the only thing that interferes substantially with the flow of that great life.

It is far from my purpose to write a treatise on Purgatory. I am concerned here exclusively with the mental attitude of the Catholic regarding the state of the soul departed from the body, and not yet admitted to the fulness of God's vision because personal sin is not fully expiated. First of all there is nothing in the Catholic doctrine on Purgatory that could make it inappropriate to apply to every dead Christian the beautiful expression that 'he fell asleep in the Lord', if he died in the faith of the Son of God, and if there were the ordinary indications that he passed out of this world in the state of grace. Though it may be presumed, according to Catholic sentiment, that many who die in the charity of Christ, have still to atone, yet such a fear, whatever its foundations and its nature, ought in no wise to render us less eager to use that dear old phrase: They are 'asleep in the Lord', all of them. The language of the Apostolic age and of the Church's liturgy are quite unhesitating in this matter. Everywhere the dying Christian is represented as falling asleep in the Lord, and there are no other terrors for him than the evil of being separated from the Lord and thus falling a prey to the dragon. The suffering of Purgatory is not one of the terrors of the dying Christian. To die in the peace of Christ, *in osculo Domini*, with the kiss from the Lord's lips on the soul's innermost consciousness, is the one overpowering fact. Whatever happens to the saved soul after its departure from the body is governed by that great fact of Christ's friendship.

It is of course one of the apparent anomalies of purgatorial atonement that there should be on the one hand suffering of spirit, and on the other hand the peace of immutable life in Christ. Yet our knowledge as to the nature of that cleansing is very limited. We know that it exists in the case of many of the faithful departed. But we know a vast deal more as to the condition of man's incorporation in Christ. This paramount reality is the one doctrine that has been worked out by the sacred writers of the New Testament with greatest completeness. The soul's destiny is forever modified by that wonderful incorporation in Christ's living organism. To view the soul's state outside it would be a most dangerous mental attitude. A Purgatory that is not life in Christ has nothing to do with Catholic dogma. For cautious as the Church is with regard to the nature of the cleansing process, its duration and quality, the exhortation to pray for the departed is constantly on her lips. In practice this is the only view of Purgatory that appeals to the Church, that makes her class it amongst her lifegiving doctrines. She wants the faithful here on earth to realise that in virtue of the great incorporation in Christ we all, living and dead, can contribute towards the increase of that divine life; and through our own sanctity here on earth, our charity, our prayers, and good works, we have it in our power to bring the divine life of the departed Christian soul to its full development of joy and glory. As to what I called a moment ago the spiritistic side of Purgatory, the state of the soul in that cleansing fire, the Church never professed to hold any explicit revelation. Purgatory is to her essentially part of the mystery of the Incarnation; it concerns the Body of Christ, with its variety of functions and affections.

One of the scriptural utterances of which Catholic theologians make use in order to establish dogmatically the existence of a purifying process for certain souls is from the First Epistle to the Corinthians: 'According to the grace of God that is given to me, as a wise architect, I have laid the foundation: and another buildeth thereon. But let every man take heed how he buildeth thereupon. For other foundation no man can lay, but that which is laid: which is Christ Jesus. Now, if any man build upon this foundation, gold, silver, precious stones, wood, hay, stubble, every man's work shall be manifest. For the day of the Lord shall declare it, because it shall be revealed in fire; and the fire shall try every man's work, of what sort it is. If any man's work abide, which he hath built thereupon, he shall receive a reward. If any man's work burn, he shall suffer loss; but he himself shall be saved, yet so as by fire. Know you not that you are the temple of God and that the Spirit of God dwelleth in you?'[1] The main idea of St. Paul here is very clear. He admits that the teachers of the New Testament may be found to do poor work on a very good foundation, Christ. Yet it is not so utterly bad work as to be a cause of eternal loss. On the other hand, the judgment of Christ will be as keen as fire. It will burn the faulty superstructure, but will leave the foundation, Christ. It is essentially the rectifying of an imperfection, not the destruction of a sinner.

The metaphors of St. Paul convey a clear spiritual principle: that God's judgments act as fire even on the just. And as the expression 'the day of the Lord' implies a judgment that is beyond the present state of mortality, theologians are justified in seeing here a general principle of which Purgatory is one of the applications. But my concern now is with the broader issue stated by St. Paul, that through all the fire and loss, there is one thing that remains unmoved and untouched, the foundation that was laid, Christ Himself. 'For other foundation no man can lay, but that which is laid, which is Christ Jesus.' My conclusion is that the one classical text in favour of the purifying process for souls lays the greatest stress on the permanency of Christ's abiding presence through all the imperfections of their spiritual work, and the subsequent cleansing by fire. More than any other province of reality, this great reality, the state of the disembodied Christian soul, is to be approached through Christ, and in Christ.

If we walk into it regardless of the grace of the Incarnation that broods over it all, we turn a mystery of mercy into a vague shadow of horror.

In strict dogmatic language there are three states of existence for the Christian. First there is the state of mortality here on earth, with its struggles and sufferings. It is for the Christian essentially a knowledge of, and participation in, Christ's Passion. Then there is the state of glory, which is indissolubly combined with the resurrection of the body, as an outcome of Christ's Resurrection. It belongs to the *Ecclesia triumphans*. Between those two states there is the transient, accidental, and less universal state of those who fell asleep in the Lord; a state that means happiness and gain, as accord-

[1] 1 Cor. iii. 10-16.

ing to the language of St. Paul it is better to be absent from the body, and to be present to the Lord. 'But we are confident and have a good will to be absent rather from the body and to be present with the Lord.'[1]

This intermediate state is less clearly described to us than the other two. Its psychological conditions are a mystery to us. It caused the first practical perplexity to the early Christians, the converts of the Apostles. The Apostolic preaching was all about the great triumph of Christ coming in glory, with the concomitant glorification of the elect, completely transformed in soul and body. But when the number of those Christians who died before the expected manifestation of Christ increased in the churches, the question began to be asked what became of them, what hopes they had of seeing Christ on the day of His power. St. Paul answers this difficulty in his first Epistle to the Thessalonians: 'And we will not have you ignorant, brethren, concerning them that are asleep, that you be not sorrowful, even as others who have no hope. For if we believe that Jesus died and rose again: even so them who have slept through Jesus, will God bring with Him. For this we say unto you in the word of the Lord, that we who are alive, who remain unto the coming of the Lord, shall not prevent them who have slept. For the Lord Himself shall come down from Heaven with commandment and with the voice of an Archangel and with the trumpet of God: and the dead who are in Christ shall rise first. Then we who are alive, who are left, shall be taken up together with them in the clouds to meet Christ, into the air; and so shall we be always with the Lord. Wherefore, comfort ye one another with these words.'[2]

Yet with all that consoling message as to the share the faithful departed will have one day in Christ's resurrection, the Apostle refrains from saying anything concerning the life of those souls in their present state of disembodiment. With St. Paul, the mystery of the resurrection is, so to speak, the only thing that matters. What is of importance, is to establish the fact that God will give the dead Christian the full privilege of the final resurrection. Whatever may be the intermediate mode of life for the soul, all due guarantee as to its happiness is given us through the assertion that such a state, as all other concerns of the baptized soul, is a thing in the Lord. In the

[1] 2 Cor. v. 8.   [2] 1 Thess. iv. 12-17.

Epistle to the Philippians, St. Paul declares most emphatically that death means life with the Lord: 'But I am straitened between two: having a desire to be dissolved and to be with Christ, a thing by far the better. But to abide still in the flesh is needful for you.'[1]

No more satisfactory formula could be found for our own minds in which to express the state and conditions of life of the faithful departed, of whatever degree of sanctity they may be, than the old expression 'asleep in the Lord'. The subdivision of this middle state into souls perfect in bliss and souls in need of suffrages is, I might almost say, a minor distinction. It does not bring about distinct kinds of existence. We might call them two unequal conditions inside the same state of existence. And it is my conviction that a very great service would be rendered to the Christian Mind if it could be brought to think of all departed Christian souls in that truly divinised fashion. Our concern with the spirits of the faithful departed is a practical one; praying for them, or even praying to them. Both these functions of spiritual life are unthinkable unless they be part of our life in Christ.

In common Catholic parlance the Church is divided into *Ecclesia militans*, *Ecclesia patiens*, and *Ecclesia triumphans;* which division comprises the Christians here on earth fighting the battles of God, the souls in Purgatory atoning for the negligences of life, and the assembly of sanctified souls in the bliss of Heaven. Such a division is quite legitimate, as it is concerned not so much with different kinds of existence, as with different conditions of happiness. The older division however gives greater satisfaction to the intellect. It means three totally different states of existence; mortal life, the disembodied life, and the risen life of the Christian. The more modern division has reference chiefly to the order of things that obtains at present, leaving out of sight that totally new mode of existence that will come to man on the day when he will rise in his flesh endowed with incorruption. If pressed too far this modern division might create the impression that there is as real a difference in the mode of existence between the soul that is still kept from the clear Vision of God and the soul admitted to that Vision, as there is between the struggling Christian here on earth and the disembodied soul of the Christian who has passed out of this world in the charity of Christ.

[1] Phil. i. 23, 24.

Yet it is evident the two differences have nothing in common. The soul in Purgatory is forever established in grace; in that state sin has become quite impossible.

The Church in her official capacity pronounces on the sanctity of a Christian's earthly life: she has the right to declare that a soul is in the glory of Heaven. But at no time could the Church pronounce in an individual case whether or not a soul is passing, or has passed, through the cleansing fire. The possible delays that keep the elect soul from the full enjoyment of beatific bliss do not really constitute an essentially different state, as all souls that are saved live in Christ unto God.

I feel sure that the reader will pardon this insistence on a view which to-day perhaps is getting less common. Yet if anything is precious to the Christian Mind, it is the consideration that life in Christ is one continuous, uninterrupted flow, from baptism until the glorious resurrection of the Last Day.

CHAPTER XV

Christ the Judge of the Living and the Dead

THE rôle of Judge has been attributed to God at all stages of religious faith. Not only does man expect fair dealing for himself on the part of God, but he considers the Divinity as holding the office of judge over mankind; rewarding the good, punishing the wicked, and redressing the balance of good and evil in His own good time. This idea pervades the writings of the Old Testament. 'Far be it from Thee to do this thing, and to slay the just with the wicked, and for the just to be in like case as the wicked. This is not beseeming Thee: Thou, who judgest all the earth, wilt not make this judgment.'[1] Thus spoke Abraham as he walked with the Lord on the way to Sodom, and as he prayed that the guilty city might be spared for the sake of fifty just men if perchance such a

[1] Gen. xviii. 25.

number could be found there. 'The just shall rejoice when he shall see the revenge: he shall wash his hands in the blood of the sinner. And man shall say: If indeed there be fruit to the just: there is indeed a God that judgeth them on the earth.'[1]

Belief in the great day of Judgment at the end of the world is one of the most constant themes of the teachers and seers of Israel: 'Then shall the just stand with great constancy against those that have afflicted them and taken away their labours.'[2] 'Wherefore expect me, saith the Lord, in the day of My resurrection that is to come; for My judgment is to assemble the Gentiles and to gather the kingdoms and to pour upon them My indignation, and all My fierce anger: for with the fire of My jealousy shall all the earth be devoured.'[3] In the mind of the seer 'the day of darkness and of gloominess, the day of clouds and whirlwinds'[4] is not always the last day of the world: it may be any time in which God gathers up the crimes of men as in a bundle, and throws them into the furnace of His anger, without bringing mankind as a whole to His bar. Yet the idea of a universal retribution and settlement of accounts at the end of mankind's history is so forcibly stated by the prophets that the point needs no further elaboration here.

The concepts then of God as the great Judge, and of the universal judgment at the end of the world, could in no wise be called specifically Christian, i.e. flowing from the central doctrine of the Incarnation. Christ found these beliefs well established, and He lent them the weight of His authority. The end of the world with its concomitant judgment was an idea familiar to the people that thronged to hear Him. He gave it greater splendour and luminousness through the clearness of His statements, and the definiteness of the parables in which He embodied that teaching. The parable of the wheat and cockle, where 'the harvest is the end of the world and the reapers are the Angels', presupposes in the minds of the listeners a high degree of faith in the Last Day, besides its being a statement of the great truth in words of matchless effectiveness: 'Even therefore as cockle is gathered up and burnt with fire: so shall it be at the end of the world.'[5]

Yet in this matter of God's rôle as Judge, Christ has done some-

---

[1] Ps. lvii. 11, 12.   [2] Wisdom v. 1.   [3] Soph. iii. 8.   [4] Joel ii. 2.
[5] Matt. xiii. 40.

thing more than throw additional light and brilliancy on an ancient tradition; He appropriated the doctrine in a way He has not followed in other matters. He Himself is the great central figure, He is the Judge, the Judgment Day will be essentially His own Day. He will come in glory with the Angels, and mankind will be brought to Him. His followers and friends will sit with Him, as His assessors, and the dividing between the good and the wicked will be done entirely on Incarnation lines, if I may use the expression. The blessed are those who gave Him to eat when He was hungry, gave Him to drink when He was thirsty, visited Him when He was in prison. The wicked owe their reprobation to the neglect of those good offices towards Him. For St. Paul as well as for the other writers of the New Testament, the Great Day spoken of by the prophets of old has a new significance, not only a new splendour. It is the Day of the Lord. The world's condemnation is merely part of it. The great fact of that day is the triumphant manifestation of Christ.

I am thus justified, I think, in placing the doctrine of the Judgment amongst the specifically Christian doctrines, because it is so inseparably united with Christ's person, so completely identified with Him, that the idea of Judgment such as we find it at the end of the Old Testament differs as much from the concept of Judgment at the end of the New Testament as the graces of the ordinary Providence differ from the graces of the Incarnation. Here we have more than the elevation of a pre-existing idea; we have a complete transformation. Judgment will be done, as was the belief of Patriarchs and Prophets, but it will be judgment by a Man, as St. Paul puts it in his discourse on the Areopagus: 'And God indeed having winked at the times of this ignorance, now declareth unto men that all should everywhere do penance. Because He hath appointed a day wherein He will judge the world in equity, by the Man whom He hath appointed; giving faith to all by raising Him up from the dead.'[1] This transference of the divine judicial function to the Son of God as Man, is solemnly announced by Christ Himself: 'For neither doth the Father judge any man: but hath given all judgment to the Son.'[2] It belongs properly to a dogmatic treatise on the Incarnation to explain this handing over of the function of judge to the Son. It is

---

[1] Acts xvii. 30, 31.   [2] John v. 22.

part of the mystery of the elevation of Christ's human nature through the Hypostatic Union, as explained in the third chapter of this book. But without any deeper investigations into that glorious truth of Christ's exaltation as Man, such words as are here quoted ought to suffice to establish the contention thus put forward, that the general doctrine of God's judicial power has been profoundly modified and affected by the Incarnation.

The deepest modification of the pre-existing belief is of course the fact that it will be Christ in the glory of His manhood who will execute all judgment. It will be His mighty voice as Man that will open up the graves, and call all generations to His judgment seat: 'Amen, amen, I say unto you, that the hour cometh, and now is, when the dead shall hear the voice of the Son of God; and they that hear shall live. For as the Father hath life in Himself, so He hath given to the Son also to have life in Himself. And He hath given Him power to do judgment, because He is the Son of man. Wonder not at this: for the hour cometh, wherein all that are in the graves shall hear the voice of the Son of God.'[1]

But there is more than this wonderful handing over to Christ of the divine prerogative. The great Judgment at the end of time is essentially a justification and glorification of Christ Himself, who has been the most reviled and the most illtreated of all that ever lived on this earth. Such is Christ's own bold confession at the moment of His humiliation, when He stood as a captured malefactor before the high-priest. 'And the high-priest rising up, said to Him: Answereth thou nothing to the things which these witness against thee? But Jesus held His peace. And the high priest said to Him: I adjure thee by the living God, that thou tell us if thou be the Christ, the Son of God. Jesus saith to him: Thou hast said it. Nevertheless I say to you, hereafter you shall see the Son of Man sitting on the right hand of the power of God, and coming in the clouds of heaven. Then the high-priest rent his garments, saying: He hath blasphemed, what further need have we of witnesses? Behold, now you have heard the blasphemy: What think you? But they answering said: He is guilty of death.'[2]

Christ's appearance in the glory of a judge will arouse an immense lamentation in mankind, a wail of remorse and despair, because they

---

[1] John v. 25-28.   [2] Matt. xxvi. 62-66.

have so obstinately rejected Him. 'Behold, He cometh with the clouds, and every eye shall see Him; and they also that pierced Him. And all the tribes of the earth shall bewail themselves because of Him. Even so. Amen.'[1] In the second place, mankind will be judged in regard to Christ's presence here on earth, either in His own Person, or in the person of His followers. 'And when the Son of Man shall come in His majesty, and all the angels with Him, then shall He sit upon the seat of His majesty. And all nations shall be gathered together before Him; and He shall separate them one from another, as the shepherd separateth the sheep from the goats: and He shall set the sheep on His right hand, but the goats on His left. Then shall the King say to them that shall be on His right hand: Come, ye blessed of My Father, possess you the kingdom prepared for you from the foundation of the world. For I was hungry, and you gave Me to eat: I was thirsty, and you gave Me to drink: I was a stranger and you took Me in: naked and you covered Me; sick, and you visited Me: I was in prison and you came to Me. Then shall the just answer Him, saying: Lord, when did we see Thee hungry and fed Thee: thirsty, and gave Thee drink? And when did we see Thee a stranger and took Thee in? or naked and covered Thee? Or when did we see Thee sick or in prison and came to Thee? And the King answering shall say to them: Amen I say to you, as long as you did it to one of these My least brethren, you did it to Me. Then He shall say to them also that shall be on His left hand: Depart from Me, you cursed, into everlasting fire, which was prepared for the devil and his angels. For I was hungry and you gave Me not to eat: I was thirsty and you gave Me not to drink. I was a stranger and you took Me not in: naked and you covered Me not: sick and in prison and you did not visit Me. Then they also shall answer Him, saying: Lord, when did we see Thee hungry or thirsty or a stranger or naked or sick or in prison and did not minister to Thee? Then He shall answer them, saying: Amen I say to you, as long as you did it not to one of these least, neither did you do it to Me. And these shall go into everlasting punishment: but the just, into life everlasting.'[2]

It could hardly be asserted that Christ speaks here of the judgment of such people only as knew His law and Gospel, and not of the

---

[1] Apoc. i. 7.   [2] Matt. xxv. 31-46.

generality of men. The words of the Gospel are as comprehensive
and general as they could possibly be. Every human creature seems
to be included in the great tableau. St. Paul, in the Epistle to the
Romans, speaks expressly of God's judgments over Jew and Gentile
irrespective of their actual and positive knowledge of the Gospel. Yet
he too makes of the judgment of such people a thing intimately connected with Christ and His Gospel. 'For when the Gentiles, who
have not the law, do by nature those things that are of the law;
these, having not the law, are a law to themselves: who shew the
work of the law written in their hearts, their conscience bearing
witness to them: and their thoughts between themselves accusing
or also defending one another, in the day when God shall judge the
secrets of men by Christ Jesus according to my gospel.'[1] No doubt
a more perfect comprehension of the truth of the Incarnation by
which God assumed human nature, would remove all intellectual
difficulties, and would show to us how justly and fitly mankind's
sins against itself are sins against Christ's humanity.

As a third element in the new doctrine of the Judgment, such as
it is through the Incarnation, I ought to mention Christ's part in
destroying the power of Antichrist. 'And then that wicked one shall
be revealed; whom the Lord Jesus shall kill with the spirit of His
mouth and shall destroy with the brightness of His coming; him,
whose coming is according to the working of Satan, in all power and
signs and lying wonders; and in all seduction of iniquity to them
that perish; because they receive not the love of the truth, that they
might be saved. Therefore God shall send them the operation of
error, to believe lying.'[2]

From the preceding passages, and other texts more or less
explicit, but all tending towards the same presentment of the end of
human history, it is evident that the last great spiritual crisis of mankind will be an almost victorious opposition to the spirit of Christ,
an opposition embodied in a man, Antichrist, who will succeed
temporarily in supplanting the Gospel of Truth with diametrically
opposed maxims. The name 'Antichrist' ought to be taken in its
strict signification of an essential and reasoned opposition to Christ
in His specific character. Now the coming of Our Lord in the rôle
of Judge is not only a destruction of that arch-enemy of Christ, but

---

[1] Rom. ii. 14-16.   [2] 2 Thess. ii. 8-10.

an actual single combat of the two, the true and the false Christ. St. Paul's expression, 'whom the Lord Jesus shall kill with the spirit of His mouth', implies more than a destruction of Antichrist's person and empire. It points to a vehemence of action on the part of the Son of God against that wicked man, to which there is no parallel in the Scriptures. Through the Incarnation the mystery of the last Judgment has become a triumphant struggle in which the God Incarnate shows His invincible superiority over a fiendish and horrible incarnation of the spirit of evil.

Finally, there is another very profound modification of the universal doctrine of the Judgment to be found in the constant promise of Christ, and the constant teaching of the Apostle that Christ's elect will judge the world with Him. 'And Jesus said to them: Amen, I say to you that you, who have followed Me, in the regeneration when the Son of Man shall sit on the seat of His Majesty, you also shall sit on twelve seats judging the twelve tribes of Israel.'[1] St. Paul's ironical advice to the Corinthians is a good instance of his practical application to daily life of the glorious philosophy of the Incarnation. They were having paltry litigations before secular judges, but he bids them rather to make the most insignificant among them their arbitrators in trivial temporal matters, since every Christian ought to be fit for the much higher rôle of judging the world of spirits and men with Christ. 'Dare any of you, having a matter against another, go to be judged before the unjust; and not before the saints? Know you not that the saints shall judge this world? And if the world shall be judged by you, are you unworthy to judge the smallest matters? Know you not that we shall judge angels? How much more the things of this world? If therefore you have judgment of things pertaining to this world, set them to judge, who are the most despised in the church. I speak to your shame. Is it so that there is not among you any one wise man, that is able to judge between his brethren? But brother goeth to law with brother, and that before unbelievers.'[2]

This assessorial privilege of the elect is more than a share in the common triumph of Christ and His Gospel. It is part of their mystical union with Him, a union first hidden, as Christ is hidden, then revealed, as Christ is revealed. 'For you are dead: and your life

[1] Matt. xix. 28.　　　[2] i Cor. vi. 1-6.

is hid with Christ in God. When Christ shall appear, who is your life, then you also shall appear with Him in glory.'[1] The triumph of the saints on the last day was an idea dear to the Jewish mind. 'The just shall shine, and shall run to and fro like sparks among the reeds. They shall judge nations, and rule over people; and their Lord shall reign for ever.'[2] But the personal glorification of Christ in Himself, and in His members, is a specifically Christian presentment of the last Judgment. 'When He shall come to be glorified in His Saints, and to be made wonderful in all them who have believed; because our testimony was believed upon you in that day.'[3]

I think I have given the leading points that make of the faith in the Judgment an entirely new thing through the Incarnation. It is our duty as Christians to bring our thoughts into conformity with these glorious transformations of a belief, which is as old as the world, and which belongs even to the natural man. A keen sense of justice belongs to the Christian more than to any other man; but it is a thirsting for the vindication of truth and goodness which is personified in Christ, the Judge of the living and the dead. The most monstrous injustice, as well as the most cunning falsehood will be brought to light and literally exposed to universal execration by the Son of God. 'Therefore fear them not. For nothing is covered that shall not be revealed: nor hid, that shall not be known.'[4] He Himself has suffered so much from the injustice and hypocrisies of man, that we feel intuitively that in Him we have a fellow-sufferer when our sense of justice is offended and exposed like a raw wound to the brutalities of the world. St. Paul shows how we ought to make a practical use of this wonderful outcome of the Incarnation. Misunderstood and misjudged by his own converts, the remembrance of Christ's judicial rôle enables him to rise superior to that great affliction of mind. 'But to me it is a very small thing to be judged by you or by man's day. But neither do I judge my own self. For I am not conscious to myself of anything. Yet am I not hereby justified; but He that judgeth me is the Lord. Therefore, judge not before the time; until the Lord come, who both will bring to light the hidden things of darkness and will make manifest the counsels of the hearts; and then shall every man have praise from God.'[5]

[1] Col. iii. 3, 4.   [2] Wisdom iii. 7, 8.   [3] 2 Thess. i. 10.   [4] Matt. x. 26.
[5] 1 Cor. iv. 3-5.

CHAPTER XVI

Putting on Christ

IN that section of this book which deals with St. Paul's arguments in favour of the living Christ, as opposed to the dead Law, a good deal has already been said concerning the position of the whole ethical order under the Incarnation. But as a clear and firm grasp of this subject is of paramount importance for the formation and cultivation in us of the Christian mind, I feel bound to devote a separate chapter to this subject. It will be the natural place for the development of many points of view which otherwise could not be brought under one heading. All through St. Paul's letters there are expressions of intense vividness and originality and almost unexpected, so boldly do they cut across our ordinary mode of thinking. They are the voice of the Christian Mind, and though they may seem to lack cohesion, they all proceed from the same principle; the identification of Christ with the general ethical order, through the Incarnation.

Ethics comprise man's moral development, in himself and in his relations with other men; as with institutions like the family, the state, and mankind as a whole. Even man's duties towards God are part of natural ethics. The Christian Schoolmen have done little original work in this matter of ethics, as the keen intellects of the Greek philosophers had almost completed the work for all generations to come. Our own theologians however have done splendid work in systematising the rules and laws of the supernatural life of grace, working out the harmonies between natural ethics and supernatural grace. But this meticulous completeness of the Christian ethical system as we now possess it would seem to preclude our finding in the Apostolic writings statements enough to enable us to work out in similar detail that transformation of all things ethical in Christ. For instance, can we expect to find in St. Paul a statement on the virtue of martial courage in terms of the Incarnation, in the way he states purity in such terms when he tells us that our bodies are the members of Christ? It is not my contention that we can find the whole ethical order so explicitly restated by the New Testament writers. Yet something of every general class of ethical duties has been thus restated by them as occasion arose; and there can be no doubt that the whole ethical order could have been so treated, down to the *species specialissima* of moral virtues. Everything that is good and true, is good and true in Christ. What has been said explicitly by the Apostolic writers is a guidance to us in other matters which they have had no occasion to touch upon. Thus, to come back to the example mentioned above—martial courage—neither St. Paul nor any of the other writers seems to have had opportunities of inculcating it to the disciples of Christ. Yet when one bears in mind how St. Paul treated kindred subjects, such as purity of body and conjugal fidelity, things he states boldly in terms of the Incarnation, one can easily surmise what words he might have used in the other case. The Christian soldier would have been bidden to be brave in Christ, because Christ also was brave when He fought the powers of evil. It is in this transformation of the ordinary duties of life in Christ that there is so much scope for our Christian Mind, without any danger of a merely arbitrary application of the graces of the Incarnation to such purposes.

It is within the scope of this chapter to cite some of those casual statements that lift the duties of life from the ethical plane to the plane of the Incarnation, and also to point out further possible applications of the same principle. But there is an important consideration which finds its natural place here, and which is helpful in understanding St. Paul's mind. It is a well-known psychological phenomenon that man's sense of intimate relationship with Divinity (excuse this rather pagan term) is not necessarily the same thing as a keen moral sense. Many religions full of faith and of the worship of the Divinity are practically severed from all ethical obligations; man is not expected to be true, and pure, and just, because he is religious, and worships God or gods. The old pagan religions were non-ethical, if they were not anti-ethical. A section of the Jewish people in the days of Christ, whilst still keenly religious, were strangely non-ethical. The same phenomenon has been quite striking at various periods in the history of Christian nations. But the man who made it into a theological system was Martin Luther. For him a keen sense of man's friendship with God and His Christ was not only compatible, both in theory and practice, with a non-ethical state, but that very friendship was made the excuse for discarding all natural morality as superfluous. This is technically called antinomianism, which, in the case of Christian sects, may be defined as the doctrine that in the Gospel dispensation the ethical law is of no obligation.

St. Paul had a double task to fulfil. On the one hand, he had to preach to the world man's freedom in Christ: on the other, he had to insist on man's ethical obligations. He makes the two things one by considering all ethical obligations as functions of our life in Christ. His blows from the shoulder on the law of Moses, or rather on the abuses in its application, might easily have led to anti-nomianism; St. Peter signalises the danger: 'And account the long-suffering of our Lord, salvation; as also our most dear brother Paul, according to the wisdom given him, hath written to you: as also in all his epistles, speaking in them of these things; in which are certain things hard to be understood, which the unlearned and unstable wrest, as they do also the other scriptures, to their own destruction.'[1] But St. Paul himself is fully aware of the possible abuse of a most divine privilege. He foresees the tendency to make liberty in Christ a cloak for malice. 'For you, brethren, have been called unto liberty: only make not liberty an occasion to the flesh, but by charity of the spirit serve one another. For all the law is ful-filled in one word: Thou shalt love thy neighbour as thyself.'[2]

More powerful than such yearnings are the deeper principles on which St. Paul bases the identity of life in Christ with the whole ethical order. A Christian through his baptism has become so com-pletely one with Christ, that moral transgression should become a thing of the past; it is simply incompatible with his new character. If the Christian sins grievously, it is as if Christ died again. This is the central thought of so much that St. Paul writes, chiefly in his Epistle to the Romans: 'For in that He died to sin, He died once; but in that He liveth, He liveth unto God. So do you also reckon that you are dead to sin, but alive unto God in Christ Jesus our Lord. Let not sin therefore reign in your mortal body, so as to obey the lusts thereof. Neither yield ye your members as instruments of iniquity unto sin; but present yourselves to God, as those that are alive from the dead; and your members as instruments of justice

[1] 2 Pet. iii. 15, 16.   [2] Gal. v. 13, 14.

unto God. For sin shall not have dominion over you; for you are not under the law, but under grace. What then? Shall we sin, because we are not under the law, but under grace? God forbid! Know you not that to whom you yield yourselves servants to obey, his servants you are whom you obey, whether it be of sin unto death or of obedience unto justice. But thanks be to God, that you were the servants of sin but have obeyed from the heart unto that form of doctrine into which you have been delivered. Being then freed from sin, we have been made servants of justice.'[1]

Such doctrine, far from weakening the ethical order, gives it a divine basis, and though it does not give man impeccability, it opens out to him the prospects of a sinlessness that is a participation in Christ's sinlessness. A more complete identification of the ethical order and life in Christ could not be imagined. That such texts could have been made use of by the German reformer in order to establish his antinominian views is the most impertinent of all the perversions of the Scriptures. Where the refined intellect of St. Paul sees absolute incompatibility between the Christian's regenerated soul and sin, the coarse mind of the German heresiarch sees a complete emancipation from all moral ties. Far from there being even a vestige of antinomianism in St. Paul's theology, there is in his teaching a distinct belief in a relative sinlessness in the Christian, in virtue of his regeneration in Christ, not the Lutheran sinlessness that comes from man's incapacity of doing any good, a shifting and a denying of all responsibility, but a positive sinlessness made of spiritual strength caused by the abundance of our grace in Christ. 'And they that are Christ's have crucified their flesh, with the vices and concupiscences.'[2]

St. Paul speaks of a great spiritual possibility, of a thing accessible to man in virtue of the Incarnation. Rejecting on the one hand a mere system of laws, an ethical order grounded on no life-giving person, the great Apostle has before his eyes more than an ethical order of a higher rank, more even than an ethical order based on the will of Christ; he contemplates as an ordinary Christian privilege the happy state of such absolute identification with Christ that the breaking of the moral order practically does not exist. Such no doubt was St. Paul's own condition, and such is the condition of

<hr />

[1] Rom. vi. 10-18.   [2] Gal. v. 24.

thousands of Christ's chosen ones at all periods of the Church's history. Thus this profound principle is the highest elevation and transformation of the ethical order through the Incarnation. With such a principle to start from, the daily tasks of human life ought to assume in our eyes the golden brilliancy of the light of the Hypostatic Union as they did with St. Paul himself, as I shall show now, quoting from his letters.

The Christian's duties towards his fellow Christian have been expressed by St. Paul in Incarnation terms more frequently and emphatically than any other forms of moral obligation, as was to be expected. The noble expression *in visceribus Iesu Christi* is of Pauline origin: 'For God is my witness how I long after you all in the bowels of Jesus Christ'.[1] To love in the bowels of Christ is more than to love for the sake of Christ, it is even more than to enter into His sentiments. It is a community of feeling between Paul, Christ and fellow Christian, so intimate as to be best expressed through the bold metaphor of the identity of the organs of love; a metaphor too daring outside that supernatural order which is based on the Incarnation. Yet with regard to the God Incarnate we feel instinctively that such language is not only permissible, but that it alone expresses adequately the sublime truth, our love for our fellow Christian.

Man's conformity to the Incarnation is to be for ever the pattern for us in treating with our brethren. 'Wherefore, receive one another, as Christ also hath received you, unto the honour of God.'[2] Which of us could ever exhaust the practical applications of such a recommendation? We are bidden to look on men as Christ has looked on them, and we are to make our elevation in the Incarnation the measure of the honour we pay our brother. All divisions amongst Christians are condemned for ever by this piercing cry of St. Paul's heart: 'Is Christ divided?'[3] All undue prevalence of merely human considerations, human personalities, are made for ever ridiculous by that other drastic apostrophe: 'Was Paul then crucified for you? Or were you baptized in the name of Paul?'[4] If Christians understood what they owe to Christ, how totally they belong to Christ, how their whole spiritual glory is Christ's own life in them, they would shun all divisions, all vaingloryings as an insult, nay, as an outrage done to Christ.

[1] Phil. i. 8.   [2] Rom. xv. 7.   [3] 1 Cor. i. 13.   [4] 1 Cor. i. 13.

In virtue of this total appropriation by the Son of God of each individual Christian, the last thing we ought to do is to judge our brother, or to interfere with his legitimate liberties. 'Who art thou that judgest another man's servant? To his own lord he standeth or falleth. And he shall stand: for God is able to make him stand. For one judgeth between day and day: and another judgeth every day. Let every man abound in his own sense. He that regardeth the day regardeth it unto the Lord. And he that eateth eateth to the Lord: for he giveth thanks to God. And he that eateth not, to the Lord eateth not and giveth thanks to God. For none of us liveth to himself; and no man dieth to himself. For whether we live, we live unto the Lord: or whether we die, we die unto the Lord. Therefore, whether we live or whether we die, we are the Lord's.'[1] It is all very glorious doctrine; the highest application of the loftiest principles of the Incarnation; yet the occasion for propounding it was anything but a grave crisis, it was merely a minor difficulty that had arisen, whether Christians might be allowed to eat meat that came from pagan sacrifices and was being retailed in the city shops. St. Paul declares that the Christian is free to do in this matter as he pleases. His liberty is unassailable. Yet as a charitable precaution, it is better not to eat of that meat, if thereby a weak brother be scandalised; for it is a grievous thing to sadden one for whom Christ died. 'For if, because of thy meat, thy brother be grieved, thou walkest not now according to charity. Destroy not him with thy meat, for whom Christ died.'[2] 'And through thy knowledge shall the weak brother perish, for whom Christ hath died?'[3] Look at thy brother, remember that the Son of God died for him. You will be slow to make use even of a right, if by so doing you are in danger of hurting him. After all, is not Christ there with His own grand example, not pleasing Himself even in good things? 'Now, we that are stronger ought to bear the infirmities of the weak and not to please ourselves. Let every one of you please his neighbour unto good, to edification. For Christ did not please Himself; but, as it is written: The reproaches of them that reproached thee fell upon me.'[4]

But these concessions to the dictates of charity in no wise impair the radical privilege of Christian liberty. Liberty is one of the con-

[1] Rom. xiv. 4-8.   [2] Rom. xiv. 15.   [3] 1 Cor. viii. 11.   [4] Rom. xv. 1-3.

cepts which can bear being worked out to any extent on Incarnatiou lines. 'For he that is called in the Lord, being a bondman, is the freeman of the Lord. Likewise he that is called, being free, is the bondman of Christ. You are bought with a price: be not made the bondslaves of men.'[1] Even the subjection we owe to our teachers in the faith does not mean their domination over our minds and hearts. In the truest sense, the whole spiritual organisation of the Church is for the sake of the governed. Christ alone truly owns us. 'Let no man therefore glory in men. For all things are yours, whether it be Paul or Apollo or Cephas, or the world, or life, or death, or things to come. For all are yours; and you are Christ's; and Christ is God's.'[2]

That same Christ is man's head and ornament: 'But I would have you know that the head of every man is Christ; and the head of the woman is the man; and the head of Christ is God. [3] Expressions like this, which at first sight seem so casual, for there'has been question of behaviour at prayer, give us the measure of St. Paul's faith in the applicability of the Incarnation to every human problem, even the smallest. Again there was question of collecting alms for the poorer brethren. Out comes this high note with its triumphant ring: 'For you know the grace of our Lord Jesus Christ, that being rich He became poor for your sakes; that through His poverty you might be rich.'[4]

St. Paul defends himself against the charge of instability of promise and purpose, a grave charge against an Apostle. He thinks at once of Christ, as personifying the stability of God's promises. 'Whereas then I was thus minded, did I use lightness? Or the things that I purpose, do I purpose according to the flesh, that there should be with me *It is*, and *It is not*? But God is faithful; for our preaching which was to you, was not *It is*, and *It is not*. For the Son of God, Jesus Christ, who was preached among you by us, by me and Sylvanus and Timothy, was not: *It is* and *It is not*. But, *It is*, was in Him. For all the promises of God are in Him, *It is;* therefore also by Him. Amen to God, unto our glory.'[5] In order to express his successes and failures in the apostolate he uses the curious metaphor of a smell, which may be fragrant or just the reverse. He, Paul, is the

[1] 1 Cor. vii. 22, 23.   [2] 1 Cor. iii. 21-23.   [3] 1 Cor. xi. 3.
[4] 2 Cor. viii. 9.   [5] 2 Cor. i. 17-20.

odour of Christ. 'Now thanks be to God, who always maketh us
to triumph in Christ Jesus and manifesteth the odour of His knowledge by us in every place. For we are the good odour of Christ
unto God, in them that are saved and in them that perish. To the
one indeed the odour of death unto death: but to the others the
odour of life unto life. And for these things who is so sufficient?'[1]

Hospitality is made a divine thing because the guest is received
and treated as Christ Himself. 'And you know how, through infirmity of the flesh, I preached the Gospel to you heretofore: and your
temptation in my flesh. You despised not, nor rejected: but received me as an angel of God, even as Christ Jesus.'[2] Gratitude for
kindness received counts on the riches of Christ as a repayment.
'But I have all and abound: I am filled, having received from Epa-
phroditus the things you sent, an odour of sweetness, an acceptable
sacrifice, pleasing to God. And may my God supply all your want,
according to His riches in glory in Christ Jesus.'[3]

The relations between master and slave are put on the same
supernatural and yet humanising basis. 'Servants, be obedient to
them that are your lords according to the flesh, with fear and
trembling, in the simplicity of your heart as to Christ. Not serving
to the eye, as it were pleasing men; but, as the servants of Christ,
doing the will of God from the heart. With a good will serving, as to
the Lord, and not to men. Knowing that whatsoever good thing
any man shall do, the same shall he receive from the Lord, whether
he be bond or free.'[4]

It is doubtful whether there is any other passage in the letters of
St. Paul superior in spiritual beauty to his statement on marriage;
that most difficult of human problems. Nowhere does the Apostle
give us a deeper insight into the meaning of the Incarnation than
when he treats of the duties of man and wife: 'Let women be subject
to their husbands, as to the Lord. Because the husband is the head of
the wife: as Christ is the Head of the Church. He is the Saviour of
His body. Therefore as the Church is subject to Christ; so also let
the wives be to their husbands in all things. Husbands, love your
wives, as Christ also loved the Church and delivered Himself up for
it: that He might sanctify it, cleansing it by the laver of water in the
word of life. That He might present it to Himself, a glorious

[1] 2 Cor. ii. 14-16. [2] Gal. iv. 13, 14. [3] Phil. iv. 18, 19. [4] Eph. vi. 5-8.

Church, not having spot or wrinkle or any such thing; but that it should be holy and without blemish. So also ought men to love their wives as their own bodies. He that loveth his wife loveth himself. For no man ever hated his own flesh; but nourisheth and cherisheth it, as also Christ doth the Church.'[1]

Purity and temperance, the most elementary virtues of the reformed man, become in the mind of St. Paul something infinitely more than mere clean living. They are actually part of that divine cleanliness of Christ's own body. The frankness of the Apostle's language does not allow us to overlook its unsparing directness. 'Meat for the belly and the belly for the meats; but God shall destroy both it and them. But the body is not for fornication, but for the Lord; and the Lord for the body. Now God hath both raised up the Lord and will raise us up also by His power. Know you not that your bodies are the members of Christ? Shall I then take the members of Christ and make them the members of an harlot? God forbid! Or know you not that he who is joined to a harlot is made one body? *For they shall be*, saith He, *two in one flesh*. But he who is joined to the Lord is one spirit.'[2]

It is in connection with purity of life St. Paul uses the beautiful phrase I have taken for the title of this chapter. 'Put ye on the Lord Jesus Christ.' The Apostle considers the Son of God in the matchless whiteness of His body and soul, and covers himself with it as with a spotless garment. 'Let us walk honestly, as in the day: not in rioting and drunkenness, not in chambering and impurities, not in contention and envy. But put ye on the Lord Jesus Christ: and make not provision for the flesh in its concupiscences.'[3] His own body is for ever stamped with the virginity and cleanliness of Christ's body: 'From henceforth let no man be troublesome to me; for I bear the marks of the Lord Jesus in my body.'[4] Warning the Ephesians against the rampant lubricities of their pagan surroundings he clinches the matter with this simple phrase: 'But you have not so learned Christ.'[5]

Unworldliness and other-worldliness become, under St. Paul's pen, most positive spiritual realities. Christ crucified and Christ glorified is to him unworldliness and other-worldliness; and

---

[1] Eph. v. 21-29.   [2] 1 Cor. vi. 13-17.   [3] Rom. xiii. 13, 14.
[4] Gal. vi. 17.   [5] Eph. iv. 20.

wherever we may go, nowhere shall we find anything comparable
to the matchless power which the Incarnation mystery gives to
St. Paul to express his own contempt of the world. Many a man of
genius has said hard things against our vulgar world, but by comparison their words are mere human embitteredness. The Christian
mind has a triumphant coign of vantage from which it looks down
upon the world, without degrading itself with any sort of resentment. 'With Christ I am nailed to the cross. And I live, now not I;
but Christ liveth in me. And that I live now in the flesh: I live in the
faith of the Son of God, who loved me and delivered Himself for
me.'[1] His courage in battling with his manifold enemies comes from
the same source. 'Always bearing about in our body the mortifica-
tion of Jesus, that the life also of Jesus may be made manifest in our
bodies. For we who live are always delivered unto death for Jesus'
sake; that the life also of Jesus may be made manifest in our mortal
flesh.'[2]

Men of the stamp of St. Paul are well aware of their usefulness.
They know that whilst they have life and strength they are profitable
to many. Death to such men is a kind of disappointment, as it puts
an end to their activities. But here again the mystery of Christ
provides the highest philosophy. 'For God hath not appointed us
unto wrath: but unto the purchasing of salvation by our Lord Jesus
Christ. Who died for us: that, whether we watch or sleep, we may
live together with Him. For which cause comfort one another and
edify one another, as you also do.'[3] 'For to me, to live is Christ:
and to die is gain. And if to live in the flesh, this is to me the fruit
of labour. And what I shall choose I know not. But I am straitened
between two: having a desire to be dissolved and to be with Christ,
a thing by far the better. But to abide still in the flesh is needful for
you.'[4] I consider that this more than philosophical indifference to
life and death is one of the choicest flowers of the Christian Mind;
but it is pathetic for any man who is not a believer in the Incarnation
to try and copy such an attitude. Activities here on earth are
expressed in terms of Christ. 'My little children, of whom I am in
labour again, until Christ be formed in you.'[5] Our sufferings are
sufferings in Christ, our consolations are consolations in Christ.

[1] Gal. ii. 19, 20.   [2] 2 Cor. iv. 10, 11.   [3] 1 Thess. v. 9-11.
[4] Phil. i. 21-24.   [5] Gal. iv. 19.

'For as the sufferings of Christ abound in us, so also by Christ doth our comfort abound.'[1] But even when we rest, our rest from labour is something divine. 'But we are confident and have a good will to be absent rather from the body and to be present with the Lord.'[2]

Such then are some of the practical applications of the treasures of the Incarnation to the problems of life and death. The brilliant galaxy of thoughts assembled in this chapter, and coming from all parts of the Pauline letters, have a strictly practical bearing on life. One thing is clear: we have to inform our lives with the Incarnation not merely by way of imitation, but by accepting it as a vital element of activity and courage. We have nothing of our own. 'For see your vocation, brethren, that there are not many wise according to the flesh, not many mighty, not many noble.'[3] But let no man be disheartened over such destitution. We Christians have an immense advantage to start life with. 'But of Him are you in Christ Jesus, who of God is made unto us wisdom and justice and sanctification and redemption.'[4]

CHAPTER XVII

The Christian Mind, the Church, and the Eucharist

I HAVE omitted of set purpose from the preceding chapter several fine passages found in St. Paul's Epistles which at first sight seem to be of the same trend. The texts thus held over have reference more especially to Christ as a power, I might almost say as an executive, amongst the faithful. Christ is to be trusted and dreaded because He steps palpably, even visibly, into the life of His followers, not merely as a living and lifegiving ideal and principle, as a power of grace, but as one who rewards and punishes, helps those of goodwill, and warns the faithless. It is easy

[1] 2 Cor. i. 5.   [2] 2 Cor. v. 8.   [3] 1 Cor. i. 26.   [4] 1 Cor. i. 30.

to see how this executive power adds considerably to the reality of the grace of the Incarnation.

The first of such passages occurs in connection with the excommunication of the incestuous man at Corinth. 'I indeed, absent in body but present in spirit, have already judged, as though I were present, him that hath so done. In the name of our Lord Jesus Christ, you being gathered together and my spirit, with the power of our Lord Jesus: to deliver such a one to Satan for the destruction of the flesh, that the spirit may be saved in the day of our Lord Jesus Christ.'[1] Then there is St. Paul's profession of his great powers as an Apostle of Christ in the Second Epistle to the Corinthians: 'For the weapons of our warfare are not carnal but mighty to God, unto the pulling down of fortifications, destroying counsels, and every height that exalteth itself against the knowledge of God: and bringing into captivity every understanding unto the obedience of Christ; and having in readiness to revenge all disobedience, when your obedience shall be fulfilled. See the things that are according to outward appearance. If any man trust to himself, that he is Christ's, let him think this again with himself, that as he is Christ's, so are we also. For if also I should boast somewhat more of our power, which the Lord hath given us unto edification and not for your destruction, I should not be ashamed.'[2] Then there is St. Paul's threat to the same Corinthians to make them feel the power of Christ, in spite of the apparent weakness of Christ, unless they change their conduct. 'Do you seek a proof of Christ that speaketh in me, who towards you is not weak, but is mighty in you? For although He was crucified through weakness, yet He liveth by the power of God. For we also are weak in Him: but we shall live with Him by the power of God towards you. Try your own selves if you be in the faith; prove ye yourselves. Know you not your own selves, that Christ Jesus is in you, unless perhaps you be reprobates? But I trust that you shall know that we are not reprobates. Now we pray God, that you may do no evil, not that we may appear approved, but that you may do that which is good and that we may be as reprobates.'[3]

The first and second texts just quoted are easily understood. The third passage is of a typical Pauline style, and a short commentary will not be amiss. St. Paul evidently was not satisfied with his dear

[1] 1 Cor. v. 3-5.   [2] 2 Cor. x. 4-8.   [3] 2 Cor. xiii. 3-7.

Corinthians. 'Do you seek a proof of Christ that speaketh in me, who towards you is not weak, but is mighty in you?'[1] Apparently they were under the illusion that, in vulgar parlance, his bark was worse than his bite. 'Therefore I write these things, being absent, that, being present, I may not deal more severely, according to the power which the Lord hath given me unto edification and not unto destruction.'[2] St. Paul gives them a warning. He bids them not to be deceived by the apparent weakness of Christ crucified, and of His poor apostle. For behind that weakness there is the tremendous power of His resurrection. That power Christ means to apply, both immediately, and through His apostle. But there is one condition for the execution of this power. It is put into motion as a chastisement for those only who are Christ's. If a man is not Christ's, if he has been cut away from Christ, the Son of God disdains to show His power towards him. Such a man is a reprobate, and the worst thing that could happen to a Christian is this, that he has become such that Christ's power does not reach him any more, that Christ is powerless towards him. So if the exercise of power with which St. Paul threatens the Corinthians were to remain without its castigating, its visible effects, it would be a terrible revelation of their spiritual state, it would show the fact that they are reprobates. Then comes that wonderful change of St. Paul's heart: he is ready to risk his own reputation, to see his power without its effect, to appear a reprobate himself, rather than to see his children suffer from the effects of his excommunication. 'Now we pray God that you may do no evil, not that we may appear approved, but that you may do that which is good and that we may be as reprobates.'[3] It is evident that St. Paul had a clear intuition of Christ's executive power in redressing evil amongst the faithful themselves.

Christ's power in helping the Apostle, and in fact every Christian, in the hard struggle against evil is of course part of the general confidence in God. Christ is God, and we trust Him to help us. 'Let not your heart be troubled. You believe in God; believe also in Me.'[4] It could not be said that practical faith in the power of the Son of God is a specifically Christian thing, except in the sense that we give to the Incarnate Son of God the same confidence that we give the Father. No man knew better than St. Paul how to rely on

[1] 2 Cor. xiii. 3.   [2] 2 Cor. xiii. 10.   [3] 2 Cor. xiii. 7.   [4] John xiv. 1.

the power of Christ, in his manifold temptations. 'And He said to me: My grace is sufficient for thee: for power is made perfect in infirmity. Gladly therefore will I glory in infirmities, that the power of Christ may dwell in me. For which cause I please myself in my infirmities, in reproaches, in necessities, in persecutions, in distresses, for Christ. For when I am weak, then am I powerful.'[1] But the power of Christ mentioned in these texts is something more specifically Christian. It is based on the personal relation of the Son of God with the regenerate soul. Its efficacy depends on man's intimacy with Christ. One that is a 'reprobate' will not be reached by that specific power of Jesus. It also differs from the power of judgment, as judgment embraces the good and the bad, the Christian and the infidel, the living and the dead. It is essentially Christ's power over His own mystical body the Church, to keep it pure and healthy. The act of excommunication on St. Paul's part was only one manifestation, I might almost say, a negative manifestation, of a power that is a most positive, a most life-giving thing; Christ's unceasing energy in building up His own mystical body, the Church. 'For no man ever hated his own flesh, but nourisheth and cherisheth it, as also Christ doth the Church: because we are members of His body, of His flesh and of His bones.'[2]

Christ is powerful amongst us according to the degree of our faithfulness to Him. 'I am the true vine; and My Father is the husbandman. Every branch in Me, that beareth not fruit, He will take away: and every one that beareth fruit, He will purge it, that it may bring forth more fruit.'[3] His great work is the sanctification of the individual souls that are the mystical members of His body; and to that work He brings an infinitude of power, an influence that is something *sui generis*, the life-force of an organism carried to infinite potentiality. It is a power both beneficent and unsparing, of which we have a divinely inspired account in the message delivered by St. John to the seven churches, in the opening chapters of the Apocalypse. There Christ strikes hard in the very souls of His people. His speech is 'a sharp two-edged sword' that comes out of His mouth. He kills with death the children of a false prophetess. He vomits out from His mouth the angel of the Church of Laodicea. But I must ask my reader to meditate for himself on that most

[1] 2 Cor. xii. 9, 10.   [2] Eph. v. 29, 30.   [3] John xv. 1, 2.

dramatic section of our inspired Books. There he will see the Son of God in a new rôle, the rôle of executive sanctity. It is Christ's rôle in His Church. The power He exercises is not just that power of help on which we trust in all difficulties: it is immanent in the body of the Church, not external to it. Christ stands 'in the midst of the seven golden candlesticks'.[1] He moves them about with a strong arm and He fights against His own careless disciples 'with the sword of His mouth'.[2]

It is no small part of the Christian Mind to have a keen realisation of that work of executive sanctity which the Son of God carries out with unceasing activity and unsurpassable power inside His Church, He Himself being the life that energises everything and directs everything. There is nothing we ought to dread more than the misfortune of putting obstacles to the glorious flow of life in the Body of Christ through personal infidelity to grace, or through reluctance to conform to the mind of the Church. Nothing punishes like stunting a life process, and there is not a life that is more vigorous than Christ in His Church. 'I know thy works, that thou art neither cold nor hot. I would thou wert cold or hot. But because thou art lukewarm and neither cold nor hot, I will begin to vomit thee out of My mouth.'[3] If we have the Christian Mind, our zeal and fervour to do the works of Christ is more than an ordinary generosity in the service of God. It is a specific love of the life of Christ in us and in the Church, with its necessary counterpart of fear lest we should at any time put obstacles to that glorious, but unsparing force. We are in dread of the two-edged sword, lest it cut us off like putrid members.

Here I find the opportunity of writing down one of St. Paul's most powerful passages, setting forth that absolute reciprocity between our life and Christ's life, founded on the larger mystery of Christ's indwelling power in us and in His Church. 'A faithful saying: for if we be dead with Him, we shall live also with Him. If we suffer, we shall also reign with Him. If we deny Him, He will also deny us. If we believe not, He continueth faithful, He cannot deny Himself.'[4] The doctrine of the Church, which Christ builds on Peter, the Rock, is of course a specifically Christian doctrine. It is so intimately connected with the Incarnation that the Church with-

[1] Apoc. i. 13.   [2] Apoc. ii. 16.   [3] Apoc. iii. 15, 16.   [4] 2 Tim. ii. 11-14.

out the Incarnation is not even thinkable. For the Church is essentially and intrinsically the Body of Christ, of God Incarnate. 'And He hath subjected all things under His feet and hath made Him head over all the Church, which is His body and the fulness of Him who is filled all in all.'[1] But as the Christian Mind always takes the practical view of more abstract dogma, I consider that a realisation of the activities of the Son of God inside His Church, activities of mercy and severity, is a pre-eminently practical view. Our obedience to the Church, our love and devotion, our daring and enterprise in her cause, as well as our humble service in the lower grades of usefulness, will spring from such a conviction as from their natural fountain head. 'But doing the truth in charity, we may in all things grow up in Him who is the head, even Christ: from whom the whole body, being compacted and fitly joined together, by what every joint supplieth, according to the operation in the measure of every part, maketh increase of the body, unto the edifying of itself in charity.'[2]

What I have said of the Church applies with equal truth to the doctrine of the Eucharist, which is inseparably connected with the doctrine of the Church. It is a dogma specifically Christian in tenor, and as original as the Incarnation itself. It is part of the mystery of the Son of God. The attitude of the Christian Mind, as something different from the mere intellectual acceptance of the dogma, and even as something different from the actual partaking of the sacrament, is less easily described on account of the vastness of the subject. We may view the Eucharist and make it a most real activity in so many different ways; and the saint is still to be born who has applied to his soul all the treasures which are hidden therein. The Eucharist is the life of Christ, the death of Christ, the resurrection of Christ; it is the companionship of Christ and the blessing of Christ; it is the triumph of Christ, as well as His sweet humility. Christ in the Eucharist is food and drink; He is priest and victim, He is our introduction to God, and our badge of brotherhood with man. It is in the Eucharist that we have a practical demonstration of the vital possibilities of the fruits of the Incarnation.

The Church does so much with the Eucharist; and who knows what she will do with it in future ages? From time to time a real

[1] Eph. i. 22, 23.   [2] Eph. iv. 15, 16.

flash of genius comes to her, and she sees what new use she can make of her great treasure. The modern frequency of Benediction with the Blessed Sacrament is one of those glorious intuitions concerning the possibilities hidden in her ancient and carefully cherished treasure, the Body and Blood of Christ.

To St. Paul's mind the dominant feature of the Eucharist mystery is the death of the Lord, shown forth in it: 'For as often as you shall eat this bread and drink the chalice you shall shew the death of the Lord, until He come.'[1] But he sees other spiritual virtues in it. The Eucharist is the sacrament of union between the faithful. 'The chalice of benediction which we bless, is it not the communion of the Blood of Christ? And the bread, is it not the partaking of the Body of the Lord? For we, being many, are one bread, one body: all that partake of one bread.'[2]

The Eucharist is also the line of division between the Christian and the pagan world as represented by its sacrifices. St. Paul has recourse to the Eucharist to decide in a peremptory way what ought to be the Christian's mental attitude towards the much mooted question of the meat that came from the heathen sacrifices. 'But the things which the heathens sacrifice, they sacrifice to devils and not to God. And I would not that you should be made partakers with devils. You cannot drink the chalice of the Lord and the chalice of devils: you cannot be partakers of the table of the Lord and of the table of devils.'[3]

I do not intend to pursue further the possible practical developments of the Christian Mind with regard to the Eucharist, simply because the subject appears to me well nigh inexhaustible. For all practical purposes the Eucharist is, to the Catholic mind, Christ on earth, with an infinite adaptability to human needs. We need not wonder then if the Church uses the Eucharist as her daily spiritual currency in the Kingdom of God, to purchase grace and salvation for the living and the dead.

[1] 1 Cor. xi. 26.   [2] 1 Cor. x. 16, 17.   [3] 1 Cor. x. 20, 21.

Conclusion

ON the First Sunday after the Epiphany the Church has the following Introit for Mass: 'Upon a lofty throne I saw a Man sitting, whom a multitude of Angels adore singing together: Behold Him the name of whose empire is for ever more.' This liturgical text is not taken from any book of the Scriptures yet no words could be a more fitting *finale* to this book, whose sole aim is to further the enthronisation of the God-Man in the minds of men, as He is enthroned in the intellect of the Angels, and also to foster confidence in the final victory of the ideals of the Christian Mind.

One of the chief tragedies of our time is that even men who hold the Catholic faith with true loyalty may have their outlook on the world practically uninfluenced by a directly Christian philosophy. Their minds are carried away by merely secular politics, and even when they 'practise their religion', as the phrase goes, they are quite devoid of that humility and reserve of judgment which a living faith in the rôle of Christ as the Judge of the living and the dead ought to produce in our minds. Let them open the book of St. John's *Revelation*, and they will find there terrifying descriptions of world cataclysms. It matters little what are the special events there prophesied. The blackest forebodings of the seer are not gloomier than the events of our own days. But what is for our instruction above all things is this, that the seven last plagues, with all the other events described in the vision, are contained in the book whose seals the Lamb alone can break. Whichever way we read the Apocalypse, one thing is in no need of special interpretation: it stands out as clear as the noontide sun. The history of the world is a judgment of the Son of God. Through all the upheavals of heaven and earth, one scheme is carried through with absolute inerrancy, the Kingdom of Christ. 'And the seventh Angel sounded the trumpet: and there were great voices in heaven, saying: The Kingdom of this world is become our Lord's and His Christ's, and He shall reign for ever and ever.'[1] The power of the Son of God, ruling nations, overruling the politics and diplomacies of even upright men, and leading them on to higher purposes, is surely a most

---

[1] Apoc. xi. 15.

direct and practical consequence of the Incarnation. Yet few even amongst the devout give that power the place in their minds which belongs to it. They are devout in Christ, but not powerful in Christ. Yet if the Son of God is anything, He is the first and greatest World Power. In these great and sanguinary debates of men, in which there is no man to lead his fellows to peace, it is the unspeakably great privilege of the Christian Mind to see 'a Man sitting upon a lofty throne, whom a multitude of Angels adore', and the Name of that Man is JESUS.

THE PERSONALITY OF CHRIST

Published in 1914, just after the outbreak of the First World War, this book was described by its Author as 'an unconventional rendering of the Third Part of the Summa', and its purpose as 'neither exegetical, nor apologetical, nor devotional, but strictly theological'. In actual fact it is a not too technical presentment of the Christology of St. Thomas Aquinas, filling the gap between the ponderous treatises De Verbo Incarnato of professional theologians and the more popular works of exegetical and devotional writers.——Editor.

Cum librum cui titulus *The Personality of Christ* a Revmo P. Anschario Vonier, Abbate Congregationis Nostrae, anglico sermone exaratum, Revmus P. Abbas Thomas Bergh, Censor a Nobis deputatus, recognoverit et in lucem edi posse probaverit, facultatem facimus ut typis mandetur, si iis ad quos pertinet ita videbitur.

Datum Sublaci in Protocoenobio S. Scholasticae, die 26 Junii, 1914.

D. MAURUS M. SERAFINI, O.S.B.
Abbas Generalis

D. ISIDORUS M. SAIN, O.S.B.
a Secretis

Nihil obstat.

FRANCISCUS M. CANON WYNDHAM
Censor deputatus

Imprimatur.

EDMUNDUS CANON SURMONT
Vic. Generalis

Westmonasterii, die 26 Aug., 1914

CHAPTER I

The Metaphysics of the Incarnation

FROM the very beginning of Our Lord's earthly life there appears the substitution of the personal element for the purely legal element. He is a mysterious personality, and the whole success of His religion lies in His being trusted, followed, understood; the main precept of His religion is of love for one another. Instead of material legal observances He established the more fundamental laws of the human heart: mutual understanding, mutual support, mutual love: 'Bear ye one another's burdens, and so you shall fulfil the law of Christ.'[1] It is the triumph of His grace to keep human beings in the oneness of religious faith without imposing upon them any strict obligation of uniformity in external ascetical practice. He Himself is the unifying force of Christianity. His first disciples followed Him in the simplicity of their new friendship, carried away by His ineffable charm. No doubt they gloried in being the followers of so great a rabbi, and yet they had no external observance to distinguish them as a school. How could they be the followers of a teacher without fasting, while the disciples of John and of the Pharisees fast so frequently? How could any man be another's disciple unless he displayed some badge of that man's leadership, whether by fast, or ablution, or prayer? But it was to be the achievement of this new rabbi to attract disciples whose only observance was to believe and have confidence in Him, and to have friendship and love for one another: 'By this shall men know that you are My disciples, if you have love one for another.'[2] 'Can the children of the marriage fast, as long as the bridegroom is with them? ... But the days will come, when the bridegroom shall be taken away from them, and then they shall fast in those days.'[3] Fasting has its part in the formation of a Christian. But you are not Christ's disciple simply because you may fast four times in the week, whilst John's disciples fast only thrice, and the Pharisees twice. 'By

[1] Gal. vi. 2.   [2] John xiii. 35.   [3] Mark ii. 19, 20.

this shall men know that you are My disciples, if you have love one
for another.'

The early attraction to Christ and fellowship with Him have all
the joyous liberty of a nuptial feast; attachment and fidelity are all
the surer because the nuptials are bright and gay; serious work is to
follow the feasting, but the memory of that joyful event will remain
an undying bond. The peace and the prosperity of the Christian
cause are thus summed up. All conversion, all holiness, must be
associated with Christ's Person and the fellow men with whom our
lot is cast. Sanctity may indeed have various secondary manifestations. With some souls consciousness of Christ's Person is the predominating factor; with others thought and action are concerned
more directly with visible human persons; but always it is persons
who count, and genuine religion is in danger where legal observances of any sort begin to crowd out the personal element, when all
spiritual efforts are directed towards the scrupulous carrying out of
a system of observances for their own sake without a personal
objective.

The spirit of Christianity, despite its ascetic purity, is diametrically opposed to such a material conception of the ethical life, and the
temporary successes it may obtain are but the harbingers of final
catastrophe. It is Our Lord's exclusive privilege to be Law, or better
still to be a substitution for all law. The human mind is jealous of
such a position because it resents being bound to a person; but as
Christ's Person is Divine, for it is the Second Person of the Trinity,
such resentment is entirely unwarranted in His regard. The Pharisees took umbrage at Our Lord's Person much more than at His
doctrine. Abstract laws or external observances never arouse hatred
or jealousy, love or sympathy, in the measure in which a person
arouses such feelings.

The great theological doctrines concerning Our Lord's Person
have an intimate connection with His spiritual position in the world,
because He is nothing if not a Personality. His grace is nothing if not
a gift of love and mutual understanding. There is no profit from the
Gospel unless it be the perfecting of the human mind and heart.
Any man may invent an ascetical system and find others to submit to
it, but no man can make of his own person the irrevocable voice of
conscience, the all-satisfying food of heart and mind; Our Lord is

the only Person who ever could. None but He can make the relations of other men with their fellows the badge of true discipleship; and no one questions His authority and right to do so. Therefore the teachings of theology about Our Lord's Person ought to be of intense interest to every one of His followers, and His being a Divine Person should fill us with unbounded joy. The history of Christian sanctity records an intense personal love for Christ in innumerable souls. The question may be asked, however, whether such deep personal friendship with One who is not of this world would be at all possible if He were not a living Divine Personality. Is not this personal love of Christ, as history reveals it, a psychological proof of His Divine reality? One thing is certain: nothing like it exists elsewhere; the personalities of non-Christian religions do not enter into the human consciousness in the way that Christ does.

It would be a great mistake then to think that what we might call the metaphysical truths of the Hypostatic Union are barren and unpractical dogmas; on the contrary they are indispensable to any rational explanation of Our Lord's relations with the human race. There belongs to Christ a kind of multiplicity of spiritual presence that makes Him the personal friend of millions of souls; yet His is also a universality of presence and action which interferes in no way with the intense individuality of His relations with souls. Such is the Christ of experience and history. In His humanity He has for all practical purposes the illimitability of Divinity itself; He is truly the Universal Friend, and yet no one was ever such an exclusively personal friend to particular members of the human race. Such intense individuality with such comprehensive universality has but one explanation: Hypostatic Union, the mystery of one human nature existing through one Divine personality. In these days more than ever, philosophical minds dread the rule of a mere individual, however holy he may be. It does not seem as if any individual being could ever be such as to give complete satisfaction and security to other minds and wills. So we constantly find in modern systems the substitution of the ideal for the individual. Such efforts are anything but blameworthy; for it is certain that no merely human individual could ever become a practical, life-giving, completely satisfying ideal for the human race. On the other hand, modern theologies are quite wrong in applying that process of substitution to Christ; there is no need to substitute an ideal Christ for the historic Christ, precisely because the Christ of the Gospels, the Christ of Catholic theology, possesses in truth and reality an infinitude of Personality. There is no limitation in Him. Without that infinitude of Personality, as far as mankind is concerned, an ideal Christ might indeed be preferable to a concrete personal Christ.

This is why I say that the great metaphysical principles underlying the doctrine of the Hypostatic Union are of immense practical import. Individual souls may not make of those great truths an actual study; they simply possess Christ, and are happy in the possession. But for the philosophical mind that wishes to consider Christ's relations with mankind, the metaphysics of the Incarnation are indispensable.

Chapter II

The Christ of the Gospels, of Christian Theology, and of Christian Experience

IT may be said of Our Lord that His written life is far from being proportionate to His place in the world of souls. To a very great extent love for Christ is independent of the Gospels taken as mere narratives. In most cases, love for Christ exists in the human soul long before the books of the New Testament have been taken up as a spiritual study. Children of tender years will kiss a crucifix with the reverence of deepest love, because it is the image of Our Lord; and it would be an entire disregard of facts to say that the boy of six loves Him so much because he has been made to understand the sublime charity of His Crucifixion from the gospel narrative. A deeper comprehension of the love-drama of Christ's death is almost exclusively the achievement of more mature spiritual development. Nor is this the peculiar characteristic of childhood's love for Our Lord; the observation holds good much more generally. For millions of men and women Christ is a great living Personality, dominating their innermost thoughts; yet with nearly all of them it is perfectly true to say that it is not the habitual perusal of the Gospels that has given to Him such a place in their soul. Their knowledge of the Gospel is not a very intimate one; they are satisfied with its general facts, whilst Christ Himself is a very definite power in their lives. If the study of Our Lord's written life be made a special practice by a Christian, it is because the Gospel speaks to him of One whom he already loves and knows, just as the lover takes the keenest interest in being told of the affairs of his beloved.

It seems paradoxical, yet it is evident to all observers of spiritual things, that no one profits by the Gospels unless he be first in love with Christ. The Sacred Text is no adequate explanation of the place Christ holds in the hearts of men. The New Testament may account for the spiritual portrait of Christ which Christian men and women hold enshrined in their minds, but it does not account for the power with which Christ sways the hearts of millions. From time to time there are enthusiastic Gospel campaigns throughout the world. The Scriptures are widely distributed in cheap editions; the words of Christ are seen everywhere, even the ubiquitous billposter is pressed into service to bring the Christian message before the eyes of passers-by. These manifestations of zeal, however laudable, are generally short-lived precisely because they seldom succeed in stirring any deep conviction. There are nations in Europe that live in the faith and love of Christ, but it may safely be asserted that, in the vast majority of the good Christians of those countries, any textual knowledge of Our Lord's sayings is conspicuous by its absence. For them Christ is not a text, but a living Person whose actual presence has infinitely more spiritual influence than any recorded saying of His; and if the Gospel text is at times like a sword of fire in the soul it is because it is interpreted in the living love of Christ.

On the other hand, it is true to say that the Christ of the human soul is not greater than the Christ of the Gospels. It is easy enough, for instance, to see what Christ was to the soul of a Teresa or Catherine. Those great mystics have left very clear records of their faith and love for Christ. Yet the 'Divine Master' of St. Teresa's writings is not greater than the 'Master' of the Gospels. She did not create in her intense religious consciousness a Christ not warranted by the sober Gospel narrative. She may speak of the Spouse of her soul with greater enthusiasm than the Evangelist; but she never describes a greater personality than did he. The soberness of an official historian belongs to the narrator who has lived with Christ or His disciples. The enthusiasm is found in the ordinary worshipper for whom the record of the historian is more a canticle of love than a source of love. But such enthusiasm never assumes anything about Christ's merits which cannot be stated in the exact language of the Evangelist. It has been said with great truth of certain religions that they are like inverted pyramids balanced on their apex. The great monument broadens out as it leaves the almost invisible starting-point. So the religious consciousness of the race has evolved a vast religious personality from a being of much smaller compass. But such a comparison would be quite unfair to the position of Christ in the world. The Christ of our Eucharistic Congresses is not greater than the Christ of St. John's Gospel. The Christianity of the Gospels is as broad as the Christianity of the *Summa* of St. Thomas. With regard to Christ there is no gradual broadening of a religious ideal until it embraces the whole extent of the human mind. But where the enlargement comes in is the efficacy and vividness of Christ's Personality as realised by human souls. No books, even divinely inspired, could create in the human consciousness such a living presence of the God-Man.

It is the conviction of all Christians that Jesus enters into the secrets of their hearts, and they are answerable to Him for their innermost thoughts. Christ is not only the object of their worship, He is also the voice of their conscience; and more than that, He is their Judge, He is the arbiter of their eternal destiny. Here again it could not be said that the Christian conscience has evolved a Christ not warranted by the authentic historical records. We have endless utterances in the sacred Gospels and the Apostolic writings stating most clearly Christ's judicial powers. 'For neither doth the Father judge any man, but hath given all judgment to the Son.'[1] It is the common teaching of theologians that there is in man a life that is inaccessible to the gaze even of the greatest spirits. God alone can read the secrets of that inner life; it is the most incommunicable portion of our being; it is there that we prove our individuality.

[1] John v. 22.

The stronger a character is, the less ready is he to reveal that inner self. Perhaps in a whole life-time a man may find only one friend to whom he opens the citadel of his thoughts; it may even be asserted that most men go through life with their hearts sealed. Readiness to manifest one's innermost thoughts, unless it be to a thoroughly trustworthy and sympathetic listener, is not a sign of manliness; it belongs to the superficial characters, to people who have no depth of their own. Now it is into that centre of our life that Christ has penetrated. It is impossible for a Christian to doubt the universality of the God-Man's knowledge of the secrets of our hearts. Are we not habitually convinced of Christ's human way of discerning the secrets of our conscience? For us it is essentially a human knowledge possessed in a human and created manner. To speak in metaphors, we know that every one of our thoughts falls into the scales of supreme justice, but the scales are Christ's human mind and human heart; the deviation of the balance is a human movement—a created factor. Such is the Christ of practical Christian experience.

CHAPTER III

Christ and Comparative Religion

CHRIST'S Personality is all-important in the religion of Christ. 'Who is He?' and 'What is He?' are vital questions for Christianity. A religion outside the circle of that wonderful Personality may be a most respectable system of morals and even of doctrines, but it is not Christianity. It would be like *Hamlet* without the Prince of Denmark.

Christian religion can never be put on a par with other religious systems, for it is not just a system but a Person. It cannot come within the scope of the science of Comparative Religion, because its essential facts—those which differentiate it from the other religions of the world—are the manifestation of a divine genius of infinite originality. Comparative Religion is a branch of human learning I revere deeply. I cannot conceive anything more fascinating than to trace the sources and relationship of the religious systems of mankind. But when all has been discovered and compared, the fact remains that there is only one such being as Christ known to the religious world. The 'Christ-idea', such as it is found in the Gospels, in Christian theology and Christian conscience, is so profoundly original that it defies all comparison. I say 'Christ-idea' instead of 'Christ' in order to remain within the scope of science. Science, being concerned with experiment and observation, can observe the Christ-idea in the world, for it is not something hidden under a bushel; it is seen around us in the world of to-day; it is the easiest of all tasks to find out from history what it was in the past. Nothing could show more clearly this deep originality of the Christ-idea and its unique position in the world of religion than the great religious strifes within the Christian pale itself that are still filling the world with their echoes. Is it as conceivable that Mohammedans, for instance, should quarrel amongst themselves as to whether there were one or two persons in their prophet; or whether the divine person in him had absorbed the human person; whether there was a human will besides a divine will in him? Yet Christians have taken, and are still taking, sides in those very questions with a passion that comes from strong feeling on those subjects. Our very dissensions are evidence that the Christ-idea has no parallel in the other religions of the world.

The science of war, on land and sea, is a definite branch of knowledge. Books are written on it, and mastered by young officers. But a Napoleon and a Nelson are not merely masters of the theory of war, they are epoch-making geniuses, who change the very science of war into something different from what it was before. Such personalities cannot be cramped within the definitions of any martial system. So Christ cannot be classified by the science of Comparative Religion, because He is what He is in the religious world through His Personality, which has such characteristics as cannot be found elsewhere. Originality and classification exclude each other. But is anything more deeply original than the Christ-idea? No doubt there is much in the practical Christian religion that resembles the tenets and practices of other religious systems. There is in mankind a vast store of religiousness, which is part of human nature itself, or may be derived from simpler and more universal forms of piety existing in some remote and primitive state of human society. Then there is the natural expression of religious awe, analogous to the fear of their masters shown by the higher animals. There are again certain subtle laws of the human spirit in its higher operations, which will be followed almost similarly, whether the ascetic be a Buddhist or a Christian monk. Thus, in the effort of thought, the spiritual man will make use of the same external means, whether he be in Tibet or in Spain. But such things are merely the basic elements of all asceticism. They may be compared amongst themselves and classified by the student. Being found everywhere, they lack originality. But the moment Christ comes on the scene there is something quite new happening in the religious world. Christ wins the spiritual battle by making use of the old, well-worn spiritual weapons; but there never was a victory like His victory, because it consists in this, that He should 'draw all things unto Himself'. He establishes His Personality, and His success is complete only when men have begun to understand who He is and what He is: 'I have manifested Thy name to the men whom Thou hast given Me out of the world. Thine they were, and to Me Thou gavest them; and they have kept Thy word. Now they have known that all things which Thou hast given Me are from Thee: because the words which Thou gavest me I have given to them; and they have received them, and have known in very deed that I came out from Thee, and they have believed that Thou didst send Me.'[1]

Spirituality is indeed indispensable to Christian sanctity; but the essence of Christian sanctity is an intimate relationship with Christ's Personality. Spirituality is a common possession of all mankind; it reveals mankind at its best, and therefore it is a necessary equipment for Christ's elect. At the same time there is a vast amount of genuine spirituality outside the Christian circle. I might say that even with the Christian soul its spirituality may be greater at times than its essential Christian holiness, as there is no practical or theoretical contradiction in the supposition that, even with good men, the efforts after spiritual life may be many times more vigorous than their efforts to enter into personal relationship with Christ. I might even say that they are spiritual men rather than definitely Christian

[1] John xvii. 6-8.

men, if we take the word 'Christian' to stand—as it ought—for what is characteristically Christ's work. The practical realisation of the Christ-concept in the work of sanctity admits of infinite gradation even where there is Faith, and Hope, and Charity. The Christian world is most prosperous when it possesses its Christ most fully. This principle of Christ's Personality once grasped changes the life of the spirit and lifts it up to a plane of wonderful supernaturalness. Spirituality itself may still be considered as a basic element, but life in Christ is the glorious secret of a new dispensation.

Chapter IV

Christ the Wonderful

A GREAT deal of man's happiness comes from the power of admiration. To admire something is like a stream of fresh water flowing over the soul's surface; children are so happy because for them there is so much to wonder at. The deep solemnity of their untarnished eyes is the solemnity of wonderment. Woe to the man who has nothing to wonder at! His soul has lost all freshness, and his eyes are lustreless and vacant. If at any time of our lives we cease to wonder, the fault must be all ours. The world in which God has placed man is an eternal wonder; admiration is the only thing which establishes a kind of equality and proportion between man and the vast world in which he lives. We do not fully understand the marvels of the universe. Indeed we see very little of the universe; each one of us lives in a very small corner of it; the universe is not ours, but it becomes ours through admiration—being so immensely greater than ourselves, we wonder at it, and our wonder grows as the immensity of the universe opens out more and more to the ripening intelligence. What we lose in proportion we gain in admiration, and we feel all the happier through our wonderment. It is the saddest thing in the world to have one's lot cast with people who have lost the gift of admiration. It is the cruellest and darkest captivity of the heart; it is external and internal darkness. It is the hardest purgatory of the soul; it would be hell itself but for the hope that the day will come that will set us free from the companionship of the unwondering souls, and place us amongst the spirits whose life is unending admiration. Let me be surrounded with children and infants, whose every movement and utterance is the expression of some wonderment, and I shall feel that my heart swells again with a happiness it has not known since childhood.

Christ the Son of God could never be man's eternal life if He were not man's eternal wonder. A Christ whom we could fully comprehend, whom we could understand through and through, could never be our life and our hope because we could not wonder at Him any more. It is an indispensable condition of all true and lasting admiration that its object should be greater than our knowledge of it; and the growth of knowledge, far from touching the limits of the marvellous, should convince us more and more of their inaccessibility. Love, no doubt, is born from knowledge and understanding; but short-lived and fragile would be the love which would be merely commensurate with knowledge and understanding. Love is actually noblest and strongest when we know enough of a person to realise that there is in him vastly more. If a brave man's motive is explained to me, I shall admire his courage and unselfishness, not so much on account of what he did, as on account of the character which his deed reveals. But if I knew the man to be incapable of another such act, I could not love and admire him any more; in fact my sentiments towards him are shaped much more by the reserves I suppose him to possess than by what I know he has done. We find strong love for Christ the Son of God, a love fresh as a spring morning and unchanging as the eternal hills, only where there is the belief in His divine nature, because there alone the created spirit has scope for endless wonderment. To make of Christ a merely human being is to deprive Him of the attribute of incomprehensibility. Such theology would be the cruellest science, destroying in the soul the most life-giving element of religion—that wonderment which makes it 'old yet ever new'.

All great admiration comes from depth. We marvel at what we know to be unfathomable and inexhaustible. Our Lord is indeed the Wonderful because in Him there is a never-ending succession of spiritual regions, the one more astonishing than the other. Our Lord is not a simple personality, He is indeed something very complex, something very deep, and only abnormal minds demand a simple Christ, so simple indeed as to leave Him without grace and divinity. The first article of the Christian creed concerning Our Lord's Sacred Person asserts that He is one Person in two Natures. This duality of natures in Christ makes Him the Supreme Wonder, in whom deep calls unto deep. There is in Him a human nature full of grace and truth; but when that human nature is explored it at once provides evidence of something deeper still—the divine nature. And this duality is the most general expression for the multiplicities of beauty which Catholic theology has undertaken to describe. Our Lord has all the perfections of man, He has the perfections of Divinity itself, and He has a perfection which is all His own—something between angelic perfection and Divinity. This gradation of perfections in Our Lord's Person, so noticeable in Catholic Christology, is what makes Him so wonderful; it is like a mountain range rising up higher and higher; when you have reached one summit you find yourself at the foot of a more towering giant. Abnormal minds reject these multiplicities as burdensome; they crave for a simple Christ, but the simplicity they crave for is like the characterless transparency of common glass compared with the scintillation of the hard diamond with its innumerable facets. But we find in practice that the most innocent and loving of Christ's faithful revel in the doctrine of Christ's twofold nature, because a simple and loving follower is a born admirer, and his only fear is lest perchance a day might come when he could not admire any more. In this spirit then let us try to understand the wonderful multiplicity of Christ's perfections such as it is taught by Catholic theology.

In following the teachings of Catholic theology concerning Our Lord's Person we are like one who explores the course of a river. There are two ways of doing it. First, after sailing for days on the broad expanse of the ocean, he comes to the mouth of some mighty Amazon, where it is difficult for a time to distinguish the river from the open sea. Up he sails towards the river's source, borne onward by the inflowing tide as it contends for mastery with the current. After many days of voyaging, the river will lose its individuality; he has now not one but many rivers to explore; it is the water-shed which interests him more than the main stream of the river. But, if the traveller chooses, he may begin his expedition on the mountain-top, follow one water-course, go down with it to the main stream, and then sail down the great river knowing that sooner or later he will find himself on the boundless ocean. This second way of exploration would be more thrilling than the first, because the traveller thus descending from the mountain fastness towards the sea, passes from marvel unto marvel till all the waters are merged in the vast ocean. This example illustrates the natural mode for man to find out the marvels of the Son of God. There is first His external human life; it is the mountain stream, fresh, powerful, of heavenly transparency, running in the deep ravines of His human sufferings. This mountain stream of the mortal life is merged into the river of His spiritual life, His sanctifying grace, His angelic perfections of intellect, His glorified body; this again, vast and powerful though it be, is finally absorbed by the infinite ocean of His Divinity.

St. Thomas Aquinas acts not as the second but as the first explorer: he begins from the ocean, the Divinity, and follows up the great system of waters to the human sources of Christ's life. A glance at the disposition of the Questions and Articles in the Third Part of the *Summa* shows clearly the movements of this great theological explorer. He begins with Hypostatic Union—the presence of the Infinite Godhead in Christ; then he speaks of His sanctifying grace and supernatural virtues. He treats of Christ's grace as the Head of the human race, of His knowledge, angelic and human; then of the human power of Christ's soul, of His prayer, His priesthood, His adoption, His predestination, His adoration, His mediation. He is still in the main stream with the tidal movements of the ocean swelling its waters. Finally he comes to Christ's human life: His virginal conception, His nativity, His baptism, His doctrine, His miracles, His passion, His death, His resurrection, His ascension. I must crave the reader's indulgence for keeping to this simile of a water-course. But in order to be fully applicable to the present subject, instead of supposing a system of converging streams that come down from the mountains, we must imagine a system of streams flowing on level land so that the tides might come up to the very spring of the most humble brook. Nature has no such water system as far as I know; if it had, it would be a splendid illustration of a great mystery: the merely human actions of Our Lord, besides flowing towards the infinite ocean of Divinity, are constantly being swollen by its tidal movements rushing along their channels and mixing with the waters of human sanctity. A tidal river has a double nature, so to speak: first there are its own waters, and then there are the waters of the sea carried along the fresh waters of the stream. So in the wonderful Christ there are main-stream and tributaries, but over them all there flow the waters of Divinity. No doubt it is this penetration of Divinity into every human act of Christ that compelled St. Thomas to navigate his theological river from sea to source.

I shall adopt the Angelic Doctor's method in the instruction of those for whom this little treatise is written. The devotional method, however, which is essentially one of progressive wonderment, begins with the 'Hail, full of grace'; and from the Virgin Mother, the sweet daughter of David, it journeys through the mysteries of Our Lord's human life to that of the Word who dwells in the bosom of the Father, passing from sweet admiration to inexpressible wonder. It is not the only instance where the theoretical presentment of heavenly things follows an opposite course to that of their practical realisation.

CHAPTER V

An Attempt at Defining Personality

IN these days the word 'personality' is one to conjure with. The power of personality is the theme of every popular work of fiction and biography. A theologian is of all writers the one who might be seen biting his quill in embarrassment for lack of a better term, for his contemporaries have robbed him of this word and given it a different meaning. The term 'personality' holds as great a place in theology as in literature, but the rôles it acts are vastly different. It is true that the more modern meaning of personality—a powerful individualistic character—is not unwelcome to a theologian, for his

Christ is the most attractive of persons; but he has a much older right to define the term, and in his attempt to explain Christ's attractiveness he has to delve down in the hidden mysteries of much more austere concepts. It is with this view of personality, as the austere and solid foundation of being, that he is primarily concerned.

John Locke's definition, or rather description, of 'person' is as good as any other, outside the Aristotelian and scholastic sphere of thought. 'This being premised to find wherein personal identity consists, we must consider what "person" stands for. Which, I think, is a thinking intelligent being, that has reason and reflection, and can consider itself as itself, the same thinking thing in different times and places; which it does only by that consciousness which is inseparable from thinking, and as it seems to me, essential to it: it being impossible for anyone to perceive without perceiving that he does perceive.'[1] With Locke, the orthodox theologian agrees that a person is essentially 'a thinking, intelligent being; that has reason and reflection, and can consider itself, as itself, the same thinking thing in different times and places.' The scholastic applies a similar definition to Deity itself, to the pure angelic spirit and to man. Yet, to the scholastic mind, Locke's definition of a person is not adequate. The scholastic asks with Locke why it is that a thinking being can think of itself, as itself; but his answer to that question shows him to be the deeper metaphysician. The English philosopher says that a thinking being thinks of itself, as itself, 'by that consciousness which is inseparable from thinking.' He makes consciousness the reason of self-consciousness ('to consider itself as itself'), which is evidently tautology. It is as if I defined my power of running through that movement that makes me run. The scholastic, though defining a person as a thinking being with self-consciousness, has a deeper underlying metaphysical element which saves him from Locke's tautology. Self-consciousness, deep and mysterious as it is, is not so deep and so mysterious as self-being. It is merely a result of self-being. Now, the scholastic maintains that self-being underlies self-consciousness, as the cause underlies its effect, and that a person is constituted primarily through self-being, through the fact of having one's being as an exclusive and total property.

[1] *Essay concerning Human Understanding*, Book II, Chap. 27.

We all know Tennyson's immortal verses describing the gradual formation of the individual self-consciousness.

> The baby new to earth and sky,
>   What time his tender palm is prest
>   Against the circle of the breast,
> Has never thought that 'this is I.'
>
> But as he grows he gathers much,
>   And learns the use of 'I,' and 'me,'
>   And finds 'I am not what I see,
> And other than the things I touch.'
>
> So rounds he to a separate mind,
>   From whence clear memory may begin,
>   As thro' the frame that binds him in
> His isolation grows defined.
>
> This use may lie in blood and breath,
>   Which else were fruitless of their due,
>   Had man to learn himself anew
> Beyond the second birth of Death.[1]

Yet this very evolution of the thought of the isolated 'I' supposes an isolated possession of existence at the start. Now it is that perfect appropriation of being by the 'I,' long before there is a conscious distinction of oneself from other beings, the scholastic considers as the thing that makes a person. Scholastics are divided amongst themselves how to explain such an exclusive appropriation of being. Such differences of opinion cannot detract from the metaphysical value of the main principle, that a person is radically and eternally *sui juris*, a rational being with rights and responsibilities that can never be shifted on to someone else's shoulders. Personality means incommunicable appropriation for weal and for woe of one's deeds. The highest manifestation of personality is moral merit and demerit; the fact through which a free act of the rational will is so entirely the property of the rational agent that, in the last instance,

[1] *In Memoriam.*

God Himself cannot be held responsible for it without contradicting Himself. Moral responsibility is well calculated to open out to us a view of the might of personality. Let us remember that both highest bliss in heaven and profoundest misery in hell are states for a spirit which God Himself could not transfer to another spirit without injustice. Self-consciousness is not so deep and so permanent a thing as moral responsibility, that all-important factor of Christian philosophy. A man may be perfectly conscious of doing a certain act without his being responsible for it, as there is the possibility of his not being a free agent in the matter. The fact of moral responsibility is the most immediate result of the element that makes a person. Moral responsibility is not that element itself, but it is its first-fruit. In moral responsibility we show that we have our being in our own hands. How could I ever be made to answer eternally for any moral act of mine, if that act were not mine to the exclusion of every other moral or ethical partnership? Self-consciousness is near the root of our being, but it is not yet the root; and there is even the possibility of the act of which I am conscious not being entirely my own. Moral responsibility is much nearer that root, for it implies in the last instance an exclusion of every other created will from my act. But it is not yet the root, just as the will is not the whole man, the whole spirit. The root from which it springs is personality. A person is essentially a rational being that has responsibility, or, anyhow, may acquire it in time.

Moral responsibility is—to my mind—the natural key to the mystery of personality. It may be objected that moral responsibility, especially when considered as stretching into the next world, is too theological a concept to be made the starting-point of the quest for personality. My answer is that I am writing a theological book, not a philosophical one, for people to whom the moral responsibility implied in the words 'merit' and 'guilt' is an intellectual certainty. Moral responsibility and self-consciousness seem almost to touch in the phenomenon of the consciousness of duty, of the conviction—intellectual if there ever was one—embodied in the notion: 'I ought'. Yet the two things, though converging, are still different. Moral responsibility is a fact quite independent of inner consciousness, or rather we know that we have the merit or the guilt of our practical answers to the 'I ought' according as we have followed the inner voice or disobeyed it. There is an old scholastic axiom, *Actiones sunt suppositorum*—'Acts belong to the person.' Nothing could be truer, if we bear in mind the mystery of personal responsibility for our deeds. I should describe personality, then, as that reality within the creature that makes his acts to be entirely his own, i.e., with his full responsibility—a responsibility stretching into eternity. It matters comparatively little how we explain that great appropriation of being that underlies responsibility. That it is a wonderful and potent reality is clear to all those who admit moral responsibility. That it is a reality that pervades and dominates our whole being is manifest from the results of responsibility, affecting our whole life for weal or for woe. It is necessarily what schoolmen call a 'substantial' reality, a reality that is not merely accidental but one that is co-extensive with the individual being itself.

I must here say a few things to remove certain misgivings that might arise at hearing such expressions as 'appropriation of being,' 'exclusive possession of being,' 'exclusive responsibility of one's moral acts.' Is it not the first rudiment of piety to believe firmly that our being is the property of God, from whom we have received it; that our good acts, especially those of the supernatural order, are the work of the Spirit of God within our own soul? The answer to such difficulties will be a further illustration of the greatness of created personality. Nothing is truer than the fact that all our being comes from God, by creation. But God's creative power is at its best, so to speak, in the production of a being that is so complete as to have a responsibility all of its own, just as He has responsibility. Pantheism, which means emanation of things from God, as opposed to creation of things *ex nihilo*, is warded off most conclusively by that duality of responsibility. That God should be able to produce outside Himself a being, whose very constitution brings about within itself a responsibility that may put it eternally into opposition to Him who made it, is the greatest achievement of His creative power. So likewise with the share of God's grace in our moral acts, both natural and supernatural. No amount of divine *influxus* will ever take away the fact that it is my own act. St. Thomas would say that the power of divine grace is of such a nature as to make my act more mine than ever. That is his constant answer to objections about the preservation of free will under the influence of grace. Just as God's creative act at its highest results in a personality distinct from Him; so God's act of supernatural elevation results in a meritorious deed that is the free will's own glory.   I have already said that even amongst the Schoolmen there are accidental divergences of opinion as to the precise definition of that far-reaching element in the created being that makes for absolute duality between God and His rational creature, even when God fills His creature with the graces of His own Spirit.

The older philosophy takes personality to be something entitatively static. The modern philosophies make it something practically all dynamic. The older philosophy has this advantage over her modern sisters, that she does the one thing and omits not the other. She has all that love of life which is the characteristic of dynamic philosophy. But underlying the transient phenomena of conscious life there are for the Schoolmen the stable elements from which life with its endless variations flows, and which give it continuity and oneness. Personality is one of those static elements; perhaps the principal one; it is the centripetal power in our very complex individualities—precisely because it is static. Such stability is not only perfectly reconcilable with the perennial flow of our conscious psychic life, it is its salvation; just as the deep banks of a river keep it from becoming a useless swamp. Or better still: personality, the static in man, is to consciousness, the dynamic, what the mighty mountain range is to the stream; in its sublime and austere solitude flows the winding stream with all the charm of its rippling motion and babbling song.

Before concluding this chapter I want to emphasise once more that the thing which I call moral responsibility is not personality itself, but it is an element of personality; and in its striking manifestation of freedom, responsibility sends a piercing shaft of light into the mysterious abyss of personality.

CHAPTER VI

The Replacement of Human Personality by Divine Personality in Christ

IT is the oldest and truest expression of the philosophy of the Incarnation to say that in Christ there is no human personality, but that the human personality in Him has been 'replaced' by Divine Personality. The great struggles of orthodoxy against Nestorianism resulted in the adoption of this formula by the Church. Christ is a human individual nature, but without a human personality; in Him the Divine Personality of the Word performs the functions of the human personality, and infinitely more, as behoves a Divine Personality. The maintenance and reality of the one individual human nature, detached as it were from its congenital and native element of created personality, and endowed with Divine Personality, is a dogmatic clarification resulting from the Church's long strife with Eutychianism and its various ramifications. The separability of personality from the individual rational nature by Divine Omnipotence, and its 'replacement' by a Divine Personality, must always be primary factors of our Christian metaphysics, if we are to give an intelligible account of Hypostatic Union.

Any sanctification, any unction of the Spirit, any grace in Christ that is not a substitution of human personality by the Personality of the Word, is not Incarnation, not Hypostatic Union; it is merely one of the ordinary works of supernatural grace. There are no limits to the powers of the Holy Ghost, to the ways in which He may elevate the rational creature above its own plane to a similarity with God; but sanctifying grace carried to its millionth degree could no more be Hypostatic Union than the most perfect cultivation of my voice could be a training of my mathematical powers. Hypostatic Union is a marvel of a different order from grace though not so different as not to have certain secret affinities with it, which would make them compatible in the same rational being. Hypostatic Union requires first of all the absence of a congenital element in the individual nature: its native created personality. All other supernatural elevations produced by the Holy Ghost, far from starting with the absence of some natural endowment, presuppose every native perfection and responsibility. The missing, or rather discarded created element, finite personality, is not elevated or glorified by the Holy Ghost; it is directly 'replaced' by a reality of the same order but of infinite superiority, the Personality of the Word. The ideas contained in the terms 'elevation' and 'replacement' well express the functions of ordinary sanctification, even of the highest order, and Hypostatic Union. In ordinary sanctification the Holy Ghost elevates to a higher plane the existing realities of the rational creature; in Hypostatic Union the Second Person of the Trinity takes the place of a created element that would be there in normal circumstances.

Such replacement could never come about in a creature, unless the replacing Personality were Infinitude itself. First, infinite power is required to interfere with the element of personality in a created being; for only a God of infinite creative power could make a responsible personality exist outside Himself. Personality is God's divinest work, and as He alone places it within the creature, He alone can give it a substitute. Secondly, such replacement requires what I might call infinite subtleness on the part of the Person thus superseding inside an individual created nature its congenital personality. Thirdly, there must be in the replacing Personality an Infinitude of personal worth, precontaining in its oneness all the personal worth possible in a creature, that accrues to an individual rational nature from its privilege of being such and such a person, with respective rights and responsibilities stretching into eternity. Now, our masters in theology are far from being blind to the fact that not to possess its native congenital personality would be to the rational nature an immense disadvantage, unless the substitute be not only infinite, but also such as to precontain in itself what it comes to replace. Suppose it to be a metaphysical possibility that my personality could be replaced by the personality of an angelic spirit, it is doubtful whether I would be the gainer or the loser. A finite spirit could never replace within me a congenital, essential element of my being without my being less myself. But with the second Person of the Trinity, in whom all things are as in their eternal prototype, Christ's humanity has acquired boundless riches of personal worth, though it be without a created personality. For Divine Personality is infinitely congenital to it. Nothing short of this substitution of Divine Personality for created personality will do justice to the traditional view of Christ, the Son of God. I make so bold as to say that Hypostatic Union, thus stated with theological exactness, is indeed worthy of the admiration of the keenest intellect. The whole difficulty resolves itself into this question: Is it possible for Infinite Personality to perform the function of finite personality in an individual created nature?

It is in this, and in no other sense, that God is said to become man. No doubt many minds, unacquainted with Christian theology, think of a transformation of Godhead into manhood when they hear the phrase, and they naturally revolt from it at once. Their mental recoil would be more than justified if Incarnation were such a transformation. But that the statement should mean that Divine Personality 'does duty' for a created personality within a human nature they seem hardly to realise; yet that surely sheds quite a different light on the matter. Other theologies, while admitting an Incarnation, at best speak of a mere indwelling of Godhead in the Man Christ, an indwelling of vague character, and bristling with metaphysical difficulties. Catholic theology, the child of the great Councils of the fourth, fifth, and sixth centuries, by adopting the 'replacement' of personality by Personality, whilst defining the bond that links Godhead and manhood in Christ, has not burdened man's intellect with a revolting metaphysical novelty. That there are within the human individual separabilities, if not actual separation of realities, is admitted in every system of philosophy. No philosopher could dream of man as of a non-composite being. Our dogma, it is true, goes to the root-separabilities, and thinks of Deity as capable of replacing certain created elements, while avoiding any pantheistic consequences.

CHAPTER VII

The Permanence of Christ's Human Nature

THIS short chapter is written to explain how the concept of a Divine Person absorbing and replacing the individual human nature in Christ would be pantheistic, whilst there is no pantheism, but a most glorious assertion of God's 'personalness,' in the replacement of human personality by the Personality of the Word. It is the oldest and most sacred of Christian dogmas that in spite of this mysterious substitution of personality, Christ's human nature is as perfect and as intact as my own. His humanity has indeed been supremely elevated by every kind of supernatural grace, but it has not been replaced—nothing in it has been superseded. How an individual nature is a distinct reality from personality I have already explained. But it remains to be shown how the Incarnation could never be a substitution of nature without its giving rise to monstrous philosophical consequences, whilst there are no such alarming results with the substitution of personality.

Nature is essentially the stream of life, born in the mountain fastnesses. It is all movement, all activity. Modern philosophies, being essentially dynamic and phenomenalist, are nature philosophies; they are hardly ever personality philosophies; they only busy themselves with modes of acting, without bothering about modes of being, and in their own generation they have been wise enough. Now, the idea of a stream suggests to me another comparison, which I think very useful in this most abstruse matter. I must crave the reader's pardon for suggesting an analogy between man's mechanical achievements and this most spiritual subject, Hypostatic Union. But have we not a great authority to justify the use of similitudes? 'And with many such parables He spoke to them the word, according as they were able to hear.'[1] Engineering skill has replaced the original banks of many a stream with artificial embankments. There is no end to the resources of the engineer; if he be given time and money, he might replace the banks of the Rhine with

[1] Mark iv. 33.

stone dykes all the way from Switzerland down to the North Sea. But no engineer, even with an empire to finance him, would ever replace the stream itself by one of his own invention.

Let the stream stand for individual nature. That God should in His own Person be personality to it is like replacing the original banks of the river with others more durable. But that Godhead should replace nature itself would mean that the river is no longer the river it was; it has lost its identity. It would not be a stream of life that comes from earthly sources; it would be simply an outflow of Divinity.

But to return to more exact thought; life, while remaining human, cannot be replaced by a Higher Life, thought cannot be replaced by Higher Thought, consciousness cannot be replaced by Higher Consciousness; but human life and thought and consciousness may be appropriated by a Higher Owner. The function of nature is to live; the function of personality is to own.

Chapter VIII

'Amen, Amen, I say to you, before Abraham was made, I am'[1]

THE text that I have chosen for the title of this chapter is one of the many passages of the Gospel narrative that show how even medieval theology, with all its high metaphysics of the Incarnation, never goes beyond the theology of the Evangelist himself. It may state the matter in different terms, but it does not state anything beyond the inspired writer's teaching.

The above text is quite clear; its authority is undoubted; the Jews saw the purport of Christ's solemn asseveration: as He gave Himself the age of the Deity itself, they picked up stones to punish the blasphemy. This declaration of unchanging divine existence, implied in the words 'Before Abraham was made, I am,' was not spontaneous

[1] John viii. 58.

on the part of Christ, but was brought about by the Jews' allusion to the death of Abraham and to Christ's comparative youth. It was the Jews, not Christ, who introduced the subject of Abraham. The unexpected turn the controversy took shows how clear to Christ's consciousness was the realisation of His own superiority to time and space. I now quote a casual remark of St. Thomas, which he makes in connection with something else, but which shows that his mind habitually moved in the atmosphere of St. John's Gospel. The doctrine contained therein is a logical consequence of the metaphysical principle laid down by St. Thomas for the understanding of the Hypostatic Union; yet it is a natural commentary on our Gospel text. 'Although the human nature in Christ be something new, nevertheless the personality [*suppositum*] of that human nature is not new, but eternal. And because this name *God* is predicated of the man [Christ] not in virtue of the human nature, but in virtue of the personality, it does not follow that [in the Incarnation] we introduce a new God. But such a consequence would follow, if the man [in Christ] had a created personality, as those who put two persons in Christ [Nestorians] are compelled to assert.'[1] Before Abraham was made, Christ *is*, because eternal Personality takes the place of created personality. The reality represented by 'is' belongs to personality. Christ has eternal Personality, therefore He *is* eternally.

Christ's human nature did not exist from eternity; it was formed in Mary's womb. But it exists in virtue of an eternal existence, the Divine Personality. Suppose a man, having lost his eye or his hand, had afterwards the eye or hand restored to him by Divine Power. That eye or hand would be much younger than the man's whole organism. At the same time the new member would share the age of the entire body, as it shares its general vitality and power of existence. This comparison is used by St. Thomas to illustrate how there is oneness of being, oneness of existence, and therefore oneness of age in Christ's Personality; though there be in Him the human element, inserted at a given period of history into the vitalities of Divine Personality. The Article of the *Summa*,[2] from which this comparison is taken, may be considered to reach the sublimest height of the metaphysics of the Incarnation. To the question 'Whether there is only one Being in Christ,' the answer is in the affirmative. The re-

[1] *S. Th.* III, Quest. xvi, Art. 2, ad 3.   [2] *S. Th.* III, Quest. xvii, Art. 2.

placement of personality which I have spoken of has been defined by Catholic Councils. They provide an adequate formula to enable us to state the mystery. St. Thomas has drawn all his conclusions from that great ecclesiastical definition. All our views of Christ, all our love for Him, are not only modified by it, but actually born of it. But when St. Thomas raises the question whether there is only one existence, one Being in Christ, he evidently does a daring thing, which might seem to be hardly authorised by the original language of the Councils. Yet his bold answer is the only one that does justice to words like those of the text: 'Amen, Amen, I say to you, before Abraham was made, I am.' That human organism that speaks, IS, exists, has being, in virtue of the existence that is Eternity itself; just as the miraculously restored eye lives in virtue of the life of the older organism. For St. Thomas, the conclusion that eternal existence is the existence of the nature formed in Mary's womb seems to offer no difficulties. He arrives at it as calmly as you arrive at the conclusion that you want food when you are hungry. Existence follows personality, he says; for ultimately it is only a personality that makes a rational nature exist. Now, Christ's human nature has Divine Personality; therefore it has Divine Existence. It is God, because it exists through God's existence. Such is the meaning of that wonderful Article I have cited. Its calmness is as surprising as its speculative sublimity. Like the Divine Master who thought it no profanation to utter the words, 'Before Abraham was born, I am,' in spite of the uproarious tumult it raised amongst the Pharisees, St. Thomas, the great master of theology, thinks it no exaggeration to say that Christ's humanity has the same existence as the eternal God. After all, it is a smaller truth than to say that it has the same Personality as the eternal God.

CHAPTER IX

How completely Our Lord's Human Nature is Divine

ST. THOMAS asks himself: 'Is Hypostatic Union natural to Christ as man?'[1] One sees the meaning of his interrogation. We have seen that Hypostatic Union is nothing else than the personal existence of the Word being directly the existence of Christ's soul and body. The meaning of St. Thomas's question, then, is this: How far is this union between Divine Personality and human nature natural to the human part of Our Lord's Person? First of all, it could not be natural in the sense of its flowing as it were from the human part of Christ; a creature of whatever rank could never have in itself the power of such a union. It all comes from above. There is, however, another aspect. Our Lord's humanity was never without that divine existence; neither His soul nor His body existed even for one instant in an un-divine way; and it is on that account that it may be said that Hypostatic Union is natural to Our Lord as man, because as man He never knew any other sort of existence. It does not seem to imply contradiction that an adult human personality should be at a given moment hypostatically united with a divine Person. But in that case, Hypostatic Union could not be called natural, as it succeeded a created human personal existence, and the mother of such an hypostatically assumed human nature could not truly be called the Mother of God. Our Lady, on the contrary, is truly the Mother of God, because her Child never existed otherwise than as the Son of God.

However, we have not exhausted the subject yet. There is one more way for Our Lord's human nature to be naturally divine, more excellent than the mere fact of His never having been anything but divine. It is this: the mode of Our Lord's formation in the womb of His Blessed Mother was such that the result had to be human nature with divine existence. She conceived by the Holy Ghost, and conception by the Holy Ghost is necessarily the origin of a nature that

---

[1] S. Th. III, Quest. ii, Art. 12.

must have divinity. This is clearly expressed in the archangel's message to Our Lady. 'The Holy Ghost shall come upon thee, and the power of the Most High shall overshadow thee; and therefore also the Holy which shall be born of thee shall be called the Son of God.[1]' He shall be called the Son of God, precisely because the Holy Ghost will overshadow her; so that Our Lord as man is God, in virtue of His conception through the Holy Ghost. In Hypostatic Union, therefore, the human nature is as divine as divine can be, not only because it always has been divine, but because, through the laws of its conception it had to be divine. 'The grace of Union is natural to Christ in regard to His humanity on account of the propriety of His Birth, as He was conceived by the Holy Ghost, so that He might be the natural Son of God, and of Man.'[2]

We ought never to think of Christ's humanity as in any way separable from His Divinity, as prior to it, or as being the object of a predestination by itself. It was always divine, and according to St. Paul's energetic expression 'Christ Jesus ... being in the form of God, thought it not robbery to be equal with God.'[3] In the supposition that a living, grown-up person were hypostatically united with a divine Person, human personality would then be 'swallowed up' by Divine Personality. But such a union would differ in many things from the Hypostatic Union that is in Christ; the greatest difference being that in such a case the human nature would not be divine by the very laws of its conception and birth. The hypothesis might safeguard Hypostatic Union, but it would not be Christianity, and the mother of the privileged human being would not be the Mother of God; she would be the mother of a man who became God, which is a totally different thing. The Church in her struggle with Nestorianism established the doctrine not only of the substitution of Divine Personality for human personality in Christ, but also the title of Mary to divine maternity, because her Son was conceived in such wise as to be necessarily God. In our hypothetical case the man thus elevated to Hypostatic Union, though truly the Son of God, would owe endless gratitude to God for the favour. In the Hypostatic Union that is in Christ it could not be said that His sacred humanity owes a debt of gratitude for its privilege. It has Divine Personality,

---

[1] Luke i. 35.   [2] S. Th. III, Quest. ii, Art. 12, ad 3.
[3] Phil. ii. 6.

divine existence, through the laws of its birth; 'Propter proprietates
Nativitatis ipsius,' says St. Thomas.

Nothing short of Hypostatic Conception can give us a complete
idea of Christ. His flesh is all divine, and from the very beginning of
the Nestorian controversies, the champions of orthodoxy appealed
to the mystery of Christ's Body in the Eucharist as an argument in
favour of the personal union in Christ being from the very start.
'This very fact that we acknowledge that the only begotten Son of
God died in His flesh, rose and ascended into heaven, qualifies us for
offering the unbloody sacrifice in the Church and, by participating
in the holy flesh and precious blood of the Redeemer, for receiving
the mystical blessing so as to be sanctified. We receive it not as a
common flesh, nor as the flesh of an eminently sanctified man, or of
one who has received dignity by being united with the Logos or by
divine indwelling, but as the true life-giving and proper flesh of the
Word. For since He is, as God is, in His own nature life, and is
become One with His own flesh, so has He imparted to this flesh a
life-giving power.'[1] This profession of faith, formulated in the
Council of Alexandria A.D. 430 under the presidency of St. Cyril,
preparatory to the great Ephesine Council, shows how clear and
definite the views of Christian thinkers were as to the extent of
Christ's divineness.

There is one more consideration that finds a natural place here:
St. Thomas says that Hypostatic Union is something created.[2] This
doctrine, strongly emphasised by Aquinas, whilst containing a world
of wisdom, might easily be misleading, as apparently implying an
inferiority of divineness for Christ's humanity. That Hypostatic
Union is a created thing ought to be clear to everyone, after a little
thought. In Hypostatic Union Divine Personality replaces human
personality; what is more to the present purpose, Divine Personality is united with an individual human nature. Now such a union
is brought about by God's creative Omnipotence, uniting the two
extremes into the One Ineffable. If creative Omnipotence were not
to intervene, a human nature could never have divine existence,
Divine Personality, except in the pantheistic sense. Personal being
outside God is always the result of a creative act of God. Now the

---

[1] Hefele, *History of Councils*, Book IX, Chap. 1, Sec. 13. (Eng. trans. Vol. III, p. 30).
[2] *S. Th.* III, Quest. ii, Art. 7.

circumstance that personal being pre-exists—namely, the second Person of the Trinity—does not alter the case. It had to be given to an individual human nature, and such bestowal, or uniting, supposes as much a creative act as the production of personal being *ex nihilo*. In this sense Hypostatic Union is something created, *aliquid creatum*. It is the result of a creative act, though implying a series of infinitudes. To be a created thing and to be a finite thing are not necessarily synonymous. Philosophers admit degrees in infinitude; in order to explain Hypostatic Union exhaustively every kind of infinitude would have to be pressed into service: it is deep calling unto deep. But one thing is certain: it has no finite element, though it be a created marvel. Christ's human nature no doubt has finite elements, but that which makes the nature divine, Hypostatic Union, is all Immensity and Infinity.

CHAPTER X

'The Word was made flesh'

THE commonest theological formula stating the Mystery of the Incarnation is this: 'God was made man.' We have scriptural authority for it in the words of St. John: 'And the Word was made flesh.'[1]

In the Sixteenth Question of the Third Part of his *Summa*, St. Thomas makes an exhaustive study of the various formulas that express the wondrous mystery. It shows amongst other things how various were the aspects of the mystery known to the great thinker. Now the formula 'God was made man' has his full approval. It is a true statement. His interpretation is this: 'God is said to have been made man, because a human nature began to have being in the personality [*suppositum*] of a divine nature that pre-exists from all eternity.'[2] In other words, for God to become man is in fact a Divine Personality doing duty for the personality of a particular

[1] John i. 14.   [2] S. Th. III, Quest. xvi, Art. 6, ad 1.

human nature. Such office Divine Personality did not perform from all eternity, but began it in time, though the hour had been eternally predestined. So it is quite orthodox to say: 'God became man.'

Many of us might feel easier in our minds with that other formula 'Man became God,' as it seems better to express the elevation of human nature through Hypostatic Union, broadening the manhood without narrowing the Godhead. Yet in his next Article St. Thomas rejects the formula as misleading.[1] His reasons are even better expressed in the Thirty-third Question, where he treats of Christ's conception.[2] I here summarise the argument. We say with great propriety of language that *God became man*; but we cannot say with any propriety that *man became God*. God merely assumed what is human; but this human element never existed before being assumed by the Word. If it had pre-existed it would have had a separate personality. Now it would be against the nature of Hypostatic Union to unite Divine Personality with a pre-existing complete human being, i.e. already having personal existence. In other words, the reason why it cannot be said that man became God is this, that the human part of Christ never had a personal existence of its own. The Godhead that created it in Mary's womb performed the functions of personality in it from the first moment of its existence. This, and no other, is the reason why the two propositions, 'God became man' and 'Man became God' are not convertible propositions. Divine Personality existed in itself from eternity, before it discharged the office of personality to Christ's human nature. But the human nature never existed before it was given Divine Personality. The moment of its creation and of its being assumed by Divine Personality is indivisible.

On the other hand, St. Thomas admits the convertibility of the two propositions: 'God is man' and 'Man is God.' It is the *factum est* ('became') the theologian does not like when Christ's humanity is spoken of in connection with Divinity. Only a pre-existing thing strictly *becomes* something new, having new relations, new functions. St. John describes in his First Chapter the life of the Word before the Word became flesh. There is no history of Christ's Humanity before it became divine. Its history starts with its being supported in existence by the Personality of the Word. But in Our Lord Man *is*

[1] *S. Th.* III, Quest. xvi, Art. 7.　　　　[2] *S. Th.* III, Quest. xxxiii, Art. 3.

God, and God *is* Man. For some minds the first formula is more prolific of spiritual consolations; for others the second is more delightful. One is as good as the other from the point of view of theological accuracy. By the first we mean that Divine Personality has replaced human personality; by the second we chiefly regard the human element having its existence through Divine Personality.

CHAPTER XI

A Scholastic Hypothesis

IT is not immensely more difficult to admit Hypostatic Union than any other supernatural grace. The moment we grant that Christ is a superman in a way in which no other human being has been or ever will be a superman, we are amongst those who can no longer have any reasonable difficulties against Hypostatic Union. The Christ of the orthodox thinker is essentially so great that He cannot be merely the outcome of a cosmic process, however prolonged and however potent that may be; Christ is what He is through a direct action, or unction, to use a scriptural word, on the part of the extra-mundane Deity. That such unction should be the communication of Divine Personality itself, instead of mere finite graces, is not a new difficulty. The supernatural order once admitted, communication of Divine Personality is merely the highest possible form of supernatural elevation.

Here I should like to mention one of the side issues of the theological doctrine of the Hypostatic Union. St. Thomas, with his masterly grip of the main question, makes various suppositions, which he answers with a view to making the central point more clear. He asks whether a Divine Person could have taken into Hypostatic Union several individual human natures. His answer is in the affirmative; for no finite number of individual human natures could exhaust the communicability of Divine Personality. In other words, the unction we call Hypostatic Union could have been multiplied a millionfold if God in His wisdom had chosen to do so, just as much lesser graces are multiplied. I dare say that to many minds Hypostatic Union is a real difficulty because they shrink from the thought of the Godhead being contained and circumscribed within the limits of a created nature. To them Incarnation seems hardly possible without a loss to Divinity itself. Their instinct is natural. No amount of spiritual advantage to the creature could ever be an adequate compensation for any loss to the Majesty of the Godhead itself. In fact such an idea implies contradiction. How could loss to God ever be the creature's gain, as all the creature's happiness is precisely in the creature's aspiration to an immutably happy Divinity? A diminished or humbled Godhead would be the creature's greatest misfortune. Hypostatic Union, however, leaves the potentialities of Godhead as infinite as before. 'The power of a Divine Person is infinite; it cannot be limited to any created thing. Therefore it cannot be said that the Divine Person took unto Himself one human nature in such wise as not to be able to take up another. For in such a case it would seem that the Personality of a divine nature would be so comprehended by one single human nature, that no other nature could have been united with the Divine Personality—which is impossible; for the Uncreated can never be comprehended by any creature. It is clear therefore that, whether we consider the Divine Person from the point of view of His power, which is the principle of the union, or from the point of view of His Personality, which is the term of the union, we have to admit that the Divine Person could have taken up another human nature numerically distinct from the one which in fact He assumed.[1] St. Thomas also conceives the possibility of a higher kind of Incarnation than the one which Faith teaches. A Hypostatic Union in which the three Divine Persons take up one single individual nature. The idea implies no contradiction. 'It is not impossible,' he says, 'that two or three Divine Persons should assume one human nature; but it would be impossible for them to assume one human hypostasis or person.'[2] With such assurances on the resources of Divinity, the main objection against Hypostatic Union falls to the ground. Hypostatic Union is infinite glory and sanctity to the human nature without its being the least fettering of the freedom of Godhead.

[1] S. Th. III, Quest. iii, Art. 7.   [2] S. Th. III, Quest. iii, Art. 6.

Even in this highest form of divine liberality we find God's free choice, which is the charm of all His gifts. Where there are many possibilities, He chooses the one best adapted for a particular purpose. Hypostatic Union is no exception to the rule of the divine deliberateness in giving. Not only is Hypostatic Union God's free election, but the kind of Hypostatic Union He determines upon shows infinitely wise thought. God is never overwhelmed by His own liberalities. In the thirteenth century, as much as in our own, there was the milk and honey temperament of the philosophical optimist, of the man who thinks that God ought always to do the best possible thing, irrespective of the final results of His divine Providence. So the hypothesis that a Divine Person might have united to Himself every human individual in oneness of personality made them ask the question why God in His charity did not do so. St. Thomas gives those big children satisfaction (if a born optimist can ever be satisfied) in the Fifth Article of the Fourth Question. If we all were united hypostatically, there would not have been the marvel of marvels, the charity of Christ dying on the Cross for us. That is one of the reasons he gives. It is a profound one, because it shows that the greatest marvel in the whole mystery of the Incarnation is, not so much the initial fact of Hypostatic Union, as the human life and death of the God-Man. 'The love of God towards men is shown not only in taking up the human nature, but especially through the things He suffered in His human nature for other men, according to Rom. v. 8, "God commendeth His charity towards us, because when as yet we were sinners, Christ died for us." This could not have taken place if He had taken up human nature in all its representatives [supposita].' [1] What glorious theology! Far from being overpowered by the doctrine of a Divine Person uniting a human nature in an indissoluble oneness, it makes the value of such exaltation subservient to the experimental sanctity of conscious life and activity.

[1] S. Th. III, Quest. iv, Art. 5, ad 2.

Chapter XII

'Instrumentum Conjunctum Divinitatis'

THE great aim of our theology is to make Christ's human nature as divine as possible whilst preserving the real distinction between His humanity and His Divinity. St. Thomas, by a rare stroke of genius, has found the theological formula that states this highest possible elevation of Christ's humanity by His Divinity for the active purposes of the Redemption. Christ's humanity is to His Divinity a living instrument, *instrumentum conjunctum Divinitatis*. A brief explanation must be given of this term. My arm and my hand are living instruments of my brain. Being vitally connected with my brain, there is practically no limit to the perfection of intelligent work my hand, with no gift of reason residing in it, may achieve. The hand of Michael Angelo has painted the Last Judgment and carved the wonderful Moses; his hand produced these masterpieces, but not his hand alone, for from his brain there flowed into his hand the mighty current of creative genius. In scholastic language Michael Angelo's hand would be the *instrumentum conjunctum* of his brain. Such is the view the Angelic Doctor takes of Christ's Humanity. Because Godhead is united with that manhood in one Person, as brain and hand are united in one organism; manhood does the works of God, just as the human hand does the works of human genius. It is easy to see that St. Thomas has practically introduced a third something between Godhead and Manhood in Christ, something that is lower than Hypostatic Union and at the same time higher than human nature, even in its loftiest state of sanctification. The technical name for this *tertium quid* is Divine Instrumentality. Highest in Christ is Hypostatic Union; below this is immensity of sanctifying grace; between the two there is Divine Instrumentality.

I shall now state this great doctrine in the words of the *Summa*; they open out wonderful horizons of spiritual possibilities, of which we the redeemed are the beneficiaries. 'The soul of Christ may be viewed in two ways. First according to its proper nature, with its powers of nature or of grace; secondly as the instrument of the Word of God hypostatically united with it. Speaking then of the soul of Christ from the point of view of its proper nature and power, whether natural or gratuitous, it has in itself the power of bringing about those effects which are natural to the soul; for instance: to rule over the body, to direct human acts, and also to enlighten through the fulness of its grace and knowledge all those rational creatures who fall short of its perfection, in a manner befitting a rational creature. But if we speak of Christ's soul from the point of view of its being the instrument of the Word united with it, then it had an instrumental power to bring about all those miraculous changes which are in any way related to the purpose of the Incarnation, which is to restore all things, in heaven and on the earth. But such changes in creatures as would bring about their annihilation are the counterpart of the creation of things out of nothing, and therefore, as God alone is able to create out of nothing, God alone has power to annihilate creatures, for God alone keeps beings in their existence lest they fall back into nothingness. Therefore we must say that the soul of Christ is not possessed of omnipotence with regard to the transmutation of created things.'[1]

We see therefore that there is only one exception to the extent of Christ's power as the living instrument of the Word: creation out of nothing and the corresponding power of annihilation could not be attributed to Our Lord as man; short of that, there is nothing which Our Lord could not do. The resurrection of the bodies at the end of the world is perhaps the highest external manifestation of Our Lord's power; it is within Our Lord's power to bring back to life every human organism, because the resurrection of all flesh is not creation out of nothing, but reconstruction out of pre-existing material. 'For as the Father raiseth up the dead and giveth life, so the Son also giveth life to whom He will. For neither does the Father judge any man, but has given all judgment to the Son, that all men may honour the Son as they honour the Father ... Amen, Amen, I say unto you, that the hour cometh and now is when the dead shall hear the voice of the Son of God, and they that hear shall live. For as the Father has life in Himself, so He has given to the Son also to have life in Himself. ... I cannot of Myself do anything. As I hear, so I judge, and My judgment is just: because I seek not My own will but the will of Him that sent Me.'[2] 'Now this is the will of the

---

[1] S. Th. III, Quest. xiii, Art. 2.   [2] John v. 21-30.

Father who sent Me, that of all that He has given Me I should lose nothing, but should raise it up again in the last day. And this is the will of My Father that sent Me, that everyone who seeth the Son and believeth in Him may have life everlasting, and I will raise him up in the last day.'[1] 'He that eateth My Flesh and drinketh My Blood has everlasting life, and I will raise him up in the last day.'[2] 'Our conversation is in heaven; from whence also we look for the Saviour, Our Lord Jesus Christ, who will reform the body of our lowness, made like to the body of His glory, according to the operation whereby also He is able to subdue all things unto Himself.'[3] 'Afterwards the end; when He [Christ] shall have delivered up the Kingdom to God and the Father; when He shall have brought to nought all principality and power and virtue. For He must reign *until He has put all enemies under His feet*, and the enemy Death shall be destroyed last. For *He hath put all things under His feet*. And whereas He says: *All things are put under Him*; undoubtedly He is excepted who put all things under Him. And when all things shall be subdued unto Him, then the Son also Himself shall be subject unto Him that put all things under Him, that God may be all in all.'[4] Texts like these—and it would be easy to quote many more to the same effect —point clearly to a power in Our Lord's Personality which is not the power of the Godhead itself, but belongs to His Manhood; and yet it is a power which is almost omnipotent. The Scholastic formula—*Instrumentum Verbi Dei*, the instrument of the Divine Word—expresses the most wonderful thing in the simplest terms.

As I have already insinuated, from this central principle there flow many spiritual possibilities; and now I want the reader to pay great attention to another doctrine of St. Thomas which is its natural corollary. Our Lord's life, death, resurrection, and ascension are the instruments of Divinity for our sanctification, our life, our resurrection and our ascension. It is clear, of course, that Our Lord is our model, in His life, death, resurrection, and ascension. It is also clear that through His life and death He atoned for us, merited for us, prayed for us; such influences of Our Lord on mankind are called moral influences, moral causes. But there is more, and there must be more, if the language of Scripture and Catholic

[1] John vi. 39-40.   [2] John vi. 55.   [3] Phil. iii. 20, 21.
[4] I Cor. xv. 24-28.

tradition are not to be treated as mere hyperbole. Christ's death is our life; Christ's resurrection is our resurrection. On this matter nothing more instructive has been written than the Forty-eighth Question of the Third Part of the *Summa*: 'On the way in which Our Lord's Passion brought about our salvation'. It contains six Articles: First, 'Whether Christ's Passion caused our salvation by way of merit?' Second, 'Whether by way of atonement?' Third, 'Whether by way of sacrifice?' Fourth, 'Whether by way of redemption?' Fifth, 'Whether it is proper to Christ alone to be the Redeemer?' To all these questions St. Thomas gives an affirmative answer. The sixth and last Article asks 'Whether Christ's Passion brought about our salvation efficiently [*per modum efficientiae*]?' To which he answers: 'There is a twofold efficient agency, viz. the principal and the instrumental. Now the principal efficient cause of man's salvation is God. But since Christ's Humanity is an *instrument of the Godhead* ... therefore all His actions and sufferings operate instrumentally in virtue of the Godhead for the salvation of men. Consequently ... Christ's Passion accomplishes man's salvation efficiently.'

In the same Article St. Thomas suggests a difficulty in this theory. There is no effective bodily action except through contact; but Christ's Passion could not have contact with all men; therefore He could not bring about the salvation of all men by means of a physical efficiency. I quote his answer literally: 'Although the Passion of Christ be a bodily phenomenon, it has spiritual power from the Divinity that is united with it, and therefore it has efficiency by means of a spiritual contact—that is to say, by faith, and the sacrament of faith.' This last clause, 'by faith, and the sacrament of faith,' means that faith in individual souls by which they are saved is caused by Christ's Passion, as by an efficient cause. To receive faith is to be touched by Christ's Passion. With still greater clearness is this doctrine stated in the Sixth Article of the Fiftieth Question, where St. Thomas asks whether Christ's death conduced in any way to our salvation. (By death he means, not the act of dying, but the actual state of death.) There is an obvious difficulty: from the very fact of His being dead Christ could not merit; therefore, though the dying Christ might merit, the dead Christ could not do anything for us. 'Granted,' says our Doctor, 'the dead Christ could not be the cause of our salvation by way of merit, but He could be a cause of salvation by way of efficiency, because even in death Divinity was not separated from Our Lord's Flesh, and therefore whatever happened to Our Lord's dead Body is to us a source of salvation in virtue of the Divinity united with it.'[1]

The same doctrine occurs again in regard to the causality of Our Lord's resurrection. 'Christ's resurrection,' says St. Thomas, 'is the efficient cause of our resurrection because Christ's Humanity, according to which He rose again, is in a way the instrument of His Divinity, and works by its power. And therefore, as all other things which Christ did or suffered in His Humanity are to us a source of salvation in virtue of His Divinity, Christ's resurrection also is an efficient cause of our resurrection through the divine power, to whom it belongs to quicken the dead; and this divine power by its presence has contact with all places and all times; and this virtual contact suffices to explain the efficiency of Christ's resurrection.'[2] In an earlier Question[3] St. Thomas has another application of this far reaching principle. Through it he explains how it is possible for Christ in His Humanity to be the life-giving Head to the heavenly spirits. But how could humanity be to angelic spirits the source of spiritual perfection? 'Christ's Humanity,' he says, 'in virtue of the spiritual nature, that is the Divine nature, is able to cause something not only in the spirits of men, but also in the spirits of angels, on account of its most intimate union with God—that is to say by Hypostatic Union.'[4] Christ gives something spiritual to the angels through His Humanity, but the Humanity does it in virtue of the Divinity. It is again the Divine Instrumentality.

I do not think I owe the reader an apology for keeping him so long in these high theological regions; the Church's greatest theologian can never be understood unless we grasp his principle of the Divine Instrumentality in connection with Our Lord's Humanity. But once we grasp it, it becomes a most consoling and devotional principle. We feel how near we are in our spiritual life to Christ's life, death, and resurrection. Nothing will surprise us any more in what we read in the lives of the saints of their mystical union with Christ's life. Infinite, unchanging, all-present Divinity, for whom there is no yesterday nor to-morrow, simply uses the actions of Our

---

[1] S. Th. III, Quest. l, Art. 6, ad 2.   [2] S. Th. III, Quest. lvi, Art 1, ad 3.
[3] Ibid. Quest. viii, Art. 4.   [4] Ibid. ad 3.

Lord as most beautiful tools for the sanctification of souls. Christ's death on the Cross is as truly and as directly the instrument of my sanctification in the hands of Godhead, as the pen with which I write is the cause of the letters that cover the paper. The mystical possibilities of this illuminating doctrine of St. Thomas are greater than anything we could imagine. As quoted above, the Angelic Doctor says that Christ's Humanity, precisely because it is a risen Humanity, is a fit instrument in the hands of God to bring about our resurrection. We must remember what we said at the beginning, that every instrument has a fitness of its own for a definite and specific purpose. Christ is the fit instrument of our resurrection because He is a *risen* Christ. We may say likewise that Our Lord is a fit instrument for every kind of sanctification and spiritual purification because He has suffered in His Body, because at one time His Body was a dead body; through His passion and death His Humanity acquired a most eminent fitness to be in the hands of God the instrument of the most miraculous graces and resurrections.

From all that precedes we see how the whole supernatural world rests on the shoulders of Christ's Humanity. In the whole work of our salvation and sanctification Christ's Divinity does not come in except as the highest cause. We know that His Divinity is behind it all, yet Divinity, being infinite truth and reality, never allows the Humanity to shirk any work that it may possibly accomplish. There is only one instance in which Divinity as such is directly appealed to in the work of our salvation: it is the adequate reparation given to God's offended majesty. Of this I shall say more later on. In everything else it is the Humanity that does the work. It does it indeed as the instrument of Divinity, but it does it none the less directly. To come back to our original comparison, we may navigate for a long time the stream of Christ's human life and perfections; we may see great wonders long before we have to come to the ocean of His Divinity. The thought of this omnipotence of Our Lord's Humanity ought to be to us a source of peace and rest. 'These things I have spoken to you, that in Me you may have peace. In the world you shall have distress; but have confidence, I have overcome the world.'[1]

In Our Lord Himself we see the grandest realisation of that deep spiritual principle which He enunciated: 'Whosoever hath, to him

[1] John xvi. 33.

it will be given; and whosoever hath not, that also which he think-eth he hath shall be taken away from him.'[1]

Hypostatic Union, far from making Our Lord's Humanity com-plete, requires in Our Lord's Humanity the presence of a new gift: the gift of sanctifying grace. Sanctifying grace is not Divinity itself, it is something created; it is the greatest possible resemblance to God which a spirit may possess; it differs entirely from the Divine Instrumentality spoken of above. Yet it is owing to the Hypostatic Union and the Divine Instrumentality that sanctifying grace is in Our Lord. Sanctifying grace is a necessary concomitant in Christ's soul of Hypostatic Union and Divine Instrumentality. St. Thomas devotes two entire Questions of the *Summa* to Our Lord's sanctify-ing grace. In the First Article of the Seventh Question he says that the reasons why there must be in Our Lord sanctifying grace are precisely Hypostatic Union and Divine Instrumentality. Christ's soul is united with Divinity, but Christ's soul is not Divinity itself. To be united with Divinity does not make it into Divinity, therefore it must be made as divine as possible, it must resemble Divinity as closely as possible; this is done through sanctifying grace.[2] Union between two things is conceivable only insofar as both remain distinct though united; if they became one being there would be no longer union, but absorption. Therefore, in Hypostatic Union Our Lord's Humanity remains quite distinct. This is why the presence of Divinity, far from rendering sanctifying grace superfluous, makes its possession of much greater necessity for Our Lord than for any other creature. Then again, from the point of view of Divine Instrumentality, sanctifying grace becomes an absolute necessity for Our Lord. 'Christ's Humanity,' says St. Thomas, 'is the instrument of Divinity, but He is not like an inanimate instrument, which has no action of its own, but is merely moved by a higher agent; He is, on the contrary, an instrument that is animated by a rational soul, which in the very act of being used has an action of its own, and therefore for the sake of action befitting His nature He was bound to have sanctifying grace.'[3] The whole Humanity of Christ must be thought of as being first permeated with spiritual vitalities, such as sanctifying grace, before it could be a fit instrument for man's

---

[1] Matt. xxv. 29; Luke xix. 26.   [2] *S. Th.* III, Quest. vii, Art. 1, ad 1.
[3] *Ibid.* ad 3.

sanctification in the hands of God; without those spiritual vitalities the instrument would have lacked natural fitness. To what extent did Our Lord possess sanctifying grace? Fulness of grace is constantly attributed to Our Lord. St. Thomas says it was not actually infinite grace, but it was such as to establish a kind of proportion between Christ's soul and His Divinity. He has as much grace as is necessary to make the union between the human soul and Divinity an harmonious one. God alone, therefore, could be judge of the measure of sanctifying grace that would make of Christ's Humanity a fit and harmonious instrument in the hands of Divinity.

It would be a dangerous tendency if the keen realisation of our spiritual privileges and responsibilities were to make us overlook Our Lord's Humanity for the sake of something exclusively spiritual. Catholic doctrine never detaches man's attention from Our Lord's Humanity. Christ's action as Man is the greatest spirit-reality for the redeemed soul. Where spiritual life is highest and sincerest, devotion to Our Lord's Humanity is tenderest, and the feeling of dependence on Him strongest. It may be stated as an unquestionable principle that Our Lord in His manhood is to the human spirit everything that makes it great and happy. We know little of Our Lord's relation with the angels, except that He is the head and king of angels; but to the human spirit in the present life and in the future He is much more. The expressions of the inspired scriptures, wherein are stated Our Lord's relations with man, and more particularly to the soul of man, are astoundingly energetic. Christ is made unto us wisdom, and justice, and sanctification, and redemption. He is our Life, He is our Resurrection; as in Adam we all fell, so in Christ we shall all rise; and there are a hundred other expressions that all point to much more direct and real influence of Our Lord on every soul than we commonly suppose.

Chapter XIII

The Dynamic Purpose of Hypostatic Union

THE presence of the Second Person of the Godhead in the individual human nature is essentially, though not exclusively, dynamic; it is essentially a power that elevates the assumed individual human nature. Perhaps this view has become slightly obscured even amongst Catholic theologians of more modern times; but there is no doubt as to the position which it held in the Christology of St. Thomas Aquinas. His dynamic view of Hypostatic Union is certainly very refreshing. In more recent works the view taken of the presence of the Divinity in the individual human nature is exclusively what I might call static. Theologians accept the fact of the Hypostatic Union, of the presence of the fulness of Godhead in Christ's Humanity, and there they remain. From such presence they all conclude the infinite moral dignity of Christ. A human nature that bears within itself the fulness of Godhead, that is united hypostatically with the Second Person of the Trinity, shares in the infinitude of sanctity and dignity proper to Godhead itself. They say, for instance, that Christ's sufferings had infinite atoning power because they were the sufferings of a human organism hypostatically united to Godhead. But beyond that communication of infinite moral worth the more recent theologies know little of an influence of the Divine Person on the human nature in Christ. This is what I mean by the static view of the Hypostatic Union.

Now the two terms 'static' and 'dynamic' are not contradictory; the same thing may be partly static, partly dynamic; so I should say that the view of St. Thomas combines the static and the dynamic. For him Hypostatic Union is indeed the presence of the Divinity in an individual human nature, but it is a presence full of activities, full of vital influences; it is more than a mere communication of moral worth; it is an elevation of all the vital powers of Christ's Humanity, natural and supernatural. This is merely another presentment of his beloved principle that Christ's Humanity is in all things *instrumentum conjunctum Divinitatis*. Divinity, through that intimacy of presence implied in Hypostatic Union, has become the master of

Christ's Humanity in a way that is not possible outside that mystery. Owing to that complete and wonderful mastery, God accomplishes in Christ works of the spiritual order, of which it would not be possible for any created nature to be the agent unless it were hypostatically united with Divinity. To put the matter more simply I may say: Hypostatic Union is not a thing that exists for its own sake, but it is the necessary means of rousing an individual human nature to such a height as to make it capable of accomplishing the work of human redemption and sanctification. It is a marvellous manifestation of God's power. Christ's human soul and body, through being united hypostatically with the Second Person of the Trinity, have acquired unparalleled fitness to be an instrument in the hands of God for every spiritual marvel. Outside Hypostatic Union no human nature could ever possess such fitness. No amount of sanctifying grace could give it, and it may even be said that this fitness is precisely the whole aim of Hypostatic Union.

It is easy to see how the older view, which I call in modern phraseology the dynamic view of Hypostatic Union, considerably affects Christian piety. The Man Jesus whom we love is the main object of the whole of our Christology. In His Humanity He atones for our sins; in that Humanity He directly forgives our sins; in that Humanity He directly raises from their corruption those that are spiritually and physically dead; in that Humanity He is the Father of the whole spiritual world to come. How can a man do these things? It is the old objection. No man can do it, unless he be hypostatically united with God; but being once hypostatically united with Divinity, man has a native fitness to do all those things. He does them in virtue of His Divinity, it is true; but it would be wrong to think that by this expression, 'in virtue of His Divinity', is meant an exclusively divine action, in the sense that only God who dwells in Christ does it. No, it is that human being called Jesus who does it, and He has become capable of doing it simply because He is hypostatically united with Godhead; without such union He could never do such works.

The merely static view of the presence of Divinity in Christ through Hypostatic Union might easily lead to a concept of Christ's Personality that accentuates the duality of natures in Him at the expense of the union of the two natures. With all due reverence, might I be allowed to say that there is a danger of our thinking of Christ 'in layers', with the consequent feeling of unreality? The older theology was as firm a believer in the differences of the two natures in Christ, the divine and the human; but the two natures were not two exclusive levels of life in Christ's Personality; there is a most intimate compenetration of activities in the two natures, the divine nature using the human nature as its *instrumentum conjunctum*, as my mind uses my hand, according to the favourite simile of St. Thomas. The identification of the two natures, and their fusion into one entity, is the old Eutychian heresy, the most subtle aberration of man trying to understand the psychology of Christ. St. Thomas has shown how it is possible to conceive a compenetration of the two natures that is not a fusion, viz. in the compenetration of mutual activities.

The Son of Man stands before us in the fulness of Divine Power; and Divinity, far from diminishing His manhood, has given that Humanity undreamed of fulness and strength, that will make every human heart in this world and in the next find shelter in Him, as the birds of the air find shelter in a mighty tree.

CHAPTER XIV

The Two Wills and the Two Operations in Christ

A STUDY of the theological controversies of the early ages of the Church reveals a different temper from that of the controversies of a later date. Christians were evidently deeply interested in Christ's Personality and psychology—I might almost say in Christ's intimate life. Perhaps it is more congenial to the Eastern mind to analyse its God than to analyse itself. Western doctrinal upheavals have always been more about practical things; about good works, sanctity, and sacraments. We are indebted, however, to the East and its theologians for that most perfect Christology which is the Church's greatest treasure. Controversies about the two wills and

the two operations in Christ were the last stages of the great theological battle; the sixth and seventh centuries are full of them, they
had even their repercussions in politics. The technical name for the
heretical opinion in that matter is Monothelitism, which means
oneness of will; while the Church decided for a duality of wills and
a duality of operations in Christ. The Council of Ephesus had
defined the oneness of Person in Christ; the Council of Chalcedon
had defined the duality of natures in Him. Christ has a divine nature
and a human nature in one Personality. That new doubts should
have sprung up is comprehensible enough; Christ's will was always
one with His Father's will, Christ's actions were always in obedience
to His Father's commands; so it would seem that, in spite of the
duality of nature, there was oneness of will and oneness of operation. The error was a subtle one, and even the holiest men might be
deceived. After all, oneness with God's will is highest sanctity. The
Latin Church, whose theology prevailed in the long run, considered
that oneness of will and oneness of operation would be a partial
renewing of the older heresy of Eutyches. Will and operation are
nature's best jewels; if they are only one in Christ and not two,
duality of nature is of little avail; so there are in Christ the divine
will and the human will; the divine operation and the human
operation.

So much for the historical and dogmatic statement of the question.
But duality of will and operation in Christ is a point of theology full
of interest to those for whom the Christ-psychology is the most
entrancing of psychologies. The Eastern mind that fell into Monothelitism overlooked a distinction which many other minds have
overlooked: the distinction between the will as a power and the will
as an object. There can never be identification of powers, but there
may be identification of objects. When I say that my will and some-
body else's will are one, I mean to say that we strive after the same
object, that we love the same object, that we agree about the same
object; so in Christ there never was, and there never could be, two
wills in the sense of two conflicting and contradictory objects:
whatever was willed by Divinity was also willed by Humanity. Such
an identification of will is a perfection; but, on the contrary, fusion
of wills as powers would be a great loss; in fact it would be the
destruction of nature.

But there is one question which is of utmost importance both in Christ's psychology and in our own; how far is that oneness of object preserved in the reluctance of our will when we have to do a hard thing which we know to be God's will, i.e., the object of God's will? That there was such a reluctance in Christ is evident from His prayer and agony in the garden.[1] That there was a tremendous struggle in Christ's soul at that hour is evident from the sweat of blood. Yet oneness of will with the Father's will was part of Christ's unalterable sanctity. The solution of this apparent contradiction lies in the distinction between the higher human will and the lower human will. The higher will is made of reason, the lower will is made of sensations and impressions. The two wills may follow different lines—opposite lines even; it is the mind in conflict, which is not always a struggle between good and evil, but is as frequently between a higher and a lower good. Now oneness with the divine will is preserved through the stability of the higher will; that it should carry out its purpose even against the most persistent reluctance of the lower will of the feelings. Such was Christ's oneness of will. 'Abba, Father, all things are possible to Thee; remove this chalice from Me: but not what I will, but what Thou wilt.'[2] That duality of will which the Catholic Church adopted as part of her Christology is really the most admirable trait in our theology of Christ, because in it we find the glorification of human freedom wonderfully combined with the oneness of the divine purpose.

St. Thomas Aquinas, who is as great a believer in the duality of wills and operations in Christ as any other theologian, has conceived another oneness of will besides the oneness of object. I quote him literally: 'The operation which is of the human nature in Christ, as far as it is the instrument of Divinity, is not different from the operation of the Divinity; for the salvation through which Christ's humanity saves is not different from the salvation through which His Divinity saves.'[3] In this sentence we have practically all that oneness in Christ's life we want; it is a deep concept to say that there are not two savings in Christ, one accomplished by His Divinity and one by His humanity; on the contrary, it is all one act, owing to the wonderful instrumental elevation and influence, made so much of by

---

[1] Matt. xxvi. 36-46; Mark xiv. 32-42; Luke xxii. 39-46.
[2] Mark xiv. 36.   [3] S. Th. III, Quest. xix, Art. 1, ad 2.

St. Thomas. No doubt thoughts of that kind had been vaguely present in the Eastern mind. Salvation was God's work, God's will, God's love; it could not think of a dual salvation. But it was reserved to a Western genius to show more clearly how with a duality of wills and powers there could be oneness of operation.

CHAPTER XV

Christ's Knowledge

OUR theology of Christ's knowledge is guided by a twofold completeness in Christ. He is entirely human, and He is a principle of life to the whole human race. The various kinds of knowledge which theology attributes to Our Lord are as indispensable to His twofold rôle as our nerves and sinews are indispensable to us in order to make our bodies healthy, active and agile, whose very life is a feeling of refreshing well-being.

At first sight the theological conclusions in this matter may seem arbitrary; it might appear as if the theologian had fallen into the trap that lies in the way of every idealistic hero-worshipper and millennium dreamer: you simply make your hero the embodiment of every beautiful abstraction; once in the dreamland of sanctity, there is no more reason to draw the line than there is in fairyland. A mountain of gold is as easily imagined as a house of gold. As Christ is The Ideal we simply invest Him with all the spiritual glories we can think of, and then we call the fantasy theology. Such, I say, might be the sceptical attitude of even a reverential lay mind towards a theologian's wisdom. However, a careful study of the reasoning of our masters in sacred wisdom reveals a quite different temper: it is not that of the idealist, it is that of the psychologist. If the theology of Our Lord's knowledge postulates various kinds of knowledge in Our Lord, it considers them as life-functions, not as the ornaments of an infinitely privileged nature. Theology simply says that without those various degrees of knowledge Christ could never be entirely human, that He could never be the life of the whole human race. So little has the naïve love of the hero-worshipper for the accumulation of glories set the standard in this matter, that, on the contrary, this very question has acquired a kind of secondary celebrity in the history of theology on account of a retraction of St. Thomas. In his earlier works the Doctor had held the opinion that in Christ there was no kind of acquired knowledge of the experimental order. This view he later retracted as being contrary to a deeper understanding of the workings of Christ's human nature.

Before proceeding, I must give the reader a synoptic view of the various kinds of rational knowledge of which Catholic theology speaks. The classification is short, including only four members. But it is a classification which is absolutely indispensable to theology; without it many of the revealed truths would be unintelligible. First and highest is the uncreated divine knowledge; the knowledge which God has of Himself and of everything else besides. Then, coming to rational creatures, there is the blessed vision of God, technically called 'Beatific Vision'. It is an entirely supernatural, I might almost say an entirely miraculous, kind of knowledge, granted only to the spirits perfect in charity, who have reached the goal of eternal fixity in goodness. By means of this knowledge a spirit, whether human or angelic, is enabled to see God in His own native splendour, and he is enabled to see in God many things of which He is the origin. After that we come to spirit-knowledge properly so-called. A pure spirit, i.e., an angel, is created with the full knowledge of all things that are equal to him or lower than himself, besides a partial knowledge of beings higher than himself. This knowledge does not depend, in its essentials, on sanctity; even a fallen spirit retains it. Such knowledge is complete in the spirit's mind from the first moment of his existence. No new ideas come to the spirit, except by special grace. But there may be new applications of the innate idea. The spirit's perfection is such as to postulate that initial fulness of wisdom. The fourth kind of rational knowledge belongs to the human spirit, in its state of union with the body. It is the knowledge acquired by the mind through the infinitely varied instrumentality of the senses. It is the wonderful schooling through the external world, with its ever new experiences and surprises, not to speak of its great lessons and possible discoveries. I need not enter into all the varieties and degrees that may be found within each of these four categories or planes of intellectual activity. I mention, as it were, four continents, but I lay no claim to having said anything as to the manifold wonders that may be hidden within their boundaries.

Leaving alone the first kind of knowledge, God's knowledge in Himself and of Himself, which is a divine and unchanging act, the three other kinds of knowledge, created knowledge, may vary endlessly in extent and vividness according to the sanctity or perfection of the invididual, human or angelic. Moreover—and this is a point of utmost importance in theological matters—the three kinds may be in the same mind at the same time, and regarding the same objects of knowledge. In other words, there is no apparent contradiction in the assumption that a human being may know all about another human being, at one and the same time in the vision of God, in the angelic mode of knowledge, and in virtue of sense observation. Each mode of knowing would convey something which the others fail to do; and the more perfect mode would not render useless the services of the less perfect, because the less perfect mode often represents its object in a more natural and proportionate way. Daily experiences supply simple analogies. I may learn of some clever piece of mechanical skill from a friend's description or from reading; both the book and the friend give me a very good idea of the invention. After that I may go to the town where it is on view and look at it myself. Though I walk up to it with a very good image of it in my mind, when I actually come to see it my store of experiences is the richer for the sight. I may then begin a process of mental investigation; I try to fathom the principle of the invention. I may succeed in following in my own mind the road which the original inventor followed in his, and I may be led to the same conclusions, thus sharing the knowledge which its maker had before he put his ideas into execution. Here we have three different modes of knowing the same object; far from excluding or superseding each other, they help each other towards a fuller comprehension. This is of course a mere analogy to illustrate a much higher train of thought: how, for instance, there may be new intellectual gratification in meeting the thing, that was seen in the light of God's vision as a reflection in a mirror, outside God, in its own native individuality, through another and lower mode of knowledge.

In Christ there are simultaneously all the aforesaid kinds of knowledge: there is the infinite, divine knowledge of the Godhead; there
is the threefold created knowledge of beatific vision, angelic cog-
nition, and human experience and ratiocination. In our thoughts on
the Incarnation there is the constant danger of being overwhelmed
by the fact of Christ's Divinity, as if it were the all-absorbing and all-
effacing splendour of Christ's wonderful Personality. But we ought
to bear in mind the great truth that Divinity was united with the
Sacred Humanity, not so much for the sake of that union, however
adorable it may be, as for the sake of the great human life such a
union rendered possible. So in this matter of knowledge, the presence of the divine mind in Christ's Person, far from rendering
superfluous the glories of the human mind, has no other end in view
than precisely the perfection of that human mind. This is why
St. Thomas says that if in Christ's Person there had been divine
knowledge only, Christ's soul would have been in the dark, and its
being united with the Godhead would have been a useless privilege.
Hypostatic Union took place in order to cause in Christ's human
soul such bliss, such light, as to make of it in its turn the direct
source and cause of all the bliss and all the light that will flood the
minds of the elect in the clear vision of God for all eternity. It would
not seem as if such height and power of beatific vision as to make it
the efficient cause of beatific vision in all other human minds would
be possible, unless Divine Personality, the Wisdom of God the
Father, were united with that created mind. Unless Christ had been
endowed with beatific vision He could not have been perfectly
happy in Himself; He could not have become the efficient cause of
our own vision of God; He could not have possessed that twofold
completeness of glorified humanity that makes Him what He is.
This same principle of Christ's entirety makes it imperative on the
theologian to ascribe to Him a most complete and far-reaching
intellectual knowledge, which cannot have its origin in the experiences of sense, and which at the same time is not beatific vision.
Christ's human mind must have been fully developed, must have
possessed every kind of perfection a created intellect can possess,
independently of the gift of God's vision, simply because it is the
intellect of One who has the double privilege of being God-Man
in Himself, and King of the whole human race, and indeed of the

universe of spirits. The whole created intellectual world is subject to Him, because in Him the human intellect has acquired unparalleled perfection through the proximity of the Godhead.

It was precisely this incontrovertible fulness of intellectuality that made it seem doubtful whether there was any room for the workings of the ordinary human mind in Christ. Why should one so full of direct intellectual perceptions learn from the store-house of sense observations? St. Thomas himself was impressed by such considerations, as I have said already, but he realised what we all learn when Christ is the habitual subject of our thoughts: the necessity of keeping Him as human as possible, in spite of the sublimities of the Hypostatic Union, or rather, because of those very sublimities. That Christ's human intellect should be filled with pure spirit-knowledge of all things belongs to the entirety of His representative rôle, embodying in Himself the whole human nature. But He would not have been quite human if He had not behaved and acquired knowledge just like other human beings. Christ's human brain is the most powerful and active that ever was. Intellectual genius belongs to Christ more than to any other historical personage. He may be called the greatest thinker, the greatest philosopher, without any impropriety of language. He possesses in the most eminent degree that which makes great men so powerful—a serene, wonderfully penetrating mind, at the service of a will of infinite resolve and considerateness. The higher kind of knowledge only comes in as a kind of reserve when the organic brain of Christ—for such is the expression best suited to interpret the theology of St. Thomas in this matter—has done all it could do in virtue of its own superlative excellency. How far a created human brain under the elevating influence of Hypostatic Union can go in its potentialities is of course a matter for admiring reverence rather than for dogmatic diagnosis. St. Thomas says that Christ knew through the sheer penetration of His human intellect all that can be known through human induction and deduction.[1] (Such are not his words; but such is his meaning.) In Christ the human mind attains its ideal perfection and power. The process of deduction and induction in Christ's mind was a progressive process, not an instantaneous one, just as Christ's brain reached its maturity not instantaneously but progressively. He acquired

[1] *Cf. S. Th.* III, Quest. xii, Art. 1.

knowledge as He grew up.[1] 'And Jesus advanced in wisdom and age, and grace with God and man.'[2] It is a universally admitted principle that Christ, through the combined clarities of the three kinds of created knowledge here described, knows everything that concerns the human race. The whole of mankind's nature with its life and free will is reflected in Christ's mind as in a mirror. St. Thomas thinks that such knowledge actually constitutes an infinity of knowledge, as the free acts of the human individuals go on for all eternity. Such special and determined kind of infinitude is not above the grasp of a finite intellect, as it is infinitude in one direction only, not infinitude all round. What Catholic theology is at pains to show is that complete mastery of mankind by the Son of Man through which our race is deified.

The theology of Christ's knowledge has received a strange actuality in our own days from unexpected quarters. Protestant theologians are at a loss how to explain Christ's abasement. This vexed question is called the Kenotic problem: How did Christ 'empty' Himself? More than one Anglican theologian explains Kenosis as if it involved deficiency in knowledge. In order to humble Himself Christ is supposed to have been lacking in knowledge, or anyhow to have turned away from knowledge—to have shut His eyes for a time to the things which He knew. Catholic theology is as great a believer in Christ's abasement as any other theology, but it never felt the need of curtailing Christ's spiritual and intellectual privileges in order to make of Him 'a high Priest who can have compassion on our infirmities'. Fulness of knowledge, on the contrary, makes of Christ the High Priest. To make of the absence of knowledge a means of sanctity is a theological device peculiarly distasteful to the Catholic mind; above all, one cannot see how the Son of God made Man could have gained anything by willingly ignoring the facts of His Divine Son-ship. Even if it had been possible for Him to exclude such knowledge from His mind, it would have been loss, not gain, to His cause, as His life must necessarily have been lowered through this very forgetfulness of His divine origin. It is a very strange phase of present day thought to look to ignorance instead of to knowledge for moral progress, as does the older theology.

There is only one way in which Catholic theology admits a kind

[1] S. Th. III, Quest. xii, Art. 2.   [2] Luke ii. 52.

of voluntary limitation of His knowledge by Christ. It distinguishes between actual and habitual knowledge. I may know a thing and yet not actually consider it; I may even make an effort of will and turn away my mind from the actual consideration of an object, and in this sense it may even be profitable to sanctity 'to ignore'. Thus if I am asked to perform a difficult act of kindness there might be human considerations of such a nature as to reconcile me with the performance of my duty. Such lower considerations I discard; I turn my mind away from them and fix it on higher motives, less alluring and less potent, perhaps, but infinitely purer. In this case my spirituality has gained through a restriction of actual knowledge. In Christ there was likewise actual knowledge and habitual knowledge, at least in the inferior modes, although Catholic theology is most constant in asserting that He realised His Divinity constantly, unceasingly, with His whole being; but it is not against Catholic teaching to say that Christ, in the lower sphere of His mental powers did not always actually consider all the things He knew. We are even permitted to think that Christ in His great struggle with sin, of set purpose turned His human attention away from the glorious vision of the triumph of His Cross in the world of souls, in order that He might drink the cup of bitterness with more heroic constancy. In this sense we may grant that Kenosis is compatible with Christ's knowledge. It is not exactly ignorance, but rather an absence of attention. It is perhaps that very thing which Anglican divines are striving after, when they attempt to make of ignorance in the Son of God an occasion of greater heroism. We may grant to them that Our Lord at certain periods, and of set purpose, turned His human attention away from considerations that would have filled Him with gladness, if He had allowed them to force themselves on His mind.

CHAPTER XVI

'In Christ'

T HE phrase 'in Christ' occurs nearly eighty times in St. Paul's
epistles; frequently it is translated into 'by', 'through', 'for the
sake of Christ'. Yet such alterations ought not to deprive us
of the wealth of mystical meaning contained in the original phrase
'in Christ'. We have a right to the literal application of the Pauline
expression. To alter it into anything less emphatic is to tamper with
our spiritual inheritance. Let us first dwell on the deep originality
of the phrase, on its strangeness, if we compare it with ordinary
human speech. No doubt it is this very strangeness that may have
led the translators to adopt less significant prepositions in place of
'in'. One can hardly think of a phrase—whether in English, German,
French, Italian, Latin, or Greek—describing some one's influence
on another, with the co-operation of a third person, where the
preposition 'in' would be correctly employed to express the mode
of that third person's intervention. Thus I may feel most anxious
about the conduct of a favourite brother of mine. No concern in the
world is nearer to my heart than his salvation from moral ruin. One
redeeming feature is his affection for our sister, a paragon of virtue
and love. In her is all my hope. Both for my sake and her own she
follows the scapegrace; she wins him back through her sisterly tact.
No words could describe my gratitude to her; I feel that she alone
has made this salvation possible; yet my speech would be foolish if
I were to say that I saved my brother 'in' her. I saved him 'through'
her, and more I could not say.

Yet St. Paul prefers the first form of speech. God saves me, not
through His Son, but *in* His Son. It is not merely an idiosyncrasy of
the Apostle's style—in fact the idiosyncrasy would be little short of
a barbarism—it is a necessity of his theology. Let us take as an instance
a magnificent passage in the Epistle to the Ephesians. (I keep the
prepositions as they are in the Greek text.) 'But God who is rich in
mercy, for His exceeding charity wherewith He loved us, even
when we were dead in sins, hath quickened us together in Christ, by
whose grace you are saved; and hath raised us up together, and hath

made us sit together in the heavenly places in Christ Jesus, that He might show in the ages to come the abundant riches of His grace, in His bounty towards us in Christ Jesus. ... For we are His workmanship created in Christ Jesus in good works, which God hath prepared that we should walk in them.'[1] The most remarkable association of words in this passage is the verse: 'And He hath made us sit together in the heavenly places in Christ Jesus.' The Douai translator for one found the reduplication of the 'in' too much for him, and he calmly translates 'in the heavenly places through Christ'. In fact, in ordinary grammar the phrase would sound ludicrous; but nowhere do we find St. Paul guilty of a careless use of prepositions. He distinguishes carefully between the preposition of instrumentality and the preposition that marks inclusion. Note, for instance, his phrasing in this passage: 'For if you have ten thousand instructors in Christ, yet not many fathers. For in Christ Jesus by the Gospel I have begotten you.'[2] The Greek and the Latin discriminate clearly between the two prepositions. The constant use of the unwonted term 'in' simply points to a spiritual truth, clearly perceived by St Paul, and for which no doubt there is no received phraseology in the ordinary language. Christ's co-operation with God in the sanctification of the elect is expressed almost invariably by St. Paul, not as an action of God *through* Him, but as an action of God *in* Him. 'For God indeed was in Christ reconciling the world to Himself.'[3] The action of God is confined within Christ's Personality, and making Him what He is, is God's way of saving and sanctifying the human race. 'In whom all the building fitly framed together groweth unto an holy temple in the Lord.'[4]

CHAPTER XVII

Christ All in All

INTELLECTUAL and philosophical ages are the high-water mark of human progress. They rise and fall with their blessings and dangers, as all the other manifestations of the activities of progressive humanity rise and fall, according to unknown rules,

Eph. ii. 4-10.   [2] i Cor. iv. 15.   [3] 2 Cor. v. 19.   [4] Eph. ii. 21.

almost with the regularity of the ocean tides. One of the blessings of a philosophical age is the love of the 'universal', for what is beyond the narrow limits of time and space. An unphilosophical, a positive and materialistic age, has no love except for the particular fact, the thing that has avoirdupois, or the thing that can be measured by an equivalent in hard cash. But this very love for the universal, which is the trait of a reflective generation, has its dangers: it leads to various systems of thought, to various 'isms' before which there stands almost as a danger signal, the Greek prefix 'pan'. Pantheism, as one instance, is the most common intellectual sin in a philosophical age. The philosophical temper likes oneness in all things. We are all one God, we are all one Mind, we are all one Spirit, says the philosophical mind that has the defects of its qualities, an excessive love for the universal.

May I be forgiven for coining an expression that represents a good deal of vague thinking and feeling in our times—times in which the drift of human evolution sets in the direction of philosophical thought—I will call it 'pan-christism'. We are all Christ's, we are all instances of the Incarnation; we are all sons of God; there is a Christ within us all, etc. Phrases like these are as common in the writings and speeches of religious men of our own days as the criticisms of the day's weather are common in daily social intercourse. The aberration is the defect of a great quality, the shadow cast by a great light; men are reluctant to make of a person quite outside themselves the principle of their higher life, though that person be of surpassing excellency. The very fact of 'outsideness' puts even the very personification of human excellency at a disadvantage with regard to our own intimate life, if that personification be a concrete individual. At bottom, all pantheistic and 'pan-christic' tendencies come from this deep-rooted aversion of the spiritually minded to make of an isolated individuality the principle of one's most intimate life.

Against pantheism Christianity has the indwelling of the Holy Ghost; that great spiritual fact which brings man nearer to God than pantheism itself, as through it man is not only near God but above himself—above the potentialities of his own natural level, an elevation quite unthinkable in the metaphysics of ordinary pantheism, where man is divine through the laws of his own spirit, and where as a logical consequence ascent is impossible, as man is already part of the Deity. If Christianity had no such spiritual fact as the indwelling of the Holy Ghost in the human soul, its fight with pantheism would have a poor chance of success. Modern pan-christism is born from a narrowing of Christ's spiritual position. Let us give Christ the position of traditional Catholic theology, and we shall find in Him the life-giving principle of what is highest in us; we shall find Him at the very root of our being, and yet we shall not feel tempted to break down the barriers of His wonderful individuality, with a view to making Him less personal and more communicable to us. One thing I may note here: pan-christism is an aberration that comes from a lingering faith in, and love for, Christ, but is unsustained by deep Christology. Now our theology of Christ is not just a tale with a purpose, written to refute, redress, or silence an error. Orthodox and scholastic Christology received its completion long before the tendencies I call pan-christism. Yet Catholic Christianity such as it is to-day is to pan-christism what the indwelling of the Holy Ghost is to pantheism—its cure, its refutation, but above all its higher and healthier alternative.

A literal interpretation of many of Christ's utterances points decidedly to the universal relationship of His person with the human race: 'Father, the hour is come; glorify Thy Son, that Thy Son may glorify Thee: as Thou hast given Him power over all flesh, that He may give eternal life to all whom Thou hast given Him.'[1] 'My Father worketh until now, and I work. Hereupon therefore the Jews sought the more to kill Him, because He did not only break the sabbath, but also said God was His Father, making Himself equal to God. Then Jesus answered and said to them: Amen, Amen, I say unto you, the Son cannot do anything of Himself, but what He seeth the Father doing; for what things soever He doth, these the Son also doth in like manner. For the Father loveth the Son, and sheweth Him all things which Himself doth, and greater works than these will He shew Him, that you may wonder. For as the Father raiseth up the dead, and giveth life; so the Son also giveth life to whom He will. For neither doth the Father judge any man, but hath given all judgment to the Son: that all men may honour the Son, as they honour the Father. He who honoureth not the Son honoureth not

[1] John xvii. 1, 2.

the Father who hath sent Him. ... For as the Father hath life in Himself, so He hath given to the Son also to have life in Himself: and He hath given Him power to do judgment, because He is the Son of Man.'[1] 'Now this is the will of My Father that sent Me, that every one who seeth the Son, and believeth in Him, may have life everlasting, and I will raise him up in the last day.'[2] 'The bread that I will give is My flesh for the life of the world.'[3] It would be easy to multiply quotations that would establish beyond doubt the fact that Christ constantly attributes to Himself not only a universality of relationship with the human race, but a relationship of life, a relationship of light, He being to all men of good will what is most intimate to them; spiritual life and spiritual light.

This filling up of creation by Christ is a cherished idea with St. Paul in the Epistle to the Ephesians. 'He [God] hath subjected all things under His [Christ's] feet: and hath made Him head over all the Church, which is His body, and the fulness of Him, who is filled all in all.'[4] 'To know also the charity of Christ, which surpasseth all knowledge; that you may be filled unto all the fulness of God.'[5] 'He [Christ] that descended is the same also that ascended above all the heavens; that He might fill all things. ... Until we all meet into the unity of faith, and of the knowledge of the Son of God, unto a perfect man, unto the measure of the age of the fulness of Christ.'[6] This idea of fulness stands for the greatest spiritual facts in the New Testament. 'And of His fulness we all have received, and grace for grace.'[7] 'For in Him [Christ] dwelleth the fulness of the Godhead corporeally.'[8] Consummate sanctity is, in the language of the New Testament, to be filled with the Holy Ghost. When therefore we see Christ spoken of so insistently as a filling up of the capacities of the spiritual world, we are confronted by a spiritual fact of the highest importance—a fact as great as the filling up of the human heart by the Holy Ghost, a fact that is the parallel of that fulness of the indwelling of Divinity in Christ Himself. If there is the indwelling of the Spirit of God in man, there is also the indwelling of Christ in man's heart. 'That Christ may dwell by faith in your hearts'[9] is a saying as pregnant with the realities of true spiritual immanence as that other phrase: 'Know you not that you are the temple of God,

---

[1] John v. 17-27.   [2] John vi. 40.   [3] *Ibid*. vi. 52.
[4] Eph. i. 22, 23.   [5] Eph. iii. 19.   [6] Eph. iv. 10, 13.
[7] John i. 16.   [8] Col. ii. 9.   [9] Eph. iii. 17.

and that the Spirit of God dwelleth in you?'[1] There is nothing that a mystical lover of Christ could desire more than that such phraseology should be taken literally. Christ's lover may not possess the theological training that enables the mind to conceive psychic possibilities of such a nature as will make the literal interpretation of the texts the most obvious interpretation; but his spiritual instincts will all be in favour of as intimate an indwelling of Christ in the human race as possible. The idea of the 'fulness' is for his mystical powers; the idea of the *instrumentum conjunctum Divinitatis* is for his reasoning powers. The two ideas complete each other.

'As Thou hast sent Me into the world, I also have sent them into the world. And for them do I sanctify Myself, that they also may be sanctified in truth. And not for them only do I pray, but for them also who through their word shall believe in Me; that they all may be one, as Thou, Father, in Me, and I in Thee, that they also may be one in Us: that the world may believe that Thou hast sent Me. And the glory which Thou hast given Me, I have given to them; that they may be one, as We also are one; I in them, and Thou in Me, that they may be made perfect in one: and the world may know that Thou hast sent Me.'[2]

The Pauline idea of God's merciful operations taking place within Christ's Personality, deep as it is, is not deeper than the Johannine view expressed in this passage. St. John states most unequivocally the doctrine of our being Christ's fulness, the *pleroma* of the Greek text. I do not think that we could find anywhere in the scriptures words more pregnant with mystical significance or more illuminating as to the real meaning of our being sanctified *in* Christ, our being the 'filling up', the *pleroma* of Christ. In the Epistle to the Colossians we find St. Paul making the same juxtaposition of that twofold presence in Christ; the presence of God and the presence of the Elect. 'For in Him dwelleth all the fulness of the Godhead, corporeally; and you are filled in Him, who is the head of all principality and power.'[3] 'I in them, and Thou in Me'; such is the double 'filling up' constituted by the mystery of the Incarnation.

The *pleroma* is essentially a glory that is inside Christ, not outside Him. The first chapter to the Colossians makes this perfectly clear. After saying that Christ is the image of the unseen God, that all the

---

[1] 1 Cor. iii. 16.   [2] John xvii. 18-23.   [3] Col. ii. 9, 10.

heavenly powers are created in Him, are kept together in Him, that He is the head of the Church, the Apostle says, 'Because in Him it has well pleased the Father that all fulness should dwell.'[1] This indwelling of the *pleroma* in Him is the union of the Divine, the Angelic order and the Elect in Him. Christ therefore has a threefold *pleroma*, and all three dwell within Him. Between Christ, the second and the third *pleroma*, there is interaction, i.e. Christ 'fills up' the angelic world and the Church, and He is 'filled up' by them. His dwelling in a created spirit is the created spirit's dwelling in Him: 'He that eateth My Flesh and drinketh My Blood abideth in Me, and I in him. As the living Father hath sent Me, and I live by the Father; so he that eateth Me, the same also shall live by Me.'[2] This mutuality of indwelling between Christ and His elect is clearly a New Testament idea. In Eph. i. 23 Christ is said to be 'filled all in all', passively. In Eph. iv. 10 Christ is said actively to 'fill all things'. Finally, in Col. ii. 10 the faithful are said to be 'filled in Him', passively. In the light of that mutuality of indwelling, so clearly stated in St. John's Gospel, these various modes of speech easily point to the same spiritual reality, a wonderful compenetration of Christ and the Elect.

Another parallelism worth remarking is found in St. Paul's expression in 1 Cor. xv. 28, where he describes the consummation of all things after the Final Resurrection, when God will be 'all in all.' Now this phrase is used with regard to Christ as a predicate in Eph. i. 23; only instead of saying that Christ is 'all in all', St. Paul says that He is 'filled all in all'. 'And when all things shall be subjected unto Him [Christ], then the Son also Himself shall be subjected unto Him that put all things under Him, that God may be all in all.'[3] This is the formula for the true 'pantheism' of Christianity. 'And He [the Father] hath subjected all things under His feet, and hath made Him head over all the church, which is His body, and the fulness of Him who is filled all in all.'[4] This is also our true and most consoling 'pan-christism'.

[1] Col. i. 19.   [2] John vi. 57, 58.   [3] 1 Cor. xv. 28.
[4] Eph. i. 22, 23.

CHAPTER XVIII

Christ's Reserves

THERE may be a practical difficulty for many minds to find happiness in that hierarchy of sublimities that constitute the God-Man, as such a hierarchy with its division of glories and attributes may not be attractive to our nature; yet the mystery of Christ ought to be the sweetest of all mysteries. It has therefore occurred to me that the hierarchical gradation of sanctities and glories in Christ could be best expressed through the English word 'reserve'; they are so many reserves of graces and glories that make Christ's Personality so intensely loveable. When we live with people whom we believe to be possessed of high moral or intellectual qualities, who have done brave deeds or said wise things, our ordinary daily intercourse with them has wonderful charm, as we feel that there is in them a great reserve of superior power. This is the kind of simile I would fain propose to those who would draw near to the Son of God. He is the Son of Man. He is a perfect man; you will find in Him all the charms of perfect humanity. Go deep into that humanity and love it tenderly; very soon you will find that behind the humanity there is a wonderful reserve of grace that is more than human. You feel its presence, though it may not act directly; but there is such a majesty in that humanity as to make it clear that the humanity is passing into something more than human. There is the Divine Personality deeply concealed underneath the created glories and graces, but suggesting those infinite vistas and possibilities of which it is so refreshing for the created spirit to catch a glimpse. Christ's human limitations are sweetly and gradually merged into the infinitudes of His Divine Personality. We enter into Him as Man, His humanity is the door, we go out of His Humanity into His angelic life, into His divine life, and our mind finds indeed its pasture in Him: 'I am the door: by Me if any man enter in, he shall be saved; he shall go in and go out, and shall find pastures.'[1]

Nothing could be more refreshing than to read St. John's Gospel in the light of this idea of reserve. The Jewish mind is puzzled and

[1] John x. 9.

irritated by this wonderful personality of Christ. They cannot make Him out; they quarrel amongst themselves about Him; they feel, in spite of themselves, that there is something extraordinary behind His human appearance. It is not only His miracles that are extraordinary, His whole personality is an enigma. His enemies, in true Jewish fashion, have a ready explanation for this incomprehensible masterfulness of the hated Rabbi: He is possessed by an evil spirit: 'The Jews therefore answered and said to Him: Do we not say well that thou art a Samaritan, and hast a devil? ... Now we know that thou hast a devil. Abraham is dead, and the prophets; and thou sayest: If any man keep my word he shall not taste death for ever. Art thou greater than our Father Abraham, who is dead?'[1] 'But a dissension arose again among the Jews for these words. And many of them said: He has a devil, and is mad; why hear you him? Others said, These are not the words of one who hath a devil. Can a devil open the eyes of the blind?'[2]

The Gospel of St. John is in fact full of assertions on Christ's part as to the presence in Himself of glories that do not appear to the eye. 'Amen, Amen, I say to thee that we speak what we know, and we testify what we have seen; and you receive not our testimony. If I have spoken to you earthly things, and you believe not; how will you believe if I shall speak to you heavenly things? And no man hath ascended into heaven, but He that descended from heaven, the Son of man who is in heaven.'[3] It might be said without exaggeration that the whole trend of Christ's discourses, as well as the Baptist's testimony in the fourth Gospel, is this: there is more in this man than appears to the eye; even His miracles, great as they are, do not give the measure of His greatness; but they entitle Him to be listened to even when He says that He and the Father are one. Quotations to that effect could be multiplied so as to make of this chapter a kind of résumé of St. John's Gospel. A few more must suffice. 'And it was the feast of the dedication at Jerusalem, and it was winter. And Jesus walked in the Temple in Solomon's porch. The Jews therefore came round about Him, and said to Him: How long dost thou hold our souls in suspense? If thou be the Christ, tell us plainly. Jesus answered them: I speak to you, and you believe not; the works that I do in the name of My Father, they give testi-

---

[1] John viii. 48, 52, 53   [2] John x. 19-21.   [3] John iii. 11-13.

mony of Me.'¹ 'I and the Father are one. The Jews then took up
stones to stone Him. Jesus answered them: Many good works I
have shewed you from My Father; for which of those works do you
stone Me? The Jews answered Him: For a good work we stone thee
not, but for blasphemy; and because that thou, being a man,
makest thyself God. Jesus answered them: Is it not written in your
law: I said, You are gods? If he called them gods, to whom the word
of God was spoken (and the scripture cannot be broken), do you
say of Him, whom the Father hath sanctified, and sent into the
world: Thou blasphemest; because I said I am the Son of God? If I
do not the works of My Father, believe Me not. But if I do, though
you will not believe Me, believe the works; that you may know, and
believe, that the Father is in Me, and I in the Father. They sought
therefore to take Him, and He escaped out of their hands.'²

From the fierce antagonism of the Pharisees let us come to the
good-natured perplexity of the disciples themselves, of Philip, the
ingenuous questioner in the Gospel, and let us hear the divine answer
given with wonderful playfulness. 'If you had known Me, you would
without doubt have known My Father also; and from henceforth
you shall know Him, and you have seen Him. Philip saith to Him:
Lord, shew us the Father, and it is enough for us. Jesus saith to him:
So long a time have I been with you, and have you not known Me?
Philip, he that seeth Me, seeth the Father also. How sayest thou?
Shew us the Father? Do you not believe that I am in the Father, and
the Father in Me? The words that I speak to you I speak not of Myself: but the Father who abideth in Me, He doth the works. Believe
you not that I am in the Father, and the Father in Me?'³

CHAPTER XIX

The Hiding of Christ's Godhead

IN our chapter entitled 'Christ's Reserves' we have tried to give
such a view of His complex Personality as to make contemplation
of Him a sweet and gradual ascent from one winsomeness to

¹ John x. 22-25.   ² John x. 30-39.   ³ John xiv. 7-11.

another within that human nature in which, according to St. Paul, Godhead had taken up a bodily abode: 'For in Him dwelleth all the fulness of the Godhead, corporeally.'[1]

There is one theological truth which is of importance if we are to relish the mystery of Christ, and it is this: though His Personality be an ever-ascending succession of spiritual sublimities, there was during His mortal life a check put on those sublimities by God's omnipotence, lest through the presence in His soul of such marvellous vitalities He should not be a sharer in our common state of mortality. St. Thomas, always so reluctant to admit exceptional interposition of God's providence, is compelled to admit that God prevented the higher graces in the soul of Christ, such as Beatific Vision, from making themselves felt according to their full possibilities. It is evident that the presence of such a gift as the clear vision of God within a human spirit ought, by all ordinary laws, to dispel any cloud of sadness. To see God face to face, as Christ saw Him, is a happiness so intense as to raise the subject's soul and body above the sphere of sorrow and suffering. Yet Christ was sorrowful in the deepest and holiest regions of His soul. He suffered in His body, He suffered in every one of His mental faculties. We have therefore to admit a psychological miracle in Christ, the only psychological miracle within Him known to theology. It is a miracle of wonderful subtlety, showing clearly what possibilities there must be in the human soul. Beatific Vision and the other spiritual sublimities were all there, in full activity; all the treasures of wisdom and knowledge were within His intellect. 'In whom are hid all the treasures of wisdom and knowledge.'[2] And yet by a direct intervention of God, as St. Thomas says, they did not flow over; they were kept back from certain regions of Christ's soul, from certain powers of His body, in order that He might be able to suffer and to merit, to be sorrowful and afraid, for the redeemed. It was a psychological miracle, because it was the suspension of effects that should have naturally followed; and I say that it is the only miracle in Christ's Person. His Person as such is not exactly a miracle, it is a marvel, the greatest of all wonders; but it is not the suspension of any laws: it is, on the contrary, the application of the highest laws of God's power.

[1] Col. ii. 9.   [2] Col. ii. 3.

The modern rationalist may find it difficult to see in the Jesus of Nazareth who was obedient to His parents, the Christ of St. Paul as He is described in the Epistles to the Ephesians and the Colossians, though, as a matter of history, the aforesaid Epistles were written before the Gospel of St. Luke. We admit that without a direct miracle the Christ in whom 'it hath well pleased the Father that all fulness should dwell' could not have been the boy who sat among the doctors at the age of twelve, asking questions and receiving answers from them. There was in Him another kind of reserve, taking reserve now in its active meaning; there was a miraculous keeping back of the glories of His Godhead from certain regions of His Personality. This is what is meant by the constant theological expression that Christ was at the same time *comprehensor* and *viator*— that is to say, a seer of God and a wayfarer, a pilgrim abroad and a guest in His Father's house. 'And no man hath ascended into heaven but He that descendeth from heaven, the Son of man who is in heaven.'[1] He was at the same time full of the eternal life and subject to the agonies of human death; the highest regions of His soul were thrilled with the joys of the Blessed Vision, and those same regions were saddened with the sight of the world's iniquities; for it would not be generous to think of Our Lord's soul having happiness in its highest faculties and sorrow merely in its lower powers. His sorrow was a divine sorrow, for it was sorrow for the creature's theological guilt; and as such it had to be in the noblest part of His soul, where there was the joy of Beatific Vision.

But such division of soul and spirit, such blending of light and darkness, is a miracle, and, as I have said, it is the only abnormal thing in Christ's Personality. The anomaly ceased when He gave up His soul to the Father on the cross.

[1] John iii. 13.

CHAPTER XX

The Form of a Slave

CHRIST'S attitude towards physical and mental suffering is of immense practical significance for man's daily life, as well as for the progress of civilisation. In our own much vaunted humanitarian age it becomes a very pressing question on the Christian theologian to know how far the wonderful victories over physical pain, won by modern science, are in harmony with the gospel of the Cross. I think it well worth while therefore to give in some detail the theological teaching concerning Christ's attitude towards pain and suffering. Morbidness, even *in excelsis*, is unforgiveable, and it is perhaps all the more deleterious to healthy soul-life because it is stretched into infinitude.

By Christ's body we mean the whole extent of Christ's sensitive life, which, more than any other human life, is a wonderful synthesis of all that is beautiful in the physical world. No human intellect can fathom the possibilities of an organism vivified and elevated by a soul so perfect as was Christ's soul. That suffering and death should enter into such an organism is a thought more appalling than that sin should have been found in the angels of God. It is only our familiarity with the mystery of the Cross that makes us look on Christ's sufferings as on an obvious natural phenomenon. The wondering compassion of the saints who are overawed and stirred in their souls with the thought that God suffered is by no means a misplaced sentiment. For Christ, in His Humanity, was entitled, by all the laws of the Hypostatic Union, to an absolutely divine immunity from pain and suffering. Divinity itself could never be subject to any kind of suffering whatsoever. It would be the worst of all blasphemies to say that God, in His own life, could experience any contrariety. No gain to creatures could come from the Creator's loss, as there is nothing so profitable to the finite being as that infinitude should inhabit the region of unassailable bliss, to which every creature may tend as to the unalterable felicity. With Divinity suffering is an absolute contradiction in terms, both from the point of view of God's life and God's sanctity. A strong God, as well as a holy God, is infinitely above every conceivable sort of disappointment. Now this separation from sorrow is Christ's natural condition from the very laws of Hypostatic Union. The divinity of Christ's Person is in itself such an exemption from the ordinary laws of mortality that no exclamation of surprise on the lips of the lover of Jesus at seeing Him suffer and die can be too strong.

Theology starts with the assertion that Christ's normal condition would have been unassailable bliss of mind and invulnerable glory of body; that both mind and body in Him should have become a prey to pain and sorrow and death is the result of a miracle. Through an act of His omnipotence, Christ in His own person suspended the natural law of Hypostatic Union, the law that makes complete bliss of mind the immortality of the body. Through the fact of Hypostatic Union Christ's human mind was endowed, from the very first moment of its own self-consciousness, with the clear vision of God, commonly called Beatific Vision. Now, such a completeness of blissful contemplation brings with itself a quickening and a glorifying of the whole bodily organism, such as theology teaches will take place in the glorious resurrection of the elect at the end of the world. A glorified mind means a glorified body, by a natural concomitance or causality, which theologians call *redundantia*—a flowing over of the higher bliss into the lower powers. This *redundantia* is a natural psychological law. In Christ, however, this law was miraculously suspended by His own omnipotence. The term 'miracle' taken technically is not too strong to describe this great spiritual anomaly in Christ's Personality. A miracle is a suspension of the results of the ordinary laws, either material or spiritual, by a direct divine interposition. Fire, whilst remaining fire and keeping its activity, and yet not burning a naturally combustible object, like straw, within its range, is a miracle. Both the fire and the straw must remain in their native state if this condition is to be verified. If divine omnipotence were to change the nature of the combustible thing, making it fireproof, there would be no suspension of laws; it would not be the kind of miracle that would necessarily need divine omnipotence. My reader will readily forgive this digression if I remind him of my aim in all this: Christ's birthright of immunity from suffering. Such was that immunity that its suspension belongs to the class of miraculous effects best instanced by fire and straw keeping their respective properties and not burning when brought into contact.

Nothing but faith in Christ's immunity could make us grasp the meaning of scriptural expressions like this in St. Paul's Epistle to the Philippians: 'For let this mind be in you, which was also in Christ Jesus: who being in the form of God, thought it not robbery to be equal with God: but emptied Himself, taking the form of a servant, being made in the likeness of men, and in habit found as a man. He humbled Himself, becoming obedient unto death, even to the death of the cross.'[1] All the humiliation and abasement of the Incarnation lie in this teaching. The union of the Second Person of the Trinity with a finite created nature could never be considered as the 'humiliation'. It is, on the contrary, one of the masterpieces of God's omnipotence. Moreover, Divinity itself could not be 'abased' without infinite loss to the whole creation, besides its being inherently impossible, as I have said already. But that Christ should appear under the form of a servant, as a slave, was indeed humiliation and abasement unfathomably deep. The Risen Christ, the Christ of to-day, has no shadow of humiliation. Hypostatic Union with a glorified human nature, such as was postulated by the very laws of Christ's Beatific Vision, would have lacked completely the element of humiliation.

I will now quote St. Thomas himself: 'By the power of Christ's Divinity, as by a special dispensation (*dispensative*), bliss was so kept back in the soul that it did not over-flow into the body, lest the power of suffering and of dying should be taken away from Him. And in the same way the delights of the vision were so restrained in His mind, as not to over-flow into the sensitive powers, lest thereby sense-suffering should be prevented.'[2] A very striking corollary to this doctrine is given by Cardinal Cajetan, when he comments on the doctrine of St. Thomas on Christ's Transfiguration. So convinced are those great thinkers of the miraculous nature of Christ's capacity to suffer, that Cajetan, in speaking of the momentary glory of Christ's body in the Transfiguration, considers such a manifestation a new miracle, because the first miracle—the miracle of the suspension—was to be of so permanent a character, that its cessation even for a moment meant another interference on the part of

---

[1] Phil. ii. 5-8.   [2] Quest. xv, Art. 5, ad 3.

Omnipotence: 'Let us grant therefore that both phenomena were miraculous; I mean that Christ's body should not shine with glory, and that it so shone in the Transfiguration. But the former is part of the first and, so to say, universal and prior (*antiquum*) miracle that took place in the Incarnation, by which was suspended that communication of glory from the Soul to the Body of Christ, in order that He might have a passible body. ... The latter phenomenon belongs to a special miracle, by which was granted that moment, to the passible body, the power of shining.'[1]

After establishing the principles of Christ's natural immunity from suffering, and of His natural right to highest beatific bliss of soul and body, our theology inquires how much of human pain and sadness Christ took upon Himself. For the miraculous suspension was anything but a wanton courting of human misery. That He should take as much and no more than was necessary for the aim of His Incarnation is to be taken for granted, on the principle that He acted with consummate wisdom and prudence in everything, as He is the Incarnate Wisdom of God. In the Fourth Article of Question Fourteen, St. Thomas has an exhaustive study as to the kind of human infirmities and passibilities which it was fitting that Christ should take upon Himself. The ruling principle is the raising up of the human race through the Incarnation. Only such infirmities were to be assumed which were co-extensive with the race itself, and whose healing therefore in Christ would affect the healing of the whole race. Infirmities that come from individual causes, not universal racial causes, Christ had not to take upon Himself. St. Thomas quotes hunger and thirst and death as racial infirmities. Other infirmities called illness are not racial; they come from particular causes. However widespread those causes may be, they are not universal and co-extensive with the race itself. It would be difficult, at this time of day, to say what limitations in our bodily well-being are racial, and what are of less comprehensive an origin. No doubt a human organism with just the racial limitations in it, without any vestige of decadence that comes from heredity, would be a marvellous fount of life. Yet, in strict theology, Christ's body was such. His own personal wisdom and mode of living made any suffering that comes from an ignorance of the art of life absolutely unthinkable.

[1] Card. Cajetanus: *Commentarium* in *S. Th.* III, Quest. xlv, Art. 2.

Christ's human life was a supremely refined one, from this absence of any hereditary taint. His body had been fashioned by the Holy Ghost Himself from a stainless human blood. Moreover, as St. Thomas points out, as fulness of grace and wisdom was as necessary to the work of the Incarnation as suffering, Christ could never have allowed in Himself any defect that would have interfered in the least with such a perfection of holiness and knowledge: there was no ignorance in Him, no mental tardiness, no contradiction between the higher and the lower powers. Though such defects may be racial in their extent, yet Christ took exception to them, as they are in opposition to consummate sanctity. We owe great thanks to our theology for having kept Christ on this serene height of bodily purity and health; for having made it possible for us to find in Him at the same time the most perfect example of patience in pain and suffering, as well as the undying fount of spiritual and bodily health.

It is evident from all this that nothing is less in conformity with the Christ idea than the accumulation of hereditary infirmities that burden mankind. Christ banished them from His own body; so it is a Christian policy, so to speak, to banish them from the human race to any extent human means may allow. On the other hand, when such infirmities have taken hold on us, their patient endurance becomes closely allied with Christ's patience on the Cross. For though He did not take such infirmities on Himself, He willingly took those older and more universal infirmities that are the parents of newer forms of suffering. To a suggestion that it would have been more generous of Christ to take on Himself every kind of human weakness, in order to heal them all, St. Thomas answers: 'All particular defects in men are caused by the corruptibility and passibility of the body, with the addition of certain particular causes. And therefore as Christ healed the passibility and corruptibility of our body by the very fact of taking them on Himself, as a consequence He has healed all the other defects.'[1]

Christ's body is a source of life through its matchless perfection of nature and grace. St. Thomas frequently insists on the causes of this most heavenly constitution of Christ's bodily frame: the active generative cause and the passive material element. The Holy Ghost Himself is the first, and Mary's most pure blood is the second of the

[1] S. Th. III, Quest. xiv, Art. 4, ad 1.

two total causes of Our Lord's human body. Who can tell the riches of health and life and grace hidden in an organism of such origin? Significantly St. Thomas teaches that Christ is the head of men both through His soul and His body: 'Therefore the whole Humanity of Christ—that is to say both according to soul and body—exerts an influence on all men, both with regard to soul and with regard to body; but principally the soul, and secondarily the body.'[1]

CHAPTER XXI

The Great Transition

CHRIST'S passing at the age of thirty from ordinary human life into one of power, claiming to be that of the Son of God, was abrupt and unexpected. Nothing in His daily existence had prepared His townsmen for this sudden exchange of rôles. That He was the village carpenter is evident from the phrase on the lips of the people of Nazareth, quoted by St. Mark. 'And when the sabbath was come, He began to teach in the synagogue: and many hearing Him were in admiration at His doctrine, saying: How came this man by all these things? and what wisdom is this that is given to Him, and such mighty works as are wrought by His hands? Is not this the carpenter, the son of Mary, the brother of James and Joseph and Jude and Simon? Are not also His sisters here with us? And they were scandalised in regard of Him.'[2] St. Joseph was dead, and Jesus had succeeded to His foster-father's modest business. St. Matthew makes the people of Nazareth say: 'Is not this the carpenter's son?',[3] whilst St. Mark's text points clearly to the fact that Jesus Himself had followed the parental avocation.

Adam Bede has become the classical instance in English literature of the noble son of the soil, grand in his simple manhood, for whom it was God's will that he should be a good carpenter. There is no profanity in thinking of Christ going about His work at Nazareth in the simple uprightness of a strong and straightforward man, to whom

---

[1] S. Th. III, Quest. viii, Art. 2.   [2] Mark vi. 2, 3.   [3] Matt. xiii. 55.

the great secrets of His spiritual life were never a temptation even
to look mysterious and secretive. The Gospel narratives are documents of supreme good taste. The element of useless mysteriousness, of irritating secretiveness, is entirely banished from them. The
apocrypha, on the contrary, boldly exploit a situation so full of
possible thrills for the vulgar mind; a human being that is a God, and
yet of set purpose hiding His identity, with just enough hints and
glimpses given to the entourage to make the pose intriguing, till
finally the veil falls. No other human being ever had the noble
quality of reserve in the degree possessed by the Divine Carpenter,
the Son of David. But when the hour of His manifestation came, it
came with incontrovertible clearness and irresistible power. It came
as an immense surprise to Christ's friends and acquaintances. In
their bewilderment they had the one explanation always at hand for
embarrassed family circles—sudden insanity. 'And when His friends
had heard of it, they went out to lay hold on Him; for they said: He
is become mad.'[1]

Our Lord's Baptism at the hands of John, and the great fast with
its mysterious temptations, were events still unknown to the world
at large. John alone had seen the heavens opened, had heard the
voice from above. The calling of the first disciples, with such
irresistible imperiousness, was Christ's first assertion of His Divinity. A few days later there was the miracle at Cana, the 'beginning
of signs'. From that day Christ's progress was rapid and overpowering: 'But He being gone out, began to publish and to blaze
abroad the word; so that He could not openly go into the city, but
was without in desert places; and they flocked to Him from all
sides.'[2] The hatred of the Pharisaical clique, and their conspiracy to
destroy Him, are events that already belong to the first months of
Christ's public appearance. 'And the Pharisees going out, immediately made a consultation with the Herodians against Him, how they
might destroy Him.'[3] The abruptness of this transition from the
normal human existence into an all-bewildering manifestation of
superhuman powers, whilst perfectly compatible with the principles
of Hypostatic Union, contradicts any theory that makes of Christ's
ascendancy the gradual evolution of a saintly life and superior
personality.

[1] Mark iii. 21.   [2] Mark i. 45.   [3] Mark iii. 6.

Jewish tradition, the outcome of the Jewish love for the marvellous and mysterious, was all in favour of a Christ whose origin
would be wrapped up in impenetrable mystery: 'And behold, He
speaketh openly; and they say nothing to Him. Have the rulers
known for a truth that this is the Christ? But we know this man,
whence He is: but when the Christ cometh, no man knoweth
whence He is.'[1] No prophet's home life and early upbringing were
so clearly known as Christ's. 'Jesus therefore cried out in the
temple, teaching and saying: You both know Me, and you know
whence I am; and I am not come of Myself; but He that sent Me
is true, whom ye know not.'[2] Everybody in Jerusalem knew that He
belonged to the class of the illiterate: 'And the Jews wondered, saying: How doth this man know letters, having never learned?'[3] The
sudden reputation of the young teacher had no doubt produced a
great eagerness and curiosity as to His antecedents. But there was
nothing extraordinary to discover, nothing to marvel at. The most
ordinary, the most uneventful, past was the only thing to satisfy the
inquisitive busybody. No religion indeed aims so little at the marvellous for its own sake as the religion of Christ. The ordinary is
the rule, but there is no limit as to the spiritual worth that may be
found within this ordinariness of human conditions. It is precisely
this complete ordinariness of His previous life that was the great
stumbling-block to the Jewish mind. The greatest miracles seemed
powerless to efface that first fact. The men of Nazareth were
scandalised in regard of Him. 'Is not this the carpenter, the son of
Mary, the brother of James and Joseph and Jude and Simon? Are
not also His sisters here with us? And they were scandalised in
regard of Him.'[4] 'And when the men were come unto Him, they
said: John the Baptist hath sent us to Thee, saying: Art Thou He that
art to come, or look we for another? (And in that same hour He
cured many of their diseases and hurts and evil spirits; and to many
that were blind He gave sight.) And answering, He said to them:
Go and relate to John what you have heard and seen; the blind see,
the lame walk, the lepers are made clean, the deaf hear, the dead
rise again, to the poor the gospel is preached. And blessed is he
whosoever shall not be scandalised in Me.'[5] This last verse seems a

[1] John vii. 26, 27.   [2] John vii. 28.   [3] John vii. 15.   [4] Mark vi. 3.
[5] Luke vii. 20-23.

strange conclusion to that enumeration of miraculous deeds of the highest order, such as the raising up of the dead. But it finds its natural commentary in the analogous passage of St. Mark, where Christ's nearest acquaintances are said to have been scandalised with regard to Him, though they admitted the fact of the mighty works wrought by His hands. All this goes to show how completely Christ took His countrymen by surprise when He began to 'manifest His glory'.[1]

Christ had His 'zero hour'. 'And Jesus saith to her: Woman, what is that to Me and to thee? My hour is not yet come.'[2] Before that hour had come no power in the world, except the prayers of His mother, could open His lips, or get Him to reveal the ineffable secret of His Personality. But when He knew that the hour had come, the secret unburdened itself from His breast with the rush of a mighty stream. This complete mastery of Christ over His own feelings, His own destiny, expressed in the term 'My hour', is a cherished idea in the Gospel of St. John. Besides the passages just quoted, where it refers to the great transition from obscurity to Divinity, it marks other new phases of Christ's career. 'They sought therefore to apprehend Him: and no man laid hands on Him, because His hour was not yet come.'[3] 'These words Jesus spoke in the treasury, teaching in the temple: and no man laid hands on Him, because His hour was not yet come.'[4] 'But Jesus answered them, saying: The hour is come that the Son of Man should be glorified.'[5] 'Before the festival day of the pasch, Jesus knowing that His hour was come, that He should pass out of this world to the Father; having loved His own who were in the world, He loved them unto the end.'[6]

There is an apparent contradiction in the Gospels in this matter of Christ's manifestation. His birth was surrounded with the elements of the miraculous; yet not once is an appeal made to it in Christ's later career. It is hardly credible that the vision of the shepherds on the night of the Nativity, and the visit of the wise men from the East, left no traces on the popular imagination. After all, thirty years is not a long period, and for a people like the Jewish nation the marvellous is remembered with infinite care and delight.

[1] John ii. 11. [2] John ii. 4. [3] John vii. 30.
[4] John viii. 20. [5] John xii. 23. [6] John xiii. 1.

No doubt the traditions survived; perhaps even they acquired volume and strength with time. But there is one providential circumstance told in the Gospels which alters the case completely: the precipitate and prolonged change of abode of the family round which there had been the momentary glory. The disappearance into Egypt of the Holy Family as told by St. Matthew, deprived the glorious tale of its hero, and instead of making the reputation of Mary's Son, it helped to swell the volume of fair legends that made everybody look to the immediate coming of the Messiah. Far from helping Christ's cause, they went against Him, as the fact of His having been born at Bethlehem was not known. 'Of that multitude therefore, when they had heard these words of His, some said: This is the prophet indeed. Others said: This is the Christ. But some said, Doth the Christ come out of Galilee? Doth not the scripture say: That Christ cometh of the seed of David and from Bethlehem the town where David was? So there arose a dissension among the people because of Him.'[1] If the memory of the vision of the shepherds and of the star had survived, the carpenter from Galilee was to be the very last person to be associated with it. There was no such interruption in the traditions round the person of John the Baptist. 'And fear came upon all their neighbours; and all these things were noised abroad over all the hill country of Judea. And all they that had heard them laid them up in their hearts, saying: What an one, think ye, shall this child be? For the hand of the Lord was with him.'[2] He was in the desert, it is true, but never far from the hills that had re-echoed the marvels of his birth. 'And the child grew and was strengthened in spirit; and was in the deserts until the day of his manifestation to Israel.'[3] It is not surprising therefore to find that the moment he showed himself to the world, without any miracle or signs on his part, he should have been thought to be the Christ by the most sincere Jews. 'And as the people were of opinion, and all were thinking in their hearts of John, that perhaps he might be the Christ; John answered, saying unto all: I indeed baptize you with water; but there shall come one mightier than I, the latchet of whose shoes I am not worthy to loose. He shall baptize you with the Holy Ghost and with fire.'[4] John's birth co-incided closely enough with the period of the visit of the magi;

[1] John vii. 40-43.   [2] Luke i. 65, 66.   [3] Luke i. 80.   [4] Luke iii. 15, 16.

nothing was easier than to associate him vaguely with the events of Christ's birth. It is certainly a surprising thing that this offspring of the tribe of Levi should have been hailed as the Christ with such readiness, when it was one of the staunchest beliefs of the Jewish people that Christ would be the son of David.

But if anything becomes clear, through the careful analysis of the New Testament documents, it is this: the Son of Mary was the very last man who would have had the benefit of the Messianic legends and hopes, so ripe in the Jewish nation of His day. He had to stand on the strength of His own divine powers. To say that Christ owed His success to a clever use and exploitation of the popular Messianic expectations of the day is an open contempt of written history.

CHAPTER XXII

Christ's Sincerity

CHRIST'S life is the greatest of all biographies. It contains the root-elements of every biography worth reading: intense sincerity pitted against the elementary human passions of jealousy, pride, avarice, and cowardice; and these elements are found in their greatest intensity. It would be an immense spiritual loss to us if the fact of Christ's omnipotent control over His own destiny were envisaged by us in a sense that would diminish the sincerity and reality of the Christ-tragedy. We could never love deeply and perseveringly one in whose career there are unrealities, even if the unrealities were there for the highest motive. Thus if the treason of Judas had not been to Christ a disappointment as keen and as human as any betraying of confidence might be to me, the Lord's Passion would not be able to rivet my wondering sympathy. But we easily fall a prey to our limited imagination, when our thoughts are busy with Christ. We put the operations of His Godhead where He had withdrawn them. The impression that after all Christ had it in

His power to avoid all the evils that befell Him, sometimes paralyzes our attempts to penetrate more deeply into the wonderful human sequence of the great biography. Now, though it is the saint's constant wonderment that Christ, having it in His power to escape from His enemies, did not escape, such a consideration is conducive to a deeper love of Christ only when it is coupled with the consideration that the exercise of such a power would have meant a redemption inferior to that under which we live now. If Christ did not exert His power, it was because there were grave reasons for Him to act thus, and the reasons were connected with man's greater spiritual welfare.

The primary fact in Christ's history is His 'taking the form of a servant, being made in the likeness of men, and in habit found as a man.'[1] It is the all-pervading element of the great biography, it is the one great fact which nothing could alter, because God had decided that for mankind's salvation such a form of incarnation was best. As great men are born with their talents, as they are born into a definite state of human conditions, and as nothing can alter this primary fact; so likewise Christ had to appear in the form of a servant. It was undoubtedly in God's power to have chosen an incarnation that would not have started with the form of a servant, but with the glory of an heir; but the former having been selected, for the higher spiritual exaltation of the human race, Christ's life was bound to turn out a tragedy. That is why Our Lord's life may easily be studied according to the canons of ordinary human biography, and why it is found to be of all biographies the greatest. When I use the expression 'ordinary human biography' I do not forget Christ's miraculous powers. But taking for granted a miracle-working Christ, as you take for granted, say, a preternaturally far-sighted statesman, I say that, according to the canons of human biography, a Christ who out of charity for man persisted in keeping hidden within Himself His Godhead, and who had to win faith in His Godhead by miracles, must almost inevitably become the world's greatest tragedy. From the moment Jesus makes His first public appearance up to the sealing of His sepulchre by public authorities, 'lest perhaps His disciples come and steal Him away',[2] there is nothing that need surprise us. Once we have understood the character of the Pharisee, we can foresee that there is little chance for Christ.

[1] Phil. ii. 7.   [2] Matt. xxvii. 64.

This is the reason why men of every school of thought are able to make of the Gospels their life study. Even the rationalist, who does not believe in Christ's Divinity, is found to say true and illuminating things concerning the psychological sequence of His human career. No one but a madman would deny that Christ stood among His contemporaries with a power and a majesty such as no other man ever possessed. A little good will would be enough to identify Christ's superhuman position with His power of miracles. But this superhuman attitude once accepted, the Gospels are a human biography. Christ's claim to be the Son of God explains the jealousy of the Pharisee, because He was to all appearances a man, and because He supported His claim with undoubted miracles: 'I and the Father are One. The Jews then took up stones to stone Him. Jesus answered them: Many good works I have shewed you from My Father; for which of those works do you stone Me? The Jews answered Him: For a good work we stone thee not, but for blasphemy; and because that thou, being a man, makest thyself God.'[1] 'The chief priests, therefore, and the Pharisees gathered a council and said: What do we, for this man doeth many miracles? If we let Him alone so, all will believe in Him; and the Romans will come and take away our place and nation.'[2] Nothing could express better the whole situation than those words. The miracle-worker, being a man, claims oneness with the Father; let Him suffer the death of the blasphemer. His miracles are a danger. The Pharisee, the man who sins against the Holy Ghost, ought to be our chief character-study in connection with the Gospels. Once we have fathomed him we can easily see that the Son of Mary is doomed to death, unless He depart from that great reserve that makes Him hide His Divinity. Judas, Pilate, Herod, the mocking soldiery, the scourging, the crowning with thorns, the crucifixion, become events that explain themselves naturally, through the ordinary elementary hatreds and weaknesses of human nature.

There are many passages in the New Testament pointing to the part played by Satan in bringing about Christ's death on the Cross. It is a favourite theme with writers of all periods to make the drama of our Redemption reach its climax when the Devil knows that he has destroyed his own kingdom, when he finds out that the Christ

[1] John x. 30-33.   [2] John xi. 47, 48.

murdered at his suggestion was the Son of God, and that the death on the cross, invented by satanic jealousy, was God's pre-ordained means of saving mankind. We may easily grant such dramatic presentment of the Redemption without there being occasioned by it the least flaw in the human sequence of events in the Christ-biography. Satan's co-operation with man's act, far from superseding human activity or filling up gaps in the causal series of human events, depends entirely on human perverseness and wickedness for its efficacy. The powers of darkness cannot work except in darkness, and the dark conscience of the Pharisees was more than ready to receive the suggestions of the spirit of wickedness. Satan's share in the Crucifixion, far from rendering the Christ-tragedy less human, gave it on the contrary an additional human cruelty and grimness, as Satan's work is always to stir up the deepest and darkest instincts of the corrupt human heart.

What we all ought to bear in mind is the human origin and the human sequel of this tragic drama. Once it is granted that 'it behoved Him in all things to be made like unto His brethren, that He might become a merciful and faithful high priest before God'[1]— that the best Redemption was the most absolute identification of Christ with ordinary human conditions, there was enough love and enough hatred in man to bring about the Christ-tragedy. How in God's wisdom the prescience of it all could become the will of His heart does not belong to the created plane of thinking. On the one hand there is the clear fact of human sin, the greatest of all sins, the sin against the Holy Ghost, which is the full and direct human cause, and to all appearance the total cause of Christ's death. On the other hand there is the fact of revelation that it was the Father's will that mankind should be saved by that death on the Cross. No finite mind is able to grasp the harmonious interlocking of those two great causes: an infinitely holy will and an immensely perverted will. Infinitude of power and wisdom is the only explanation. 'The Father delivered up Christ; and Christ gave Himself up out of charity; and therefore They are praised for it. But Judas betrayed Him for greed, the Jews from envy, Pilate gave Him up out of worldly fear, and therefore they are blamed.'[2] No more felicitous and succinct statement could be framed to include the causalities at

[1] Heb. ii. 17.   [2] S. Th. III, Quest. xlvii, Art. 3, ad 3.

work in Christ's fate than this simple answer of St. Thomas to an objector who could not see how the Father and Judas could both be said to have delivered up the Son of God. In the same Article the Doctor defines the Father's rôle in Christ's Passion: 'God the Father delivered up Christ to suffering in a threefold way: Firstly, as far as He in His eternal will pre-ordained Christ's passion to be the deliverance of the human race. Secondly, as far as He inspired Christ with the willingness to suffer for us, pouring Charity into Him. ... Thirdly, not saving Him from suffering, but leaving Him at the mercy of His persecutors.'[1] Christ's own share in bringing on Himself the great storm is thus analysed by St. Thomas in the first Article of the same Question: 'One is the cause of an event indirectly, when one does not prevent it, when one could: just as a man is said to drench someone else, because he does not shut the window through which rain comes in, and in this way Christ was the cause of His own suffering and death. For He could have prevented them, firstly checking His enemies, so as to render them incapable or unwilling to kill Him. Secondly, because His spirit had power to preserve intact the nature of His body, lest it should succumb to any injury, which power Christ's soul possessed because it was united with the Word of God in oneness of Person. Therefore, as the soul of Christ did not keep from His body the hurts inflicted on it, but rather willed that His bodily nature should succumb to such injury, He is said to have laid down His life, or to have died willingly.'[2]

But again, Christ could not have exerted such power without our Redemption being less bountiful; and if He was to give Himself to man without reserve or restriction, He had to be the helpless prey of man's darkest passions. The Father would have sent Him twelve legions of angels, if He had asked, in virtue of His birthright. But how could one with twelve legions of angels surrounding Him turn round and look at Peter with a look that drew the truest and warmest tears that were ever shed by human eyes? 'And Peter going out, wept bitterly. And the men that held Him mocked Him and struck Him, and they blindfolded Him and smote His face.'[3] It is from the midst of such a gathering of lowest humanity that Christ won back

[1] *S. Th.* III, Quest. xlvii, Art. 3.   [2] *Ibid.* Art. 1.   [3] Luke xxii. 62-64.

the faithless disciple to a penitent love that was to be stronger than death.

Chapter XXIII

Christ's Way of Perfection

CHRIST'S mortal career is a most complete and perfect act in itself; it has a fulness that makes it a source of life for all ages to come.

It is perhaps not too much to say that the general tendency of the human mind is to belittle the importance of the individual life—I mean the mortal career of individual people. Man soon begins to dream of possible new existences, where things might be done and duties fulfilled which have been omitted and neglected during the first mortal life. One need only remember the doctrine of the migration of souls, the most wide-spread theory of the Hereafter we know of; no doubt, as most human lives seem so worthless, man's innate wish for better things makes such beliefs part of the human optimism. Christianity is indeed of all religions the most optimistic; but its optimism never degenerates into a wishful thinking; it is essentially this, that it thinks highly of the possibilities of the one mortal life of which we are certain, as being the only chance for each individual. Christianity constantly reins in the human imagination, only too prone to overlook the blessings of the present hour for the fairy tales of uncertain existences in the future.

Christ's mortal life has become to His Church the beginning and the end, the Alpha and the Omega, the source of all grace and the consummation of all sanctity. There is no re-acting of that great life; it has been acted once, and the drama was indeed a delight to the eyes of God and of the angels. Christ Himself insists emphatically on the importance of His one life, to do the work of His Father: 'And Jesus passing by, saw a man who was blind from his birth. And His disciples asked Him: Rabbi, who hath sinned, this man, or his parents, that he should be born blind? Jesus answered: Neither hath this man sinned, nor his parents; but that the works of God should be made manifest in him. I must work the works of Him that sent Me, whilst it is day: the night cometh, when no man can work. As long as I am in the world, I am the light of the world.'[1] 'I have glorified Thee on the earth; I have finished the work which Thou gavest Me to do. And now glorify Thou Me, O Father, with Thyself, with the glory which I had, before the world was, with Thee.'[2] This same theological idea is one of the leading thoughts in that most perfect résumé of Christology, the Epistle to the Hebrews. 'Then said I: Behold I come to do Thy will, O God. He taketh away the first, that He may establish that which followeth. In the which will, we are sanctified by the oblation of the body of Jesus Christ once. And every priest indeed standeth daily ministering, and often offering the same sacrifices, which can never take away sins. But this Man, offering one sacrifice for sins, for ever sitteth on the right hand of God; from henceforth expecting until His enemies be made His footstool. For by one oblation He hath perfected for ever them that are sanctified. And the Holy Ghost also doth testify this to us; for after that He said: And this is the testament which I will make unto them after those days, saith the Lord. I will give My laws in their hearts, and on their minds will I write them: and their sins and iniquities I will remember no more. Now where there is a remission of these, there is no more an oblation for sin.'[3]

In another chapter I shall show how this oneness of life in Christ is not contradicted but rather emphasised, by the doctrine of the Holy Eucharist; but there is one remark I should like to make here. It is my impression that certain pious souls have not been proof against that weakness of the human mind mentioned above; the tendency to multiply lifetimes, because the first span of life some-how seems to lack fulness and sufficiency. Not a small amount of modern eucharistic literature is tainted with this attitude. Good and pious men make of the Eucharistic Presence a kind of second existence of Christ, a kind of mortal career that goes on for ever and ever, a kind of self-abasement on the part of the Son of God, even greater than His first abasement. Now, I would be the very last person to put a check on the enthusiasm of Christian feeling

---

[1] John ix. 1-4.   [2] John xvii. 4, 5.   [3] Heb. x. 9-18.

about the great sacramental marvel. With St. Thomas Aquinas I say here:

> Quantum potes, tantum aude;
> Quia major omni laude,
> Nec laudare sufficis.[1]

At the same time there is the great fact that Christ's mortal career was all fulness, and that through His resurrection He entered into glory for ever. The presence and existence of Christ in the Holy Eucharist are not a human presence, a human existence, in the sense in which He was present or existent in His mortal days. It is not even a presence or existence that resembles in any way Christ's glorified presence and existence in heaven, such as He is now. It is a presence, an existence, which is absolutely new, infinitely different from any known mode of presence and existence.

People who talk of the Eucharistic Presence in language that could not apply to anything except an ordinary human life could do nothing better than study that Question in the *Summa* which treats 'of the way in which Christ is in this Sacrament'.[2] It contains eight highly metaphysical Articles. Let me quote from the Seventh: 'Whether Christ's Body, as it is in this Sacrament, can be seen by any eye, at least if it belong to a glorified body'. 'Strictly speaking,' he says, 'Christ's body, according to the manner of existence which It has in this sacrament, is not discernible either by sense or imagination, but by the intellect only, which is called the spiritual eye. It is moreover perceived differently according to the differences of intellect. For as the mode of existence according to which Christ is in this sacrament is entirely supernatural, it can be seen in its proper state by the supernatural intellect—I mean the Divine Intellect; and as a consequence it can be seen by the glorified intellect of either angel or man, which in virtue of that participated glory of the Divine Intellect in them, see things that are supernatural in the vision of the Divine Essence. As for the intellect of man still in his mortal career, it cannot see It except by faith, as is the case with all

---

[1] Strive thy best to praise Him well;
Yet doth He all praise excel;
None can ever reach His due.

Sequence: Lauda, Sion'.

[2] *S. Th.* III, Quest. lxxvi.

things supernatural. Even the angelic intellect, left to its natural resources, is unable to see It. Consequently the demons cannot through their intellect perceive Christ in this sacrament, except by faith, to which they pay unwilling assent.'[1]

Church history is full of marvellous events centring round the consecrated elements of the Eucharist, such as palpable flesh taking the place of the consecrated Host, or warm blood issuing forth from the sacramental species, or even the Eucharistic Bread taking the form of the Divine Infant, for the consolation of the faithful or the conviction of the doubter. St. Thomas treats of the objective value of such miraculous phenomena in the Eighth Article of the same Question. His explanations are satisfying; the phenomenon is either a subjective impression in the beholder, or an objective preternatural effect surrounding the consecrated species. But the real substance of Christ's Body does not come into the phenomenon; it remains hid in its inaccessible mysteriousness. 'Such transformed sacramental elements,' he says, 'have sometimes been enclosed and at the suggestion of many bishops, preserved in a pyx, which it would be wicked to think of with regard to Christ in His proper semblance. (*Quod nefas esset de Christo sentire secundum propriam speciem.*)'[2] This energetic condemnation of the idea of Christ being held a prisoner, as it were, in material surroundings, though it be under a Eucharistic transformation, shows how repugnant to Catholic theology are ways of stating the Eucharist Presence in other terms than those of the sacramental Transubstantiation.

There are two distinct points of doctrine with regard to the great Christian Eucharist. The first point is the Real Presence: Christ is really present. This is the point over which Christians are divided, some being satisfied with a mystical, spiritual presence of Christ's body, whilst others, taking the Gospel literally, hold that besides the mystical spiritual presence, Christ's bodily reality is there, and that in fact the spiritual, the mystical reality is the effect, the outcome of the bodily reality thus present. This first point suggests nothing as to the manner of that bodily presence. The second point is an exclusively Catholic point; it has long been part of the Catholic theology on the blessed Eucharist, and the Council of Trent raised it to a Catholic dogma. It is the dogma of Tran-

---

[1] *Ibid.* Art. 7.   [2] *Ibid.* Art. 8.

substantiation; the dogma, I might say, of the mode of Christ's presence. Christ is in the consecrated elements because the consecrated elements have been changed, transubstantiated into Christ's Body and Blood by God's omnipotence. This is no mere taking up of His abode in the bread and wine as the Lutheran theory of impanation would have it. It is easy to see how the Catholic doctrine of Transubstantiation removes the mode of Christ's Eucharistic Presence into the region of the mysterious and miraculous beyond any other theory. A Catholic ought to be the very last man to apply to Christ's Eucharistic Presence modes of speech that sound incongruous, except when applied to the normal, natural human life, with its lights and its shadows, its trials and its virtues.

I have risked wearying the reader with the refutation of certain aberrations of Catholic piety, because I feel how important it is for our spiritual well-being to go back constantly to Christ's mortal life, to find there not only every virtue and every example, but also finality of virtue and of example. 'Who in the days of His flesh, with a strong cry and tears, offering up prayers and supplications to Him that was able to save Him from death, was heard for His reverence. And whereas indeed He was the Son of God, He learned obedience by the things which He suffered; and being consummated, He became, to all that obey Him, the cause of eternal salvation.'[1] In another chapter I shall show the relationship between the Eucharist and Christ's life and death. But whatever that relationship, Christ, like all other *viatores*, pilgrims on earth, had only one earthly life, one human life, one life of prayer, struggle, merit, and edification for His brethren: the life of thirty-three years in Palestine. Everything in the spiritual order, not excepting the Eucharist itself, comes from that great life, and goes back to it. Christ's Eucharistic Presence cannot be called a human life; it cannot be said to show forth human virtues; it cannot be regarded as containing ethical perfections that might be a pattern to the Christian, or in any way superior to the perfections of His mortal career. It is a presence so eminently miraculous, so absolutely beyond the laws of humanity, that God alone is able to watch the pulsation of that hidden life.

In order to remain faithful to my programme of describing the Christ of theology, I have to confine myself to that aspect of His

[1] Heb. v. 7-9.

life, the theological aspect. We are happily in possession of excellent works, endless in their variety, on the historical and spiritual aspects of the great life. Now one aspect which, to my mind, constitutes something deeply interesting for the religious thinker, is the circumstance that Christ led an ordinary social life, with the duties appropriate to refined and civilised humanity. He differs from the Baptist; He is not a solitary, an ascetic, a priest of the Levitical tribe; He is the Son of David, of the tribe of Juda, of royal descent. 'For He of whom these things are spoken is of another tribe, of which no one attended the altar. For it is evident that Our Lord sprang out of Juda; in which tribe Moses spoke nothing concerning priests.'[1] This ordinariness of Christ's life is a fact of such significance that I do not hesitate to call it its theological aspect, because it is an immense acquisition to the history of human sanctity that the Son of God on earth should have led a life not different in its external arrangements from the ordinary social life of the men of His time and His social standing. 'Is not this the carpenter, the son of Mary?'[2] This exclamation on the lips of Christ's nearest acquaintances shows well how completely human He had made Himself, and how unprepared the Jewish mind was to receive its heaven from the hands of an artisan whom they had met daily for years past.

Nothing could be more suggestive, from the point of view of the history of spirituality, than the differences between the career of the Baptist and of Christ. The Baptist was essentially a Jewish saint from beginning to end; Christ was not the kind of saint the Jew admired or could understand. John the Baptist was never doubted by the people, his mode of life was such as to make every word that fell from his lips a rule of faith. The Pharisee indeed might say of John; 'He hath a devil.'[3] But then John had never spared them. 'Ye brood of vipers, who hath shewed you to flee from the wrath to come?'[4] Such had been his apostrophe. As for the people themselves, their faith in the Baptist was implicit. 'And it came to pass that on one of the days, as He (Christ) was teaching the people in the temple and preaching the gospel, the chief priests and the scribes, with the ancients, met together, and spoke to Him, saying: Tell us by what authority dost thou these things? Who is he that hath given thee this authority? And Jesus answering said to them: I will also ask you one

[1] Heb. vii. 13, 14.	[2] Mark vi. 3.
[3] Matt. xi. 18.	[4] Matt. iii. 7.

thing. Answer me: The baptism of John, was it from heaven, or of men? But they thought within themselves, saying: If we shall say: From heaven, He will say: Why then did you not believe him? But if we say: Of men; the whole people will stone us: for they are persuaded that John was a prophet. And they answered that they knew not whence it was. And Jesus said to them: Neither do I tell you by what authority I do these things.'[1] That one of so perfect a life should give testimony of One whose mode of living in the world was like any other man's was indeed a great puzzle to Christ's contemporaries. Christ was at an enormous disadvantage with the Jewish mind, owing to this ordinariness of life. His miracles, His wonderful teaching, were no compensation to the Jewish temperament for that absence of ascetical austerity. It was rather a scandal to them that one with an ordinary kind of life should do wonders and speak such wisdom. Had He been among them, 'not eating and drinking,' the miracles would have been hailed with enthusiasm. 'And going out from thence, He went into His own country; and His disciples followed Him. And when the sabbath was come, He began to teach in the synagogue. And many hearing Him were in admiration of His doctrine, saying: How came this man by all these things? And what wisdom is this that is given to Him, and such mighty works as are wrought by His hands? Is not this the carpenter, the son of Mary, the brother of James and Joseph and Jude and Simon? Are not also His sisters here with us? And they were scandalised in regard of Him.'[2] 'And they come to a house, and the multitude cometh together again, so that they could not so much as eat bread. And when His friends had heard of it, they went out to lay hold on Him; for they said: He is become mad.'[3] That spiritual greatness was possible within the ordinary conditions of human society was a truth not yet realised. That a man could sit down to dinner with His host, and at the same time read the secrets of the heart of those that approached Him was a lesson still to be learned by men. Jesus had multiplied signs and wonders, but He failed to win the confidence of the Jews; John had done no sign, and yet his word was of immense weight. 'If I do not the works of My Father, believe Me not. But if I do, though you will not believe Me, believe the works: that you may know, and believe, that the Father is in Me, and I in the Father.

[1] Luke xx. 1-8,   [2] Mark vi. 1-3.   [3] Mark iii. 20, 21.

They sought therefore to take Him: and He escaped out of their hands. And He went again beyond the Jordan, into that place where John was baptising first; and there He abode. And many resorted to Him, and they said: John indeed did no sign. But all things, whatsoever John said of this man were true. And many believed in Him.'[1]

St. Thomas treats of the characteristics of Christ's life in the Fortieth Question of the Third Part of the Summa: *De modo conversationis Christi;* 'The Manner of Christ's Living'. I quote from the Commentary of Cajetan on the Second Article, as it embodies in a few words the essence of Christian theology on Christ's practical life among men. 'Take notice and fix in your mind this doctrine, that Christ was an example of perfection in all things that belong necessarily to salvation. From this conclude that in those things which have no necessary relations to salvation, things that have no intrinsic goodness, but are good merely as means to an end, such as obedience, poverty, and other such practices, we ought not to ask from Christ more austere things, as if they were more perfect. But what we ought to find in Christ are the things that belong to the final purpose of the Incarnation; whether such things be austere practices or not, matters little.' The perfect life is indeed an infinitely wise life, because all its phases and all its duties are determined by this one consideration. It was a wisdom of life the Jew could not understand; for him a garment of camel's hair was the spiritual marvel. It is only the children of wisdom that can see the beauty of that other life. 'The Son of man is come eating and drinking; and you say: Behold a man that is a glutton and a drinker of wine, a friend of publicans and sinners! And wisdom is justified by all her children.'[2]

I shall once more quote Cajetan, summing up the doctrine of his great master St. Thomas. The terseness of the theologian is very helpful, as it is so important for us all to take a true and sober view of Christ's glorious life, the divinely authentic pattern of human perfection. 'Christ quite appropriately adopted social life as His way of living on earth, not solitary life. Such is the thesis of St. Thomas, and this is its proof. Christ was bound to adopt such a mode of life as would best suit the purpose of the Incarnation. The purpose of the

---

[1] John x. 37-42.   [2] Luke vii. 34, 35.

Incarnation is best served by social life. Therefore Christ was bound to choose social life as His life. The purpose of the Incarnation is threefold: first, to give testimony of the truth; second, to save sinners; third, to bring men to God. Now, all this means social life.'[1]

CHAPTER XXIV

God Meeting God

PERSONALITY, in the sense of its being a great entitative reality, is, as I have said so often, at the root of all the metaphysical momentum of Hypostatic Union. Personality, in the sense of its being a living, overpowering influence, is at the root of all our sanctification and exaltation in Christ. The two views are not separable in practice, as Christ is a Divine Person, through that wondrous replacement of personality so much spoken of in this book, for our sakes, in order that we might reach highest human perfection in Him.

Personality, in so far as it signifies a rational being with distinct rights and claims, with a distinct ethical estate as its inalienable property, is at the root of that part of Christology called Christ's Priesthood. This third view of personality is not separable from the two preceding views in practice; but it is the predominating view when we come to approach Christ's Atonement—Christ's sacerdotal rôle. Theologians have written whole folio-volumes on this one subject: the Priesthood of Christ. It is no easy task then to compress so great a thesis into one single chapter. However, I have a precedent in St. Thomas Aquinas, who finds that one Question comprising six Articles is sufficient, even for the theologian.[2] Besides, there is the inspired treatise on Christ's Priesthood, the Epistle to the Hebrews; a strictly theological thesis with Rabbinic arguments pressed effectively into service.

[1] Card. Cajetanus: *Commentarium in S. Th.* III, Quest. xl, Art. 1.
[2] *S. Th.* III, Quest. xxvi.

The question might be asked whether Christ's priestly office is anything different from His other offices; for instance, from His office as the mystical Head of the Church. My answer is that the distinction is not clearly drawn anywhere, either in the Apostolic writings or even in the theology of St. Thomas. Atonement, mediation, sanctification, teaching, consoling, are all functions that may be attributed to priesthood. The definition of a priest, given in the Epistle to the Hebrews, covers all such beneficent interventions on the part of the God-Man. 'For every high priest taken from among men is ordained for men in the things that appertain to God, that he may offer up gifts and sacrifices for sins: who can have compassion on them that are ignorant and that err; because he himself also is compassed with infirmity.'[1] Christ is an entirely supernatural personage: 'Whom the Father hath sanctified and sent into the world.'[2] He is the great Anointed of God; His whole bearing, His whole presence, is that of a high priest; He is a priest always and everywhere.

There is, however, the essential, the inalienable act of priesthood, that of offering a sacrifice; and it is with that function of Christ I am concerned now, as in it we find the greatest assertion of the mystery of His Personality, what I might be pardoned for calling the juridical assertion. By the replacement of human personality in Christ by Divine Personality, He is a Divine Person with a power for created life and virtue, of infinite ethical value, since they are attributable to a Divine Person. Christ's Personality is distinct from that of the Father. Christ exercised highest virtue, highest love, in the death on the Cross, and He gave glory to God through His obedience, coupled with equality of personal rights with the Father. Theologians have gone deeply into the juridical question of the Atonement; their arduous labours make one point quite clear: Christian Atonement differs, *toto coelo*, from the instinct of atonement which is practically the common inheritance of mankind. It is not the physical death, the physical blood, that is the primary thing in the Christian Atonement; it is the great personal factor of God treating with God. According to Christian theology, far from there being 'a wantonness of blood', there is in the sacrifice of Christ a divine nicety as to the measure of the immolation. The Atonement is a moral claim, meaning by the word 'moral' juridical. No Christ-

[1] Heb. v. 1, 2. [2] John x. 36.

ian can exclude from his theology such thoughts on the Redemption as are based on the juridical claims of a Divine Person.

The difference of the Christian Atonement from merely human atonements—the Jewish not excluded—is beautifully put forward in the Epistle to the Hebrews, where the personal value as opposed to the merely physical value is so strongly emphasised. 'For it is impossible that with the blood of oxen and goats sin should be taken away. Wherefore when He cometh into the world, He saith: Sacrifice and oblation Thou wouldest not, but a body Thou hast fitted to Me. Holocausts for sin did not please Thee. Then said I: Behold, I come. In the head of the book it is written of Me that I should do Thy will, O God. In saying: Sacrifices and oblations and holocausts for sin Thou wouldest not; neither are they pleasing to Thee, which are offered according to the law. Then said I: Behold, I come to do Thy will, O God. He taketh away the first, that He may establish that which followeth. In the which will, we are sanctified by the oblation of the body of Jesus Christ once.'[1]

There is a further consideration, indispensable in this matter of Christ's Atonement: it concerns the additional sanctity acquired by Christ through the obedience of the cross. The treasury of sanctity that manifested itself in His wonderful life was not to be the price of our Redemption. There had been no juridical transaction between Divine Persons as to its moral purchasing power. The Passion, on the contrary, was made the price of our souls. The following passage of St. Thomas is very illuminating: 'The original sanctity of Christ's Humanity does not prevent that same human nature, when it is offered up to God in the Passion, being sanctified in a new way— viz. as a victim actually offered then. For it then acquired the actual holiness of a victim, from the charity which it had from the beginning, and from the grace of [Hypostatic] Union sanctifying it absolutely.'[2]

[1] Heb. x. 4-10.   [2] S. Th. III, Quest. xxii, Art. 2, ad 3.

CHAPTER XXV

The Man of Sorrows

THE incomprehensible refinement of a Divine Personality is not only the most enduring motive for Christian compassion for the crucified Saviour, it is also the explanation of the greatest of Christ's sufferings. None of us can fail to be deeply affected by the story of the Passion, if our minds are habitually occupied with the infinitely sweet perfections of the Son of God made Man. Compassion for Christ crucified will remain an actual living thing in human souls as long as the world lasts, chiefly because the Sufferer was an infinitely excellent Person. Christ's personal perfections of being were also the measure of His sufferings, both in soul and mind. For such a Victim compassion enduring to the end of time is not a fruitless or groundless lament.

It is the general Christian conviction that our Saviour suffered more than any other human creature on earth. St. Thomas himself adopts this view.[1] I must confess to a certain impatience with that inferior kind of spiritual literature that seems to enjoy horror like a feast, and which has a mania for accumulating horrors. The authors of such books would write, for instance, of ten thousand years in purgatory, with as much ease as of one year. Theirs is a type of religious mind, good in itself, but hopelessly insensitive to the rights of reason. So in this matter of Christ's sufferings, one has read books written by devout men in which the accumulation of pain in Christ's life has been done with a kind of mad recklessness, with utter disregard of the Gospel narrative or of theological principles. Besides being in extremely bad taste such accumulation defeats its own end: it takes Christ's Passion out of the human sphere, and makes it profitless to us as an example and as a consolation. The thesis of St. Thomas, however, that Christ suffered more than any other single man ever did, is common Christian sentiment, and it is wonderfully helpful in the struggle of life. 'From all these causes,' he says, 'it is clear that the pain of Christ was the greatest of all pains.'

[1] *S. Th.* III, Quest. xlvi, Art. 6.

It would be difficult to assign any single cause that gives to Christ's sufferings such proportions: there are many causes at work, coming from the complexity of His wonderful Personality. His physical torments would go a long way to make of Him one of the most ill-treated human beings, chiefly if they are taken in connection with the ingratitude and the treason that brought them about. But when all has been said, in order to give the explanation of how Christ's suffering was simply and absolutely the greatest, we have to fall back on the perfection of His hypostatically united nature. Christ's body was a miracle of perfection and delicacy. His soul was the finest instrument of feeling that ever was. On a body of such complexion, tortures like those described so soberly in the Gospel narratives would assume unwonted proportions; which sufferings no special heavenly consolations seem to have sweetened, when the pain was actually on Him. In His mind, He voluntarily admitted sorrow for sin, for failure in the spiritual world, and His keen soul became its own tormentor. In this matter of Christ's mental sufferings over the sins of the world there seems to be no conceivable limits. How much did He allow Himself to be invaded by that keen internal sorrow? 'Christ,' says St. Thomas, 'in order to satisfy for the sins of all men, took on Himself sadness, a human sadness that was the greatest, as an absolute measure, but a sadness that did not go beyond the rule of sound reason.'[1] Our Doctor makes another golden remark in connection with Christ's death: 'The bodily life of Christ was of such excellency, and this chiefly on account of Divinity united with it, that its loss even for an hour would be a matter of much greater sorrow than the loss of the life of any other man for any length of time.'[2]

The Passion of Christ ought to be a subject of tender contemplation, even for the most exacting and unemotional mind. There is no place in it for physical pain merely for the sake of ruthless contempt of physical well-being. We know that it is voluntary in the sense of its not having been the only possible device God had to redeem the world; yet that there is in it a divine adaptation of perfect means to an excellent end is made manifest by the choice God made of it to be the cause of our Redemption.

[1] S. Th. III, Quest. xlvi, Art. 6, ad 2.   [2] Ibid. ad 4.

The Happiness of Christ

IT would be a most ungracious and unnatural theology which would speak of Christ's sorrows without even mentioning His joys. The contemplation of Christ as the Man of Sorrows, if it were too exclusive, would become a positive heresy, as such exclusiveness would mean that Christ was the great sufferer by a kind of ruthless fate, the personification of the *Weltschmerz*, of the world's unspoken agony. With all our faith in Christ's vicarious Atonement; with all the literalness of inspired language, such as St. Paul's 'Him, who knew no sin, He hath made sin for us'[1]; with all the bitterness of His death,—it remains a theological fact that the element of joy in Christ's human life was immensely preponderant.

We must bear in mind that in Christ there was never any striving after greater personal happiness, no struggle to escape from unhappiness. He condescended partially to put aside happiness for a time; but there is never in Him the grim stretching forward to life and light that characterises the earthly hero. His mortality and passibility were temporary arrangements of a miraculous nature, and though the cessation of such an arrangement was to be in a sense Christ's human reward, it differed profoundly from our release from this body of sin, inasmuch as we are released from a fatal and universal law, whilst Christ's glorification was the cessation of the miraculous suspension of glorification. When Christ entered into that personal glory that was His birthright, He entered into it in a spirit of triumph, with 'greater honour,' as St. Thomas says.[2] But being the heir, not a stranger, it was merely 'a home-coming' when He received the totality of His happiness. The Christ of the Gospels is as much the source of life and joy to the millions of human souls that worship Him as is the Christ of heaven. He could be no such support if His mortal existence had been unalloyed agony.

The doctrine of St. Thomas as to the fulness and the permanence of Christ's bliss is most constant and most unequivocal. His soul enjoyed beatific vision from the first moment of His conception in

---

[1] 2 Cor. v. 21.　　　[2] *S. Th.* III, Quest. xlix, Art. 6.

Mary's womb. This state of blessedness was a most exceptional favour, one conferred on no other created mind. His beatific vision was immensely greater than the vision of all other created spirits put together. As an objection the Doctor suggests: 'What befits neither man nor angel, would seem to belong solely to God, therefore it is not becoming to Christ as man. But to be always in the state of beatitude befits neither man nor angel; for if they had been created in bliss they would not have sinned afterwards. Therefore Christ, as Man, was not in the state of beatitude in the first instant of His conception.' To which he replies: 'Since Christ was both God and Man, He had, even in His Humanity, something more than other creatures—that He was in the state of beatitude from the very beginning.'[1]

What beatific vision means as a source of happiness is, of course, incomprehensible. Now, though it belongs to the theology of St. Thomas to say that Christ put limits to certain of the secondary effects of that overpowering bliss, it would imply a contradiction to say that He did not enjoy to the full the blessed vision itself. He was absolutely *beatus* in that portion of His mind where there was the vision. Again it would be contradictory to say that Christ's vision was ever interrupted. One might as well think of an interruption of Hypostatic Union itself. Such interruption, far from being helpful towards man's redemption, would have lessened its power, as it would have lessened Christ's natural dignity and sanctity. Another consideration that finds its place here is this: beatific vision can never be anything but a source of happiness. All things seen in God are seen in their divine relationship, and as such they are good, and very good. Even the sight of a sinful world, as it can be seen in God's omniscience, could never be a sad spectacle—or, anyhow, a saddening spectacle—because the blessed vision shows that if a divine ordinance be transgressed by a creature in one way, another ordinance redresses the transgression. Christ could never be saddened from what He saw in the glory of the Father. But He had inferior orders of knowledge, and according to these His soul was made sad.

Many other joys there were in Christ's human life besides that sun of brightness high up in His mind, the vision of God. How could a life of consummate virtue and sanctity be anything but a long

[1] *S. Th.* III, Quest. xxxiv, Art. 4, ad 3.

spiritual feast? But the greatest of merely human joys was, no doubt, His own immaculate Mother, in whose company almost the whole of His mortal life was spent. It is certainly a great light in itself, in matters of Christ's Personality, to reflect that He who came to save sinners spent His life, a few years excepted, with one who was pre-eminently not a sinner. It all points to the same great theological fact, that with Christ the law of happiness is the dominant, the prevailing law, the law that is followed up as far as possible. The law of suffering is submitted to as an exception, and with a wise adaptation of means to an end, whilst the law of happiness is applied with divine generosity.

CHAPTER XXVII

Christ the Strong One

THE duality of natures in Christ, made so much of in our theology, has many interesting consequences. There is in Christ duality of spiritualness; there is in Him a created and an uncreated sanctity; and, besides, there is the saintship which is His own personal acquisition. Though He be the Son of God, sharing with God the privilege of matchless sanctity, He created Himself a sanctity of His own. He acquired sanctity, just as the son of an ancient family of inexhaustible patrimony might build up for himself a great fortune by personal initiative and activity, though he be the lord of an ancient heritage. 'And whereas indeed He was the Son of God, He learned obedience by the things which He suffered; and being consummated, He became to all that obey Him the cause of eternal salvation.'[1]

Christ practised saintship in an heroic degree. He was full of sanctity, He was infinitely remote from sin, through the very elements of His wonderful Personality; yet human sanctity brought Him all the terrible consequences and responsibilities of high sanctity in this sinful world. Infinitely holy from the beginning, He

[1] Heb. v. 8, 9.

had to be holy in a human way by mixing with ordinary humanity; but human opposition and sin, as well as physical suffering, became to Him more painful by reason of His own wonderful perfection of origin. Here was divine sanctity endowed with the power of human sentiment; here was human sentiment made more keen through the presence of the infinite Purity. There is nothing so tragic as the life of a man of superior intelligence and high resolve bent on doing some great work for the men who surround him, and with the concurrence of those that are to be ultimately benefited, but being misunderstood, misjudged, distrusted all the time by those very men. Of all tragedies it is the most bitter. Such was Christ's saintship; in Him there are unfathomable depths of tragedy. His native sanctity is like a fire devouring His soul; it feeds His zeal for the sanctification of man. 'And for them do I sanctify Myself, that they also may be sanctified in truth.'[1] Human blindness, human resistance, even human sin against the Holy Ghost, are to Him the occasions of acquiring personal sanctity. Catholic theology therefore understood Christ better when it endowed Him from the very first with every kind of spiritual gift. The human patience of Christ is so great, precisely because with so much native dignity He could share the difficulties of human companionship.

There is necessarily absent from Our Lord's life an element of preponderant interest in human biographies: viz. the internal struggle between good and evil, the sifting of motives, the growth of wisdom through failure of selfish motives and untimely efforts. The element of passion, in the ordinary sense of the word, is entirely excluded from Our Lord's character. There might be the danger, therefore, that His life should appeal to us less as a living fact than as an abstract ideal. Yet Christ's life ought to be our constant solace, precisely because it was so intensely human and so intensely heroic in its human virtues. We cannot of course think for one moment of moral struggle in connection with Our Lord's Personality. He never felt any dissensions in His mind or body. But there is in Our Lord's nature an element that made of His life the greatest struggle, the greatest tragedy. It was that contradiction between His own personal sanctity and His external surroundings. He was indeed the Son of God come down from heaven, to live

[1] John xvii. 19.

amongst short-sighted, prejudiced, ignorant, and sinful men; and He came to share, so to speak, their social position. There was the great contrast between this incomparable superiority and human inferiority. Yet, the moment He enters into the world, He identifies Himself with the men that surround Him. He is not as one living amongst men and yet picking his steps carefully, raising his garment lest it be soiled, and saying to all that are near, 'Do not touch me, because I am clean.' No; He walks bravely with the sinner and the traitor, with the coward and the fanatic, for they are truly His friends. Their friendship and their good will have become indispensable to Him, if His work is to have roots in the human race. This intimate contact between Him and the common man was a necessary element in the Redemption. How could man be sanctified unless his heart had been won by God? Our Lord had to enter into the lives of His followers; He had to admit them into the hiddenness of His own life. It is in this contact between highest sanctity and human commonness that we are to find that element of conflict which lends to His life its human interest. It is no doubt a spectacle for angels to see a creature of clay, such as man is, rise gradually to the spiritual plane, through a series of disappointments in the things he had set his heart upon. But what shall we say of consummate sanctity and highest spirituality giving itself to man as a friend, to be treated by him as a friend, in his own gross way of understanding and treating sanctity and spirituality? For we shall see how the Son of God treats with man on the footing of equality; how He never uses His omnipotence to precipitate a decision to overpower a mind with the impression of His own excellency. He is determined to let Himself be found by man, as no doubt any other way of convincing him would be neither so deep nor so lasting.

The great truths of sacred theology concerning the God Incarnate are sometimes considered to be mere abstractions, incapable of giving life and colour to Our Lord's Personality. Nothing could be less true. They all enter into the very life of Christ; they make that life one of palpitating interest, precisely because they give us the key to that incomparable superiority of His nature, which superiority is of all things the one element we must constantly bear in mind if we are to understand His life.

CHAPTER XXVIII

The Master misunderstood

IT is the penalty of all real greatness to be misunderstood. The great are such because they are above their surroundings, because they see farther or even differently. In every great life there is an independence of established ways and ideas. In Our Lord's life there is this evident sign of greatness. He is misunderstood; even His own did not understand Him. There are few things more pathetic than the conversation which St. Peter had with his Master just after he had been promised the keys of the Kingdom of Heaven. 'From that time Jesus began to show to His disciples that He must go to Jerusalem and suffer many things from the ancients and scribes and chief priests: and be put to death and the third day rise again. And Peter taking Him began to rebuke Him, saying: Lord, be it far from Thee, this shall not be unto Thee.'[1] We can easily imagine St. Peter, strong in the conviction that he had his Master's confidence, and that therefore he could do what no one else would dare, administer to Him a gentle rebuke. He draws Him aside and, no doubt after a very polite introduction, comes to the matter that weighs on his mind. He has a right to look after his Master's interests, and perhaps he understands them better than the Master Himself. Jesus listens silently, and when Simon Peter has finished delivering himself of his carefully prepared rebuke, He turns round and looks at the poor man with unusual sternness. Then He says: 'Go behind Me, Satan; thou art a scandal unto Me, because thou savourest not the things that are of God, but the things that are of men.'[2] No, Peter was certainly far from understanding his Master; with all his good will and good intentions, with all his loyalty to his Master, his mind was still moving on the plane of human expediency. The divine admonitions that follow sound very much like an answer to the remarks Peter must have made in his effort to dissuade the Master. 'If any man will come after Me, let him deny himself and take up his cross and follow Me. For he that will save his life shall lose it: and he that shall lose his life for My sake shall find it. For

[1] Matt. xvi. 21-22.   [2] Matt. xvi. 23.

what doth it profit a man, if he gain the whole world and suffer the loss of his own soul? Or what exchange shall a man give for his soul? For the Son of Man shall come in the glory of His Father with His angels: and then will He render to every man according to his works. Amen, I say to you, there are some of them that stand here that shall not taste death till they see the Son of Man coming in His Kingdom.'[1] This allusion to the Transfiguration, which was to take place a few days afterwards, and in which Peter was to hold such a conspicuous place, seems to be a reversal of Our Lord's feeling towards Peter, after the sharp rebuke. It is certain that His first reaction had been one of deep disappointment at being so misunderstood by those who sincerely loved Him and whom He loved with boundless generosity. There are other passages in the Gospels where Christ expresses grief, if not anger, at being so little understood. 'Incredulous generation, how long shall I be with you? How long shall I suffer you?'[2] The very men who come to Him with their sick to be healed doubt His power and His Mission. It might be said that the tragedy of the Gospels lies in that constant misunderstanding. There is a kind of ill will in Our Lord's surroundings which Our Lord compares in one passage with the naughtiness and the sulkiness of children playing in the market place: 'We have piped to you and you would not dance; we have lamented and you would not mourn.'[3]

Certain schools of religious thought in our own days take a pleasure in explaining Christ's unpopularity by political or social motives. Christ raised His voice against the rich and the powerful in favour of the poor. His unpopularity was that of a demagogue with the ruling party. Such a view is strangely superficial. Our Lord was misunderstood by His own friends more than by anyone else. He rebuked the poor as sternly as He rebuked the rich. Many did not walk with Him any more, saying, 'This saying is hard; and who can hear it?'[4] The hard words were anything but a revolutionary speech: they were the announcement of the Holy Eucharist. There was, in fact, not a single individual who had come into contact with Christ, with the exception of His mother, who at one time or another was not a prey to doubts as to His real mission and char-

[1] Matt. xvi. 24-28.   [2] Mark ix. 18.
[3] Matt. xi. 17.   [4] John vi. 61.

acter. His crucifixion was a scandal even to the most persevering friend. 'All you shall be scandalised in Me this night.'[1] Our Lord spared no effort in trying to gain the confidence of a few. Why is it that Our Lord had such difficulty in gaining a following entirely devoted to Him, when it is the achievement of any agitator to gather round him in a few days crowds of men who believe in him blindly, and are ready to die for him? There is not a trace of such over-powering ascendancy over men in Our Lord's life. Doubt, suspicion, diffidence, are on every side. Peter indeed boasts that he is ready to follow Him to prison and to death, but the Master answers his boasting with a sad smile.

'I am come in the name of My Father and you receive Me not: if another shall come in his own name, him you will receive.'[2] Leaders of all sorts, with human causes or human interests, coming in their own names, have indeed done what Christ could not do: they have won desperate followers. If the Gospels were the imag-ined tales of naïve men they would have represented their hero as a man of irresistible power over his followers; his manifold miracles would have been given as the explanation of a devotedness unto death on the part of the followers. Instead, we have miracles in plenty, but there are as many, if not more, signs of unbelief. The explanation is this: Christ had no human cause to defend; He was no partisan; He came, as He says, in the name of His Father, with the fulness of truth, not with a political or social idea. He came with all ideas, and it would seem that the ordinary human mind has diffi-culties in trusting another that is not one-sided, but complete and absolutely wise, taking in every view of things. Man easily follows isolated impressions and ideas, as an animal follows irresistible instincts; but it is only the highest enlightenment that makes man love faithfully the fulness of truth, the truth of God in its manifold forms and presentment. John the Baptist had no difficulty in getting a faithful following, in spite of his austerities; it was because he had a definite, an exclusive mode of life; whilst Christ required from His disciples every perfection of mind and heart. Man's loyalty is always partisanship; faith in Christ, on the contrary, is enlighten-ment of mind and charity of heart. To arrive at a perfect faith in Christ, man has to give up what it is most difficult to part with, his

[1] Matt. xxvi. 31.   [2] John v. 43.

partisan attachments. The Jews by whom He was surrounded were passionate partisans; everyone expected a Christ that would be the glorification and triumph of his own partisan ideal; but Jesus goes back to the fundamental universal non-partisan principles of life and sanctity, and He is met on every side with angry looks because He does not join in the race with the fanatic and the zealot. The Holy Ghost brings the Kingdom of God, not the triumph of the Jewish nationality. The Spirit of God knows no boundaries; He is the Spirit of the Greek as well as of the Jew; His is the only movement Christ came to establish. All popularities are popularities of parties; to substitute for party universal charity and love is the surest way to be misunderstood.

CHAPTER XXIX

The Christ Tragedy

CHRIST'S career has all the characteristics of a tragedy; He was born to be the consolation of Israel, and He proved to be the 'child set for the fall and for the resurrection of many in Israel, and for a sign which shall be contradicted.'[1] Israel had been living in the hope of a child conceived and born of a Virgin, bearing the glorious name of Emmanuel, to be a sign of God's omnipotent favour to His people in distress. But, like many other long-expected scions of ruling houses, He proved to be His people's misfortune and curse: 'His blood be upon us, and upon our children.'[2]

History, so full of the cruellest tragedies, has none like the tragedy of Christ. The hope for which Israel lived became its curse through that awful misunderstanding which the Gospel calls blindness of heart. St. Paul in the Epistle to the Romans has dramatised the terrible irony of events with the genius of a Sophocles: 'I speak the truth in Christ; I lie not, my conscience bearing me witness in the Holy Ghost; that I have great sadness and continual sorrow in my heart. For I wished myself to be an anathema from Christ, for my

[1] Luke ii. 34.   [2] Matt. xxvii. 25.

brethren: who are my kinsmen according to the flesh; who are Israelites: to whom belongeth the adoption as of children and the glory and the testimony and the giving of the law and the service of God and the promises; whose are the fathers and of whom is Christ, according to the flesh, who is over all things, God blessed for ever. ... What then shall we say? That the Gentiles who followed not after justice have attained to justice, even the justice that is of faith. But Israel, by following after the law of justice, is not come unto the law of justice. Why so? Because they sought it not by faith, but as it were of works; for they stumbled at the stumbling-stone, as it is written: Behold, I lay in Sion a stumbling-stone and a rock of scandal, and whosoever believeth in Him shall not be confounded. Brethren, the will of my heart, indeed, and my prayer to God is for them unto salvation. For I bear them witness that they have a zeal of God, but not according to knowledge. For they, not knowing the justice of God and seeking to establish their own, have not submitted themselves to the justice of God.'[1] But nothing shows more clearly the bitterness of the tragedy than St. Luke's picture: 'And when He drew near, seeing the city, He wept over it, saying: If thou also hadst known, and that in this thy day, the things that are to thy peace; but now they are hidden from thy eyes. For the days shall come upon thee; and thy enemies shall cast a trench about thee and compass thee round, and straiten thee on every side, and beat thee flat to the ground, and thy children who are in thee. And they shall not leave in thee a stone upon a stone; because thou hast not known the time of thy visitation.'[2]

It may be said with perfect theological accuracy that the primary motive of Christ's coming turned out a tremendous failure; a failure which Christ tried to avert with all His might. We are too apt to think that Christ courted failure in order that prophecies might be fulfilled; that His sacrifice on the Cross might become possible. No doubt it is difficult for our limited minds to see how an event which God has chosen to be the means of some great good does not become, through the fact of that divine choice, a necessary and unavoidable event, from which there is no escape; and if efforts at escaping it are made, they look very much like so many sham movements. As it was written that Christ should die to save mankind, we find it

---

[1] Rom. ix. 1-5; 30-33; x. 1-3.   [2] Luke xix. 41-44.

difficult to believe that His efforts to win the Jewish nation to His love were of tremendous sincerity. He is very persistent in reminding His disciples of this His failure, in order to teach them not to be discouraged at their own future failures in the Apostolate; in fact, the memory of his Master's failure ought to keep the Christian from being too self-confident even in his zeal for Christ. 'Amen, Amen, I say to you; the servant is not greater than his Lord; neither is the Apostle greater than He that sent him. If you know these things, you shall be blessed if you do them.'[1] 'If the world hate you, know ye that it hath hated Me before you. If you had been of the world, the world would love its own; but because you are not of the world, but I have chosen you out of the world, therefore the world hateth you. Remember My word that I said to you: The servant is not greater than his master. If they have persecuted Me, they will also persecute you. If they have kept My word, they will keep yours also.'[2] 'And when they shall persecute you in this city flee into another. Amen I say to you, you shall not finish all the cities of Israel till the Son of Man come. The disciple is not above the master, nor the servant above his lord. It is enough for the disciple that he be as his master, and the servant as his lord. If they have called the good man of the house Beelzebub, how much more them of his household?'[3]

In this utterance we have an allusion to one of the saddest instances of Christ's powerlessness against Pharisaical envy, and no doubt the sense of failure rankled deep in His heart. 'Then was offered to Him one possessed with a devil, blind and dumb; and He healed him so that he spoke and saw. And all the multitude were amazed and said: Is not this the Son of David? But the Pharisees, hearing it, said: This man casteth not out devils but by Beelzebub the prince of the devils.'[4] To have Himself recognised as the Son of David would have been Christ's triumph; to be the Son of David meant everything to the Jewish mind. But instead there is the other extreme, the lowest depth of moral depravity—to be an associate of Beelzebub. Confronted with such consummate wickedness of thought, Christ speaks of the hopelessness of saving such men. 'Therefore I say to you: Every sin and blasphemy shall be forgiven men, but the blasphemy of the Spirit shall not be forgiven. And

[1] John xiii. 16, 17.   [2] John xv. 18-20.
[3] Matt. x. 23-25.   [4] Matt. xii. 22-24.

whoever shall speak a word against the Son of Man, it shall be for-given him; but he that shall speak against the Holy Ghost, it shall not be forgiven him, neither in this world nor in the world to come.'[1] This attitude of the Pharisaical mind, even more than the death on the Cross, brings home to us the horror of the Christ tragedy. Repeatedly Our Lord makes it clear, both by word and deed, that He had it in His power to escape from the hands of His enemies, but nowhere do we find it said by Him that it was within His power to win His enemies to His love. He did all He could, and He failed. 'If I had not come and spoken to them, they would not have sin; but now they have no excuse for their sin. He that hateth Me hateth My Father also. If I had not done among them the works that no other man has done, they would not have sin: but now they have both seen and hated both Me and My Father. But that the word might be fulfilled which is written in their law: They have hated Me without cause.'[2] Twice St. Mark, when describing Christ's controversies with the Pharisees, hints at the feelings of this des-pairing sadness that clouded Christ's heart: 'And looking round about on them with anger, being grieved for the blindness of their hearts.'[3] 'And the Pharisees came forth, and began to question with Him, asking Him a sign from heaven, tempting Him. And sighing deeply in His spirit, He saith: Why doth this generation ask a sign?'[4]

The sin against the Holy Ghost marked, if one may use this expression, the limits of Christ's spiritual power: He shrank back helpless; He became its victim, because the Pharisee, confirmed for ever in that state of mental perverseness, became the direct author of His crucifixion and His death. After the resurrection of Lazarus, some who had been the witnesses of the miracle went to the Pharisees and told them of the miracles that Jesus had done. 'The chief priests, therefore, and the Pharisees gathered a council and said: What do we, for this man does many miracles? ... From that day therefore they devised to put Him to death.'[5] 'Judas there-fore, having received a band of soldiers and servants from the chief priests and the Pharisees, cometh thither with lanterns and torches and weapons.'[6]

---

[1] Matt. xii. 31, 32.   [2] John xv. 22-25.   [3] Mark iii. 5.
[4] Mark viii. 11, 12.   [5] John xi. 47, 53.   [6] John xviii. 3.

The sin against the Holy Ghost is one of the stark facts of the New Testament most deserving of the attention of the critic and theologian. It is a phenomenon that stands out in its hideous nakedness as prominently as Christ's Cross itself; with this difference however, that the Cross is surrounded with the halo of eternal hope, whilst the sin against the Holy Ghost is everlasting reprobation, begun here on earth. It made the Cross and got from it not blessings, but only curses. Blasphemy against the Son of Man was turned into praise of the Son of Man at the foot of the Cross; but those dark blasphemers against the Holy Ghost, the Pharisees and their confederates, blasphemed more than ever: 'And they that passed by blasphemed Him, wagging their heads, and saying: Vah, thou that destroyest the temple of God and in three days dost rebuild it; save thy own self. If thou be the Son of God, come down from the cross. In like manner also the chief priests, with the scribes and the ancients, mocking, said: He saved others; Himself He cannot save. If He be the King of Israel, let Him now come down from the cross, and we will believe Him. He trusted in God; let Him now deliver Him if He will have Him; for He said, I am the Son of God.'[1] This blasphemy is the strangest mental aberration: they admit the fact that He saved others, that He worked miracles; they make use of this uncontested power of His to deride His apparent present helplessness; the former signs of God's presence in Christ are now made the occasion of a satanic gibe: 'He trusted in God; let Him now deliver Him, if He will have Him.' From such perverseness there is no hope of return.

Chapter XXX

The Humane Character of Christ

CHARACTER is the one element in the human individual that gives power over one's fellows. It makes all other gifts useful; without it, the most brilliant mind is a mere toy in the hands of caprice. Character binds our various gifts into one mighty

[1] Matt. xxvii. 39-43.

organism capable of every effort. Take one of the most brilliant of human minds that ever was, St. Paul's: his intellect was of the highest rank, though at the same time its very boldness was a danger to its usefulness. But the one element that binds all his thoughts together is his intense earnestness and unselfishness of character. Whatever St. Paul says belongs to the permanently living literature of mankind, precisely because you feel underneath it all a most potent character, in whom there is not a single weakness.

So with Christ: there is in Him His human character. We cannot love Him with a lasting love until by meditation we have discovered what manner of Man He is. We know Christ to be the fulness of Godhead; we know Him to be the Wisdom of God. We know Him to be the Judge of the living and of the dead. We know Him to be the great wonder-worker. But all these magnificent, infinite attributes become a living, fascinating power to us only if we have understood His character. Without this understanding such colossal gifts fill us with awe rather than bring us consolation.

It is an old experience of mankind, this transformation of our judgment of character. You hear of a man who is making himself a name with his brilliant gifts, his great activities—perhaps in the political sphere. Looking at the man from a distance, as one looks on a stranger, those very qualities may irritate you. You think him haughty, selfish, unscrupulous, precisely because he is putting forward brilliant, dazzling gifts. Now if it be your good fortune one day to make the man's personal acquaintance, to be admitted amongst the circle of his friends, your prejudices will most likely disappear, because you then come to see the man's true character, you find out how his extraordinary gifts are reinforced by more solid qualities; how he is a patient human being after all; and the charm of his character makes you love the man whom those exceptional endowments had rendered suspect to you.

Now, even with Christ, there is what I might call the striking, the overpowering aspect of His Personality. It is built on such a massive scale. He is God; He is the Victor over Death and Hell. He comes in the power of His Father, with the angels of God, at the voice of the archangel, with the sound of the trumpet of God, to judge the living and the dead. His mortal life is full of mighty contrasts; His birth is amongst the angels; He is set for the rise and the fall of many. His death is tragedy on a colossal scale, with rent rocks, and darkness over all the earth, and the dead stirring in their graves. His resurrection is made known to the disciples by an angel whose countenance is like unto lightning. There is the danger of such greatness producing nothing but awe-inspired faith, when the proper and perfect attitude of Christ's disciple ought to be sweet and affectionate love, a friendship more gentle than the love of man for woman. And spiritual experience teaches that those only rise above mere wondering faith who have taken the trouble to make Christ's personal acquaintance; and thus have gained an insight into His intimate character. This they do by studying closely His sacred Gospels, trying to find out the real meaning, the real intentions of Christ, in every one of His deeds and sayings. The tears shed over the sorrowing widow who had lost her son, or the tears shed over the death of His own friend Lazarus, are as important to the comprehension of Christ's Personality as the miraculous Resurrection of Easter. The one makes Him glorious; the other makes Him lovable. Or, to keep to the Resurrection, Christ's interview with Mary Magdalene at the sepulchre, His sweet salutation to the holy women, are as important as the glorious and overpowering apparition of the angel that announced the great victory over death. They reveal Christ's character; they make the ineffably sublime most attractively human. Up and down the Gospel narrative there are those traits, those flashes of humanity, which reveal Our Lord's character, and which unite all the sublimities of His wonderful Personality in the one, sweet, most loving and most lovable Jesus of Nazareth—the city of flowers. It is a study which we have to do ourselves, which every Christian who wants to grow in the personal love of Christ has to take up from the start. Nothing can replace in our spiritual life the constant perusal of the Gospel narrative with a view to treasuring up the character traits of the Son of God. The Gospels themselves are written in such wise as to facilitate their study even by the simple and ignorant. They are a series of character sketches whose chronological order is made almost entirely subservient to the more important rôle of portrayal. It is a pity that in spite of the multiplication of excellent exegetical works our knowledge of Christ's intimate life does not grow apace. I am the very last man to withhold the due meed of praise from the results of modern scholarship, which tries to make the text of the Gospels clearer by submitting it to the ordinary canons of textual interpretation. Such labours have established more firmly the antiquity, authenticity, and majesty of the Gospels. At the same time, it has to be admitted that the text of the Gospels can fulfil, and does fulfil, its main mission without the elaborate apparatus of modern scholarship. The Evangelists give us a picture of Our Lord, such as they knew Him; and this picture every man, woman and child is free to behold. It would take too long to give here what I consider the character traits of Christ, scattered as they are throughout the four Gospels. I must ask the reader to do this for himself. Certainly nothing could be more profitable to our souls than to write out for ourselves such a collection of sayings and acts as would endear Christ to us.

The Holy Ghost Himself has given us the key to Christ's personal character in an immortally beautiful passage of the Prophet Isaias— a passage which has all the more importance as the Evangelist St. Matthew quotes it in circumstances that show well that in it we have the main elements of Christ's natural disposition. 'Behold my servant; I will uphold Him. My elect: my soul delighteth in Him. I have given my spirit upon Him: He shall bring forth judgment to the gentiles. He shall not cry, nor have respect to person, neither shall His voice be heard abroad. The bruised reed He shall not break, and smoking flax He shall not quench: He shall bring forth judgment unto truth. He shall not be sad nor troublesome, till He set judgment in the earth; and the islands shall wait for His law.'[1] In the Gospel this quotation follows an account of Pharisaical fault-findings, and Christ's endeavour to spare their feelings. 'At that time Jesus went through the corn on the sabbath: and His disciples being hungry began to pluck the ears, and to eat. And the Pharisees seeing them, said to Him: Behold thy disciples do that which is not lawful to do on the sabbath days. But He said to them: Have you not read what David did when he was hungry, and they that were with him: how he entered into the house of God and did eat the loaves of proposition which it was not lawful for him to eat, nor for them that were with him, but for the priests only? Or have ye not read in the law that on the sabbath days the priests in the temple break the

[1] Is. xlii. 1-4; Matt. xii. 18-21.

sabbath and are without blame? But I tell you that there is here a greater than the temple. And if you knew what this meaneth: I will have mercy, and not sacrifice: you would never have condemned the innocent. For the Son of Man is Lord even of the sabbath. And when He had passed from thence, He came into their synagogues. And behold there was a man who had a withered hand. And they asked Him, saying: Is it lawful to heal on the sabbath days? that they might accuse Him. But He said to them: What man shall there be among you, that hath one sheep: and if the same fall into a pit on the sabbath day, will he not take hold on it and lift it up? How much better is a man than a sheep? Therefore it is lawful to do a good deed on the sabbath days. Then He saith to the man: Stretch forth thy hand. And he stretched it forth, and it was restored to health, even as the other. And the Pharisees going out made a consultation against Him, how they might destroy Him. But Jesus, knowing it, retired from thence. And many followed Him, and He healed them all. And He charged them that they should not make Him known. That it might be fulfilled which was spoken by Isaias the prophet.'[1]

We know what is meant when it is said of anyone that he is regardless of his fellow man's feelings and interests. Inconsiderateness is the incapacity or unwillingness to admit that our fellow men are creatures of flesh and blood like ourselves; that the humblest of them, if their heart be crushed, will groan; and that from their flesh will flow, warm, red blood, if they be pricked, just as it is with ourselves. One can be so regardless from high motives as well as from low, but the motive does not change the case. One may be a 'bully' in the pursuit of offices and lucre; and one may be a 'bully' in the pursuit of an ideal, even a spiritual ideal. A man may become so absorbed in some spiritual scheme as to make other men, as well as things, subservient to it; making mere tools of them for the furtherance of his own purpose; keeping in view some general plan, while entirely regardless of the rights, the happiness, the needs of individuals. The Pharisee is an example. With him men do not count; it is the law, the ideal, the general result that is everything.

Now it is precisely in this that Christ differs *toto coelo* from that 'spiritual bully', the Pharisee. With Our Lord the ideal is identified with the happiness, the salvation, the well-being of individual souls.

[1] Matt. xii. 1-17.

This divine consideration both for the rights and possibilities of every human being is essentially His character. He does not force His disciples to keep pace with Him, striding on rapidly towards a high, abstract goal. Such may be the conduct of a human leader. Nor does He put before them anything too great to achieve. He only expects them to love Him, to be faithful to Him, and give faithful testimony of Him when the time comes. He rejects energetically any mere ideology; the ideal of a kingdom, the ideal of some great spiritual estate. His ideal is that they love Him, that they love each other, that they believe in His love for them. His Personality is the ideal. He considers that His life's work is well done, when they have come to believe in Him and to love Him. Most great men have failed in this respect. Their schemes have been their idols; they have utilised the best men merely as tools; and as a consequence no one remained to love them or weep over their death.

Christ is God indeed, Christ has all knowledge and all power; He has all things given into His hands. But all these gifts He uses only to give eternal life to the humblest and poorest, in order that He may be loved by the simplest, that He may strengthen the weak reed, that He may rekindle the smoking flax. 'Before the festival day of the pasch, Jesus knowing that His hour was come, that He should pass out of this world to the Father: having loved His own who were in the world, He loved them unto the end. And when supper was done (the devil having now put into the heart of Judas Iscariot, the son of Simon, to betray Him), knowing that the Father had given Him all things into His hands, and that He came from God, and goeth to God, He riseth from supper, and layeth aside His garments, and having taken a towel, girded Himself. After that, He putteth water into a basin, and began to wash the feet of the disciples and to wipe them with the towel wherewith He was girded.'[1]

[1] John xiii. 1-5.

CHAPTER XXXI

Christ's Place in Men's Conscience

IT is an indisputable fact that Christ has become part of the psychology of many different races; He has entered deeply into their mentality. This Christian ethos is more than mere religiousness; it is more than a grip on doctrinal theories; it is more than a group conscience; it is something intensely personal; it is essentially the consciousness of One outside the individual, yet deeply concerned with the life of the individual; of One who is an historic personality, and has at the same time the pliability of an ideal. No dream, even of a Celtic imagination, was less limited in its possibilities than is the Christ ideal of the Christian races. At the same time see the wondrous individuality of that ideal. Since the advent of Protestantism we may differ as to the practical means of approaching Christ, and renewing our own lives in Him. But as for their views of Christ, taken as a whole, there is little difference between Catholic and Protestant races.

It would be as stupid, as it is unnecessary, to minimise the differences between the mentalities, let us say, of an English evangelical and of a French nun. In religious temperament they are at the antipodes; yet in the love of the Master they are one and the same. No one would be so uncharitable as to suspect the evangelical Englishman of hypocrisy; no one would dream of accusing the sweet-faced religious in a French convent of insincerity. Temperamentally the two are worlds apart; at the same time, their life in Christ expresses itself in identical language. We have here a phenomenon worthy of serious attention: how Christ's Person has remained practically unimpaired in the Christian conscience in spite of that great upheaval of Christian sentiment, that great schism in the Church He founded, which is called the Reformation. If anything were required to show the extent of the hold Christ has on His predilect people, this circumstance would show it. For the breach between the Protestant and the Catholic mind is profound; it is almost incurable. Yet the gulf is not in what the Master is felt to be to man, but in the practical conception of what man ought to be to the Master. The French nun conceives herself to be Christ's bride, and she sacrifices herself even as Christ was sacrificed. The English evangelical thinks more of Christ's benefaction to him than of an equal return of blood for blood.

Various races have expressed Christ differently. This need not make us sceptical. There are such diversities and profundities in Christ's character as to warrant the most various expressions of His life. At one time His divine attributes will appeal more to the mind of man; the first few centuries are especially rich in instances of this. Then His crucifixion will be the most conspicuous feature of Christian contemplation; the Middle Ages lived on the height of Calvary. At other periods His personal love is the preoccupation of the devout. The best explanation of these varieties of approach is the ordinary psychological one: such views of Christ suit the temper of the period. Christ has all the elasticity of an abstract ideal; the created mind that conceives Him shapes Him to the image of its own higher and purer part. Nevertheless, in doing so, the mind holds more than an empty ideal, it holds a true substance, because Christ in Himself is all that it has conceived.

One of the results of a well-balanced religious education is to respect the way in which other souls love Christ, speak to Christ, and speak of Christ, whilst making use of one's own liberty to approach Him differently. There is no disloyalty in not joining in specialised views of Him, even if such views are for the time being the attraction and devotion of the greater number around one. Few there are who express to themselves Christ wholly; it may even be questioned whether anyone can do so. I mean expressing Him not in His innate, interior state of being—for no finite mind could do that —but expressing Him in that fulness, such as faith proclaims Him. There is nothing one ought to be more careful about than to accuse any Christian of holding an imperfect, a defective view of Christ. For no Christian deliberately limits Christ in his heart and mind. He grasps what he can; he depicts Him to himself according to his need and temper of mind. He hardly ever draws the line sharply. He feels that He is a Man, but a Man with endless reserves of the Higher Life, with the inclusion of Divinity itself. Even if the uninstructed were to affirm that he does not believe Christ to be God, I should still hesitate in my heart to believe him, and give him the benefit of the doubt. For in his ignorance, to deny that Christ is God is not quite the same as disbelieving the Incarnation; most likely, if it were put to him that Christ is God without ceasing to be man, this view of the Godhead, as a kind of glorious reserve in Christ's manhood, would express his own unformulated thoughts.

Christ could not be the living power He is without deeply modifying the ethical sense of the nations that worship Him. There are certain precepts which we all speak of as precepts of the Gospel, because they are so strongly emphasised in the New Testament. But precepts alone would not be enough to create a new and universal ethical sense. Ethical sense, in a healthy and normal state, gives peace to those that possess it and conform to it in practice. It is part of man's innermost nature, it belongs to the vital elements of his being. No set of precepts, however wise, could create the ethical sense. Precepts, in order to be living things, must be expressions of the hidden ethical sense of man; they do not cross his aspirations, they merely elevate them. Now, the lessons of history are that wherever the name of Christ is alive, there we find profound ethical assurance and certainty, besides ethical simplicity and directness, all of which results in great ethical peace.

There is, in practice, very little difference between the Utopian state of ethical perfection and evangelical perfection. The kindliest, purest, strongest man of the Utopian ideal is not kinder, purer, and stronger than the perfect disciple of Christ. Do we not all dream of Christian nations as living in simplicity amongst Nature's pure harmonies, and endowed with every virtue that comes, as it were, from close contact with Nature? Has not Christianity flourished most vigorously amongst the ethically healthiest races of the world, and is not decline in a nation's ethical health also decline in that nation's Christianity? All that ethical well-being is necessarily Christ's property: it is His most precious possession here on earth; it is part of His Kingdom; and He has proved Himself to be the Living God through the fact that He has grafted Himself so easily, and as it were so naturally, on the purest ethical sense the world possesses. I do not think that there could be a movement in the world more anti-Christian than that of separating the ethical sense of mankind from Christ; representing Christ as antagonistic to it, and trying to make it self-sufficient.

Christ is the King of Peace, because in Him man's ethical needs are satisfied. He has not brought a law only; He has brought more. He has brought life. It is very significant that the deepest laws of human nature—which are not so much laws as elements of life—have come to be considered as the elementary precepts of Christianity. We speak of the man who violates them in his own person as a bad Christian; and, as I remarked a moment ago, in practice there is no difference between the voice of Nature and the voice of Christ. In practice a man is acting against the precepts of Christ, not only when he does not forgive his enemy, but also when he is intemperate or lazy. The intensest human love, as well as the renouncement of all things sensual, is Christ's life; and nothing could be more hurtful to the cause of Christianity than to make of renunciation Christ's law, and of Nature's true and legitimate joys the world's law. They are both Christ's, expressing one and the same life in a variety of functions. The mystical nuptials of the cloistered virgin and the pure love of conjugal life are equally Christian in character, though they may represent a difference of spiritual perfection. The founder of a religion not wholly divine could not have hit on the secret of thus making Nature's laws in the conscience of men and women part of His own sanctity. He would have singled out one ethical point, one ascetical practice, as the special badge of his followers. Not so Christ; the Christ who has lived among the nations for centuries. He has become to them the fulness of every moral perfection, the ideal of every purity; He rebukes them in their hearts for every kind of transgression. Christ, and 'He crucified,' is to mankind profound ethical peace. If there is no peace for the wicked, there is no peace either for the man who has lost the just balance in the practice of good. The fanatic is just as empty of the peace of God as the profligate himself. There is no harmony in his soul; there is no joyfulness in his eyes, however good his intentions may be. He is without peace in Himself, and he is the enemy of his neighbour's peace.

It would seem almost impossible, humanly speaking, to have as one's ethical ideal a God crucified, without the danger of an extreme ethical severity, without a fanatical courting of the harrowing and the dreadful. Yet, Christ crucified has been a greater source of joyful peace than any other ethical ideal. This comes from the divinely rational measure of Christ's crucifixion. Christ's cross is the wisdom of God; its measure is God's providence. There is no wanton display of physical endurance in Christ's Passion; there is no in-human contempt for physical pain; but there is a strong, patient endurance of just so much pain as was indispensable to achieve a spiritual result. Every pang of that divine pain had its own object in view, and once the object was attained, the pain was discarded as a tool that burns the hand that uses it. Christ's Passion was indeed enveloped in the sweetness of God's Wisdom. Christ crucified is the source of the ever-refreshing stream of human life, because His crucifixion, taking place in the very centre, as it were, of God's wisdom and prudence, is an eternal delight to the minds that con-template it. It is the most wondrous proportion between means and end; it was Christ's highest moment of mortal and created spiritual life; and whilst His lips were parched with the thirst of His agony, His spirit was quickened within Himself, and thus refreshed it went forth into the world of spirits, to announce the good news of the Redemption to those spirits that had been incredulous in the days of Noah. Christ suffered, as a Divine Person ought to suffer, with patient wisdom, yielding reluctantly to the encroachment of pain on His own natural happiness; yet yielding bravely, because doing so meant salvation to the souls He carried in the bosom of His love.

CHAPTER XXXII

Christ and the World's Progress

IT would be the greatest theological mistake to consider Christ's Humanity merely as a vessel of rare material in which Divinity dwells in a state of repose, as in a consecrated tabernacle. On the contrary, the Humanity of Christ is raised through that sublime indwelling to the highest realisation of all the potentialities of human nature. Christ is manhood made exceedingly great in itself through the participation of Personal Godhead. Godhead has achieved in Christ such an elevation of humanity as to bewilder the heavenly intelligences. Any raising up, therefore, of mankind is strictly within the movement and the grace of Hypostatic Union. To confine this elevation merely to the internal graces, to the directly mystical part of man, would not do justice to the great fact that God became man. The advancement of humanity on every possible line of progress, spiritual, mystical, intellectual, and material, is the only true and adequate view of the practical meaning of the Incarnation for mankind. There is indeed in Christ's personal life a preponderance of the spiritual and mystical, a constant reminder of the one important thing—salvation of one's soul. In Himself He demonstrates that temporal failure is of small account in the great work of Atonement. But there is no condemnation of the material order of things; there is no spiritual or mystical onesidedness; there is with Him no such ascetical view of the life of sanctity as to make it unlikely *a priori* that a great temporal empire might be based on the principles of the Gospel—an empire whose practical administration would be impregnated with the Spirit of Christ.

No abuse of temporal things or of intellectual progress by man can ever counterbalance the fact that Eternal Wisdom and Power became Man, making use of temporal things and of a human intelligence; and therefore, through the infinite superiority of His one Personality over the whole human race, making His use of temporal things and His knowledge of created secrets an unassailable title to the possession of the earth. If the earth belongs by right to the best, who has a firmer hold on it than the One who is infinitely superior to His fellows? It is true that intimacy with, and love for, the mystical life in Christ frequently begets in simple souls a kind of suspicion of all temporal progress, as being a hiding and an obscuring of Christ's sovereignty. Such suspicions are certainly not the fulness of the spirit of Christian wisdom. Why should civilisation be a danger to the Christ ideal? The most Utopian age would still fall short of the human possibilities contained in the personal union of the Second Person of the Trinity with human nature in Christ. It is not at all certain that a lower state of civilisation is more favourable to the prosperity of Christian faith than a highly advanced civilisation. It would be very ungenerous of us to think that the Man-God would feel ill at ease in a world full of enlightenment and philanthropy. Some of us seem to have a lurking fear lest the civilisation initiated by Christian ideals should outgrow those very ideals, and that it should become greater than the Christ who founded it. This is a very ungracious attitude of mind, and one that nothing in Christ's mortal life, nothing in our Christology, justifies.

That Christ chose poverty, failure, and the Cross, is no indication that He abdicated that sovereignty over the world that is His from the simple fact that He is the one being in whom manhood is united to Godhead itself, through oneness of personality. In His teaching He refers to Himself as the King of the world, to whom all power has been given. His sayings concerning detachment from temporal things are such as might well be taken to heart by a director of big business, without such admonitions interfering with the man's efficiency. The eight Beatitudes are a practical code of spirituality for every conceivable state of human life and every sort of honest enterprise. Riches, which can so easily be an almost insurmountable obstacle to the acceptance of the kingdom of God, have become, in Christ, the object of a special act of God's power, to take from them their hardening influence: 'Then Jesus said to His disciples: Amen, I say to you that a rich man shall hardly enter into the kingdom of heaven. And again I say to you: It is easier for a camel to pass through the eye of a needle than for a rich man to enter into the kingdom of heaven. And when they had heard this the disciples wondered very much, saying: Who then can be saved? And Jesus beholding, said to them: With men this is impossible; but with God all things are possible.'[1]

It is true that Christ calls some of His followers to the imitation of His own intensely spiritual life—a life that discards as far as possible the use of temporal things. But Christian tradition has always considered such calls to be a special grace, a special vocation, and nothing warrants the assertion that it was Christ's intention that the majority of those who receive His name are meant to follow this more detached mode of life. Those who do renounce all things will always be, as they have always been, a very small minority of the Christian people. Above all, the practice of what is called evangelical poverty—i.e. of that external renunciation of temporal things— if properly understood, far from being an obstacle to the progress of human civilisation, has been one of its most potent levers of

[1] Matt. xix. 23-26.

action. It is a constant principle of our Christology that Christ of His own free choice adopted a life of comparative poverty and of exclusively spiritual powers. It was one of the many alternatives He could have followed. He had in Him such powers as would have made Him the first and greatest in every sphere of human power and influence. Hypostatic Union includes them all, and much more. The choice Christ made of what might be termed an exclusively spiritual career ought not to make us forget how much else there was in Him, not so much in a state of dormancy as in a state of expectation, to become active under other circumstances when the work of His spiritual Atonement would be accomplished.

CHAPTER XXXIII

The Power of Christ

CHRIST'S Person is the real inwardness of the Church. The Church, in the words of St. Paul, is 'His body and the fulness of Him who is filled all in all.'[1] All the powers of the Church, all her rights and duties, are conditioned by this Personality-view of Christ. The Church has no authority outside it; no mission besides it. As a matter of fact, Christ's Personality and His Church are inseparable; they are what is called in logic convertible ideas—one concept includes the other. The Church is not just an empire of which Christ is the King, because an empire may be composed of free men and slaves; the Church is the union of souls in Christ. There may be in the Church on earth administrative power, but this is conditioned in its operations and in its extent by the personal relations of souls with Christ. The power is given to Peter to win souls to Christ, and keep souls in Christ, and his power is so great precisely because the object of it all is so great—the restoration of all things in Christ.

If the power of the Catholic Church, or of the Papacy, were to exert itself on objects entirely outside that personal relation of souls

[1] Eph. i. 23.

with Christ, the abuse would very swiftly bring its Nemesis in the form of some great religious cataclysm. The nature of ecclesiastical power may assume a stern mood, but its sternness can never be anything but a reflection of Christ's own merciful severities. 'Behold, this is the third time I am coming to you: In the mouth of two or three witnesses shall every word stand. I have told before and foretell, as present and now absent, to them that sinned before and to all the rest, that if I come again, I will not spare. Do you seek a proof of Christ that speaketh in me, who towards you is not weak, but is mighty in you? For although He was crucified through weakness, yet He liveth by the power of God. For we also are weak in Him; but we shall live with Him by the power of God towards you. Try your own selves if you be in the faith; prove ye yourselves. Know you not your own selves, that Christ Jesus is in you, unless perhaps you be reprobates? But I trust that you shall know that we are not reprobates. Now we pray God that you may do no evil, not that we may appear approved, but that you may do that which is good and that we may be as reprobates. For we can do nothing against the truth, but for the truth. For we rejoice that we are weak and you are strong. This also we pray for, your perfection. Therefore I write these things, being absent, that, being present, I may not deal more severely, according to the power which the Lord hath given me unto edification and not unto destruction. For the rest, brethren, rejoice, be perfect, take exhortation, be of one mind, have peace. And the God of peace and of love shall be with you. Salute one another with a holy kiss. All the saints salute you.'[1]

Chapter XXXIV

The Finding of Christ

THE dominion which the Almighty gave to man at the beginning of all things over 'the fishes of the sea, and the fowls of the air, and the beasts, and the whole earth, and every creeping

[1] 2 Cor. xiii. 1-12.

creature that moveth upon the earth,'[1] is not only inexhaustible in its resources, but also unlimited in its possible developments. Mother Earth whilst feeding her children is not always equally known by her children, and perhaps the race of men that will know her perfectly is not to come for thousands of years yet; but if such a race actually does come, the earth it will tread will not be a different one from that on which we now move. Their dwellings will stand on the same ground as that dwelt upon by primitive man in his rude huts. Now this is a parable to convey the attitude of the human race, or even of Christian peoples, towards the God-Man, the Second Adam, the great foundation, as St. Paul calls Him, on which we all build up our spiritual dwelling. Christ is meant to be discovered by the world as the earth is to be conquered by man. We have to find out His treasures, His secrets, His spirit; and the success of that discovery has as many phases as man's conquest of the earth. There was never any intermittence in the earth's subjugation by man; but how different has been man's dominion at various periods! So Christ has always been possessed by man; but how different has been at various times that blessed possession of Him!

To some minds it may be a scandal to find Christ is loved and comprehended so spasmodically, with such variability; yet such is the fate of creation in general. Christ is God's great spiritual creation, more wonderful than any material creation; why then should we be surprised at the endless ebb and flow of the human mind and heart with regard to Him? He must be contradicted as well as loved. He must be misunderstood as well as hailed with Hosannas. He must be the sweet food of the world as well as the rock upon which men shall be broken. He is the fulness of God's creation; we go in and go out from Him; we find pasture in Him, according to our taste and talent. That continual presence of His spirit and truth in the Catholic Church does not alter the fact that Christ is man's conquest with a great variety of success; for even inside the Church the practical comprehension of His spirit, and the practical application of His great law of love, have, metaphorically speaking, their periods of savage primitiveness, and periods of high civilisation. Faith in Him is like the unchanging earth; growth in His holiness, with its gifts of wisdom and understanding, admits of

[1] Gen. i. 26.

endless developments, failures, and triumphs. History speaks of different civilisations, as well as of the differences between barbarism and culture. Some of the greatest civilisations seem to be older than all known forms of barbarism; nothing prevents our thinking in that way of God's great spiritual creation—Christ. The earliest record of man's conquest of Christ is one of high sanctity—the holiness of the primitive Church. There were other sanctities, or rather other periods of holiness—sanctity being essentially the same whatever its form, yet with differences as great as those between various civilisations. Oneness of spirituality is not a monotonous uniformity, and provided it be the same Christ, the same Faith, the same spirit of God, even the strictest orthodoxy will welcome any fresh manifestation of man's conquest of Christ.

Christ is not like those men—and heaven knows how many such there are of superficial character, who are seen through at a glance and make little impression upon their fellows; they are not the men that will ever be contradicted or misunderstood. Christ is the Man behind whose human countenance there is the infinite Godhead; the Man who speaks, not of the present hour only, but of the end of the world: 'And He said: So is the kingdom of God, as if a man should cast seed into the earth, and should sleep and rise, night and day, and the seed should spring and grow up whilst he knoweth not.'[1]

CHAPTER XXXV

Christ the Father of the World to come

CHRIST'S religion is indeed a religion of the present world; it has finality in this world, though it has not its ultimate finality here. It gives happiness here on earth, though the happiness it gives is not ultimate happiness. Such indeed are the advantages of Christian spirituality that none better could be devised for a race which would have no higher world to look forward to, as Christian ethics contribute to human life the highest sum of happiness. The

[1] Mark iv. 26, 27.

purpose of Christianity is sanctification, which means everything holy and true and beautiful. Its end is life everlasting; not that it has no other interests except those of the invisible world, but its sanctification is such as to bear everlasting fruits. If the invisible world were Christianity's first and last finality, there might be the danger of exaggerated other-worldliness. The end and finality of Christianity is a sanctity which must needs take into account the present world; while its ultimate result is eternal life.

It may be said truly that a desire for heavenly glory is part of sanctity. But it is not a part of the effort of sanctity—who could make an effort to ascend to heaven?—it is the natural consciousness that our present sanctity finds its consummation in eternal glory. This is why we find in Christian spirituality the double phenomenon of Christ being present with us, filling our hearts with His love, and of that kind of yearning for the absent friend whom we hope to find in heaven. No more incomplete view of Christianity could be given than to define it as a striving after a Christ who lives in the heavenly world. Christianity is life with Christ here on earth; and where highest sanctity has flourished, there has been the greatest actual presence of Our Lord. The question might be asked how, in practice, a religion would shape the minds and hearts of men if it had no finality in this world, but had it all in the next? To say the least, it would reduce everything human to the level of merely utilitarian means; it could not love anything here on earth for its own sake; it would be the dwarfing and warping of all human generosity; and no doubt with logical minds the disaster would go further still, as the conviction would grow stronger that man has no direct means of ascending into heaven. But such is not Catholicism. It is an effort at human spirituality, at human sanctity, at a perfection to be acquired here in this life. Its eternal results are not indeed a matter of indifference to the saint; they are of the utmost importance to him, for his sanctification is essentially the perfection of his own immortal soul. But it may be quite safely asserted that, even with the greatest saint, the thought of his going to heaven is only one of many, kept in its proper place by the more urgent need of doing the deeds of charity, of finding Christ in his own heart, of speaking with Him, and of being happy in His company. The thought of heaven itself has always been held as one of the main considerations which make the present life happy and perfect. It helps sanctity; but our efforts are not for the heavenly mansions, they are for sanctity. Over and over again experience teaches us that Christ's religion is a wonderful balance of transcendent philosophical wisdom: the crucified God teaches merciful tenderness for physical suffering; the Word who is in the bosom of the Father is the most perfect human being, reigning in heaven at the right hand of the Father; His religion is the religion of the present world's happiness. Besides His throne in heaven He has His real presence in the Eucharist; and the unsatisfied craving of highest Christian sanctity is not so much to find Him as to see Him, because sanctity has already found Him, but being of this world it has not yet seen Him.

The relation between sanctity here on earth and eternal life might be considered from various points of view. Just now I want to insist on the psychological aspect—I mean the attitude of the Christian saint towards the blessedness of heaven. It is certain that no saint has any experimental knowledge of what awaits him in heaven; his desires for heaven, whatever they may be, are not of the things he has tasted and wants to taste again; even when most intense, those experiences are immensely inferior to the real thing. To have a desire for heaven proportionate to the excellency of heavenly bliss, one would have to imagine one of the elect who has lived in heaven and come back to mortal life—a supposition that is evidently contradictory in its terms. It may be doubted whether it is at all possible to strive for an unknown thing; one might wait for it, wondering all the time what it will be, but striving for it with eagerness of mind and heart does not seem possible. This is why Christian sanctity is essentially an effort to possess Christ, to taste His sweetness; because, while He may not be fully known, He is not utterly unknown. It may be said that every stage of sanctity has a realisation of Christ's Presence that gives it there and then entire satisfaction. But heaven and its glorious mysteries are always beyond man's realisation. They are never his possession here on earth as Christ is. Christ is a kingdom within ourselves; heaven is a kingdom outside ourselves; and it is the inward kingdom that makes Christ's soldier happy in all his battles. I do not think a high spirituality is at all possible without that kingdom of God within us, whose peace surpasseth all understanding. To put it still more clearly, a spiritual system with no results in this life, with no gain in this life, but which would be merely an effort towards, and an expectation of, a life after death, would be a great psychological blunder. Our Lord's religion is no such failure.

CHAPTER XXXVI

Christ's Mortal Life and the Eucharist

CHRIST'S real Presence in the Blessed Eucharist and His continued Sacrifice on the altars of the Catholic Church stamp His Personality with an originality as great as is Hypostatic Union. The Christian Eucharist, under its twofold aspect of food and sacrifice, is an inimitable concept; this alone would suffice to put Christianity outside the categories of Comparative Religion. The Christ of the Eucharist has been made the subject of specialisation in theology. Scholastic treatises on the wonderful sacrament, and the not less wonderful sacrifice, are as comprehensive and as important as the treatises on the Incarnation itself. Here I am concerned with one aspect only of that great spiritual marvel: the relation between Christ's mortal life and His eucharistic life. All the moral perfection, all the sanctity, all the merit, all the atonement of which the God-Man is capable were consummated in His one mortal life. Our Redeemer is no exception to the great law of finality, which seems an inherent element of human life. How then are we to view this prolongation of Christ's presence on earth? How are we to view that endless repetition of His Sacrifice on the altars of the Church from sunrise to sunset, until the end of the world? The measure of our redemption was full when Christ had shed the last drop of His blood; why then this ceaseless repetition? It may seem a paradox, yet the truest way to state the matter is to say that the eucharistic renewing of Christ's death is a result of that infinite fulness of redemption that is in His mortal life. Because Christ merited infinitely, and atoned with a generosity superabundant, we have the real Presence, we have the daily Sacrifice of the Christian altar. The Eucharist is the Christian's greatest privilege simply because It enables Him to enter into direct and physical communion with Christ's life and death. And this privilege Christ merited for His faithful through the excess of His atoning love. To detach the Eucharist from His mortal life would be the greatest aberration in our view of Christ. In the very earliest controversies about Christ's Divine Personality, the orthodox theologians challenged Nestorius to explain the Christian Eucharist without Divine Personality. How could we eat the flesh of one who is not God? Between Hypostatic Union and Transubstantiation the relation is most intimate, and it would certainly imply a contradiction if a human organism that had not Divine Being were to be the supernatural food of spirits. After all we have here the *instrumentum conjunctum Divinitatis* in its highest manifestation.

Although we know little as to the aptitude which Christ's Humanity gained through its life and death, to be the Eucharist of the Christian people, yet the whole genius of our theology warrants the supposition that Christ became most eminently fitted for this rôle through His life and death. His mortal career gave Him consummate fitness, in every sense, to be the Author of life to souls. Now, as this life is essentially a personal relationship with Him, the great object of all the merit of His sanctity was union with Himself; He merited that we should be in Him, and He in us. The Eucharist is the grandest and truest result of His holiness, as it is the grandest and truest union with the Person of Christ. All the Sacraments derive their spiritual power from Christ's death. That one of them, instead of merely containing Christ's grace, contains Christ Himself, shows the wonderful efficacy of His death. In the Eucharist, the Personality, which is the pivot of Christianity, has become not only a centre and a source of grace, but a means of grace. The protestant argument against the Eucharist in general and the Sacrifice of the Mass in particular, being based on the all-sufficiency of the Sacrifice of Calvary, would be best met by emphatic insistence, not only on the all-sufficiency, but on the infinite superabundance of the Cross. To the protestant mind all-sufficiency applies to the work of Christ; it never means that all-sufficiency of the soul's mystical contact with the great sacrifice. We grant him the all-sufficiency he acknowledges; indeed we grant it more liberally than he; we grant the all-sufficiency of a work so great that it breaks its bounds, and becomes the all-sufficiency of a more real contact with Christ our Redeemer.

CHAPTER XXXVII

The Majesty of the Eucharistic Presence

PRESENCE means the existence of a being in a given part of the material universe. When we speak of presence we must of necessity imply a certain position or relationship with regard to a material world. If there were no matter, but only spirits, there could be no question of either presence or absence; there would be question only of distinct spiritual individualities, which would be neither near nor distant with regard to each other, but each one would exist by itself, having power to admit into or exclude from communication with its own intellectual life other co-existing spirits. Presence and absence are essentially and radically connected with space, and space is dependent upon matter.

Now, though a spirit could not be said to be present or absent, with regard to a fellow spirit, if they both remained outside the material universe, they are present or absent from each other in virtue of that material world. For one spirit may be in one part of the material universe, and another spirit in another part, in which case there is real distance between the two. But how, and why, is a spirit in the material universe when his nature is entirely immaterial? The answer is this. A spirit is said to be in a certain place, simply and solely because he exerts certain activities, produces certain effects, in that place; either on a material thing in that place, or even on the spiritual thing already connected in a similar way with that place. If the spirit stops exerting his activity in this way, this very cessation is in itself infinite distance from the spot where he was truly present the instant before. The spirit comes and goes, not through local movement, as a bodily thing, but through action or cessation of action on a bodily thing.

God and the angels are present in the way thus described. There-fore, if a spirit can exert his activities on various parts of the universe at the same time, he is really simultaneously present to those various parts of the universe. The more perfect a spirit, the more numerous are the parts of the universe where he can be present at the same time. God, being a spirit of infinite perfection, is accordingly simul-taneously present in every part of the material universe; as every part of the universe needs His sustaining power. The human soul, at least in its present state, is the last and lowest among the spirits. Its main activity is to give life to the body, therefore it cannot be out-side the individual body to which it belongs. So much for the presence of spirits. They can be really present to the lowliest sort of matter, and yet remain infinitely superior to it. They are not con-taminated by matter, but they invest matter with their sweet activity. Such a presence is a noble attribute of theirs; it is the majesty of their spirituality.

Coming now to the presence of bodies, their being present any-where in the material universe comes from their imperfection, not their perfection; for their presence is such that they cannot escape. A material thing must of necessity occupy one definite part of space in the universe, and when the body thus occupies one given place it cannot at the same time be outside that portion of space. It is the subjection of a bodily creature which is the slave of space, whilst a spirit is the king over space. It is true our glorified bodies in heaven, and above all the glorified body of Our Lord, are given wonderful powers of agility, so as to transport themselves from one part of the material world to the other with the rapidity of thought. This is a certain liberation from subjection to space. Yet even then it will be impossible for the glorified body to be at the same time in two places.

Now the wonder of wonders in the matter of presence; a majesty of presence almost akin to that of God's Presence, which is every-where and yet transcends all things, is Christ's Eucharistic Presence. Though Our Lord's body in its glorified condition has only one natural, spatial presence in the universe, viz. heaven; nevertheless God, in His omnipotence, has given It a supernatural power of non-spatial presence, which it enjoys at the same time as its natural spatial presence. As the only rule for this supernatural, non-spatial presence is God's omnipotence, there is no limit to the number of places in the universe where it may exert itself simultaneously. It is no more a humiliation than the omnipresence of God; on the contrary, it is a perfection of state too high for even angelic acumen. That God should dwell on high, and yet inhabit the lowest nature—this is the majesty of divine presence; it is first and greatest. That the Son of Man should have ascended bodily into heaven, and yet should be bodily present in every corner of the world—this is the majesty of the eucharistic presence; it is the second greatest presence, the merciful majesty of eucharistic presence.

Chapter XXXVIII

The Blood of Christy

ALMIGHTY God has made man's salvation and sanctification depend on the pouring out of the Blood of His only-begotten Son. Our Lord's life, up to the shedding of His Blood, was a life of immeasurable sanctity, a life of an infinite moral perfection. Yet it is not to any previous act of that wonderful career that our Redemption is due. The humility of His birth, the hidden prayer and obedience of His thirty years at Nazareth, the zeal and labour and bitterness of His public preaching, did not win the salvation of mankind. We know, of course, that all those years of Our Lord's life were infinitely meritorious; we know with less certainty in what manner those merits of the God-Man benefit the human race; we do know, however, that it is not through them we were bought back from the servitude of Satan. Our price, the price of our redemption, is essentially the precious Blood of the unspotted Lamb. The Blood of God's Son poured out like water, the Blood of God's Son drunk by man—this and nothing else was to be our redemption and our sanctification.

In making the Blood of His Son the price and vehicle of every grace, God has shown wonderful knowledge of the mysteries of human nature—if one may use these words with regard to One who has made human nature. Our blood is our human individuality. We are what we are through the communication of the blood of our parents. Our far-reaching differences of temperament and power come from the blood that flows in our veins. It makes us of what nature we are: apt for good, or prone to evil. Neither the philosopher nor the theologian can lay too much stress on the phenomena of heredity—phenomena that invariably point to the fact that it is man's blood that contains the germs of parental depravities or perfections.

In the Blood of the Son of God we have a Blood of absolute human purity—a Blood that carries no germs of evil, but is filled, through the laws of human heredity, with every perfection, because it is Blood from an Immaculate Mother. The Blood of Our Lord is precious, primarily on account of Mary's spotlessness, through the immunity from all concupiscence, which was Our Lady's privilege. That Our Lord's Blood should have been endowed with absolute human purity we owe to Mary. Had she had the seeds of sin, the *fomes peccati*, in her blood, Our Lord's Blood might still have received purity from above; but it would not have had human purity, it would not have been precious as a human blood. But now, thanks to Mary's spotlessness, Blood flowed in the veins of Our Lord that came down from Adam, and had nothing in itself except what was purest and noblest in the human race from the beginning. Besides this accumulation of human perfections, the Blood of Our Lord was made still more precious through the indwelling of the Spirit of God. It had divine heredity besides human heredity. The Spirit of God had filled it with the fulness of Divine Life, when it was already precious as the product of Mary's noble life. In this twofold heredity we have the key to the mystery of the Precious Blood; we know now why both its atoning and sanctifying power are infinite. St. Paul, in one of his pregnant sentences, makes it easy for us to remember the whole theology of the Precious Blood. 'For if the blood of goats and of oxen and the ashes of an heifer, being sprinkled, sanctify such as are defiled, to the cleansing of the flesh, how much more shall the Blood of Christ, who by the Holy Ghost offered Himself unspotted unto God, cleanse our conscience from dead works, to serve the living God?'[1] The Blood unspotted, filled with the Holy Ghost,

[1] Heb. ix. 13, 14.

poured out through that very generosity communicated to it by the Holy Ghost, purifies the conscience, not externally, but internally by raising it, ennobling it—in a word, by making it serve the living God.

The Blood of Our Lord is drunk by our soul in the mystery of the Holy Eucharist, is drunk by that highest and innermost part of ourselves, where spiritual temperament, or conscience, is to be found; and it gives to that part of our being, by a new kind of heredity, its own nobility; it makes us have God in our blood. When you are in contact with a Catholic people, with multitudes of the faithful (for the masses are the best guide in these things), you find a refinement of thought, a depth of feeling in things spiritual, a keen insight into heavenly matters, which are painfully wanting in non-Catholic populations. You ask yourself why there is this gulf between the mental states of two families of people, geographically and racially perhaps so near. There is only one answer possible: it is in the Blood—in the Blood that is drunk by the Catholic people, that has been drunk by their fathers and their fathers' fathers.

The Blood of Our Lord, wherever it is found, must produce great confidence in God; that is its primary and principal effect. Not only does it give us confidence through the belief that we have been bought at so great a price, but it gives confidence by a kind of heredity, a psychological transformation in the spirit that receives it. We become spiritually, supernaturally, sanguine. We expect everything from God, precisely because we have in our veins that precious Blood that makes the Heart of the Son of God throb with unlimited confidence in the goodness of the Father.

CHAPTER XXXIX

The Optimism of the Incarnation

THE fact of Hypostatic Union should alone turn the scales in favour of religious and theological optimism. How could mankind be a doomed race after the Personal Union of Divinity with even one member of that race? How could our prospects be hopeless when we consider that man is God, and that God is man? (With St. Thomas, I may be permitted to make use of these two convertible propositions in order to express the privilege conferred on humanity.) The Godhead of Christ is a fact of infinitely greater reality than all the accumulated sinfulness of the human race. A race in which a Divine Person could be fittingly enshrined through a union such as is Hypostatic Union could not be radically corrupt. It is true there is only one individual nature of that race thus united. All the same, with God as his brother, man's future must be a bright one. By all the laws of logic, an infinitude of good-ness, such as is the property of Christ's Personality, is for the human race—the race to which Christ belongs—a vastly more significant fact than that immense accumulation of moral deformities which make up mankind's history. If mankind has, as we know it to have, spiritual enemies of a higher order and of preternatural perverseness, one could hardly think of a more cunning way for them to wrong man than by blinding him to the fact of that overwhelming sanctity which is in Christ, and which can never have an opposing moral evil of equal size.

But there is more than the presence among us of a Brother who is a Personality of infinite perfection; He is not only a Presence that gladdens us by its glories, but He has come to us in the infinitude of His grace with unreserved determination to work out our salvation. He has come with infinite resolve to take away sin, to destroy death, to give life: 'Blotting out the handwriting of the decree that was against us, which was contrary to us. And He hath taken the same out of the way, fastening it to the cross; and despoiling the princi-palities and powers, He hath exposed them confidently in open shew, triumphing over them in Himself.'[1] Who would dare accuse the Apostle of using hyperbolic language? Such a deed, described by St. Paul as accomplished by the God-Man, changes for ever the relative strength of moral good and moral evil. Mankind's moral good, from the very fact of the Incarnation, is infinitely greater than mankind's guilt. All men put together could never commit sin that would be a dark blot as large in size as that bright sun—Christ's sanctity. But there is more than that: the sin of man has been posi-tively assailed by Christ; He has destroyed it in His own Body, He

[1] Col. ii. 14, 15.

has swallowed it like a poison, and, though He died through sin, a higher life for man emerged from His death.

We are all used from our childhood to these expressions of confidence; all the same, we find it difficult to live in the serene optimism of the Epistles of St. Paul. After all, we say, souls are lost even now, and perhaps in large numbers. How is such optimism compatible with that dreadful terror? Is not every preacher at pains to impress us with the terrifying number of those who go to perdition? Now I have no opinion as to the relative numbers of the saved and the lost. Our Lord has warned us in the Gospels against the presumption that wants to look beyond the practical issues of our spiritual life. But if one thing is clear to me it is this: that such losses, whatever their number may be, could never take away one jot or tittle from that glorious optimism which is the Christian's birthright. I am sure of the fact that God became man, and that He put infinite energy and sincerity into the work of man's salvation; of this I am sure with all the conviction of my Christian faith. If there are human beings that are lost, I feel certain that their loss is so well-deserved that it need not excite in me the least compassion: I know that if their salvation had been possible it would have been accomplished by the Redemption of Christ. I know that if there had been good will, such good will would have become an instrument of happiness in the hands of the God-Man. Simple souls sometimes ask the question: How is it that the elect can be happy in heaven for all eternity, if there be a correspondingly long period of misery for other fellow beings—the reprobate in hell? I know it is a difficult task to convince those good souls of the mistake of transposing their present kind feelings for every suffering creature into the spirit-state of eternity; but one thing is certain; with that perfection of human nature which comes from consummate sanctity, the elect in heaven enjoy a happiness that cannot be darkened for one moment by the thought of the miseries of the reprobate. Reprobation, whatever else it may be, is not a thing that need excite compassion. It ought to be our first principle, in thinking of reprobation, that it is a state so absolutely the personal responsibility of the lost, without its being anybody else's fault, that it excludes compassion even from the Heart of the Saviour. So likewise with the sanctity of the Incarnation and the concomitant Redemption. Its efficacy is not in the least diminished through the fact of the loss of souls, even under the new dispensation; and the possibility of their being lost under the very shadow of the Cross does not limit the extent of that truth constantly expressed in the scriptures: that Christ destroyed sin completely. It may be difficult for my finite mind to reconcile these two facts; but the efficacy of God's Death on the Cross is infinite. It is the one fact which I am exhorted by every Christian authority to cherish and to keep ever before my eyes. To say that Christ's work of Redemption is in any way a failure is downright blasphemy. We may say that Christ during His mortal life failed to win the hearts of His enemies, but it could never be true to assert that the eternal loss of any human being could detract from the efficacy of the grace of the Cross.

There are strange aberrations in the minds of even good people, which no doubt come from their being too much the slaves of imagination and sentiment. It is just possible that even a holy man might have his spiritual life darkened through the thought of the loss of so many, in spite of Christ's Cross, or even perhaps through an abuse of Christ's grace. I should begin by telling such a one not to be more sympathetic than the saints in heaven, who cannot be sad-dened by this thought, simply because they see all things in the light of eternal truth. Eternal loss is not meant, and cannot be meant, to be an object of compassion, precisely because it is irremediable; if its termination could be hastened by our efforts, compassion would indeed be well employed, at least spiritual compassion; for when it is a question of mortal beings pitying spirit-beings, ordinary tender-ness of heart would be a very unreliable guide. Let the holy man exercise his works of mercy towards people here on earth, who have it in their power not to go to that place of torment. Let him pity the souls of men because they do not make use of graces whilst graces lie at their door. Such was Our Lord's compassion. It may seem contradictory that one should be exhorted to have compassion on people who run towards their own ruin, when they have it in their power to run towards life eternal, and not to have compassion on them any more when they have actually fallen into eternal per-dition. A reader might accuse me of being like a man whose heart is filled with distress because he sees a friend gambling away his family estate, but who adopts an attitude of supreme indifference towards the poor wretch when once he is in the workhouse. But the comparison is not fair. The human soul that leaves this life outside the grace of Christ no longer belongs to redeemed humanity; it no longer belongs even potentially to the mystical Body of Christ; its severance is so complete that Christ Himself, who is the Head of the human race, cannot own it any more.

We are all familiar now with the beautiful doctrine that Christ is the Head of the Church. St. Paul's theology is summed up in it. St. Thomas Aquinas, however, goes one step further, and declares Christ to be the Head of all men. In the First and Second Article of the Eighth Question in the Third Part of the *Summa*, he shows how Christ is indeed the Head of the Church, in virtue of an actual influx of His spiritual vitalities into the souls and bodies of the baptized. But these considerations are followed by an article entitled 'Whether Christ be the Head of all Men.' I quote his own words; they are wonderfully liberal: 'Speaking universally and taking in the whole duration of the world, Christ is the Head of all men. But this has various degrees. For He is first and mainly Head of those who are actually united to Him in glory. In the second place, He is the Head of those who are actually united to Him through charity. Thirdly, of those who are united to Him through faith. Fourthly, of those who are united to Him only potentially, a possibility not yet realised, but which is to be realised one day according to divine predestination. Fifthly, He is the Head of those who are united to Him merely potentially, which potentiality is never to be realised: such are men who live in this world, but are not predestined to heaven. These, however, when they leave this life, cease absolutely to be members of Christ, because they are no longer endowed with the capability of being united to Christ.'[1] Reprobation is the only power that tears man away from the sweet possibilities of the Incarnation. The reprobate lacks even the potentiality of being Christ's; he is of another world altogether. Very wisely and generously St. Thomas makes that wonderful potentiality consist in two things only: the power of Christ, and freedom of will on the part of man: 'This potentiality is founded on two things: first indeed and chiefly, in the power of Christ that is sufficient for the salvation of the whole human race; then, in a secondary way, in the freedom of will.'[2]

[1] *S. Th.* III, Quest. viii, Art. 3.   [2] *Ibid.* ad 1.

Christ—the Pride of our Race

THE fact of an individual human nature being united hypostatically with Divinity is a spiritual achievement of the highest importance entirely on its own merits. In other words, our spiritual life is raised up wonderfully, not only through what Christ did and said and taught; but the mere fact of Hypostatic Union makes us live, if we are but willing, in an entirely new world. How could we ever take a merely natural view of mankind, if we are really convinced that there has been a Man who is God—God in the inexhaustible infinitude of meaning that is implied in that very word.

The great ones of mankind have been our benefactors, not only through the things they did; their very greatness is their highest benefaction, because it ennobles the race and gives it a renewed consciousness of its excellency. Therein no doubt lies the interest of every great biography: a great man easily becomes the friend and idol of the many of more humble calibre, to whom his external activities may have been of no practical profit. So with Christ: His being God, with all the excellencies and powers implied in the Hypostatic Union, His being so great, is in itself and by itself mankind's best treasure. The world's teeming millions are not too large an assembly for One so elevated; He stands among them as distinguished as if He were alone; He is so great that the hubbub of endless throngs could never succeed in drowning the least whisper from His lips.

The emotion of the pilgrim who sits by the Lake of Galilee and says to himself with such absolute conviction, 'On these waters Christ sailed!' is but a terrestrial counterpart of that much vaster astonishment that must fill the angelic mind when it looks at mankind: 'This is the race out of which there came God!' There is a quickening of soul and body in Christ's faithful through His grace that makes of such hero-worship a unique thing, a life-giving thing. Christ is indeed our ideal, but He is also our life. Yet even as an ideal, merely as the raising up of one human individual to an infinite altitude, Hypostatic Union ought to colour with optimism the whole outlook of mankind.

To ignore in practice the fact that we are dealing with creatures who, by the very laws of their nature, are the brothers of God, is the cruellest of all lapses of memory. However mean my neighbour may be, Christ's Personality is vast enough to reach out to him; just as the lowest of God's creatures may bask in the sun. That some or even many human beings have a special kind of relationship with Christ, through their baptism, does not supersede the more elementary fact that all men are of the family of which God came. It may even be said that Christ's activities, of whatever kind, in the world and on the world, are intended as means to win man to the practical realisation that He their God is amongst them.

Conclusion

IF the New Testament is to be taken literally; if its composition, like all great literature, is the offspring of the highest thought, then we are happy people indeed. The primary and fundamental condition of our life is its being involved in Christ's Divine and infinite Personality, instead of its being merely the result of a distant action. We may not be able to understand how we are thus involved, though, even to the least educated mind, infinitude in Personality cannot mean anything short of infinitude of comprehension, an all-embracing fulness. St. Paul's *pleroma* and 'in Christ,' if taken literally, ought to change our views on the nature of our spiritual life not less radically than the Copernican theory revolutionised the world's astronomy. According to the New Testament view of spiritual life, instead of Christ revolving round us, to warm us with His grace, we move inside Him, inside His Personality. Or, pressing this comparison from physical science still further, let us say that as the all-pervading ether penetrates and enfolds our planet and keeps it in the sun's radius, so likewise Christ through the infinitude of His Personality dwells in those who have their supernatural being in Him. 'And the glory which Thou hast given Me I have given to them; that they may be one, as We also are one. I in them, and Thou in Me; that they may be made perfect in one; and the world may know that Thou hast sent Me and hast loved them, as Thou hast also loved Me.'[1] Most of us love to look at the immensities of heavenly wonders; the fascination of the starlit firmament is among the oldest joys known to man. In the spiritual, in the mystical order of things we have something greater, something more novel than the revised astronomies of modern times; but something too that human thought is slow to grasp. No doubt the indwelling of the Father in the Son, and of the Son in the Father, easily becomes the delight of a mind prone to lofty speculation; none of us have any difficulties in giving literal meaning to words that convey such mutuality of indwelling. But we may think such words are to be taken less literally when it is our neighbour, our companion in Christ's faith, who is meant as being part of that wondrous system of divine en-circlement.

The glories of the Hypostatic Union are intensely human in their aim. Hypostatic Union is not a prodigy that appears in the spiritual firmament for its own sake: the blade, and the ear, and the ripe fruit, happy children and old men basking in the sunlight here on earth, make of the immensity of the sun a quite proportionate means to an end. Quite simply, then, if my mind delights in the sublime verities of Hypostatic Union, whilst I regard and treat my neigh-bour as though he were not God's brother too, the great mystery is for me but barren speculation. There is endless food for thought in the fact that the great mystery of God, the Incarnation, the secret hidden in God from the beginning, should be indissolubly associated with Simon the fisherman, with Mary the woman with the seven devils, with the Samaritan woman who had five husbands and a sixth who was not hers. They are figures and types of the humanity which will be Christ's conquest. 'Now Jacob's well was there. Jesus there-fore, being wearied with His journey, sat thus on the well. ... There cometh a woman of Samaria to draw water. ... Jesus an-swered and said to her: If thou didst know the gift of God and who He is that saith to thee: Give Me to drink; thou perhaps wouldst

[1] John xvii. 22-23.

have asked of Him, and He would have given thee living water. ...
And immediately His disciples came. And they wondered that He
talked with the woman. Yet no man said: What seekest thou? or:
Why talkest thou with her? ... I have meat to eat which you know
not. ... My meat is to do the will of Him that sent Me, that I may
perfect His work. ... Behold I say to you: Lift up your eyes, and see
the countries; for they are white already to harvest.'[1]

Sun of Justice, Word Incarnate, Thine is the blade, Thine is the
ear, Thine is the ripe corn in the ear. Grant me to love Thy harvest,
for which Thou shinest in the heavens in the glory of Thy Hypostatic Union; keep my feet from trampling on the rising blade,
whilst my intellect gazes at Thy beauty in the blue firmament; keep
my hands from plucking ruthlessly the ear that is whitening, whilst
I walk through life full of the rapturous thoughts of Thy being God.
Make me to understand that Thou didst become Sun for the sake of
the blade, that Thou seest the possibility of a true worshipper of the
Father where I harden my heart and turn away my eyes. May my
mind return thanks to Thee for the delights of the thought that
Thou art one with the Father, by generously accepting my oneness
with my brother in Thee; and let me make some return for my
glorious freedom to go in and to go out in the infinitude of Thy
most sweet Personality by cheerfully accepting Thy great Law, O
Thou most long-suffering of Friends,—'Bear ye one another's
burdens, and so you shall fulfil the law of Christ.'[2]

[1] John iv. 6-7; 10; 27; 32; 34.   [2] Gal. vi. 2.

THE VICTORY OF CHRIST

Of this book Abbot Vonier himself wrote in 1934 (the year of its publication), 'I am convinced that there is hardly a subject of Christian doctrine so appropriate to the needs of our day as the revealed truths concerning the defeat of the empire of darkness by Christ the King'. How much more that message is needed in our own time when people are disillusioned and downcast by the material and spiritual ruin following two world wars, and apprehensive of greater catastrophe in the future! The triumph of Christ is an important aspect of the Redemption, and this supreme achievement of our Redeemer is known only to faith. But theology can help to a fuller understanding of revealed mysteries, and in this vital matter of Christ's power over evil an increase of knowledge will give, not only mental satisfaction, but greater courage to endure the trial of faith. In the twenty years preceding the writing of The Victory of Christ *the Abbot produced a dozen books. His splendid optimism, therefore, is not the expression of uncritical enthusiasm, but the fruit of mature thought.—Editor.*

Imprimi potest.

MAURUS ETCHEVERRY, O.S.B.
Abbas Generalis

Nihil obstat.

GEORGIUS D. SMITH, S.Th.D.
Censor deputatus

Imprimatur.

✠ JOSEPH BUTT
Vicarius generalis
Westmonasterii, die 9 Julii, 1934

CHAPTER I

The Mystery of Christ's Glorification

THE victory of Christ is an integral part of the mystery of His glorification; it is that portion which has to do with the overcoming of all obstacles. We ought therefore to begin by laying down the general principles that guide our faith in Christ's permanent exaltation.

The glorification of Jesus Christ is truly a mystery, that is to say, a truth greater than the mind of man can encompass. Like all other mysteries connected with the Incarnation it is incomprehensible both in itself and in its setting. The fact that One who not so long ago walked on this earth, in all things resembling man, should now be in that state which is described as 'sitting at the right hand of God' is, of course, beyond human comprehension, for the exaltation is an infinite reality. Then the other aspect, the setting of the mystery, is itself a problem that defies all human anticipation and is beyond parallel. The *milieu* of the exaltation is the debased humanity from which Christ sprang, according to the flesh. It is true that Christ is raised above all whose names are mentioned in this world or the next; but being exalted, He has not left humanity behind, He has not shed it, He has not cast it away, but He has retained all His connexions with it. Humanity is as truly the setting of the mystery of Christ's elevation, as it is the setting of the Eucharist. Now I say that this is a fact that baffles us, but which we have to accept as containing in itself no contradiction: that humanity should apparently remain so unelevated when its Head, Christ, is surrounded with infinite glory. It is, of course, no greater problem than the co-existence of God and evil, or the simultaneous realities of God's omnipotence and man's abuse of the free will which the Creator has given him. Christianity is full of such paradoxes, and we must accustom our minds not to think less of the holy reality because the unholy one is by its side.

So Christ's glorification is for us the supreme reality which we see everywhere; it is not diminished through any denial of that splendour by the world: we know that Christ is in the glory of the Father. Our Lord's glorification is essentially to be conceived in terms of happiness for Himself. Through glorification He possesses in His humanity all that bliss which is due to Him in virtue of His being united hypostatically with Godhead. While on earth much of that happiness was withheld from Christ's humanity: how much we have no means of knowing. Now, there is no possible check to the inundating gladness of the Divinity. He is as happy in His soul and body as is conceivable. Any sadness or pain would be a contradiction of His state as the Son sitting at the right hand of the Father. Christians here on earth may represent to themselves Christ as a sufferer in soul and body. They may do this as a remembrance of all He endured during His earthly life. The sufferings of Christ may be said to haunt the mind of the Church, so vivid and actual is that memory. Christians may even think of Christ in the present as the One whose Name is blasphemed and persecuted, whose love is unrepaid and forsaken. The sorrow for this enmity and ingratitude of the men with whom we live may inspire in the faithful sentiments very near to sympathy, as for One who is bruised and neglected. The mystical sense of the devout Catholic enables him to feel all those things as if Christ were suffering in him and he in Christ. But it is, of course, beyond all doubt that in Himself, in His self-subsisting personality at the right hand of the Almighty, Christ is infinitely far from the contact of evil, sadness and woe. He is truly the King of Glory, and as such He rules the world with irresistible might, 'with a rod of iron', as the Scriptures love to put it.

Christ's glorification is the one article of the Creed that is to be held responsible for the Christian temperament. Our Christian outlook is what it is because we hold it as an obvious fact that Our Lord and Chief is in the glory of the heavens. Such was the mentality of the Apostles. The holy men whom the Son of God had chosen to be the foundations and the preachers of the new Kingdom went all over the world witnessing to the twofold vision of the abasement of Christ on the Cross and of the glory that followed: 'The ancients therefore that are among you, I beseech who am myself also an ancient and a witness of the sufferings of Christ, as also a partaker of

[1] 1 Peter v. 1.

that glory which is to be revealed in time to come.'[1] They announced to the world One whom they conceived as filling heaven
and earth with the splendour of His personality. Their distress was
great that men could not behold Him whom they saw so clearly with
the eyes of the spirit, that Jesus, whom God had exalted and who is
the judge of the living and the dead. They suffered in their hearts
for their newly-converted flocks, lest the dark horrors of persecution might obscure for them the vivid reality of the Christ in
majesty. For to keep this faith alive is the main task of the Christian
ministry. Glorification of Christ is the justification of the Christian
religion, even more than that religion's inward merit and perfection. To give Christians confidence in their faith, through the greatness of the splendours of eternity, is the task of apostolic men of all
times: 'You are of God, little children, and have overcome him
[Anti-Christ]. Because greater is He that is in you than he that is in
the world.'[2] Through our faith in Christ's glorification we are given
the power to rise superior to any might or pride that may try to
raise itself up in this world against God.

St. Leo has an eloquent passage on this Christian mentality in one
of his sermons on Christ's Ascension: 'Whatever in our Redeemer
was visible, passed into mysteries (through His Ascension); and
that faith might be nobler and firmer, sight was succeeded by doctrine, the authority of which might be accepted by believing hearts,
illuminated by rays from on high. This faith, increased by Our
Lord's Ascension, and strengthened by the gift of the Holy Spirit,
has not been overawed by chains, or imprisonments, or banish-
ments, or famine, or the sword, or the teeth of wild beasts, or
punishments invented by the cruelty of persecutors. For this faith,
throughout the whole world, not only men, but even women, not
only young boys, but even tender maidens, contended even to the
shedding of their own blood. This faith has cast out demons, driven
away sicknesses, raised the dead. Hence also the blessed Apostles
themselves, who, although confirmed by so many miracles, instructed by so many discourses, had yet been scared by the dreadful-
ness of the Lord's Passion, and had not received without hesitation
the truth of His Resurrection, profited so greatly by the Lord's
Ascension, that whatever before had caused them to fear was turned

---

[1] 1 Peter v. 1.   [2] 1 John iv. 4.

into joy. For they had lifted up the gaze of their soul to the Divinity of Him that was sitting at the Father's right hand; nor were they any longer hindered by the interposition of bodily vision from directing the glance of the mind to that which had neither, in descending, been absent from the Father, nor, in ascending, withdrawn from the disciples. Accordingly, then it was, dearly beloved, that the Son of Man, the Son of God, became known in a more transcendent and sacred way, when He betook Himself to the glory of the Father's Majesty, and in an ineffable manner began to be more present in His Divinity, when He became further off in His Humanity.'[1]

Christ's glory is immutable. It is now what it will be for all eternity: it acts now as it will act always. But not to all eyes is the glory manifested. To the spirits in heaven it has already noontide splendour; they see Christ exercising His power from one end of the universe to the other every hour of the present æon. To the believer on earth Christ is in the splendour of God, but neither with the eyes of the body nor of the mind can he see that effulgence. The infidel denies the glorification, and this denial makes him the un-believer he is. Christ, therefore, at the end of time will not receive greater glorification, but His glory will be manifested to all flesh. The great day of God is invariably spoken of as the manifestation of Christ's glory, as the unveiling of a wonder that existed and was present at all times, but was not seen by many. Not increase but manifestation is the difference between the state of Christ's glory to-day and that glory in the world to come. And what is true of Christ's glorification in general is true of Christ's victory, which is, as we have said, one portion of the belief that Christ sits at the right hand of God.

Chapter II

An Historical Survey of Christian Mentality

IT is clear to all that a victory truly so-called may have a double perfection, that of quantity and that of quality. A victory of quantity would only be complete when every individual being

[1] St. Leo, *Sermo* LXXIV (Migne, *P.L.* LIV).

who had been an opponent was brought into subjection by the victorious power. A victory of quality would be so complete a conquest of all opposing forces that it might be truthfully said that all hostilities were over, that all the resources of the enemy had passed into the hands of the victor, that there was no chance of a reaction, and that it would be a mere matter of time for the numerical results to appear.

Christ's victory has both these features, but not simultaneously. The victory of quality precedes the victory of numbers: the latter is delayed until a moment which is one of the Father's unrevealed secrets; the former is dated in a most precise fashion from the hour in which the Son of God rose from the dead; it is with us now, and will be with us for ever, to be supplemented in due time by the second victory, that of quantity. The Catholic mind is not indifferent to the numerical extent of Christ's achievement, but, in comparison with the qualitative intensity of the influence of Christ's work, quantitative extension holds a secondary place. We are not directly interested in the question whether many are saved or few, but we are most keenly alive to the intrinsic power of Christ's salvation, its having removed all obstacles in the way of those who want to find God. Is there any kind of evil which Christ has left unconquered; or, if He has overcome it once, has the dark power a chance of rising again? It is precisely that unrestricted universality of victory that appeals to the Catholic mind and makes the universality of mere numbers a matter of less importance. If all men were *de facto* saved by Christ, but were not saved in a supreme and irrevocable fashion from all evil, such salvation would be as nothing compared with the condition of those, many or few, who are delivered from evil, *überhaupt*, with no possible or imaginable limitation to their deliverance. It is therefore entirely in accordance with Christian sentiment to say that Christ would have laboured in vain had He left one single enemy unchallenged and unconquered.

The older and more permanent Christian sentiment is concerned more directly, though not exclusively, with that absolute kind of triumph of Jesus which is the mystery of His Resurrection. The earlier Christian period was the age when the fewness of believers was not a scandal to the Christian mind. The opposition between faith and unbelief was an evident opposition between life and death, between light and darkness. This opposition, to the mind of the Christian, did not make the light less enlightening, nor the life less vital. But even in those days of the clear ring of unchallenged redemption, the Catholic preacher was happy to point out the number of individual converts to the faith. He loved to expatiate on the manifest power of the Gospel that carries everything before it. The two African preachers, Tertullian and Augustine, each in his day, gave expression to that legitimate feeling of Christian exultation. The older writer, Tertullian, in his *Apology*, is astonishingly emboldened by the thought of the numbers of Christians then alive: 'If we desired, indeed, to act the part of open enemies, not merely of secret avengers, would there be any lacking in strength, whether of numbers or resources? The Moors, the Marcomanni, the Parthians themselves, or any single people, however great, inhabiting a distinct territory, and confined within its own boundaries, does it surpass, forsooth, in numbers, one spread over all the world? We are but of yesterday, and we have filled every place among you —cities, islands, fortresses, towns, market-places, the very camp, tribes, companies, palace, senate, forum—we have left nothing to you but the temples of your gods. For what wars should we not be fit, not eager, even with uneven forces, we who so willingly yield ourselves to the sword, if in our religion it were not counted better to be slain than to slay? Without arms even, and raising no insurrectionary banner, but simply in enmity to you, we could carry on the contest with you by an ill-willed severance alone. For if such multitudes of men were to break away from you, and betake themselves to some remote corner of the world, why, the very loss of so many citizens, whatever sort they were, would cover the Empire with shame; nay, in the very forsaking, vengeance would be inflicted. Why, you would be horror-struck at the solitude in which you would find yourselves, at such an all-prevailing silence, at that stupor as of a dead world! You would have to seek subjects to govern. You would have more enemies than citizens remaining. For now it is the immense number of Christians which makes your enemies so few—almost all the inhabitants of your various cities being followers of Christ.'[1] From the writings of St. Augustine one could cull a whole anthology of pregnant sayings concerning this

---

[1] Tertullian, *Apologetica*, xxxvii (Migne, *P.L.* I).

same power of Christianity in the political world. One of the best known is found in his *Enarratio*: 'Pay attention at least to the glory of Christ's Cross. Already that Cross which His enemies insulted is marked on the forehead of kings. The world has proved its power. Christ has overcome the world, not with iron but with wood: *Domuit orbem non ferro sed ligno.*'[1]

On the whole the Christian ages have thought more of Christ's absolute triumph, with the result that their faith has suffered no scandal either from the sins of believers or from the great numbers of unbelievers. The Middle Ages were certainly ages of faith through this very feature, the universal sense of Christ's supremacy. The external expressions of that sense are simply overpowering. They culminated in the position of the Papacy, in that unique phenom- enon which ill will describes as Papal imperialism; but which, if properly understood, is nothing else than the conviction shared by a whole civilization that all things are at the feet of the Son of God who reigns in heaven. The period we call the Renaissance is a great assertion of the final victory of Christ in the plan of the universe, and this assertion is made by Catholics and by Protestants alike, though in different ways. Protestantism narrowed down the triumph of Christ to the redemptive mission of the Son of God, and to the un- shaken confidence on the part of man that Christ's supremely effi- cacious Redemption was applied to individuals. Catholicism, on the other hand, went on, as it had done through the ages, giving a much wider interpretation to Christ's victory. The mind of Catholicism at that period is best expressed in the inscription which Pope Sixtus V caused to be cut on the ancient obelisk which by his order was placed in front of the Basilica of St. Peter, where it stands to-day: *Christus vincit, Christus regnat, Christus imperat, Christus ab omni malo plebem suam defendat.* 'Christ is victorious, Christ reigns, Christ rules. May Christ defend His people from every ill.' With all the losses which the Church had sustained through the Reformation movement there seems to be no diminution in the minds of Catholics of the unconquerable power of Christ. The Renaissance art has certainly done one thing magnificently, it has painted the triumph of Christ.

The question now arises whether we have kept that age-long

---

[1] *Enarratio in Ps. liv* (Migne, *P.L.* XXXVI).

sense of victory. It goes without saying that Catholics at least have never wavered in their faith; how could they, for Christ's triumph is an integral and indispensable portion of the Creed? The ancient Liturgy, which is exclusively a Liturgy of victory as we shall see by and by, is still in daily use without any modification; hymns of triumph are on our lips whenever we join in the official prayers of the Church. This however would not prevent sentiment and imagination from being moulded differently, so that, actually, with a theoretic faith that knows no shadow in Christ's glory, there may be much less of that exultation in the hearts of Christian men and women. It would be difficult to analyse the causes of so vast a change of mentality. Weakening of faith would be the obvious formula in which to state the origin of the sad malady; but a diminished faith is itself a result of other evil powers at work, not a cause that makes itself felt independently. The denial of Christ's position in the affairs of mankind is a comparatively recent phenomenon: we may assign to the eighteenth century the beginning of that hostile movement against the supremacy of the Redeemer. The whole of the nineteenth century and after has been the glorification of a civilization that boasts its independence of Christ, its complete self-sufficiency; in no wise will it acknowledge indebtedness to the Son of God for any of its achievements. This almost universal self-sufficiency of the political world has become a grave temptation for believers themselves. So we find everywhere instances of the apologetic attitude of Christians, of the feeling of inferiority at least in sentiment and imagination which takes many forms, from the speculative to the devotional. We have become unduly worried by the conclusions of the so-called science of comparative religion. We make of the problem of the salvation of infidels an acute theological question, much to the detriment of the doctrine of the salvation of the faithful through Christ. We too readily admire the works of the modern world, and we become unjust towards Christianity in our judgements of the Christian past. In politics we readily become the prey of slogans and we are led astray like sheep that have not Christ for their Shepherd. Not infrequently our devotional life reveals a lamentable ignorance or forgetfulness of the essential doctrines of the supernatural order as it is in Christ. The diminution of the spirit of worship in the world may be taken as the most evident sign of the decay of faith in Christ's supremacy. It is at the same time a cause and an effect. When men cease to praise Christ and to adore Him as their Lord and Master their feelings become more and more secularised; as, on the other hand, practical worldliness becomes increasingly impatient with all the duties of public and private worship.

CHAPTER III

The Fact of Christ's Victory

THE traditional Christian conception of the Son of God made Man is that of a Victor. This prerogative is a special glory, clearly definable and distinguishable from all the other privileges that adorn His Person. It is not quite the same thing as being a Redeemer or a Saviour, for both redemption and salvation might have been achieved without the specific element of victory. It is true that both redemption and salvation are very commonly spoken of as the victory of the Son of God, because in truth they were not brought about except through a great defeat of adverse powers, through a brilliant victory in the moral world. But this is not essential to the work of redeeming and saving. God might choose His elect, might save and redeem them, whilst leaving the hostile forces undisturbed in their position. But such has not been God's way through the mystery of His Son made Man. Not only are the elect chosen out of a world of evil, but that evil is overcome, is vanquished, so that it no longer has the air of a sovereign power. It might be put like this: redemption and salvation are a purchasing of individual souls from the thraldom of sin, a sanctification of individual souls who were in a state of spiritual death: victory is a successful assault on evil itself, it is the dethroning of the prince of darkness, it is a struggle followed by the discomfiture of an inimical power. The evil with which Christ had to deal was not only a disease, it was an enemy, one might say a personal enemy. It would be an inadequate concept of the beneficent action of Jesus Christ here on earth to describe Him merely as a divine healer of both soul and body. He was indeed a healer, of infinite efficiency; but the evil that met His eyes on all sides was more than bodily sores or spiritual diseases: He saw terrible, obstinate and resolute enmity pitted against Himself. We may, of course, speak of the whole of Christ's activity as a victory, from His prayers to His charity in forgiving His enemies when expiring on the Cross. But this would not give to the term 'victory' the technical significance it ought to possess when applied to the achievements of the Son of God. One is only a victor after a battle. Now Jesus Christ, besides His other great glories, has this renown, that He fought a great battle and remained the victor over a personal hostile force. We admit that the expression 'victory' may be largely metaphorical, but it is precise and exclusive in its meaning when applied to the Incarnate Son of God.

Another consideration is of importance here. The dethronement of the power of darkness could have been brought about by an act of God's omnipotence, just as, through omnipotence, all the elect could have been saved from a world of unconquered evil. Such a blow dealt by the arm of the Almighty would not have been a victory. It would have been the result of a divine fiat, as was the creation of light. But for a victory there must be a meeting of forces commensurate in some way, according to created standards. This truth is beautifully expressed by Pope St. Leo in one of his sermons on Christ's Nativity: 'For according to that fullness of time which the inscrutable depth of the Divine counsel ordained, the Son of God took on Himself the nature of mankind in order to reconcile it to its Maker, that the devil, the inventor of death, might be conquered through that very nature which had been conquered by him. This conflict, undertaken for our sakes, was fought out with great and wonderful fairness of equality; inasmuch as the Almighty Lord does battle with that most cruel enemy not in His own Majesty, but in our lowliness, opposing him by the very same form and the very same nature, which shared indeed in our mortality, but was free from every kind of sin.'[1]

Christian thinkers of the higher order are always careful in assigning the reasons why it was desirable that the Son of God should be made Man, should be born in poverty, should be persecuted, should be put to death on an ignominious gibbet, in order to

---

[1] St. Leo, *Sermo* XXI (Migne, *P.L.* LIV).

save mankind; though it is taken for an *a priori* certainty that innumerable other means were at God's disposal for the same purpose. The great Doctors speak with awe of that divine resolve, *divinum consilium*, that made God adopt the Cross as the instrument of salvation. St. Thomas Aquinas frankly admits that the real reasons of such a choice are beyond the understanding of man. It may be asserted, however, that the idea of victory is the richest and most satisfying concept applicable to this sublime matter. The Son of God put forth, not His divinity, but His humanity in the great struggle, so as to create an equality of conditions between the combatants. Of whatever kind His enemies were, to the very last they were not certain of His being the King of Glory; in fact, as the ignominy of His death became the more evident, their conviction that He was not God grew stronger. The ignorance of what Christ was in His deeper self made it possible for His enemies to pursue Him to the end in the hope of exterminating Him from among the children of men: 'For if they had known it, they would never have crucified the Lord of glory.'[1] It is certain that Christ's enemies had set out to destroy Him, to overcome Him. They wanted an evident sign that they were ultimately stronger than this mysterious and irritating personality. Crucifixion, if carried out to the full extent of its horrible possibilities, would be as loud a proclamation to the universe as human ingenuity could devise that, after all, the much-hated and dreaded man was nothing more than an ordinary mortal. From the point of view of Christ's enemies the tragedy of Calvary was certainly a pitched battle, and death won the victory. To the very last they dreaded a reversal of fortune, some unexpected act on the part of the wonder-worker, which would make His persecutors the world's laughing-stock. But St. Paul's words just quoted seem to give a wider application to that psychological state; the Apostle insinuates that the mightier minds of the evil spirits were also watching the results of the condemnation to death pronounced by Pilate. He speaks of the 'princes of the world' as being ignorant of Christ's true glory. This denomination, with St. Paul, is applicable to the unseen powers of darkness. That the Son of the Virgin was the object of determined hatred on the part of Satan from the moment He appeared in this world is revealed to us retrospectively by St. John in his apocalyptic vision: 'And there was seen another sign

[1] 1 Cor. ii. 8.

in heaven. And behold a great red dragon, having seven heads and ten horns and on his heads seven diadems. And his tail drew the third part of the stars of heaven and cast them to the earth. And the dragon stood before the woman who was ready to be delivered: that, when she should be delivered, he might devour her son. And she brought forth a man child, who was to rule all nations with an iron rod. And her son was taken up to God and to His throne.'[1] If the Son of Mary had been finally overcome by this array of hostility it would have been a defeat on His part. His enemies could have broken forth in shouts of triumph. But if Christ emerged untouched in His Person from the death struggle, His enemies had to consider themselves hopelessly beaten. The word 'victory' then is the only true description of Christ's unvanquished position.

The older Christian thinkers make of the circumstance that Jesus Christ's real nature was hidden from His enemies, human and discarnate, an inexhaustible subject of eloquence. They see in this terrible blunder made by man and Satan the true drama of Christ's fight. St. Leo has worked out the idea with astonishing fullness in his various sermons. The great Pope of the fifth century seems to take a positive delight in this aspect of Christ's Death, which we might call the 'surprise' aspect: 'And that He might loose mankind from the bonds of deadly transgression, He concealed from the devil's fury the power of His own Majesty, and opposed him in the infirmity of our lowliness. For if the cruel and proud enemy could have known the plan of God's mercy, he would rather have set himself to soften the minds of the Jews into gentleness, than kindle them into unrighteous hatred; lest he should lose the dominion over all his captives, while attacking the freedom of One who owed him nought. So he was cheated by his own malice: he brought on the Son of God a punishment which was to be turned to the healing of all the sons of men. He shed righteous Blood, which was to be a ransom and a cup for the reconciliation of the world. What the Lord chose according to the purpose of His own will, that He took upon Him. He submitted Himself to the impious hands of infuriate men, who, while busy with their own wickedness, were doing the behest of the Redeemer.'[2]

[1] Apoc. xii. 3-5.   [2] *Sermo* LXII, *De Passione Domini*, XI (Migne, *P.L.* LIV).

CHAPTER IV

The Inner Meaning of Christ's Victory

WE have proposed two possibilities regarding man's salvation from evil. The first is that God should elect His own from the midst of evil, without destroying evil as such. The second implies an act of divine omnipotence exterminating evil in all its forms at one blow. Neither of these possibilities did God choose, determining instead to save mankind through Christ, who destroyed evil, not by might, but by fighting against it as a hero. We can make a third suggestion, therefore, which has to do with the work of Christ Himself. This suggestion is often made in Christian literature, but no one has put it more beautifully than St. Thomas Aquinas, who speaks thus of the redeeming Blood of the Son of God: *Cujus una stilla salvum facere totum mundum quit ab omni scelere.* 'One single drop of that Blood can save the world from every kind of sin.'[1]

Christian theology, bearing in mind the supreme fact that the Redeemer is God, knows that the least human act on the part of Christ had value enough intrinsically to ransom man from the power of darkness, to overcome, in fact, all the world of iniquity. This assumption cannot be gainsaid. It was not necessary for the mere balancing of the ethical order that the Son of God should have taken upon Himself the great labours which He voluntarily undertook for our redemption. Nor would it be a satisfying statement to say that Christ did so much precisely with the intent that our redemption should be superabundant: that He added merit to merit, suffering to suffering, in order that there should be no possible lack of satisfaction given for sin. For we must remember that in very truth one drop of His Blood has inexhaustible power of propitiation for sin in all possible and imaginable emergencies. It has absolutely infinite redeeming virtue, and nothing can be added to that infinitude. We must then find another approach to the mystery of Christ's obedience 'unto death, even to the death of the Cross.' We must think not only of the abundance, but also of the glory of Redemption; of the Redemption that is at the same time a victory. 'To him

[1] In the hymn *Adoro Te.*

that shall overcome, I will give to sit with Me in My throne: as I also have overcome and am set down with My Father in His throne.'[1] The work of Redemption being by its very nature a victory, has for its principal result the exaltation of the Redeemer; a triumph that implies the exaltation also of the elect, which is in itself Redemption's first fruit.

Coming now to the actual relationship of effect and cause, it is, of course, impossible for man, without a special revelation from God, to know how the manner of Christ's birth, life and death overcame evil in all its aspects, and was that supreme victory which makes of Jesus the Lord of heaven and earth. For we must take it as certain that there was in the mortal career of Christ and in His death that very power which brought low all His enemies and raised Him to the throne of God: 'As I also have overcome and am set down with My Father in His throne.'[2] We may be made to understand how Jesus Christ through the manner of His life and death exercised the human virtues in the highest possible degree, how He practised charity with incomprehensible perfection; yet His behaving in so holy a way is not the explanation of His destruction of sin and Satan. We have to admit another element, quite mysterious; that of God's free determination that certain definite acts of the Son of God made Man should be the death-blow to Satan's power. Without this divine determination the theology of Redemption becomes wellnigh meaningless. We forget too readily that the Son of God came for a work that embraces the whole created universe; St. Paul describes it thus: 'In the dispensation of the fullness of times, to re-establish all things in Christ, that are in heaven and on earth, in Him.'[3] Catholic theologians, following in this universal Christian sentiment, have always maintained that in God's wisdom the way in which the Son of God died was the direct and unerring road to victory. There was in that course a divine appropriateness for so great an end: 'The passion of Christ had a result which none of His previous merits had, not on account of greater charity, but on account of the nature of that deed, which was calculated to bring about such a result.'[4] The *genus operis*, the special kind of deed done, is in the mind of St. Thomas Aquinas an indispensable factor in the

---

[1] Apoc. iii. 21.   [2] *Ibid.*
[3] Eph. i. 10.   [4] *S. Th.* III, Quest. xlviii, Art. 1, ad 3.

work of Christ's spiritual conquest. Christ is the instrument of God in this mighty work. Whatever He does or suffers is under the direct inspiration of the divine Spirit who moves Him for that very purpose. His human acts have an object far beyond their immediate moral excellency; they are the work which He came down from heaven to do, with a definite cosmic consequence that shakes heaven and earth. Through the Cross, Satan is conquered. Such is Christian faith; and it is a literal faith; that is to say, this physical reality, this stem of a tree cut from an olive grove, is to Satan more than the emblem of his defeat, it is the very weapon that defeated him, because God had so willed it.

In order to understand the psychological mystery of Christ's terrific struggle a knowledge of the psychology of the whole world of sanctity and sin is needed. There is in Christ's history, as narrated by the New Testament writers, a visible element of victory, of which the fuller exposition is reserved to a later portion of this book. The very fact that the Death of Christ was followed by the Resurrection shows clearly that the Evangelists conceived Christ's career here on earth in the light of a victory as astounding as it was unexpected. This manifest and historic victory of the Son of God has been chronicled in a human way, and it has the ordinary interest of human failure and success in the sense that we can follow the vicissitudes of fortune in this epic struggle. This palpable form of Christ's victoriousness is, of course, an integral and very important part of the main mystery of the divine triumph. But when we say that Jesus Christ in the acts of His earthly career fought a battle and won a victory, we mean more than the things man saw and the 'predestined witnesses' of the Resurrection and the Ascension beheld. Those very deeds of Jesus made Him victorious not only over His human enemies, but over His invisible enemies, over Satan and sin; it is as if on the Cross He had wrestled with sin personified in the prince of darkness. With regard to this unseen conflict we have to profess ignorance of all its phases. That there was such an assault on the forces of evil by Christ is beyond all doubt, and the deeds of His mortal life were so many tactical moves in the campaign. Christ not only merited the humbling of Satan, but He alone, by His own valour, humbled the rebel spirit in the dust; Christ proved Himself to be the stronger of the two combatants:

'When a strong man armed keepeth his court, those things are in peace which he possesseth. But if a stronger than he come upon him and overcome him, he will take away all his armour wherein he trusted and will distribute his spoils.'[1]

At the dawn of creation there was a battle in heaven between Michael and his followers on the one hand and Lucifer and his army on the other: 'And there was a great battle in heaven: Michael and his angels fought with the dragon, and the dragon fought, and his angels. And they prevailed not: neither was their place found any more in heaven.'[2] Nothing could be more remote from all our range of knowledge than the nature of such a war, spirit pitted against spirit. Still the reality of that decision of the sword of the spirit enters into the building up of our faith. We have to believe in the fall of the rebel angels. Similarly, the contest between Christ and Satan through the Cross has no parallel in our experience: but this is no reason for doubting it as an historic fact. The whole procedure of that contest between Christ and evil is a mystery, an event unfathomable by man. St. Leo again is eloquent on the recondite operations of the Saviour: 'The Lord then was delivered up to the will of infuriated enemies. In order to mock His Kingship He was compelled to carry the instrument of His death, so that the vision of Isaias might be fulfilled: "A Child is born to us and a Son is given to us and the government is upon His shoulder." (Is. ix. 6.) When therefore the Lord carried the wood of the cross, which He meant to change into the sceptre of His power, He appeared to the eyes of the ungodly utterly disgraced, but to the believers a great mystery was presented. For this most glorious victor over Satan, this most mighty conqueror of all adverse powers, carried the sign of His triumph as a brilliant ornament. He put on His own shoulders, armoured as they were with insuperable patience, the emblem of salvation, which was to be adored by all nations.'[3]

[1] Luke xi. 21, 22.   [2] Apoc. xii. 7, 8.
[3] St. Leo, *Sermo* LIX, *De Passione Domini*, VIII (Migne, *P.L.* LIV).

CHAPTER V

The Three Enemies

THERE are three hostile forces which Christian tradition considers to be the opponents of God: Satan, sin and death. Two of them are personal, Satan and sin, for by sin we must, of course, understand the sinner with his free act. Death is an impersonal evil, yet it is justifiably classed as one of the three foes of God. For this we have Scriptural warrant: 'And the enemy, death, shall be destroyed last,'[1] says St. Paul, speaking of the general resurrection. St. John, in the Apocalypse, describes death as an evil power that is finally cast into the place of reprobation. 'And hell and death were cast into the pool of fire.'[2]

It is not necessary for us to examine here the interdependence of those three evil realities. The very first page of our inspired Scriptures gives us sufficient insight into the close relationship between the manifestations of evil. Satan tempts man to sin and, the moment the rebellion against God is consummated, death becomes man's fate. Nothing more will happen on this earth in the matter of evil. The realm of evil was definitely established on the day of the Fall, through the triple tyranny of Satan, sin and death. Original sin makes all men to be radically children of wrath, and the actual sins of human beings, as they take place in the course of the centuries, are no new hideousness, but an imitation of the hideousness of that first sin. For the rebellion of Adam and Eve was the gravest sin ever committed by man: there can be no graver offence than the revolt of Adam against his Creator. Human sin cannot be defined merely in terms of human influences; in every human sin there is the diabolical element as it was in the first sin. Again, death is the work of Satan in a most direct manner. In uttering the great falsehood that disobedience could never mean death, but an illumination of the mind, the spirit of mendacity made of death the main object of his machination. He wanted man to fall into death: 'And the serpent said to the woman: No, you shall not die the death. For God doth know that in what day soever you shall eat thereof, your eyes shall be

[1] 1 Cor. xv. 26. [2] Apoc. xx. 14.

opened: and you shall be as Gods, knowing good and evil.'[1] So
Holy Writ makes the jealousy of Satan the origin of death. The Evil
One was envious of man's immortality: 'For God created man in-
corruptible, and to the image of His own likeness He made him.
But, by the envy of the devil, death came into the world.'[2] It may
seem strange to us who have so long been unaccustomed to look at
God's plans in their entirety to hear it asserted that the main
object in tempting man was to bring about his death. Yet it is not
without deep significance that Our Lord defines Satan as the arch-
murderer: 'You are of your father the devil: and the desires of your
father you will do. He was a murderer from the beginning: and he
stood not in the truth, because the truth is not in him. When he
speaketh a lie, he speaketh of his own: for he is a liar and the father
thereof.'[3] Satan's lie brought about man's death, and death was the
end he was set on. For although the interior sin of Adam was, for
himself personally, a greater evil than the physical death that was to
follow; from the point of view of Satan, if we may speak thus, death
was the more important result, for it meant the destruction of
a divine plan of immense greatness and beauty. Adam himself
recovered interior grace through repentance, but death remains as
a ruler; as St. Paul says: 'Death reigned from Adam unto Moses,
even over them also who have not sinned, after the similitude of the
transgression of Adam, who is a figure of Him who was to come.'[4]

Every Catholic writer on these dread matters is conscious of a
grave handicap: our contemporaries seem as incapable of taking a
rational view of evil as they are unable to grasp the nature of goodness. They readily accuse theologians of giving to evil an appearance
of majesty and power, when in reality it is nothing but an accidental
frailty of human nature. Dogmatists, it is said, in order to create a
raison d'être for the Redemption, have first to invent the evil that
would call for a Redeemer. But surely the ordinary human lapses
could hardly be a justification for so stupendous an arrangement as is
implied in the creed of the Redemption! Such facile assumptions
are much in vogue nowadays. But one moment's serious thought
ought to be enough to make us pause in our light-hearted diagnosis
of mankind's condition. It is evident, to begin with the obvious,
that we are in contact with only a very small section of human life.

[1] Gen. iii. 4, 5.   [2] Wis. ii. 23, 24.   [3] John viii 44.   [4] Rom. v. 14.

What do we know of the ebb and flow of the well-nigh boundless ocean of human wills, as they are in truth before God? If our experience in our very limited sphere is not of the worst, what of the unplumbed depths of the vast multitudes of human beings who in reality are as far removed from us as if they had lived and died a thousand years ago? God's eye alone can see all that happens at every moment, in every heart. What do we know of the past; what of the future?

Then there is this problem of the corporate responsibility of mankind. Do we really know how God looks at the men whom He has created? We ought certainly to be prepared for the assumption that to God mankind is a unity far beyond anything we can conceive. He sees in the last man that will be born on this planet the first man whom His hands created. The act of Adam is the act of all who are in Adam, the act of the human race which to God's eyes is a unit. The domination of Satan over that race is explained by the very first chapter of Genesis. For the order which God had created, for the order of innocence and immortality, Satan has succeeded in substituting the chaos of sin and death. The particular sins of all the children of Adam, which are all present to God's omniscience, are the result of that subversion of the original structure of grace and immortality. Sin can be spoken of in the singular, as *peccatum*, though its manifestations are more numerous than the drops of the ocean. It is always the original rebellion in one way or another, it is the stain upon our human family which is before God in its entirety as one moral factor. 'The next day, John saw Jesus coming to him; and he saith: Behold the Lamb of God. Behold Him who taketh away the *sin* of the world.'[1] The sin of the world constitutes, with Satan and death, the empire of evil. It is an active, organized and purposeful empire, because Satan dwells in sin and death. The three dark powers cannot be separated. To the end of history they appear in the same relationship in which they were first manifested, when Satan brought death into the world through the sin of the head of mankind.

[1] John i. 29.

CHAPTER VI

The Destruction of Sin

THE main doctrines concerning the destruction of sin by the Word Incarnate are known to all Christians. This dogma is so vast that the simplest statement of it is the truest. We say that God created the world, and these few words suffice for an adequate expression of the greatest of all facts—creation. We could not say more for this very reason, that all things without exception were made by God out of nothing. So likewise we say that Christ destroyed sin, and we have said everything. For truly Christ did it, and He alone did it, and He did it without leaving a single sin undestroyed. The very greatness of that work makes its dogmatic expression easy, and Christians in their millions accept this immense fact in all literalness. There can be no kind of transgression which has not been wiped away by the cleansing breath of Christ: from whatever angle we may consider sin, Christ's atoning power meets it. We may consider sin as an offence against the Divine Majesty, we may regard it as a disturbance of the moral order, we may look upon it as a slavedom of Satan, we may view it as a stain on the human soul or as a guilt deserving eternal reprobation: every one of these aspects is met by the omnipotent grace of Christ's redemptive power. It is therefore a logical consequence of this Faith among Christians to look upon despair as the worst of all transgressions. Nevertheless the subject of the destruction of sin by Christ is truly inexhaustible. Does not this doctrine fill our theological tomes? We believe in the remission of sin through Christ as we believe in the resurrection of all flesh, as we believe in eternal life; this remission is one of the basic facts of the supernatural world. My special object in this book is to bring home to the believer the implications of this great faith; to make him see what an overwhelming victory Christ gained when He brought sin to naught.

In order to understand this more clearly let us remember that sin, in its very essence, is the exact opposite of charity; that it radically destroys man's friendship with God and accordingly makes him unfit for eternal life. Remission of sin then, if it is to be complete, must mean this—that man again becomes worthy of God, worthy of eternal life, worthy of everlasting abiding with God in the splendours of Beatific Vision. Destruction of sin by Christ not only means a wiping away of guilt and stain, but it means a positive rebuilding of the broken spirit of man; man, through this Redemption is again made the temple of God. There is therefore in Christ's victory over sin more than a cleansing power, there is in it an infinite vivifying power, it is essentially a raising up of the countless multitudes of the spiritually dead. Great as is the vision of Ezekiel, it is only a pale image of the supreme reality of the might of the Son of God calling out of their spiritual tombs the souls buried in sin. The prophet beheld a limitless plain covered with white bones; he despaired of ever seeing those bones possessing life again; but what looked hopeless came to pass through the breath of the Spirit 'which came into them, and they lived: and they stood up upon their feet, an exceeding great army.'[1] Is it not a wonderful thought that every Christian may look upon the Saviour as being unceasingly in this very position of breathing life into the innumerable dead of the world? He has destroyed their sin, and He gives them life, and there is no end to that mystery of life out of death. For we must bear in mind that this incomprehensibly great work has been done by this one Person—Jesus Christ; there is no other agent, either principal or secondary, who has concurred with Him. If ever a work was the achievement of one man, this destruction of sin is; to His Incarnate Son the Father entrusted the work, to Him He left it to accomplish; Christ alone has trodden the wine-press of the world's sinfulness, and out of all nations there was not one with Him to help Him. This wonderful metaphor of treading the wine-press was at one time a very popular subject in Christian iconography; its comprehension was a great credit to the generations that loved to paint it and to gaze at it; they understood what we might call the exclusively personal factor in the work of the Redemption; for although we admit that it was in the power of God to destroy sin in many other ways, Christian faith most persistently holds that all the sins of men were put on the shoulders of the Incarnate Son of God and that He bore them on the Cross. He truly appropriates unto Himself sin and its effacement. It is therefore simply impossible to conceive of any

[1] Ez. xxxvii. 10.

personality to whom the appellation 'victorious' may be applied so truly as to the personality of Christ. The reiterated expressions of the Scriptures that God put the sins of men on Christ, that God considered Christ as being covered with the sins of mankind, are extremely significant; they point to a great mystery of appropriation by Christ. In the theology of the Incarnation we are told that the Second Person alone of the Trinity was made Man, to the exclusion of the First and Third Persons; it is the Son of God who bore our sins and died on the Cross, and Christians go to their Lord as to the One who single-handed has achieved this great victory. Was there ever a conqueror like Him? Was there ever a courage like His? What power of darkness could remain where He shows Himself? This atonement for sin in His own Person has given to Christ's humanity a new sanctity which is well described for us in matchless imagery by St. John in his apocalyptic vision: 'And His head and His hairs were white, as white wool and as snow. And His eyes were as a flame of fire: and His feet like unto fine brass, as in a burning furnace. And His voice as the sound of many waters.'[1]

This consciousness that Christ did the work of the cleansing of sin single-handed does not produce in the Christian mind a minimising of each man's burden or of each man's duty to make amends for his own sins; nor does it stand in the way of that very Catholic sentiment that Christians may be instrumental in atoning for each other's sins. It is quite in conformity with Catholic theology to speak of saintly men and women as being made victims for the sins of their brethren. Above all there is the rôle of the Virgin Mother at the foot of the Cross, entering more deeply into the mystery of the divine Victim than we can ever understand. All such participations in Christ's propitiatory work are finite, and, of course, necessarily presuppose the supreme propitiation of Christ. With the Son of God we enter into the region of the absolutely infinite, and into that sphere of atoning activity no creature, however holy, could follow Him. Whatever willingness and power there may be in Christians to work at the destruction of their own guilt is only a participation in Christ's all-sufficing and all-embracing satisfaction for sin. It is because the Son of God has destroyed sin so completely that we are able, each one in his own conscience, to repent and to atone for sin.

[1] Apoc. i. 14, 15.

In no other matter does Christianity show forth so clearly its unmatched superiority as in this, that liberation from sin is taken to be Christ's greatest gift to man. To keep alive amongst men a keen and practical appreciation of this liberation is the Church's greatest task, and in no other work does her unworldliness appear with such evidence. Life has so many external servitudes which press on men and from which they desire to be set free: there are especially the great political tyrannies of the world which may chafe the human spirit to the last extremity; racial liberations are among mankind's highest ideals, and man is justified in giving his all and his very life to set his people free from the oppression of a tyrant. To-day, as at all times, we assist at the working out of those irresistible ideals which are athirst for liberation. It is difficult for man, when carried forward on such waves of long-repressed enthusiasms for freedom from tyranny, to be made to feel that deliverance from sin is the most real freedom from oppression, far exceeding in importance any war of liberation known to history. Nothing could give us a clearer insight into the spiritual excellency of Joseph, the husband of Mary, than this, that the angel described to him at once the greatness of Jesus in terms of spiritual liberation from sin: 'And she shall bring forth a Son: and thou shalt call His name Jesus: for He shall save His people from their sins.'[1] We can readily understand the radical difference between a society that has a practical belief in the doctrine of Christ's victory over sin and a society that, either through indifference or through materialistic infidelity, has no such belief. A deeper psychological gulf than the one brought about by these two mentalities can hardly be imagined. A people that considers it to be a historic fact, transcending all other events, that Christ has delivered it and is delivering it from its sins, has within itself a fount of perennial joy which no amount of material wealth can ever replace. Worship of that great Redeemer naturally becomes the primary task of such a people, and its power of suffering adversity in temporal matters is well-nigh inexhaustible.

[1] Matt. i. 21.

CHAPTER VII

The Victory over Death

THE fact that men die must be considered as a most far-reaching thwarting of God's original plan. Death, in Catholic theology, is intimately associated with the original Fall and the sin that is inherited by all men. Man's rebellion in Paradise was a defiance of God, a demonstration that he would not die the death even if he disobeyed the divine command. So death has been considered by Holy Writ, not only as a punishment for sin, but also as an adversary of God's original plans. We may indeed find it difficult to see how an event like death should be an enemy of God; but if we bear in mind, as already insinuated elsewhere, that death was the one purpose our arch-enemy had in view when he tempted man, we shall accept more readily the literalness of Scriptural language that makes of death an enemy. It is as if Satan, by bringing in death, had made an assault on the very city of God, and had obtained possession of one of its strongholds. So we find that Christ's Resurrection from the dead is universally spoken of in Christian language as a victory over death. By this word 'victory' Christian tradition means more than the simple fact that Christ, in His own Person, rose from the dead; it means that death itself was conquered, nay, was put to death, in the energetic language of the prophet: *O mors, ero mors tua, morsus tuus ero, inferne.* 'O death, I will be thy death: O hell, I will be thy bite.'[1]

It is unquestionably certain that God attached the restoration of His primitive order to the resurrection of the promised Messiah; the death which man's rebellion brought about was to be swept away by the event of Christ's Resurrection. Here we may repeat what we have said in other connexions, that it would have been possible for God's omnipotence to heal this terrible disaster of death by a direct act of interference; but God chose another way, that the death of the One who by right was immortal, the Incarnate Word of God, should be the end of death. So we may say that if Christ in His Person had not been able to conquer death, death

[1] Osee xiii. 14.

would remain; but now He has destroyed it by showing in His own Person that death is not a permanent state, but only a passing condition. We are justified, I think, in assuming that when Satan provoked man's rebellion and thus brought in death, the evil spirit thought that God's plans had irretrievably miscarried; that death was a damage so great that it could not be repaired; that God Himself could not bring back to life that which was dead. It is certain that Christ's bodily Resurrection means infinitely more for the spiritual world than any other event except our liberation from sin; it means above all this, that God's power of making all things new, of restoring all things to their pristine perfection, is as great as His original power of creating all things out of nothing. The raising up of the dead is an entirely new manifestation of God's wisdom and omnipotence, more incomprehensible than the first creation of beings.

Now of this great divine deed of making all things live anew, Christ Jesus is the hero, as He Himself has said: 'And as concerning the dead that they rise again have you not read in the book of Moses, how in the bush God spoke to him, saying: *I am the God of Abraham and the God of Isaac and the God of Jacob?* He is not the God of the dead but of the living.'[1] So we see Christ making of the Resurrection a work which He came to do in the name of His Father; He had received from His Father the command to lay down His life and to take it up again: 'Therefore doth the Father love Me: because I lay down My life, that I may take it again. No man taketh it away from Me: but I lay it down of Myself. And I have power to lay it down: and I have power to take it up again. This commandment have I received of My Father.'[2] So likewise it is the will of the Father that sent Him that He should raise up the elect in the Last Day: 'Now this is the will of the Father who sent Me: that of all that He hath given Me, I should lose nothing; but should raise it up again in the last day. And this is the will of My Father that sent Me: that every one who seeth the Son and believeth in Him may have life everlasting. And I will raise him up in the last day.'[3]

In Christ's Resurrection there is the visible and the invisible effect: the visible result is that His bodily Resurrection is supreme and final evidence of His Godhead amongst men; the invisible

[1] Mark xii. 26, 27.   [2] John x. 17, 18.   [3] John vi. 39, 40.

effect is that death itself has been overcome in principle, a result that will be made manifest on the Last Day. In both senses Christ showed Himself supremely victorious. In our own days Christ's bodily Resurrection is still the world's great debate, because if it is proved that Christ rose on the third day Christianity is unassailable. Happily the world is full of excellent books setting forth the irrefragable evidence for that testimony. We may confine ourselves here to one aspect of this great victory: no kind of glorification merely of Christ's soul would have been truly a conquest; His body had to be alive again if His enemies were to be confounded. For like Satan of old in Paradise they had set their intent on death, that He whom they dreaded so much should no longer walk amongst men; that it should be proved that He was not God, but only man, through this very thing, death; for if He were God He certainly could not die. If He died, then He was not God. Thus did they argue in their jealousy; little did they care about His being a just man or a saint; they had no grudge against His soul, but they were determined to destroy His personality, His reputation, and death would do it most effectively. If the spirit only of Christ had been glorified, His enemies here on earth would have had every justification to proclaim Him a mere man; but if He rose bodily from the dead, then all their worst fears were true; they had crucified God.

If it be objected that those very enemies of Christ were also the men who did not believe in His Resurrection and that, consequently, they did not feel conquered by Christ, the answer is ready to hand. Whatever impression the news that the dead Galilean had appeared again may have had on the minds of those wicked men, one fact is clear, the Resurrection of Jesus is an event of overpowering certainty for the believers of all times; and it is the believer who, in the first instance, is interested in the news of Christ's victorious rising from the tomb. It is for him that this great testimony has been given. As for the unbeliever, he at least knows that faith in the Resurrection of Christ is universal. It would be difficult for us to say what was the real attitude of the men who put Jesus to death; but we cannot be far wrong if we assume that in their innermost hearts they admitted the fact of His Resurrection. They did not become believers and worshippers in the supernatural sense of the word; they lived and died as Christ's enemies. Such contradictions in the human conscience are only too possible! They died in their sin as Christ had foretold: 'Again therefore Jesus said to them: I go: and you shall seek Me. And you shall die in your sin. Whither I go, you cannot come.'[1]

Resurrection from the dead is the one classical testimony of Christianity. All other testimonies are subsidiary to this main evidence. In the first centuries of Christendom the Resurrection of Christ was almost exclusively appealed to by the preacher of the faith; even the miracles that accompanied the ministry of the Apostles were signs that Christ had risen. The same hierarchy of evidence holds good throughout the ages; whatever reasons for believing may be adduced by Christian apologists, they are only other ways of saying that Christ is risen from the dead, and there is power in those who invoke the Name of the King of Glory. Christianity, we may say, is essentially resurrectionist; its first and its last appeal to man is this: Christ is risen from the dead. The empty tomb of Christ is the temple of Christian truth; a Christianity that was not resurrectionist would be as different from what we Catholics know it to be as a people of slaves differs from a victorious nation.

We come now to the mysterious power which Christ's Resurrection possesses to conquer death in its widest meaning. Mankind is dead only provisionally; all men will rise again, will live again, and this in virtue of Christ's Resurrection: 'Amen, amen, I say unto you, that the hour cometh, and now is, when the dead shall hear the voice of the Son of God: and they that hear shall live. For as the Father hath life in Himself, so He hath given to the Son also to have life in Himself. And He hath given Him power to do judgement, because He is the Son of Man. Wonder not at this: for the hour cometh, wherein all that are in the graves shall hear the voice of the Son of God. And they that have done good things shall come forth unto the resurrection of life: but they that have done evil, unto the resurrection of judgement.'[2] In strict theology we say that Christ's Resurrection is the cause of the universal resurrection in a threefold way: it is a meritorious cause, it is an exemplary cause, and it is an efficient cause. Christ, through the charity of His death, merited His Resurrection, and in His Resurrection He merited the raising

<hr>

[1] John viii. 21. [2] John v. 25-29.

up of all men from their graves. He is, too, the pattern of that tremendous transformation, the passage from death unto life; what was done in Him will be done in all men. But theologians say more: in all these matters we are dealing with God; the Son of God is risen from the dead in virtue of His own power; He is not raised up; He Himself, through the resources of His own Personality, achieves that miracle; what He could do in Himself He can do with all flesh, all flesh has been given to Him in order that He should give life to it on the Last Day.

But the mighty circumstance that we are dealing with God in this matter of the Resurrection also warns us and puts us on our guard lest we think that we have said everything. We only know the outlines of this great mystery. Even if we had no means of bringing home to our minds how Christ, through His Resurrection, conquered death, we should still be full of enthusiasm for the great Victor. Christian tradition is so replete with the conviction that on Easter Sunday death was conquered, that it would be egregious temerity not to attach a literal meaning to those classic utterances regarding this great triumph of the risen Christ.

Chapter VIII

The Triumph over Satan

NOTHING is more familiar to Christian thought than the defeat of Satan by Christ; on the other hand, few theological subjects are more difficult to explain. Scriptural language, patristic teaching, liturgical formulas, all combine in creating in our minds the impression that Christ met a formidable adversary, a personality of evil, of immense power, and that He overcame that prince of darkness with finality. On the other hand, we find it difficult to put into exact theological language, first the fact of that evil spirit's sovereignty, and then the nature of the defeat which he is supposed to have suffered at the hands of Christ; for Satan and his followers are creatures of God; they depend entirely on Him for their very existence. Their diversity from other creatures, from the good spirits for instance, is exclusively one of will, not of nature. They are in opposition to God through their own free choice, but their natures are not altered; just as the essential nature of a bad man is not different from the essential nature of a good one. It is true that the fallen spirits have lost happiness, but this is only another way of saying that, through an act of will, they are in opposition to God. How then can it be said that Satan has power enough to be an adversary of Christ, when it is evident that by a single act of His will God could reduce the rebellious creature into the state of nothingness?

One of the explanations of Satan's sovereignty goes very deep, and it certainly must be considered as an essential portion of Christian thought. Through sin, man became Satan's subject. It is one of the tragic results of sin that it throws the sinner into the world of evil spirits, into the world of opposition. Through deliberate grave sin man abandons God, and this desertion does not remain neutral in its effects; positive hostile forces take hold of the rebel, through that hatred which Satan's perverted will exerts in every possible way. It would be very strange indeed if man, in opposition to God through an act of rebellion, could just remain where he chooses to remain, surrounded as he is with a world of active haters of God—the spirits of darkness—who are beings far superior to himself in power and in energy of hostility against God. This appropriation of sinful man by Satan is readily comprehensible: 'For by whom a man is overcome, of the same also is he the slave.'[1] Another glimpse is given us in the book of the Apocalypse, where Satan is described as the accuser of man: 'And I heard a loud voice in heaven, saying: Now is come salvation and strength and the kingdom of our God and the power of His Christ: because the accuser of our brethren is cast forth, who accused them before our God day and night.'[2] From words like these it is permissible to conclude that man's guilt gives a kind of juridical power to the devil; the power of the accuser, asking for punishment, not through a sense of justice, but from ill-will towards man. So it is said in theology that the sin of man gives Satan a hold over man, that Satan's tyranny is one of the punishments due to sin. We have, of course, to avoid anything that might have the appearance of juridical deal-

[1] 2 Peter ii. 19. [2] Apoc. xii. 10.

ings between God and Satan, as if on a footing of equality. God owes nothing to Satan, and the price of the Redemption is not paid to Satan but to God. But this much we may admit, and it will be sufficient to give a meaning to much of Christian language, that the reprobate spirit is clamouring for the exercise of God's justice, as he himself is condemned by that same justice. But when all that we can say with safety has been said, we have to grant that the words of the inspired books, as well as the current language of Christian antiquity and of ceremonial liturgy, point to a domination of mankind by Satan which is like the oppression of a human tyrant over his fellow-men. Christian language and sentiment in this matter are realistic in the extreme.

How, then, are we to visualise the breaking of that power by Christ? We can, of course, always say that Our Lord merited for man, by His deeds of sanctity, the destruction of the empire of evil. But the whole tenor of inspired literature leads us to think of a more immediate, more personal combat between Christ and Satan, a conflict adumbrated by the temptation in the desert after the fast of forty days. The *vade retro, Satana,* that concluded that encounter was to be completed by a blow from the shoulder of such vehemence that Satan reeled and never rose again. The personal power of Our Lord over the demons in His public life, His irresistible influence against which they cried out, calling it a 'torment,' shows that there was more than a moral command: there was a continuous pressure of the advancing victor: 'And behold they cried out, saying: What have we to do with Thee, Jesus, Son of God? Art Thou come hither to torment us before the time?'[1] 'And crying with a loud voice, he said: What have I to do with Thee, Jesus, the Son of the Most High God? I adjure Thee by God that Thou torment me not.'[2] 'And when he saw Jesus, he fell down before Him. And crying out with a loud voice, he said: What have I to do with Thee, Jesus, Son of the Most High God? I beseech Thee do not torment me.'[3] Here was a battle of the spirit, Christ's spirit being pitted against the proud mind of Satan. But it was on the Cross that the main action was fought out, when Christ made Himself obedient to the extremity of an ignominious end.

Christian tradition has it that the prince of darkness knows of his

[1] Matt. viii. 29.   [2] Mark v. 7.   [3] Luke viii. 28.

complete discomfiture; he knows that his cause is irremediably lost. It is therefore the Christian's privilege to consider himself in every way stronger than Satan, to have no kind of fear in the presence of unseen enemies. The contempt of the Saints for the devil is strangely at variance with the diffidence and the humility of those faithful servants of God. To make fun of Satan is one of the healthy manifestations of Catholic sentiment. It is only the unobservant who could not see the full meaning of that truly Catholic liberty to make the devil appear ridiculous. Yet the terrors of sombre spirits fill the unregenerate world; although actual devil worship may be confined to comparatively small sections of mankind, the worship of evil forces is widespread on the globe. The Christian Faith and subjection to Satan have become, through Christ's victory, an antithesis. They exclude each other as day and night, not only in purpose but also in actual life. The prince of darkness has no kind of lien over the Christian soul: he can neither hurt it nor seduce it. Through the virtue of our Baptism we enter into that implacable opposition which exists between Christ and Belial: 'But the things which the heathens sacrifice, they sacrifice to devils and not to God. And I would not that you should be made partakers with devils. You cannot drink the chalice of the Lord and the chalice of devils: you cannot be partakers of the table of the Lord and of the table of devils.'[1] There is a significant expression in St. Paul's Epistle to the Romans: 'And the God of peace crush Satan under your feet speedily.'[2] The image of St. Michael with the Dragon under his feet is familiar to all of us, but St. Paul's bold words give us the right to emulate that angelic gesture of victory. Such power, of course, comes to us only from God; nevertheless it is in us, we are enabled through the grace given to us in Baptism to trample on the spirit of darkness.

So vast a subject was bound to figure largely in patristic thought. We have in fact endless allusions to this discomfiture of Satan in the writings and sermons of the Fathers. What I have already called the 'surprise' aspect of the contest is most frequently touched upon in this voluminous literature. St. Augustine is never more eloquent or dramatic than when he is launched on this deep problem: 'It was necessary that Christ should come in hiddenness, so that He might

---

[1] 1 Cor. x. 20, 21.   [2] Rom. xvi. 20.

be the object of a condemnation; but He will come with manifestation, so that He may condemn. For if He had come in the first instance with manifestation, who would have dared to condemn Him thus made manifest? Does not St. Paul say, "If they had known, they would never have crucified the Lord of Glory". But if He had not been killed, death would not have died. The devil was vanquished by His trophy. Satan rejoiced when through a deception he had succeeded in throwing the first man into death. By seducing the first man, he killed him: by killing the last Man [Christ] he let the first escape from his snares. So the victory of Our Lord Jesus Christ was celebrated when He rose from the dead and ascended into heaven. What you heard when the Apocalypse was being read has been accomplished, the Lion of the tribe of Juda has vanquished. He is called a lion who was killed as a lamb. He is a lion on account of His courage, a lamb because of His innocence; He is a lion because He is invincible, a lamb because He is meek. And the lamb that was killed overcame the lion who goes about seeking whom he may devour. For the devil is called a lion, not on account of his strength, but for reasons of his ferocity. For the Apostle St. Peter says, you must watch against temptations, because your adversary, the devil, goes about seeking whom he might devour. And how does he go about? As a roaring lion, he says, seeking whom he might devour. Who would not fall into the jaws of that lion, if the Lion of the tribe of Juda had not overcome? You have the Lion against the lion, the Lamb against the wolf. The devil exulted when Christ died and yet he was conquered through that very death of Christ. The devil thinking he had food had taken a bait. The sight of death rejoiced him, as if he were the overseer of death. But what was to him joy, became to him a trap. The trap of the devil is the Cross of Christ. The food he thought he had swallowed was the death of Christ. And behold, Our Lord Jesus Christ is risen. Where is the death that was suspended on the Cross? Where is the insult of the Jews? Where is the boasting and pride of those who shook their heads before the Cross, saying, "If he be the Son of God, let Him come down from the Cross"? And He did more than they asked of Him in so opprobrious a fashion. For it is a greater deed to rise from the grave than to come down from the gibbet.'[1]

[1] St. Aug., *Sermo* CCLXIII (Migne, *P.L.* XXXVIII).

CHAPTER IX

An Answer to the Main Objection

So far we have not considered any of the practical difficulties which stand in the way of our whole-hearted acceptance of the doctrine of Christ's supreme victory. We shall now turn our attention to an objection which to many must seem formidable, and suggest an answer. The objection is as simple as it is far-reaching. It is that all appearances and all human experiences are against the totality of the triumph of Christ. In this matter we are confronted, not only by that sort of improbability which stands in the way of our accepting any of the mysteries of the Faith, but also by a seemingly direct contradiction between belief in an unchallenged spiritual overlordship and the realities that everywhere meet our eyes. With so much sin, with such widespread unbelief and infidelity, how could anyone not blinded by a naïve optimism believe in the victory of Christ? Are we not deluding ourselves with mere assumptions, that any religion might appropriate and claim as it own tenets? Christians, insinuates our detractor, will have to show a much larger measure of heroism, before the world will greet their Christ as a spiritual conqueror. Would it not be much wiser for Christians frankly to admit the tragedy of their religion, the appalling chasm between the ideal and the real, and be satisfied to compassionate their God for having disciples so immensely inferior to all He expects of them? Some of the less acrid of the scoffers will even say that this gives the religion of Jesus a charm all its own: an ideal God who suffers from the failures of His very unideal disciples.

Here we must remind the reader of the scope of this book. It is essentially and exclusively a work for the comfort of the believer. No one who does not hold the faith that the Son of God died on the Cross as a Victim of propitiation can really appreciate the considerations here laid down. Anyone who accepts that initial article of faith has the capacity in him to understand the supremacy of Christ's victory over evil. We might say that to be admitted to the secrets of its results in the spiritual world is the reward of faith in the Redemption through the death of God. As for the man who is either unable or unwilling to share in this great belief, it is evident that he cannot judge of human events except by human standards.

Now it is the proper characteristic of a propitiation for sin that is in the Blood of God Himself, that it atones for that very evil which is a scandal to so many, the lack of correspondence on the part of man with the redeeming love of God. This evil, like all other evils, has been atoned for by the Son of God. We may here mention a special instance of that resourcefulness of the propitiatory power of Christ which is always greater than any imaginable sin. The deicide of the Jews is the greatest sin committed by man since the Fall. It might seem to the superficial mind that it would have been almost better if God had not come down from heaven, so as not to expose man to the perpetration of a crime so heinous. Such argument might be excused if it were not evident that in that very death of God of which men made themselves culpable there is found propitiation for the deicides themselves. It is only on the presupposition of an infinitely abundant atonement for sin that we may believe in the effacing of iniquity, even when the crime is this very thing, the infliction of an ignominious death on a divine Redeemer. It is, of course, evident that, with the Blood of God at its very source as a redemptive and conquering power, Christianity has to adopt standards that are entirely different from human valuations. The world's evils can no longer be such, in the sense they would have been were there no such counter-balancing power in the moral universe as propitiation through the Blood of Christ. It may be difficult for us to understand how moral evil is thus made so insignificant. That it is so is the very essence of the Christian faith in the Atonement. Perhaps this is the most interesting, as well as the most baffling, problem propounded to the human mind; to reconcile the guilt of sin with faith in the complete wiping away of sin by the Blood of Christ. In Christian doctrine sin is atoned for by the Son of God long before it is committed by the free act of man, for Christ died to wipe away the sins of the future as well as the sins of the past. But in whatever way this great problem be solved, one thing is certain: the atoning act of Jesus is infinitely more important and weighty in the scale of moral values than all the possible sins of all men put together. This, of course, is an immediate and easily comprehensible consequence of the Incarnation, of the mystery of the God-Man. Anyone who holds that mystery is justified in believing in this immeasurable superiority of justice over sin, of atonement over offence; in one word, he has the right to live in the faith of the victory of the Son of God in spite of earthly appearances. He that has no such faith cannot lay claims to any such privilege; he cannot apply any other standards than those of human ethics.

So we may lay it down as a principle that actual human sinfulness and present-day infidelity need not, in themselves, be signs that Christ's victory is not complete. Not one of those dark realities is beyond the redeeming and conquering power of the Son of God: He has made satisfaction for all of them. We have no means of knowing what percentage of human beings actually profit by this divine victory, and will finally and eternally be saved. God has not made any confidence to man about this dread secret. But whatever be the ultimate proportion of lost and saved, one idea ought not to desert us, namely, that the numbers of the lost cannot in any way be regarded as a sign that the victory of Christ was less complete than it might have been; such calculations are merely human ways of looking at God's work. We must hold it as the only rational attitude of mind that Christ's ultimate victory could not be greater. In whatever mysterious way the kingdom of the Son of God will be compensated for the loss of the reprobate, let us take it as an indisputable theological axiom that a complete compensation does exist, so that the Son of God can truly say: 'This is the will of the Father who sent Me: that of all that He hath given Me, I should lose nothing; but should raise it up again in the last day.'[1]

To go through life with the kind of faith that is described in this book is no mere illuminism or unreasoning optimism. It is, on the contrary, the exercise of the finest gifts of the Spirit, the gifts of knowledge and understanding, which enable the Christian man to separate sentiment from truth, appearance from reality, eternal values from passing emotions. In another place we shall consider how ethical realism remains intact under a belief so intransigent regarding the nature of Christ's victory; and that it is possible to keep alive the horror of sin in a breast that glows with joy at the thought that all sins are atoned for by Christ. It is always helpful to hear the views of the great Christian thinkers in matters so

[1] John vi. 39.

challenging to human experience. Those fine intellects are proof against the disturbing influences of mere sentiment. St. Thomas Aquinas is famous for his unswerving adherence to the intellectual, and therefore true, value of Christian realities: 'Christ, through His passion, has liberated us from sins causally, in the sense that He has instituted the cause of our liberation, through which any kind of sin can be remitted, either past, present or future, as if a healer prepared a medicine to cure every kind of sickness, even a future sickness.'[1] And again: 'The charity of the suffering Christ was greater than the malice of those who crucified Him. Therefore the power of Christ to atone by His passion surpassed the guilt of those who crucified Him. The passion of Christ was not only sufficient, but superabundant, to atone for the sins of those who nailed Him on the Cross.'[2]

It would certainly have been in God's power to make the whole work of the Incarnation have this result: that all men should be preserved from sin, as the Mother of God was preserved from all sin. But such has not been God's plan. The Incarnation is given for the purpose that all men should be redeemed from the sins committed by them. This work Christ has accomplished, and He has not failed. That there should be some men who do not profit by the Incarnation in their own persons is not against the totality of the redemptive work, for no human being, endowed with free will, remains finally outside the grace of the Incarnation except through his own act.

There is a splendid example of Catholic insistence on these truths which brings out in a classical way the full meaning of Christ's victory over sin. A newly baptised adult is so completely liberated from all sin that between him and heaven there is no barrier; were he to die directly after his baptism his soul would go straight to the Vision of God, whatever his previous life might have been. The sacrament of Baptism gives him the full benefit of Christ's victory; he is in no need of any further purgation. Not to accept this doctrine would, according to St. Thomas Aquinas, be an insult to the power of Christ's death.[3]

What we have already said of sin in this chapter is, of course, applicable to the power of Satan. The victory of Christ is as com-

---

[1] S. Th. III, Quest. xlix, Art. 1, ad 3.   [2] S. Th. III, Quest. xlviii, Art. 2, ad 2.
[3] Cf. S. Th. III, Quest. lxviii, Art. 5.

plete to-day as it will ever be; Satan's power is broken; and if the evil spirit is still active, his exertions are those of the leader of a defeated and fast-retreating army. Satan is not chained up yet, as he will be at the end of time, using the apocalyptic language of St. John; he is still filled with a great anger and makes war on the saints, discomfited though he be. But we must simply admit that the evil spirits have not the least power over those who are Christ's and who are free from sin. The Fathers have tried to find popular ways of expressing the condition of an enemy who is defeated but who is still active, full of evil resolve. St. Augustine's aphorism is as telling as it is witty: 'Satan can bark, but he cannot bite.'

Christ's victory over death presents no practical difficulty. It involves the dogmatic fact of the resurrection of *all* flesh. Let us remember that through the power of Christ's Resurrection the human race in its entirety will be brought back to life irrespective of the ultimate fate of the elect or reprobate.

Once more we may emphasize the great truth that the evils conquered by Christ are finite evils, whilst the victory is truly an infinite reality. It may not be easy for some minds to adjust themselves to such modes of thought, to see, for instance, how it is an infinitely better thing for us to be assured that God by His Blood has redeemed the world than to be told that all men are saved. It ought not to be difficult, however, to realize that with God Himself at work everywhere human statistics of results would be very misleading measurements.

CHAPTER X

The Standard of Victory

THE victory of Christ is a supernatural reality which must deeply affect the thinking of Christians. If their Lord and Master is truly the triumphant King, Christians have a most efficient method of judging all things. There is simply no event, no kind of happening here on earth, which does not appear insignificant by the side of this transcending reality, the victory of Christ. This readiness to institute a comparison between the fact of Christ's glory and human things is for Christians the most natural way of enjoying their faith in the unseen triumph of the Crucified. It is not granted to the eye of the believer here on earth to behold the glory of the risen One, but there is accorded to every faithful soul one grace, that of being able to make such a comparison between earthly things and the glorious Emmanuel. The Christian always knows that nothing really matters if Christ is risen, for that Resurrection is victory without any limitations. If there be no such victory, then the Christian's lot is truly pitiable: 'If in this life only we have hope in Christ, we are of all men most miserable.'[1] But, on the contrary, if the splendid Resurrection is an historic fact, then we have every justification to account little of this world and all its works, to think little of our own perils and tribulations. The Christ who has conquered is so overpowering in His triumph that nothing can stand up against Him. We are powerful, as St. Paul was powerful, precisely through the answer of this conditional appeal: If Christ be not risen, what then? But if Christ be risen, what then? 'Why are we in danger every hour? I die daily, I protest by your glory, brethren, which I have in Christ Jesus Our Lord. If (according to man) I fought with beasts at Ephesus, what doth it profit me, if the dead rise not again? Let us eat and drink, for to-morrow we shall die.'[2] Life is simply inverted, it has an entirely different pole, according to the answers given to those questions.

But Christ being risen, His sovereignty is unquestionable: 'For He must reign, until He hath put all His enemies under His feet.'[3] This is the usual procedure of the Christian mind; it is a faith of comparisons, it is a choice between two conditions. What does all the rest matter, when we think of the glory that is in Christ? If that be true, then everything else falls into place. So in order to have the intellectual fruition of our faith in Christ's victory we are not under the necessity of beholding an actually submissive world, happy in its obedience to Christ. It is sufficient for us to be profoundly convinced of the Resurrection of Christ. By this we know that He rules the world with infallible security of justice and success. In all such matters Christian faith is aprioristic. It is an immensely greater

[1] 1 Cor. xv. 19.   [2] *Ibid.* 30-32.   [3] 1 Cor. xv. 25.

thing for us to accept the faith that Christ has redeemed mankind
than to count the numbers of the saved. It is more important for us
to know that from sunrise to sunset there is offered up a sacrifice of
propitiation on the Eucharistic altars of the Church, than to be able
to diagnose the results of such a dispensation. Again, our faith in
God's justice is our direct and infallible solution of any difficulty
brought forward against the lot of the reprobate. Our conviction of
God's justice is the one thing that shapes our thinking, not sentiment
concerning the possible state of the creature. The creature's state is
very secondary and cannot possibly be in opposition to divine justice.
Another instance of the aprioristic nature of the Christian faith is the
belief in prayer. We are certain that God has heard us, though we
cannot demonstrably show it by pointing to results that are merely
human. Such are the characteristics of the Christian faith right
through, believing in a greater reality than the human factors, and
establishing comparisons between the unseen and the seen: 'While
we look not at the things which are seen, but at the things which
are not seen. For the things which are seen are temporal: but the
things which are not seen, are eternal.'[1] So is it also with our faith
in Christ's victory. A multitude of enemies making war on Christ
here on earth in our days is a phenomenon which dwindles into
nothingness by the side of the majesty of the victorious Christ. Our
imagination may indeed feel impressed by the formidable array of
hostile forces; but our reason, illumined by faith, sees all things in
due proportion. To do this is faith's merit. The Christian to whom
this habit of mind is foreign would be a pusillanimous believer. Not
by believing in the wickedness of men, but by believing in Christ's
power to overcome all wickedness are we saved.

It is evident that in this matter Christians identify themselves with
standards of judgement that cannot be found elsewhere, and that
can only be justified on the assumption of principles which are
essential to Christianity in quite an exclusive way. We think more
of the power of God than of the state of the creature, because God's
power is immutable and inexhaustible, whilst the creature is fallible
and transient. By this we do not diminish the chance of the creature,
nor do we reduce the creature's hopes, for we start with the
assumption that God is more anxious for the creature's happiness

[1] 2 Cor. iv. 18.

than is the creature itself. The will of God to save man is deeply
earnest, whilst man has but feeble desires to escape from loss. We
know that the counsel of God cannot fail, cannot be checked by any
number of creatures abusing their freedom of choice. In this God
shows Himself to be God, not merely a demiurge. This mode of
thinking, then, we also bring to bear on the victory of Christ. For
us, as for St. Paul, the whole issue lies in this question: did Christ
rise from the dead or did He not? In other words, did Christ overcome all evil? If He did, all things are well, whatever the world may
do in ages to come. This, in a way, is a greater announcement than
if it were proclaimed that all men will be saved. For the victory of
Christ is something greater than the corporate salvation of the
human race. Christ's triumph means a conquest that goes far beyond
even the highest interests of mankind, just as the mercies of God
exceed by far all the occasions in which mercy may be needed.
There is indeed every justification for the faithful Christian's
optimism.

CHAPTER XI

Christ's Superiority

IT is not infrequently made a reproach against the traditional
Catholic Christology that there is in it an element of unreality.
The Jesus of the Gospels, and of Catholic piety, is represented
as having fought a tremendous moral battle in His suffering and
death; though it was absolutely clear to Him that the issue would be
splendid beyond all earthly comprehension, and that no power in
the world could either prevent or retard the triumph of His Person
and of His cause. No earthly hero, it is said, was ever thus privileged;
but had to plunge into the fray without such assurances being given
to him. Would it not seem that this kind of heroism rings more true
because of that very absence of any clear vision of triumphant
success? We must indeed defend the doctrine of Christ's certainties
against all comers, not only against the rationalists, but also against

the well-meaning pietist. We must say that Christ would have been not more lovable, but less lovable, if He had not been so sure of His ultimate victory. An element of doubt, of fear, would have made Him less attractive to Christian contemplation. In other words, He would have been less of a hero. This, however, we must grant, that there is a mysterious problem in Christ's certainties in the hour of His enemies and in the triumph of darkness: 'This is your hour and the power of darkness.'[1] Here is a spiritual phenomenon truly unique, and it may be said without exaggeration that the whole mentality of Christianity is dependent on this very issue: whether or not Christ, in His abasement, had complete and unshakeable knowledge of the glories that were to come to Him. For if Jesus had such an assurance, it is evident that the evils that befell Him were essentially of a provisional character, that they were not so much powers to be dreaded, as trials to be undergone. Consequently the only right attitude for Christians of all ages would be to meet the afflictions of their own times in the knowledge of their being a transient provision; not with the awe and terror that are inspired by an inexorable power.

Our Lord most certainly knew that nothing could finally hurt Him. He felt unassailable in every fibre of His being: 'For the prince of this world cometh: and in Me he hath not anything.'[2] There was in the Incarnate Son of God a perfect sense of proportion that made Him appraise the evils of the present life at their true worth. If the term 'philosopher' is justifiably applied to one whose mind is not overwhelmed by human evils, then Christ must be proclaimed the Philosopher *par excellence*. Everything in Him made Him superior to that tyranny which human suffering and death exercise over the imagination of mankind, making those dread things appear as masters of human destiny. But there was more in Christ than superiority of knowledge; there was also the power to overcome all those dark monsters. We must simply admit that the only orthodox Christology is that at all times Christ was in His own Person the unconquerable master of death and all connected with it; physical evil and also human tyranny were powerless before Him, whenever He chose to manifest His superiority.

The charm of our divine hero is in this: that He submitted to

[1] Luke xxii. 53. [2] John xiv. 30.

those evils for the sake of the redeemed, in order to show that they could not really hurt what is essential in man. According to St. Paul Christ took all human evils and death upon Himself for this very purpose, that death should lose its terrors for us, and that Satan, who utilized the gloomy prospect of death to tyrannise over man, should be deprived of his most potent weapon: 'Therefore because the children are partakers of flesh and blood, He also Himself in like manner hath been partaker of the same: that, through death, He might destroy him who had the empire of death, that is to say, the devil: and might deliver them who, through the fear of death, were all their lifetime subject to servitude.'[1] So it is infinitely more consonant with the whole scheme of our liberation that Christ should have been, as Catholic theology has always represented Him, *inter mortuos liber*, a free man among the dead; One who moved in the dark places of human existence with the light of divinity all around Him; One who could not know sin, and if He tasted death, did so with the end that death should be swallowed up in the abundance of His own life. Thus Christ never speaks of His coming humiliation without mentioning the subsequent glorification; the Resurrection on the third day is, one might almost say, a ritual formula with Him: 'Then Jesus took unto Him the twelve and said to them: Behold, we go up to Jerusalem; and all things shall be accomplished which are written by the prophets concerning the Son of Man. For He shall be delivered to the Gentiles and shall be mocked and scourged and spit upon. And after they have scourged Him, they will put Him to death. And the third day He shall rise again.'[2] Any historian of Christ's life who does not give to this aspect of the Gospels its true place, fails egregiously in his task. The insistence of Christ on His complete immunity from sin and the tyranny of the evil world makes of His career something quite apart from all other human histories. He does not just leave it to the Christian of the coming generation to find out how free He had been, He Himself makes use of every opportunity to proclaim this incontestable independence, this power to bring low all that is against Him.

There is another aspect of Christ's career upon earth which is a kindred feature to the superiority just described. It is His economy in the use of the powers that were in Him for the furtherance of the

[1] Heb. ii. 14, 15.   [2] Luke xviii. 31-33.

Kingdom of God which He came to establish. Christ had His hour, and Christ had His own way, in the work for which He had been sent, and no power could deflect Him from His course or induce Him to forestall His chosen moment: 'Now the Jews' feast of tabernacles was at hand. And His brethren said to Him: Pass from hence and go into Judea, that Thy disciples also may see Thy works which Thou dost. For there is no man that doth anything in secret, and he himself seeketh to be known openly. If Thou do these things, manifest Thyself to the world. For neither did His brethren believe in Him. Then Jesus said to them: My time is not yet come; but your time is always ready. The world cannot hate you: but Me it hateth, because I give testimony of it, that the works thereof are evil. Go you up to this festival day: but I go not up to this festival day, because My time is not yet accomplished.'[1] Is there anywhere a narrative like the Gospel story precisely in this respect: the accumulation of testimonies that the central hero has His fate in His own hands, that no one can take His life from Him without His consent? This atmosphere in which Christ moves has become, as I have said, the permanent attitude of the Christian mind; for the certainty that nothing can really hurt them was meant to be the happy condition in which all who adore the Father are expected to possess their souls. 'These things I have spoken to you, that in Me you may have peace. In the world you shall have distress. But have confidence. I have overcome the world.'[2]

It was to be expected from Pope St. Leo that he would never give any peace to his hearers on this subject of Christ's freedom to choose His own manner of life and death. The heresies of Nestorius and Eutychius had disturbed the Christian conscience. For many, the problem of how to visualize the Christ-tragedy had become acute. Was Jesus doomed to a terrible end without having a voice in the matter? Or would it not be wiser to attach no real meaning to the sufferings of the Son of God as they appear in the Gospels, the whole event being merely an external show, as the Docetists, who were akin to the Eutychians, would have it? The holy Doctor reminds his Roman audience that Christ's infirmities are the fruit of Christ's power, as from love of us He willed to be weak: 'The two natures in Christ are but one Person, and there is only one Lord, the Son of

---

[1] John vii. 2-8.   [2] John xvi. 33.

God who at the same time is the Son of Man; He took upon Himself the servile condition through a plan of love, without being subject to that condition through any law or necessity. For through an act of power He became lowly, through an act of power He became passible, through an act of power He became mortal. In order to destroy the sovereignty of sin and death He made the weaker nature capable of pain, without His stronger nature losing any of its glory.'[1]

It is no profanity to say that here is the key to the secret of Christian humour, of that sense of the innate weakness of all that tries to frighten man: 'And I say to you, My friends: Be not afraid of them who kill the body and after that have no more that they can do. But I will shew you whom you shall fear: Fear ye him who, after he hath killed, hath power to cast into hell. Yea, I say to you: Fear him. Are not five sparrows sold for two farthings, and not one of them is forgotten before God? Yes, the very hairs of your head are all numbered. Fear not therefore: you are of more value than many sparrows.'[2] The phrase 'my friends' justifies our boldness in using here the word 'humour'. Christ is surrounded by a group of men who can afford to make light of tribulation. Surely a smile plays round His lips when He says of His disciples, big strong men as they are, that it would take many sparrows to equal them in weight and worth!

CHAPTER XII

Christ's Certainty

IN the last chapter we have touched on the main principles of a most important topic in theology, the radical immunity of Christ from the powers of evil. In the present chapter we go one step further in the consideration of Christ's positive certainties concerning, not only His ultimate, but also His immediate triumph. It is taken for granted that the personality of Christ is essentially a

---

[1] St. Leo, *Sermo* XLVI (Migne, *P.L.* LIV).   [2] Luke xii. 4-7.

mystery; Hypostatic Union can never be understood by man, nor can man estimate the consequences of that Union inside the personality of the God-Man. We cannot understand how Our Lord possessed at the same time the glories of Godhead and the infirmities of Manhood; how He was omnipotent and weak; how He was impassible and passible. Nestorianism, which divided Christ into two Persons, would apparently facilitate matters as, in the hypothesis of Nestorius, one could speak independently of Godhead and of Manhood in Christ, attributing to each its respective privileges and responsibilities. But the Catholic faith in the Oneness of Person in Christ makes such independent attributions heresies. The human in Christ has always to be considered in the light of the divine; and the death of Christ is not a merely human state, but the state of a divine Person. Too frequently, I think, the analysis which devout writers pretend to undertake of what they call the 'interior life of Christ' is tainted at bottom with crypto-Nestorianism; they too readily read into Christ a life of thought and sentiment which is in reality the psychology of an independent human person, not of a human nature that is part of a divine Person. In no matter ought one to proceed with greater caution than in defining the activities of Christ's interior life. We hold, moreover, that Christ's human mind, from the first moment of His conception, had the clear Vision of God, which it never lost. This circumstance alone would place Christ beyond all standards of human comparison: no man knows what may be the workings of a created intellect when it is illumined through Beatific Vision. So we have at every turn this great fact, that Christ was absolutely certain of His future victory; the regularity of earthly seasons was no more certain to Him than the advent of His triumphant glory. He knew with utmost clearness the price of the victory; while as for the actual coming of the day of glory for Himself, it was present to His mind as a fact that was as good as accomplished. So we find in Our Lord's public utterances the constant reiteration of His certainty of victory. Of doubt and hesitation concerning this all-important issue there is not a single vestige in the sacred Gospels. At no time does Our Lord speak hesitatingly of His future, as if such hesitation were humility or meekness of heart; on the contrary, He openly glories in the fact that no man has the power to hurt Him in any way.

This attitude of Christ's mind is identical with the vaster problem of His permanent consciousness that He was the Son of God;
a consciousness that did not come to Him gradually, but was in its
noontide clarity from the very beginning of His human existence.
It is noteworthy, however, that Christ speaks more clearly and
frequently of His triumph than of His Godhead. Catholic scholarship
has had no difficulty in proving that Jesus Christ more than once
said in clear words that He was the Son of God and therefore God.
It has become the fashion with modernists to deny that Christ ever
committed Himself to such statements; but even the modernist will
not deny that Jesus of Nazareth most emphatically claimed His
coming triumph. As a matter of fact this reiterated claim has been
the occasion for many to accuse Christ of hyperbolical optimism.
'Jesus,' they say, 'certainly declared that very soon He would be
seen coming on the clouds of heaven, but generations of Christians
have lived and died without seeing the promised spectacle.'

Nothing is easier than to describe Christ's attitude of mind with
regard to His quickly approaching and absolute triumph. This victory can be identified with the doctrine of the Kingdom of God;
that Kingdom which is nigh when Christ speaks. The Kingdom is
universally represented as being supreme, not only in its claims, but
also in its efficacy. The work of the Kingdom may be a work of
cleansing and purifying, but the cleansing and the purification are
irresistible. Christ, the mighty Harvester, has the fan in His hand,
to cleanse His barn; angels are sent out to separate wheat and
cockle; the net that draws every kind of fish does not break, but the
sorting of the fish, good from bad, is rapid and efficient as a work
which it was always intended to accomplish. Unholy elements,
according to the Gospel, have no power to soil or to retard the
Kingdom of God. Now that Kingdom is to come at once, Christ's
triumph is to come at once, nay, even the judgement is to come at
once; all these expectations of Christ, all these magnificent promises need not wait for the Last Day in order to have their fulfilment.
The victory of the Cross, and the Resurrection, with the advent of
the Paraclete, fully justify Christ's declaration. If we had to read all
that Christ says concerning His victorious coming merely as so
many prophecies of His return at the end of the world and nothing
more, our lot as Christians would be hard indeed; there would be

no ground under our feet; we might almost say there would be hope without faith, because we should not have the solid substance of our supernatural liberation invisibly surrounding us on all sides. It is indeed the exclusive genius of Christianity to possess this certainty. While there is anxiety and tribulation on all sides, while there is even the hour of darkness when the evil powers are let loose, there is in the midst of it all this reality of victory; not only the hope of a future reversal of conditions, but a present vision of the Kingdom of Glory. So the martyr dies seeing Jesus standing at the Right Hand of God, as did Stephen, the first martyr; for this is ideal martyrdom, to behold the heavens opened, to gaze upon the triumphant Christ, even while a rain of stones crushes the life out of the body. Christianity has found it possible to reconcile adversity and prosperity, temptation and its issue, persecution and exaltation in one and the same person, at one and the same moment. When the powers of darkness laid their hand on Jesus, that presumption of theirs recoiled on them as a thunderbolt of death. So is it with every power that lays its hand on the members of Jesus, persecuting Christ in His brethren.

Nothing is more significant than the emphasis placed by Christ on His approaching glorification at the very moment when He stood like a criminal before the High Priests: 'And He said to them: If I shall tell you, you will not believe Me. And if I shall also ask you, you will not answer Me, nor let Me go. But hereafter the Son of Man shall be sitting on the right hand of the power of God.'[1] A greater immunity from the effects of human wickedness than the one implied in these words of Christ cannot be imagined; yet such is Christ's constant attitude during His life, and such is also the normal attitude of Christ's Church in the midst of her enemies to the end of times. There is truly no proportion between human adversity and the glory that will be revealed in us. The exaltation which Christ announces as awaiting Him without delay is out of all proportion to the indignities He suffers in the courts of the High Priest. It is one of our first Christian instincts, to perceive this disproportion between human evil and the raising up of Christ through the power of God. His sitting at the right hand of the Father is a position of such might and excellence that in very truth it is as if all

[1] Luke xii. 67-69.

His enemies were His footstool. The vastest machinations of Satan against Christ have become an object of derision to the supreme Lord of Glory. Nothing would be more contrary to Christian faith than the mentality of which St. John speaks in the Apocalypse, where men are described as overawed by the power of evil: 'And all the earth was in admiration after the beast. And they adored the dragon which gave power to the beast; and they adored the beast, saying: Who is like to the beast? And who shall be able to fight with him?'[1] A similar disproportion exists between those straitenings which are the constant condition of the Church, and her real glory, present and future. St. Paul asserts that there is no comparison between our present tribulation and the glory that will be revealed. We may extend this apostolic method of appraising things even further. Between the real sanctity and power of the Church and the world's indifference and wickedness there is no comparison: one is a divine reality, the other is a negation. The People of God, the Church, has an immortality which makes all other institutions appear ephemeral. Of that Kingdom it is said by the prophet: 'It shall break in pieces and shall consume all other kingdoms, and itself shall stand for ever.'[2]

CHAPTER XIII

Christ's Glorification through the Holy Ghost

THE external form of Christ's Resurrection is the last evidence of the resolve of the Son of God that here on earth, at His first coming, He would not show forth the majesty of the divinity that was in Him. To the eyes of the men who were privileged to behold the risen Christ the external form of the Master was the same as it had been through life; even the momentary glorification of the Transfiguration does not seem to have been repeated during the forty days which Christ spent on earth after His rising from the dead. The visions of glory and terror that belong to the

[1] Apoc. xiii. 3, 4.   [2] Dan. ii. 44.

Easter morning were not visions of Christ but apparitions of heavenly spirits; Christ Himself invariably appeared in the form to which the disciples were accustomed. This simplicity of behaviour is significant beyond words; the fact of His Resurrection was the one thing that mattered, and the time of external glorification had not yet arrived. For the purposes of Christian apologetics it is far more satisfying to see the figure of man only in the risen One, not the glory of divine majesty, because the complete identity of Personality between the dead Christ and the risen Christ is of the highest importance. If the risen Christ had appeared in the splendour of His glory that identity would have been less evident. That the Resurrection made no difference whatever in the external appearance of Christ is truly a feature of divine artistry. There is peculiar beauty in the way St. Mark records this event. For the Evangelist the supreme miracle of the Son of God is as simple as the early rising of any man after a refreshing sleep: 'But He rising early the first day of the week, appeared first to Mary Magdalen, out of whom He had cast seven devils.'[1]

The Ascension of Christ into heaven, forty days after the Resurrection, is Christ's last act here on earth, and in that act He does not break the self-imposed law of ordinary humanity. Though He is seen rising to heaven there seems, from the account given by the Evangelists, no reason why we should think of the Saviour as being suddenly glorified; so long as the gaze of His disciples followed Him He kept the normal form of humanity: 'And it came to pass, whilst He blessed them, He departed from them and was carried up to heaven.'[2]

With Pentecost we enter into an entirely new sphere of divine manifestation. All those reticences which give the Gospels their special characteristic disappear; there is no longer any question of not publishing the works of Christ, of not speaking of His Transfiguration; on the contrary, publicity has become the key-note of the new dealings of God with man. The coming of the Holy Ghost on the fiftieth day after Christ's Resurrection is the official proclamation by God Himself of the supreme victory of Christ. The descent of the Paraclete ought to be considered by us, as it was considered by the Apostles, as the external manifestation of the hidden victory

[1] Mark xvi. 9.   [2] Luke xxiv. 51.

of the risen Christ; the Holy Ghost is the herald of that victory; it
it is His mission to glorify Christ: 'He shall glorify Me because He
shall receive of Mine and shall show it you.'[1] The Holy Ghost, as
He then appeared, is a Spirit of victory. The Incarnate Son of God,
as we have seen, won the victory, but on this earth He never
assumed the glories of that triumph. That triumph has become the
office of the Third Person of the Trinity in that special manifestation,
different from all the other advents of the Spirit, which we call
Pentecost, and which, of course, is a permanent revelation. The
Paraclete is, to the end of times, the triumph of Christ personified
in a divine Person, the Holy Ghost is amongst us in the pentecostal
sense as the external proclamation of all the hidden achievements of
the divine hero, Jesus Christ. The Holy Ghost is so essentially a
manifest presence that there is a kind of necessity for the Incarnate
Son to withdraw from our sight: 'But I tell you the truth: it is
expedient to you that I go. For if I go not, the Paraclete will not
come to you: but if I go I will send Him to you.'[2] The Spirit of
Pentecost has only one mission on the earth, to manifest in every
possible way the glories of Christ, to convince the world that Christ
has overcome all evil, that the prince of this world has already been
judged by Christ. There will be no more silences, no more delays
in trumpeting forth the truth; there will be unsparing, overpowering accusation and judging of the world for its refusal to believe in
Christ. The sanctity of Christ, the merit and the justice of Christ,
will now be proclaimed to the ends of the world. 'And when He is
come, He will convince the world of sin and of justice and of judgement. Of sin: because they believed not in Me. And of justice:
because I go to the Father: and you shall see Me no longer. And of
judgement: because the prince of this world is already judged.'[3] Nor
is there any longer any consideration for the infirmity of the human
mind. Our Lord declared divine truth to the disciples gradually and
carefully, as they were far from being ready for the intense light
that was in the Master. Not so in the future; blazing light, without
mitigation of its fierceness, will be the normal condition of God's
dealings with man. 'I have yet many things to say to you: but you
cannot bear them now. But when He, the Spirit of truth, is come,
He will teach you all truth. For He shall not speak of Himself: but

[1] John xvi. 14.   [2] Ibid. 7.   [3] Ibid. 8-11.

what things soever He shall hear, He shall speak. And the things that are to come, He shall shew you.'[1] Truly the Spirit of Pentecost carries out in practice what Christ had announced: 'Therefore fear them not. For nothing is covered that shall not be revealed: nor hid that shall not be known. That which I tell you in the dark, speak ye in the light: and that which you hear in the ear, preach ye upon the housetops.'[2]

Twice during His mortal life did the Spirit appear over Jesus, and in both instances He showed Himself as the glorifier of the Son of Man. The two occasions are the well-known scenes of Christ's Baptism in the Jordan and His Transfiguration on the mountain. Both these scenes are entirely at variance with the general tenor of the Gospels, which are essentially the history of the hidden God: 'And Jesus being baptized, forthwith came out of the water: and lo, the heavens were opened to Him: and He saw the Spirit of God descending as a dove and coming upon Him. And behold a voice from heaven, saying: This is My beloved Son, in whom I am well pleased.'[3] This manifest coming of the Spirit is an event that stands between two humiliations of the Son of God, His Baptism at the hands of John and His fast and temptation in the wilderness. In the Transfiguration the Spirit appears as a bright cloud overshadowing Christ and His two companions: 'And as He was yet speaking, behold a bright cloud overshadowed them. And lo, a voice out of the cloud, saying: This is My beloved Son in whom I am well pleased. Hear ye Him.'[4] Of this vision Jesus does not want a word to be spoken before the Resurrection: 'And as they came down from the mountain, Jesus charged them, saying: Tell the vision to no man till the Son of Man be risen from the dead.'[5]

We may then rightly give to the Spirit the name of Glorifier: as such He appears on two occasions in Christ's earthly career, and as such He took possession of the Church and the world on the day of Pentecost. So the glory of Our Lord here on earth is more than the remembrance by the believers of all He is and all He did: His glory is a divine Person; the Paraclete came to do this very thing which Christ had always shunned, to appear glorious. Nothing could be further from the intentions of God than that the Name of His Son

---

[1] John xvi. 12-13.   [2] Matt. x. 26, 27.   [3] Matt. iii. 16, 17.
[4] Matt. xvii. 5.   [5] Ibid. 9.

should not be great among men. Only a few days before the beginning of the Passion Christ, whilst speaking to the people, was all at
once seized with a great fear: 'Now is My soul troubled. And what
shall I say? Father, save Me from this hour. But for this cause I came
unto this hour. Father, glorify Thy name. A voice therefore came
from heaven: I have both glorified it and will glorify it again.'[1]
Glorification, then, is the dispensation of Pentecost, and truly the
Holy Ghost is the herald of the victory of the Son of God here on
earth; He announces to the ends of the world that Christ is risen
and has conquered all things; that He sits at the right hand of God.
St. Peter and the Apostles on the day of Pentecost and ever afterwards speak of the Spirit in this strain; He has come manifestly, He
has come as the testimony of Christ's glorification. It is beyond
doubt that the event which took place on the third hour of the day
was of utmost publicity: 'And when this was noised abroad, the
multitude came together and were confounded in mind, because
that every man heard them speak in his own tongue. ... And they
were all astonished and wondered, saying one to another: What
meaneth this?'[2] Peter sees in all this the fulfilment of a promise;
Christ was humbled, now He is glorified: 'This Jesus hath God
raised again, whereof all we are witnesses. Being exalted therefore
by the right hand of God and having received of the Father the
promise of the Holy Ghost, He hath poured forth this which you
see and hear.'[3] The life of the early Church is a transport of joy in
the Holy Ghost. It is as if Christ Himself had appeared in majesty.
The Spirit has all the power of the glorious Godhead.

As the Third Person of the Trinity has become the messenger of
the Son of God in His exaltation, there can be no fear that Christ's
glory will ever suffer any diminution in this world; there is a
divine constancy in this work of showing forth who Christ really is.
Neither men nor angels have been entrusted with this mighty
message, the Spirit Himself is the Message; angels and men, as far as
they are promoters of the name of Christ, are such, not through
themselves, but through the Spirit that dwells in them. Sanctification
of souls is only another word for glorification of the Son of God, for
souls are holy in the measure in which they comprehend the greatness of the divine Victor over sin. The language of Our Lord con-

---

[1] John xii. 27, 28.   [2] Acts ii. 6, 12.   [3] Ibid. 32, 33.

cerning the work of the Paraclete is so precise and forcible that it is necessary to admit this very special glorification, besides admitting the more universal divine law that justice and truth must triumph in the end, and falsehood and iniquity, by their very nature, must sooner or later give way before the rights of truth and equity. Concerning the Son of God made Man there is more than this universal law of retribution; there is direct exaltation as the counterpart of His humiliation: 'For which cause, God also hath exalted Him and hath given Him a name which is above all names.'[1] This magnificent recompense will only appear in its full splendour on the day when Christ returns in glory. In the meantime the Spirit gives testimony that Christ is in the glory of the Father.

CHAPTER XIV

Christ's Victory and the Church

THE Spirit whom we have described as the herald of Christ's victory is Himself a mighty manifestation. He gives testimony of Christ by the assertion of His own presence on earth, and this assertion is made in an external, palpable fashion. It is admitted that the Holy Ghost inhabited the souls of the just at all times from Adam onwards; but not before the Pentecost described for us in the Acts of the Apostles had He manifested Himself in an external, visible manner for all men to see. In the Baptism at the Jordan and in the Transfiguration on the Mount, the Spirit was indeed visibly manifested, but only to a few witnesses. So far His presence had been an invisible presence in the hearts of men; on Pentecost He manifested Himself visibly, so that in all literalness of language St. Peter could say to the crowds that they had seen and heard the Spirit: 'Being exalted therefore by the right hand of God and having received of the Father the promise of the Holy Ghost, He hath poured forth this which you see and hear.'[2] What happened on that third hour of the day was not primarily a mysterious inward trans-

[1] Phil. ii. 9. [2] Acts ii. 33.

formation of man's mind, but an external sign to men that the promised Paraclete had now arrived. Right through the Acts of the Apostles we find that the coming of the Spirit, at Pentecost and later on, was to the early Christians as evident a fact as the coming of the divine Word in the flesh. The Spirit took the place which Jesus held among the disciples when He was still walking with them; the Spirit was truly that 'other Comforter' which Christ had promised: 'And I will ask the Father: and He shall give you another Paraclete, that He may abide with you for ever: the Spirit of truth, whom the world cannot receive, because it seeth Him not, nor knoweth Him. But you shall know Him; because He shall abide with you and be in you. I will not leave you orphans: I will come to you.'[1]

The Pentecostal marvel was not confined to the fiftieth day after Easter, for it was not a transient visitation of the Holy Ghost but a true abiding; thus, when Cornelius and his household had received St. Peter's instruction the Holy Spirit fell on them: 'While Peter was yet speaking these words, the Holy Ghost fell on all them that heard the word. And the faithful of the circumcision, who came with Peter, were astonished for that the grace of the Holy Ghost was poured out upon the Gentiles also. For they heard them speaking with tongues, and magnifying God.'[2] Peter was struck by the similarity of that event to the experience of the disciples in the Upper Room: 'Then Peter answered: Can any man forbid water, that these should not be baptized, who have received the Holy Ghost, as well as we?'[3] He came back to this point when asked to defend his conduct before the brethren in Jerusalem: 'And when I had begun to speak, the Holy Ghost fell upon them, as upon us also in the beginning. And I remembered the word of the Lord, how that He said: John indeed baptized with water, but you shall be baptized with the Holy Ghost. If then God gave them the same grace, as to us also who believed in the Lord Jesus Christ, who was I, that could withstand God?'[4]

The coming of the Holy Ghost at Pentecost is in every respect as great a phenomenon in the divine economy of man's salvation as the Incarnation in the bosom of the Blessed Virgin. The mode of the coming of the Spirit is different from the way in which the Second Person of the Trinity came: the Son came assuming a human nature,

[1] John xiv. 16-18.   [2] Acts x. 44-46.   [3] *Ibid*. x. 47.   [4] *Ibid*. xi. 15-17.

the Holy Ghost came by giving evident signs of His arrival which no man could deny; but the coming and the abiding, in both instances, are equally real and lasting. The Spirit came, however, not so much for Himself as to give testimony of the coming of the Second Person, the Word Incarnate. Christ had said this: 'But when He, the Spirit of truth, is come, He will teach you all truth. For He shall not speak of Himself; but what things soever He shall hear, He shall speak. And the things that are to come, He shall shew you.'[1] That the Spirit would not speak of Himself can only mean this, that His mission here on earth is complementary to Christ's mission, as the visible sign of Christ's invisible triumph; for in Christian theology Christ's triumph, as already said, is invisible, whilst the Spirit is visible. Christ will only appear at the end of time, but the Spirit has already appeared. Christ is received into heaven and will not be seen by the eye of man till the times be fulfilled: 'Whom heaven indeed must receive, until the times of the restitution of all things, which God hath spoken by the mouth of His holy prophets, from the beginning of the world.'[2] But the Spirit comes out of heaven and men see and hear Him. This visible mission of the Holy Ghost is of supreme importance in the whole of the Christian dispensation; if it were left out, the Kingdom of God on earth would be a mere ideal, not a reality; the Holy Ghost, we may say, is the Kingdom of God, not in His invisible presence, I repeat, but through what is manifest and visible. The interior graces and consolations of the Christian soul are a result of that external coming; but the presence of the Spirit is like a mighty voice proclaiming the fact that Christ is risen from the dead and sits at the right hand of God the Father in the glory of heaven.

The Catholic Church is the milieu in which the Holy Ghost carries out His mission of purification; the Church is essentially this, a people brought together by the Holy Ghost in the faith of Christ's victory. The first three thousand who were added 'in that day' were won over because of what they saw and heard and from which they concluded that God had raised up 'that Jesus whom they had crucified.' Through the Church the same work goes on over the whole world to the end of time. It is only a glorified and victorious Christ who could win adherence: not one, however holy,

[1] John xvi. 13.   [2] Acts iii. 21.

who became the innocent victim of His enemies, without power over His own destiny. The Church, then, must at all times be viewed in the light of Christ's victory; it is her very life to believe in that triumph, to feed on it, to glorify it through the Spirit that is in her. Any diminution of her faith in Christ's exaltation would be a death-blow to her; for she is not living on an edifying memory, she fights for the King of Glory whom the heavens have received. This triumphant faith is truly the continuation of Pentecost; it is as great a marvel as the signs by which the Spirit manifested Himself. The purpose of the Spirit was, in the language of St. Peter, to show forth the great fact that God had glorified His Son. As long as there are men united in that same faith the work of the Spirit knows no abatement. He does what He did at Pentecost. He shows His presence in so far as through Him we believe that Christ is risen and glorified. The Catholic Church shows forth in every act of her life something of Christ's victory; her faith, her prayers, her sacra-ments, her combats, her whole organization, proclaim that her Head is the One who has overcome all evil and has acquired eternal glory. In order to be a Church of victory she need not be without assaults from the outside, or without blemishes in her own children. But one thing is essential to her, she must be able to withstand every external adversary, and to cleanse away every sin that is found in the heart of any of her members; and this the Church has always done, and for this reason we are more than justified in proclaiming her the Church militant, which can only mean the victorious Church.

It is not without deep significance that the mystery of the Resur-rection, the mystery of the Spirit, and the mystery of the forgive-ness of sins, are shown in the sacred Gospels as united. When Christ, come back from the dead, shows Himself to the Apostles, He breathes on them the Spirit and gives them power to remit sins, for the exercise of that power is truly the complete Christian Easter. 'And when He had said this,[1] He shewed them His hands and His side. The disciples therefore were glad, when they saw the Lord. He said therefore to them again: Peace be to you. As the Father hath sent Me, I also send you. When He had said this, He breathed on them; and He said to them: Receive ye the Holy Ghost. Whose sins you shall forgive, they are forgiven them: and whose sins you shall

[1] John xx. 20-23.

retain, they are retained.'[1] The power of forgiving sin in the Church is the one great trophy which Christ brought back to His Apostles when He returned from His triumphant battle; He did not bring the grace of complete sinlessness for the Church here below, but He brought the greater grace of the remission of sins in His name, because He had conquered sin. It is as if Christ, in that moment of supreme happiness, was overpowered by what He had achieved on the Cross and in the tomb and in Limbo, the complete conquest of sin, and so His first words to His disciples are to be these: 'Whose sins you shall forgive, they are forgiven.' They are truly the words of a conqueror. Christ had forgiven sin in His own lifetime, but now, without any reservation, He makes a gift of that power to His Church, to be available until the end of time. It is perhaps an unfortunate result of our being familiarized with divine utterances that makes it difficult for us to see the transcending glory of a Gospel message like this. Had it been left to us to guess what were the first words of Christ to His disciples at so astonishing a moment, would it have occurred to us to put remission of sins in the first rank? But happily we are not asked to speak for God; the Gospels are essentially the dealings of a divine Person, and therefore dealings which are mostly unexpected and incomprehensible. Still, does it not sound as if Christ, with infinite graciousness, told His Apostles: 'Here I am once more, and since we parted I have done what I set out to do: I have destroyed sin. Therefore go forth and forgive sin wherever there is sin to be forgiven'?

We may conclude this chapter with an extract from one of St. Leo's sermons. More than anyone else this profound and enlightened thinker seems to have possessed the capacity of perceiving the supernatural reality in its entirety, without being side-tracked by the transient phenomena of human weakness. 'So then, all those things which the Son of God both did and taught for the reconciliation of the world, we do not simply know of by the history of past events, but feel even now by the power of the present operations. He it is who, having been brought forth by the Holy Spirit from a Virgin Mother, by the same inspiration makes fruitful His undefiled Church, so that through the Baptismal childbearing is produced an innumerable multitude of children of God, of whom it is said, "who were born, not of blood, nor of the will of the flesh, nor of the will of man, but of God." He it is in whom the seed of Abraham is blessed by the adoption of the whole world to sonship, and the patriarch becomes the father of nations, while the promised sons are born, not carnally, but by faith. He it is who, making no exception of any nation, forms out of every people under heaven one flock of holy sheep, and daily performs what He had promised in the words, "And other sheep I have, which are not of this fold; them also I must bring, and they shall hear My voice, and there shall be one fold and one Shepherd." For although it is to blessed Peter chiefly that He says "Feed My sheep," yet it is by the one Lord that care is taken for all the shepherds themselves, and those who come to the Rock He nourishes in such pleasant and well-watered pastures, that numberless sheep, strengthened with the fatness of love, hesitate not themselves to die for the Name of the Shepherd, even as the Good Shepherd was pleased to lay down His life for the sheep. He it is in whose suffering not only the glorious courage of Martyrs has a share, but also the faith of all who are new-born in their actual regeneration. For while they renounce the devil, and believe in God; while they pass from the old life into the new; while the image of the earthly man is laid aside, and the form of the Heavenly is put on; there takes place a certain appearance of death, and a certain likeness of resurrection; so that he who is put on by Christ and puts on Christ is not the same after the laver as he was before Baptism, but the body of the regenerate becomes the flesh of the Crucified. This, dearly beloved, is "the change from the right hand of the Highest," "who worketh all in all," so that in the case of every faithful man we may, through the character of a good life, understand Him to be the author of pious works: giving thanks to the mercy of God, who so adorns the whole body of the Church by innumerable bestowals of spiritual gifts, that by the many rays of one light the same splendour is everywhere manifest, nor can the good desert of any Christian be aught else than the glory of Christ. This is that "true light" which justifies and "enlightens every man". This is that which "rescues us from the power of darkness, and translates us into the kingdom of the Son of God". This is that which through newness of life elevates the desires of the soul, and quenches the appetites of the flesh. This is that whereby the Lord's Passover is legitimately celebrated "in the unleavened bread of sincerity and truth"; while, after the leaven of the old malice has been cast away, the new creature is exhilarated and fed from the Lord Himself. For the participation of the Body and Blood of Christ effects nothing else than this, that we pass into That which we receive; and as we have died with Him, and been buried with Him, and raised up with Him, so we bear Him throughout, both in spirit and in flesh, as the Apostle says: "For ye are dead, and your life is hid with Christ in God. For when Christ, your life, shall appear, then shall ye also appear with Him in glory".'[1]

CHAPTER XV

Christ's Sovereignty over all Flesh

THERE is in Christian faith a vast region of supernatural realities loudly proclaiming Christ's supreme victory. These are the sacramental graces. They are by their very nature of such supremacy that unless we believed in the unrestricted mastery of Christ over all flesh we could hardly conceive that such things are possible. Through the sacraments Christ sanctifies the human race by the sheer domination of His supernatural empire. It would take us too far if we were to expound here the sacramental doctrine of the Church in its entirety; though for anyone who is writing on the victory of Christ the temptation to do so is very great, for from first to last sacramental grace shows an independence of human conditions which is only possible on the hypothesis that the Son of God Himself has triumphed over all obstacles. Through water, through the laying on of hands, through bread and wine, through other words and signs, the Son of God sanctifies the world with irresistible power, asking no more of man than that he should believe and repent. What in technical theology is called the *opus operatum* of the sacrament may well be described in terms of divine victory; but the whole sacramental life of the Church, in all its aspects, presupposes that an immense wealth of spiritual powers is

[1] St. Leo, *Sermo* LXIII (Migne, *P.L.* LIV).

always available, knowing no obstacles, asking leave of no man. When Christ, for the first time, as far as we know, introduces the subject of the future sacraments, He silences the objections of Nicodemus who could not see how a man, being old, could be born again of water and the Holy Ghost. His reply is merely a statement of the immensity of the activities of the Spirit: 'That which is born of the flesh is flesh: and that which is born of the Spirit is spirit. Wonder not that I said to thee: You must be born again. The Spirit breatheth where He will and thou hearest His voice: but thou knowest not whence He cometh and whither He goeth. So is every one that is born of the Spirit.'[1]

In order to make our meaning clearer we may keep to this example of baptism as a perfect instance of the transcending sovereignty of Christ over all human beings. Water becomes an irresistible agent of sanctification under the breath of the victorious King: nothing can resist the power of baptismal water. It is worth reflecting on the mode of speech which the early Church uses with regard to this element, water. When the hearts of the people were touched by the words of Peter in the hour when the Spirit was sent forth, they appealed to him and the other Apostles: 'Men and brethren, what shall we do?' The reply is marvellously direct: 'Peter said to them: Do penance: and be baptized every one of you in the name of Jesus Christ for the remission of your sins. And you shall receive the gift of the Holy Ghost.'[2] There is no hesitation, there is no groping about; there is no uncertainty: 'be baptized every one of you in the name of Jesus Christ.' An external rite, the simplest rite in the world, will bring them into immediate contact with the great spiritual power that is seen and heard by everybody, the Paraclete: 'And you shall receive the gift of the Holy Ghost.' When the eunuch had been instructed by Philip on the road from Jerusalem to Gaza they came to a certain water; in this the man from Ethiopia sees his chance: 'And the eunuch said: See here is water, what doth hinder me from being baptized?' Philip, the deacon, has only one condition; 'If thou believest with all thy heart, thou mayest.' The eunuch makes a profession of faith that is as simple as it is comprehensive: 'I believe that Jesus Christ is the Son of God.' The scene that follows is matchless in its unquestioning acceptance of Christ's

[1] John iii. 6-8.   [2] Acts ii. 37-38.

power to sanctify anywhere and everywhere. 'And he commanded the chariot to stand still. And they went down into the water, both Philip and eunuch. And he baptized him.'[1] Again, Peter, after instructing the house of Cornelius, seeing how the Holy Spirit had come down on these catechumens, makes this remark: 'Can any man forbid water, that these should not be baptized, who have received the Holy Ghost, as well as we?'[2]

The water of baptism, then, is spoken of by the early Church as being a divine power. Water came from the pierced breast of Christ when He succumbed in the great battle, and from His Death there sprang forth the river of life, Baptism. We know that under certain conditions any human being can validly baptize wherever he may be. Any soul crying out for that Baptism is saved through its waters. The doctrine of Christian Baptism is such a stupendous assertion of Christ's power of sanctification that, unless we hold fast to our faith in His universal conquest of mankind, we could hardly bring ourselves to admit so universal a means of giving eternal life; for through this water countless millions of children are sanctified and made heirs of the kingdom of heaven; through this water all sins are washed away, and the greatest criminal finds himself clothed in the white robes of the children of God. It is not the act of man, it is the act of Christ. Faith and repentance are the only dispositions which are presupposed in the adult, to make him the fit subject of this great regeneration. Many more things we could say about the irresistible power of Baptism, of its effects, even in spite of the sins of man and the unworthiness of the ministers; for it is truly Christ who baptizes through the human ministry, and the Baptism of Christ is supremely efficacious because the dominion of Satan over mankind has been broken by Him. Infant baptism is but the natural consequence of this strong belief. To admit, as we do, that the new-born child can be given a second life incomprehensibly more lasting than the life it has from the mother's womb, is indeed to think in values which are entirely different from ordinary human standards. The child is as remote from a conscious rational act as could possibly be imagined, its physical life is of the frailest; and yet we say that through original sin its soul is in bondage to a dark power at one moment, while at the next it is translated into the kingdom of the

---

[1] Acts viii. 36-38.   [2] Acts x. 47.

Prince of Light by the sacrament of water. From that moment heaven is in the soul of that child, and the breast of that little one is the temple of the Holy Ghost; if the feeble natural life should cease, one more spirit has gone to swell the ranks of the angels that stand before the Throne of God. Well might we ask with Nicodemus: 'How can these things be?' The reply is, as always: 'Through the victory of the Son of God'.

We have already alluded to the intimate connexion between Christ's Resurrection and the power of remitting sin. The sacrament of Penance is indeed another aspect of Christ's triumph; sin is remitted because sin has been overcome by Him. The power that effaces sin committed after Baptism, is called the 'power of the Keys'. This metaphor primarily represents the Apostolic jurisdiction vested in St. Peter and his brethren; but Christ Himself, as a result of His victory, also holds the keys of life and death, of sin and grace: 'And to the angel of the church of Philadelphia write: These things saith the Holy One and the True One, He that hath the key of David, He that openeth and no man shutteth, shutteth and no man openeth.'[1] The remission of sins which Christ entrusted to the Apostles on the first Easter day is essentially destined for the believer, for him who is baptized in Christ; for the triumph of the Son of God is not only this, that He should conquer man, bringing him out of infidelity and making him His own through Baptism, but also His unlimited jurisdiction over His own and over their acts, so that He can forgive their sins without being obliged to give an account of His mercies. He is simply supreme in this matter of forgiveness because in His own Body He has destroyed all sin. The apparent facility with which the remission of sin is obtained by the faithful through the sacrament of Penance is a scandal to many; but to all those who have true understanding of the victory of Christ the unceasing murmurings of the words of absolution in the confessionals all over the world are like the music of the heavenly *cortège* that follows the triumphant Christ.

Of the Eucharist, as the sacrament of Christ's victory *par excellence*, we will speak in another chapter; in it there is the sacrificial aspect which constitutes an entirely new way for Christ's triumph to be brought home to man. The Christian priesthood with

[1] Apoc. iii. 7.

its powers and charismata, is the army of a triumphant cause. The certainties of the Catholic sacerdotal ministry cannot be understood, in fact they would be hardly tolerable, if the priesthood did not speak in the Name of One whose Name is above all other names. The Catholic contention that every marriage of Christians is a sacrament, again presupposes infinitely more than the world is ready to accept. It takes for granted that Christ's overlordship is not only an ideal of the mind, but that it is a juridical power which annuls every human undertaking that is against Christ's rights. The sanctification, moreover, of human propagation through a sacrament is hardly conceivable except through the assumption that the Son of God has power over all flesh, down to the very sources of human life.

In death we expect Christ to show forth His victory over the world, over sin, over Satan, in a most personal way in favour of each one of us. There is simply no end to the trust of the dying Christian. It is taken absolutely for granted that there can be no sort of peril or unknown evil awaiting the Christian soul on the other side, because the Son of God has overcome it all. There can be no rift in the armour of the Christian. If the chances of our encountering unforeseen dangers on our entering eternity were not more than one in a million, even that small fraction would be enough to snatch the laurels from Christ's brow; He would not be the complete Victor. But our trust in Him cannot envisage even such a remote possibility of danger. The profession of that trust is couched in terms of undying splendour by St. Paul: 'Nor height, nor depth, nor any other creature, shall be able to separate us from the love of God which is in Christ Jesus our Lord.'[1]

It is chiefly through that entirely new form of supernatural life, the sacramental graces, that the Christian people have become the worthy recipients of an encomium like the one from the pen of St. Peter: 'But you are a chosen generation, a kingly priesthood, a holy nation, a purchased people: that you may declare His virtues, who hath called you out of darkness into His marvellous light.'[2] Through the sacramental life in all its aspects the Christian people cry forth to the whole world the virtues of the divine Victor, who has made the kingdom of light to succeed the kingdom of darkness.

[1] Rom. viii. 39.   [2] 1 Peter ii. 9.

CHAPTER XVI

Christ's Victory and the Persecution of the Church

ONE of the profoundest originalities of Christianity is in this: that its divine Founder makes it a part of His message to announce every kind of hardship and contradiction as the normal condition of existence for His followers. Were it not for the optimism that makes Him declare all evil to be the road to victory, Christ might be called a prophet of evil, for none has spoken more darkly of the future. His coming as the Redeemer of mankind does not mean the holding up of the human tragedy, of the ills that are the unavoidable accompaniment of life's journey: 'Nation shall rise against nation, and kingdom against kingdom. And there shall be great earthquakes in divers places and pestilences and famines and terrors from heaven: and there shall be great signs.'[1] Wars there will be, as much as and even more than ever. The *pressura gentium*, the 'distress of nations,' seems particularly the fate reserved to mankind in the days that follow its Redemption by the God-Man. From that multitude of calamities Christ does not promise His disciples physical immunity, though He constantly promises an immunity of a much higher kind. But there is even more than this general announcement that the world would be left to its own sad destinies. Tribulations of a peculiar kind are in store for His disciples, for His Church, precisely because they are His own: 'If the world hate you, know ye that it hath hated Me before you. If you had been of the world, the world would love its own: but because you are not of the world, but I have chosen you out of the world, therefore the world hateth you. Remember My word that I said to you: The servant is not greater than his master. If they have persecuted Me, they will also persecute you. If they have kept My word, they will keep yours also. But all these things they will do to you for My name's sake: because they know not Him that sent Me.'[2] Christians will share in the identical misfortune which was

---

[1] Luke xxi. 10, 11.   [2] John xv. 18-21.

Christ's own, namely to be put to death, because men think they are doing a service to God by that. Jesus was crucified because the Jewish priesthood declared Him to be a blasphemer of God. So to His disciples Jesus says: 'These things have I spoken to you, that you may not be scandalized. They will put you out of the synagogues: yea, the hour cometh, that whosoever killeth you will think that he doth a service to God. And these things will they do to you; because they have not known the Father nor Me.'[1] Our Lord speaks of the great catastrophes and the persecutions and scandals as of things that are unavoidable: 'For these things must come to pass.'[2] Into a world thus doomed Christ sends His dear disciples, as 'sheep among wolves.' A more telling metaphor human imagination could not invent in order to describe the unfavourable milieu which this world is for the believer. So we are absolutely certain of this fact, that Christ's victory could not mean a miraculous alteration of the course of human destinies. This the Son of God never contemplated as belonging to His mission here on earth. His victory is achieved in that unfavourable milieu, *in medio inimicorum suorum*.

All this, of course, is applicable only to the present age, to the Kingdom of God in this world. In reality, Christ's victory over adverse circumstances is as complete as His triumph over sin and death. In the endless ages of eternity the absolute sovereignty of Christ will be as manifest as all His other attributes. No head will be raised up against Him. In comparison with eternity this present time of trial is as nothing. Compared with the infinitude of the glorious eternity, thousands of years of Church history, with all their records of persecution, are in reality not much longer than the thirty-three years of Christ's mortal life, when He was in the state of kenosis, of humiliation. But if by absolute reckoning the days are few, they are admittedly evil, very evil, and their darkness might obscure for us the supreme fact that Christ is truly victorious. But with His frankness in announcing the evils to come Christ invariably unites solemn assurances that nothing can hurt us. He seems to take a delight in this contrast, the mountainous form of the evils, and their complete powerlessness to do His disciples any harm: 'But a hair of your head shall not perish.'[3] It is not only the general watchfulness of God's providence, it is a direct dispensation that is the

---

[1] John xvi. 1-3.   [2] Matt. xxiv. 6.   [3] Luke xxi. 18.

cause of this preservation in the midst of cataclysms; the immunity of the elect is part of Christ's own immunity from evil. For though Christ conquered Satan, sin and death, He succumbed externally to the ferocity of His enemies. So the elect may succumb, but they cannot be hurt in their real life. Above all, the transient success of the powers of darkness is unable to produce in the faithful the impression that Christ's cause is weak; for they see with a clear vision the coming of judgement. They are not seduced, they are not led to alter their faith in Christ, to think of Him otherwise than in terms of immutable majesty. 'Then if any man shall say to you, Lo, here is Christ, or there: do not believe him. For there shall arise false Christs and false prophets and shall shew great signs and wonders, insomuch as to deceive (if possible) even the elect.'[1] This is the supreme grace and genius of Christianity: that the signs and wonders of false prophets cannot seduce the minds of the faithful.

What Christ had said repeatedly concerning the Christian's immunity from real harm in a world full of woes, has been magnificently amplified by that Spirit who was sent to announce the things that are to come: 'For He shall not speak of Himself: but what things soever He shall hear, He shall speak. And the things that are to come He shall shew you.'[2] These words of Christ make it evident that some 'showing' of future events is part of the Spirit's mission. This was done chiefly through the Revelation to St. John, called the Apocalypse: 'And the Lord God of the spirits of the prophets sent His angel to shew His servant the things which must be done shortly.'[3] The great prophecy of John, the beloved disciple, is a fit conclusion to the Scriptures, not only through the splendour of the vision, but chiefly through the greatness of the lesson it inculcates, the persistence of the Lamb's triumph in spite of every adversity and hostility. In the Apocalypse, as in the Gospels, the external conditions under which the elect live are put before us with ruthless frankness. There are dark passages like this: 'And it was given unto him [the dragon] to make war with the saints and to overcome them. And power was given to him over every tribe and people and tongue and nation.'[4] Yet with all those concessions to the powers of darkness the real issue is never doubtful; the evil powers will fight the

---

[1] Matt. xxiv. 23, 24.   [2] John xvi. 13.
[3] Apoc. xxii. 6.   [4] Apoc. xiii. 7.

Lamb with one accord, but it is all in vain; 'These shall fight with
the Lamb, and the Lamb shall overcome them, because He is the
Lord of lords and King of kings: and they that are with Him are
called, and elect, and faithful.'[1] We may, in a way, readily understand why the revelation of God to man should be crowned with a
prophetic vision of the future; it will always be the Christian's chief
practical difficulty to see a victorious Christ through the overshadowing clouds of human events. More than once the words of
the Apocalypse will be fulfilled: 'And the sun became black as sack-
cloth of hair: and the whole moon became as blood.'[2] But at no
time is the actual figure of the divine fighter obscured; He rides
forth as an invincible conqueror.

It is a striking feature of that wonderful book that no clear distinction is drawn in it between the final triumph of Christ at the end
of all time and His triumph in the actual present. Many of the
glorious scenes of victory depicted in the Apocalypse are applicable,
and have to be applied, to both states, the final eschatological state
and the present transient state of temptation. It would be distinctly
wrong not to apply to our present conditions some of the tableaux
of victory delineated by the great seer. It is the genius of St. John in
all his writings, in his Gospel, in his Epistles, in his Revelation, to
show how the mystery of the eternal life, of the divine victory,
belongs to the present time as well as to the future world; how the
eternal life is in us now, how we have the victory over the world
now, though the full meaning of that life and of that victory will be
revealed only when Christ shall appear in glory. There is no reason
why we should not apply to the Christian people of the present
time that description which constitutes one of the most famous
passages in the Apocalypse, though by a natural transition the image
moves from the present æon into the state of eternity. We could
not conclude this chapter more usefully than by quoting it here,
exhorting our readers to think of themselves as members of that
wonderful people. (One of the arguments adduced in order to prove
that St. John speaks of earthly conditions, at least to begin with, is
this: the multitude which he sees is 'of all nations and tribes and
peoples and tongues'; this formula naturally points to earthly conditions.) 'After this, I saw a great multitude, which no man could

[1] Apoc. xvii. 14.   [2] Apoc. vi. 12.

number, of all nations and tribes and peoples and tongues, standing before the throne and in sight of the Lamb, clothed with white robes, and palms in their hands. And they cried with a loud voice, saying: Salvation to our God, who sitteth upon the throne, and to the Lamb. And all the angels stood round about the throne and the ancients and the four living creatures. And they fell down before the throne upon their faces and adored God, saying: Amen. Benediction and glory and wisdom and thanksgiving, honour and power and strength, to our God, for ever and ever. Amen. And one of the ancients answered and said to me: These that are clothed in white robes, who are they? And whence came they? And I said to him: My Lord, thou knowest. And he said to me: These are they who are come out of great tribulation and have washed their robes and have made them white in the blood of the Lamb. Therefore, they are before the throne of God; and they serve Him day and night in His temple. And He that sitteth on the throne shall dwell over them. They shall no more hunger nor thirst: neither shall the sun fall on them, nor any heat. For the Lamb, which is in the midst of the throne, shall rule them and shall lead them to the fountains of the waters of life: and God shall wipe away all tears from their eyes.'[1] It is the present-day Christian who can be said to be standing before the throne and in the sight of the Lamb, clothed with a white robe and with a palm in his hand, because through his faith and his grace he is truly in the midst of the divine mystery.

CHAPTER XVII

The Holy Eucharist, Monument of Christ's Victory

WE must take it as a fundamental principle of Christian thought that the Christ who presides over the destinies of the Church is the victorious Christ; the One who said: 'Behold I am with you all days, even to the consummation of the

[1] Apoc. vii. 9-17.

world,'[1] is the conqueror of Satan, sin and death. So all the manifestations of Christ's power and presence are, by their very nature,
exhibitions of the divine victory. Even when we celebrate the memory of Christ's Passion and Death, we are invariably conscious of the
glories that followed after. So we are justified in looking upon every
one of the sacraments of the Church as a direct act of divine conquest of the human race by the Christ who dwells in glory. From
the right hand of God, through the sacraments, Jesus enters into the
very flesh and bone of the human race as an assimilating power
binding man to Himself. But there is one sacrament which may
truly be called *the* sacrament of Christ's victory, because through its
very constitution it is a monument of the great achievement of the
Son of God, our liberation from all evils through His Blood. This
sacrament is the Blessed Eucharist. In it we celebrate Christ's
triumph with a directness that leaves nothing to be desired as to the
true significance of that venerable sacrament. It is difficult to find
terms for realities so extraordinary and so new to human experience.
One would fain ask leave to coin expressions that would in a way do
justice to one's thinking, if not to the reality itself. So I should like
to speak of Christ's victory as the mystery of 'immortal death,'
mors immortalis, and this for two reasons. Firstly, the Death of
Christ is an event which, historically speaking, happened once, but
which, in the dispensation of the Christian sacrament of the
Eucharist, is perpetuated in a mystical way. Then I call Christ's
Death immortal, because immortality was so much a part of that
passing away on the Cross, that the Death of Jesus must truly be
considered as but a brief and miraculous interruption of His native
immortality. This immortality surrounds the Death of Jesus as the
waters of the ocean press from all sides on the deep keel of a ship,
urged by their natural fluidity to fill up the gap as the keel moves on.
Not mortality but immortality was Christ's natural condition even
whilst here on earth; so His Death could never be regarded as an
isolated event, but must be read in the light of the vaster event, the
rapidly-returning immortality, in other words—His Resurrection.

Nothing could happen to Christ that would necessarily end His
life here on earth; He laid it down Himself; the divinity that was in
Him could always prevent that separation between soul and body

[1] Matt. xxviii. 20.

which, in human language, means death. He Himself committed
His soul to His Father. So we have to admit that if cruelties that
would cause death to ordinary mortals were inflicted on Christ's
human nature, in His case death would not follow unless He willed
it, for as a divine Person He had full possession of that soul which
would not leave the body except by His will. Says St. Thomas:
'Christ's spirit had the power to keep the nature of His flesh, so that
it would not be crushed by any hurt whatsoever inflicted on it. This
power the soul of Christ possessed because it was united with the
Word of God in oneness of Person, as Augustine says in the Fourth
Book on the Trinity. As Christ, then, of His own accord, did not
repulse from His own body the hurt done to it, but willed that His
bodily nature should succumb to the injury, it is truly said that He
laid down His soul or that He died of His own accord.'[1] St. Leo
abounds in the same sense. 'Although the ferocity of the Jews was
aflame and ready to carry out their criminal design, yet no violence
could have been done to the temple of Christ's body had He not
allowed it Himself, because God was in Christ, reconciling the
world unto Himself. But as it was determined that another kind of
work (than an effect of the divine omnipotence) should bring about
the liberation of mankind, and as otherwise the Blood of Christ
could not have been the price of the Redemption of the believers,
had the Saviour not been laid hold upon, He allowed the godless to
stretch forth their hand against Him. He kept in check the power of
the Godhead, so that the glory of the Passion might be reached.'[2]
The Bishop of Hippo speaks in the language of the Pope of Rome, so
we read in St. Augustine's Fourth Book on the Trinity [chapter xiii]
referred to by St. Thomas: 'The Mediator did not leave His flesh
against His will, but because He willed, when He willed and as He
willed, because He was united to the Word of God in oneness of
Person. ... It is not because some power had jurisdiction over Him
that He was deprived of His bodily life, but He stripped Himself of
it: for He who had it in His power not to die if He did not want to
die, without any doubt died because He so willed, and therefore
He held in mockery principalities and powers, showing unhesitat-
ingly His victory over them in His own Person. For this was His
purpose in dying, that through the one most true Sacrifice offered

[1] S. Th. III, Quest. xlvii, Art. 1.   [2] St. Leo, Sermo LXV (Migne, P.L. LIV).

up for us, He might cleanse and abolish and extinguish whatever claim there was through our sins for the principalities and powers to make us the objects of just punishment.'[1] We see here how St. Augustine, by a natural sequence of thought, identifies the two concepts, sacrifice and voluntary death.

Coming now to the great memorial of the Lord, the divine Eucharist, it as as much the sacrament of Christ's Resurrection as of His Death, because it is the monument of that Death like unto which there is no other death. It is a commemoration of that victorious passage unto the Father, that new and supreme Passover, of which the first Passover was but a faint figure. Therefore 'as often as we eat that Bread and drink of that Cup we show forth the death of the Lord until He come'[2]; a Death that is in every respect a triumph, because the advent here alluded to is not a coming from the realm of the dead, but from the kingdom of eternal life. This phrase of St. Paul, 'until He come,' could easily have been twisted into a half-pagan meaning, into the expectation of the return of a dead hero. But Christian sentiment has been proof against any such distortion. The dead Lord's coming that is part of the Eucharistic significance, the Eucharistic 'showing forth', is a coming from the realms of glory and life. The world has never known a rite of such triumphant signification, wherein the whole meaning is a victory of unsurpassed proportions. The Real Presence lifts that rite into the region of the infinite and the divine. Nothing in the Eucharist speaks of failure or loss; everything proclaims fulfilment of the desires of the Son of God: 'And when the hour was come, He sat down: and the twelve apostles with Him. And He said to them: With desire I have desired to eat this pasch with you, before I suffer. For I say to you that from this time I will not eat it, till it be fulfilled in the kingdom of God.'[3] Christ from the supper-room sees the glorious future, the Eucharist that is food and drink in the kingdom of God, the Christian Church. So the sacrament of His Body and Blood is above all things a thanksgiving, a *Eucharistia*, for the great victory. As such its prototype appears when Melchisedech the high priest offers bread and wine: 'But Melchisedech the king of Salem, bringing forth bread and wine, for he was the priest of the most high God, blessed him, and said: Blessed be Abram by the most high God, who created heaven and

---

[1] *Loc. cit.* (Migne, *P.L.* XLII).   [2] 1 Cor. xi. 26.   [3] Luke xxii. 14-16.

earth. And blessed be the most high God, by whose protection the enemies are in thy hands. And he gave him the tithes of all.'[1] The Eucharist is the sacrifice of thanksgiving for the victory of Christ in all its manifold aspects. As it is a commemoration, the element of thanksgiving must, as a matter of course, be predominant; for the event, the liberation of captive humanity through the death of Christ, could not be remembered except with supreme gratitude. In the words of the sacred Council of Trent, the Eucharist is a pasch, a feast of rejoicing, for ever commemorating the passing from servitude unto liberty. 'Christ instituted a new pasch, when He gave Himself to be immolated by the Church through the hands of the priests under visible signs, in memory of that passage of His from this world unto the Father, when He redeemed us through the pouring forth of His Blood, when He delivered us from the power of darkness and brought us into His own Kingdom.'[2]

It is Catholic faith that the Eucharistic sacrifice is one and the same with the sacrifice of the Cross: *una enim et eadem est hostia*. There is this, however—and through this circumstance the identity of the sacrifice is not interfered with—the Eucharistic sacrifice is the *memoria*, the commemoration, of the sacrifice of the Cross, and therefore its thanksgiving, its song of praise and victory. We might be permitted to say that the Death of the Lord, the remembrance of which is the very essence of the sacrifice of the Christian altar, appears in the Eucharist chiefly from that aspect of immortality which we said belongs to it at all times. So in the same breath the Church commemorates at Mass Christ's Death, Resurrection and Ascension, as belonging to the great remembrance; because Christ's Death was truly and necessarily a passing from this world unto the Father, unto glory and majesty. In this it is different from all other deaths. And so the Eucharist, though essentially a memory of the dying of Christ, is quite naturally a triumphant act of Christ, performed on the altars of Christendom. One of the technical modes of stating the Eucharistic sacrifice is to say that the Mass applies to us all the fruits of the sacrifice of the Cross. This is simply another way of declaring the same mystery: it is the triumph, the dividing of the spoils after the successful battle. The Eucharistic sacrifice is in no way prejudicial to the redemptive efficacy of the sacrifice of the

---

[1] Gen. xiv. 18-20.   [2] Sessio xxiii, c. 1.

Cross, as the Council of Trent is careful to remind us. It is not a new merit added to those of Christ's cruel Death on Calvary. It is essentially a triumph, the celebration of a great achievement, the victory of the bloody struggle of the first Good Friday. No hymn of rejoicing is too enthusiastic, no manifestation of joy excessive, in those who are privileged to be the sharers of the Christian altar. How rightly the laureate poet of the Eucharist urges us:

> Quantum potes, tantum aude:
> Quia major omni laude
> Nec laudare sufficis![1]

Even when we celebrate Mass in a penitential spirit, for the remission of our sins, the note of victory is not less clear, because we are reconciled to God in virtue of the showing forth of the divine Blood under the sacramental veil, as it is the glory of the risen life. In this sense the Eucharist is truly a heavenly sacrifice because its two adorable elements, the Body and the Blood, are not of earth but of heaven. So Christian tradition has it that the hosts of heaven surround the altar on which the divine mysteries are celebrated.

The Council of Trent gives us another hint that makes us perceive, at least dimly, another aspect of that invincibility of glory which belongs to the Eucharist. The Council says that this immaculate sacrifice cannot suffer any stain through the iniquity of man: *Et hæc quidem illa munda oblatio est, quæ nulla indignitate aut malitia offerentium inquinari potest.*[2] In other words, the Eucharistic sacrifice is independent of human worth; the unworthy priest cannot throw a shadow into that world of light which is the Eucharist; even when he offers Mass with a sin-stained conscience, the faith of the Church, who is the real sacrificant, transcends the individual shortcomings of her minister. So the priest before his Communion prays that God look not at his sins but at the faith of the Church: *Ne respecias peccata mea sed fidem Ecclesiæ tuae.*

The partaking of that sacrifice, Holy Communion, is essentially

[1] Strive thy best to praise Him well,
Yet doth He all praise excel;
None can ever reach His due.

St. Thomas Aquinas: *Lauda, Sion.*

[2] Sessio xxii. c. 1.

and intrinsically in the nature of a banquet; it is eating the Flesh and drinking the Blood that gave life to the world; it is a participation in the Cup of the Lord, it is an eating at the table of the Lord, in opposition to the dark and sinister rites of paganism that were an enslavement to Satan: 'You cannot drink the chalice of the Lord and the chalice of devils; you cannot be partakers of the table of the Lord and of the table of devils.'[1] Festiveness is the only temper which Christians may bring to the reception of that heavenly bread; they cannot be sad, they must rejoice with the angels in heaven when eating that divine manna. It is not known to the history of Christian spirituality that the faithful ever approached the Euchar- istic table with other dispositions than those of gladness and triumph; at Holy Communion Christians join the white-robed army which stands before the throne of God and of the Lamb. To be allowed to partake of the altar, of the offering that is on the altar, is the supreme privilege of religion; it makes the distinction between the adherent of that religion and the outsider, or even the mere aspirant: 'We have an altar whereof they have no power to eat who serve the tabernacle.'[2] The servers of the Jewish tabernacle are excluded from participation in the Christian altar: such exclusion is the persistent and strictest law of the Church. The faithful, on the contrary, have this privilege: their communication in the mysteries of the altar gives to them, in the words of one of the oldest and most mysterious prayers of the Canon of the Mass, the sacrosanct Body and Blood of Christ with all heavenly benediction and grace. 'We beseech Thee, O Lord God Almighty ... that all those of us who shall receive the most sacred Body and Blood of Thy Son, through this our participation of the altar, may be filled with every kind of heavenly blessing and grace.' The words *ex hac altaris participatione* are one of the profoundest liturgical terms, difficult of translation, because they express an idea from which we have been estranged to a large extent, namely, that Holy Communion is essentially a participation in the sacrifice of the altar.

[1] 1 Cor. x. 21.   [2] Heb. xiii. 10.

CHAPTER XVIII

The Behaviour of the Believer in Christ's Victory

TOTALITY of atonement for human sin through Christ is an article of faith so vast and so astonishing that, in a way, all merely human calculations in the ethical order are upset by it. What becomes of human guilt in the face of a justice so overwhelming and so unlimited as is the justice of the atoning Son of God, who was 'made sin' for us that through Him we should 'become justice'? So there is every reason for us to ask the question: how do men who sincerely believe in atonement, in the victory of Christ, view human sin? Ought we not to expect them to make light of human sin for this very reason that in Christ Jesus it is destroyed as thoroughly as if it had never been a living act on the part of man? For let us never forget that, according to the energetic language of St. Paul, the Atonement is a destruction of sin. We can never say enough concerning the power of the Blood of Christ to do away with sin; it pursues sin and destroys it with a kind of divine fury. What then is left of sin? Has it any horror, any sting, after the passing of the Blood of the Lamb? Is not every sin committed by men in the course of the ages in a way still-born, since the Lamb of God has taken upon Himself all the sins of the world and destroyed them in His own Body on the tree of the Cross? We ought not to marvel if the minds of believers have been dazzled at times by the victory of the Cross, and have not found it easy to distinguish clearly the respective places of the two opposite powers, the power of sin and the power of the Atonement. Yet it may be asserted without fear of contradiction that universal Christian sentiment has preserved a real and sincere horror of sin, a horror that is all the greater because Christ died to wipe away all iniquity. Sin, in popular language, has crucified Christ; and that very Death of God which destroys sin makes the full hideousness of that sin appear before the eyes of all men.

We may not be able to find a key to this psychological paradox of the Christian conscience, but the fact is indubitable: in practical life faith in the Atonement has not diminished dread of sin among

Christians; it has enormously increased it. But no doubt the theological explanation is not beyond our reach. Christ has hated sin; this is the reason of His readiness to shed His blood as a cleansing from sin. Through His Spirit the Son of God instils into the hearts of Christians the very feelings that are in Himself; His own heart's horror at the very sight of sin is to be found in the hearts of those who are His. This detestation was the cause of Christ's profound humiliation, of His ignominious Death on the Cross. So there can be no other attitude for the Christian towards sin than a similar detestation, with the bitter remembrance that the Son of God was thus degraded through bearing *our* sin: 'For let this mind be in you, which was also in Christ Jesus: who being in the form of God, thought it not robbery to be equal with God: but emptied Himself, taking the form of a servant, being made in the likeness of men, and in habit found as a man. He humbled Himself, becoming obedient unto death, even to the death of the cross.'[1] The destruction of sin which Christ undertook, if fully comprehended, includes this, that through His Spirit He should produce in His followers a supernatural detestation of all iniquity, similar to His own. If, having been told that God has atoned for all sin, man were left to appraise its meaning by his sole natural resources, he might indeed be very uncertain how to do so; but such is by no means the case. Man is given a direct share in Christ's own Spirit, that Spirit of sanctity who prompted Him to offer Himself up as a pure oblation for all the defilement of the human race. The spirit of repentance for sin committed has thus become one of the main features of Christian spiritual life. It may indeed be called the human side of the Atonement, man's own share in the mystery of the destruction of sin. With our faith in Christ's victory over sin there is united our faith in the necessity of human repentance; so that there can be no question for the Christian of a falsifying of moral values, or of a minimising of ethical burdens, on account of the basic fact of the divine act that makes sin appear as if it had not been. We must therefore look upon repentance for the voluntary trespasses of the will as the human manifestation of the infinite mystery of the cleansing Blood of the Lamb. We do not, in Christian spirituality, repent isolatedly; we repent in Christ, with some of the sorrow that

[1] Phil. ii. 5-8.

filled His soul when He contemplated our infidelities towards God.

Faith in Christ's victory cannot lead to any kind of antinomianism, either in the speculative or practical order. By antinomianism is meant that aberration of man's conscience which makes him believe that he is freed from all law because he holds a privileged place, because he is the object of some quite special favour. It would be antinomianism if anyone thought himself at liberty to act as he chooses because Christ has paid the debt of punishment for all delinquencies. Now such an aberration could never be the consequence of an unquestioning acceptance of the fact that Christ has overcome all evil. Human repentance is part of that victory, as we have already said more fully when treating of the remission of sin through Christ's Resurrection. It would be of little service here to go into the historical side of this matter, and examine to what extent such antinomianism has manifested itself in the course of the life of the Church. The name of Luther naturally comes to one's mind, as the originator of protestantism is credited precisely with such a one-sided view of Christ's redemptive triumph that neither good works on the part of man, nor repentance, has any place in his scheme of human salvation. We might say that Luther's is a remarkable instance of faith in the Atonement producing the effect dreaded all along, that of making human guilt appear as nothing in face of an atoning sanctity so overwhelming as that of Christ. But, to do Luther justice, his antinomianism was only partial; his mind was bewildered by the blow that nailed all human guilt to the Cross and effaced it in the Blood of the divine Victim. But his belittling of the necessity of human repentance was not whole-hearted; it was full of compromises with the traditional Christian psychology, which, as we have seen, is a marvellous blending of God's act and man's sorrow for sin.

CHAPTER XIX

The Religion of Victory

THE basic fact of Christ's victory affects Christianity in all its forms, whether it be private religion or official worship. The Christian must think of himself as of one bought with a great price; he must think of the world as being redeemed; and he must view all the events of human history as being subsidiary to a fully-established and inflexible plan of spiritual liberation. It is therefore not too much to say that Christian religion differs not only in degree but in kind from natural religion. Owing to this presupposition of a consummated state of spiritual conquest there is in Christian worship an element that is unique and quite original. We perform acts of adoration, of thanksgiving; we pray, we intercede, we crave for forgiveness, as other religious men who believe in God have done and are doing; but we do more, because the Divine has come much nearer to us through the mystery of the Incarnation and through the advent of the Holy Ghost. It is, however, not only a higher prayer, but a different prayer, when we deal with God precisely as Christians, that is to say, in the Name of Christ and in the name of His victory. For this is the Christian's privilege, that he comes before God and remains with Him in virtue of the great conquest made by His Only Begotten Son. We may call this the dividing of the spoils amongst the followers of the divine Captain after the victorious battle. It ought to be evident, even to the least thoughtful, that the victory of Christ has brought into the supernatural world, and into man's relationship with God, an entirely new element, quite unsuspected before. Man is not only a suppliant before the face of his Maker, he is the sharer of a glorious privilege; he is fellow-heir with Christ; the good things that come to Christ through His mighty victory fall also into the laps of His brethren. Any worship that left out of consideration this supreme addition to the supernatural order, would be not only an imperfect but a positively defective Catholicism. However sincere and ardent adoration, praise and thanksgiving might be, if Catholic worship had nothing more than these functions it would not be essentially higher than ancient Judaism. But it has something that is all its own and we may call it 'the religion of victory'. We Christians ought to feel as a nation feels when, with its king, it celebrates the day of victorious peace that ends a long war. The rejoicing of sovereign and people is a common rejoicing, the advantages of the successful contest are common advantages, the glory of it belongs to every member of the nation. This is only a feeble simile of a mighty spiritual reality. Christian souls in their multitudes are fellow-victors with Christ; the day of Christ's triumphal ascending is their day of rejoicing, and the air of gladness is everywhere. There is more than that: there is the partaking in the spoils. There is in Christian religion this one thing which no other religion ever professed to possess: the claim to definite advantages on the part of the faithful because Christ has conquered. Christian prayer may be intercession and supplication, but it may also be the staking of a claim; we lay our hands on riches and we call them our own, because we belong to the kingdom of the triumphant Christ: 'But to every one of us is given grace, according to the measure of the giving of Christ. Wherefore He saith: Ascending on high, He led captivity captive: He gave gifts to men. Now that He ascended, what is it, but because He also descended first into the lower parts of the earth? He that descended is the same also that ascended above all heavens; that He might fill all things.'[1]

This is the true meaning of prayer through Christ, a new prayer, not known before, because previous to that great victory no man dared to claim a share in the gifts of God. This is indeed the innermost meaning of Catholic liturgy. Liturgy is more than worship, it is worship plus that great claim of which we have spoken just now. If there were no justification for such a claim there would not be, properly speaking, a Christian liturgy. When the Catholic approaches God, he approaches Him in the Name of Christ, in the name of His merits, in the name of Redemption, in one word: in the name of Christ's victory. The formula *per Dominum nostrum Jesus Christum* acquires true meaning precisely through this claim which Christian faith inserts into religion, and which no religion ever possessed before. 'And in that day you shall not ask Me anything. Amen, amen, I say to you: if you ask the Father any thing in

[1] Eph. iv. 7-10.

My Name, He will give it you.'[1] They do not ask, and yet it is granted; they ask in Christ's name, and it is granted. Could there be a clearer pronouncement concerning the Christian's right to possess the riches of the Son of God? Catholic liturgy, therefore, is more a celebration than a supplication; it speaks to God, it reminds Him of all that has been achieved; it is a direct entering into the treasure house of God; it is a free partaking of the banquet of God. Unless we had this sense of spiritual possession which comes to us through Christ's conquest, we should have no true liturgy, we should have only the ordinary human prayer.

It is obvious, then, that the whole sacramental system, with the blessed Eucharist as its centre, is an evident embodiment of this new relationship between God and man; what we have said in a preceding chapter on the victory of Christ through the sacraments, and through the Eucharist in particular, is only another way of expressing the leading idea of this present chapter. The great theological notion of the *opus operatum* could be called the doctrine of man's claims on God, in virtue of Christ's conquest. Through the *opus operatum* we receive the best and the most perfect gifts without asking for them. We receive them, not through supplication, but through celebration, through an official act which we perform with absolute certainty as God's ministers. With a firm step we enter into the Holy of Holies, carrying the prize of the divine victory, and there is the distribution of these gifts of the risen Christ on a scale truly divine. It was to be expected of course, that the denial of the sacramental theology of the Catholic Church would mean a complete reversal of conditions in man's intercourse with God; such a denial must of necessity be the end of what we call here the religion of victory. It is to be remarked, however, that interference with the sacramental doctrine of the Church on the part of protestantism was not so radical as might appear at first sight. Under a disguise, and under different names, some of the reformers really clung to the doctrine of the *opus operatum*, of a distribution of divine favours beyond the merits of man's acts. No greater blow could be dealt to the Christian economy of grace than a refusal to admit divine largesses which are far in excess of man's merit, whether this be through the sacraments or through some other channel; it would

[1] John xvi. 23.

reduce the position of the victorious Christ to that of a mere auxiliary of man instead of the Prince of Glory who enriches all those who follow Him.

Although the religion of victory shines with greatest brightness on the sacramental life, it would be wrong to think that the other acts of the supernatural life of the Christian are devoid of that quality; besides the divine claim, the Christian has the ordinary powers of prayer, of supplication, of intercession; but these powers in their turn have been transformed and elevated through the very fact of Christ's victory. The Christian prayer has a perfection all its own through this divine circumstance, that it is 'through Jesus Christ.' The Christian implores divine forgiveness whenever he has sinned; but his cry for mercy is not like the repentance of other men, because his prayer for forgiveness becomes part of a divine advocacy, of a confident prayer that is more than intercession or supplication: 'My little children, these things I write to you that you may not sin. But if any man sin, we have an advocate with the Father, Jesus Christ the just. And He is the propitiation for our sins: and not for ours only, but also for those of the whole world.'[1] Whatever is indispensable to the life of the soul, whether as an individual or as a member of society, comes through a divine promise, through that settled estate which is called Christ's inheritance; the Father gives it to us because He loves us, and He loves us because we love the Son; we are expected to ask, but the asking is not the cry of the outcast, it is a reminder that we are the sons of God and the lovers of Christ, and as such we expect to be heard. 'Because I go to the Father: and whatsoever you shall ask the Father in My name, that will I do: that the Father may be glorified in the Son. If you shall ask Me anything in My name, that will I do.'[2] 'If you abide in Me and My words abide in you, you shall ask whatever you will: and it shall be done unto you.'[3]

If we call divine praise 'liturgy', as we ought to do, then of course the identity between the religion of victory and the liturgy is manifest. Our hymns to God and His Christ must be songs of victory, for we are like those who come home after having overcome the enemy and who have loaded themselves with spoils. It may perhaps be urged as an objection against the idea of complete originality which

[1] 1 John ii. 1, 2.   [2] John xiv. 13, 14.   [3] John xv. 7.

we claim for Catholic liturgy that most of its texts are the Psalms
and Canticles of the Old Testament. Has Christianity really a worship different in kind, if the bulk of its liturgy is borrowed from the
Jewish religion? Such an objection could only be made by those who
are strangers to the Catholic doctrine of Scriptural inspiration. The
Old Testament is the preparation for the New Dispensation; the
Psalms and the Prophecies are full of Christ; Christ is in the
Canticles of David and in the Canticles of Moses. He explains to the
disciples, after the Resurrection, all that those ancient hymns say
of Him; it is a supreme evidence of His being the expected Messiah.
We should not be surprised, therefore, that the Christian mysteries
are celebrated and expressed most effectively when we make use of
the language of the Old Testament. But the liturgical prayers and
hymns which are the composition of the Church herself, i.e. of her
pontiffs, doctors, saints and poets, are one long canticle of victory.
A slight change may, no doubt, be noticed in some of the modern
compositions, where the note of condolence with the offended God
is more noticeable. But this nuance is so slight that it cannot make
a difference to the universal song of praise that rises day and night to
the throne of the victorious Christ. There is no need to quote from
the liturgical books of the Church, for every prayer might be cited
in evidence of the Church's true spirit. One well-known canticle,
however, may be alluded to: the *Exultet* of the Holy Saturday celebration. 'Let the angelic choirs of heaven now rejoice; let the
divine mystery rejoice; and let the trumpet of salvation resound for
the victory of so great a king. Let the earth also rejoice, illumined
with such splendour; and, enlightened by the brightness of the
eternal king, let it feel that the darkness of the whole world is dis-
persed. Let also our Mother, the Church, rejoice, adorned with the
brightness of so great light; and may this temple resound with the
loud voices of the people.'

CHAPTER XX

The Victory of the Christian

IT is one of the most permanent features of Christian spiritual literature to describe the higher life in terms of victory. Not only the supreme fidelity of martyrdom is hailed as a victory, but every advance of man in the supernatural life is the defeating of an adverse power. In Christ Himself this wide application of the metaphor of victory to all the phases and acts of the spiritual order would not be a correct reading of the facts. The Son of God made Man had no opposition to defeat, no darkness to overcome, in His own interior life. He was sinless and infinitely above all the allurements of human temptations. He had the clear vision and the perfect possession of God; so that it cannot be said of Him that He had the gifts of faith and hope, as He was already *in termino*, in that very centre towards which other men are led gradually by faith and hope. His internal charity was no struggle to Him as He was perfect in all things. His struggle, and therefore His victory, was in the external work which the Father had given Him to do, the work of Redemption, as we have said in a previous chapter. In this, then, we differ from our Redeemer. The whole supernatural order without exception is not congenital to us as it is to Christ. It is grafted on a raw, desperately undivine nature, and to begin with we are strangers and foreigners to grace. So it is true to say that the supernatural dispensation is not held by us except through a constant struggle, is not made use of except through effort, and every step forward, every achievement in our spiritual life, is truly a victory. Fidelity unto the end is described as such by the Spirit of Jesus: 'To him that shall overcome, I will give to sit with Me in My throne: as I also have overcome and am set down with My Father in His throne. He that hath an ear, let him hear what the Spirit saith to the churches.'[1]

The grace of Christ in the souls He has conquered is not only abundant, it is multifarious. It has never escaped the masters of the life of the spirit that there is a variety of ways within the one great dispensation of Christian sanctity. For some centuries the distinction

[1] Apoc. iii. 21, 22.

between the active and the contemplative way has been much stressed, perhaps unduly; still the distinction has the advantage of bringing before our eyes the great fact of the variousness of the grace of Christ. But there is no grace, to whichever way it belongs, that is not a conquest of the soul by the Spirit, a surrender of man's mind and will to a higher Power; nay, a victory within man's own intimate personality, one side of the human individuality rising superior to the other.

In this matter Catholic supernatural life parts company with the majority of modern psychologists. Our higher life as Christians is essentially a state that does not belong to us; it is in every instance a conquest; it is the sovereignty of an external power, not the expression of our own self or the development of what is in us. This, of course, is evident in the whole sphere of the supernatural *per essentiam*, in the supernatural properly so-called; in faith, hope and charity, the workings of the sevenfold Spirit within us. In all these activities we are conquered by God, we are led into captivity by God, we are taken hold of in a most masterful way by God, we are no longer our own. Faith is a power that, in the words of St. Paul, 'bringeth into captivity every understanding into the obedience of Christ.'[1] St. Thomas Aquinas, commenting on these words, says very aptly that in faith we submit to a stranger, to a truth that is not of our native soil, and therefore we are the captives of a victor: *Et inde est quod intellectus credentis dicitur esse captivatus quia tenetur terminis alienis.*[2] Hope is the brave deed of throwing oneself forward into the Unseen in spite of all human experience. Charity is the unselfish preference given to the One who is not ourselves. It is always and everywhere victory, both active and passive; we are conquered by God, and we conquer God. St. Paul felt keenly the adventitious origin of our whole supernatural life: *Vivo ego, jam non ego, vivit vero in me Christus*, 'I live, yet not I, but Christ liveth in me,'[3] this is his best known exclamation, revealing the constant attitude of his mind. Even when he breaks forth into enthusiastic praise of the new light that shines in the Christian's heart, he is all at once sobered by the thought that such a treasure is, after all, reposing in hearts that are very fragile receptacles: 'For God, who commanded the light to shine out of darkness, hath shined in our

[1] 2 Cor. x. 5.   [2] QQ. Disp. XI, De Veritate. Quest. xiv., Art. 1, ad 9.
[3] Gal. ii. 20.

hearts, to give the light of the knowledge of the glory of God, in the face of Christ Jesus. But we have this treasure in earthen vessels, that the excellency may be of the power of God and not of us. In all things we suffer tribulation: but are not distressed; we are straitened: but are not destitute.'[1]

Even those perfections of man which seem to belong to him with a more assured claim, his moral endowments, are still under the law of conquest as truly as the higher order. We cannot be the 'foursquare man,' the *homo quadratus*, of the philosopher without an unceasing struggle: 'Now then it is no more I that do it: but sin that dwelleth in me. For I know that there dwelleth not in me, that is to say, in my flesh, that which is good. For to will is present with me: but to accomplish that which is good, I find not. For the good which I will, I do not: but the evil which I will not, that I do.'[2] This division in man is profound and permanent. There is a discontent in us as there was in Paul: 'Unhappy man that I am, who shall deliver me from the body of this death?'[3] But there is no antagonism so violent between the flesh and the spirit, between the lower powers and the higher, as not to be overcome by the grace of Christ. Christian asceticism is essentially optimistic; right through the ages there is the sound of the canticle of the innumerable people who stand before the Lamb, clothed in white robes and with the palms of victory in their hands. From the hero of the ascetical golden age, the hermit of the early centuries, to our own more complicated civilization, there is the faith in man's power, through the grace of Christ, to be immaculate before God: 'He that shall overcome shall thus be clothed in white garments: and I will not blot out his name from the book of life. And I will confess his name before My Father and before His angels.'[4] The metaphor of the white garment belongs to the New Testament, and its meaning is this: innocence through victory; the elect are in white garments because they overcame.

All we have said in this book concerning Christ's victory has a direct bearing on the individual life of man. We share in Christ's triumph now, here on earth, through that newness of life which comes to us from the Resurrection. 'Now if we be dead with Christ,

[1] 2 Cor. iv. 6-8.   [2] Rom. vii. 17-19.
[3] Rom. vii. 24.   [4] Apoc. iii. 5.

we believe that we shall live also together with Christ. Knowing that Christ, rising again from the dead, dieth now no more. Death shall no more have dominion over Him. For in that He died to sin, He died once: but in that He liveth, He liveth unto God. So do you also reckon that you are dead to sin, but alive unto God, in Christ Jesus our Lord.'[1] Just as there is no limit to Christ's sovereignty, so there is no limit to the possibilities of Christian sanctification, of the Christian's power to rise superior to all darkness and the captivity of sin; we not only worship the victory of Christ, but we are partakers of its virtue in our own mind, in our own members. This superiority of the Christian to all evils is, of course, a commonplace in New Testament thought; but though it be such a universal idea it is none the less marvellous. The victory of Christ operates in us; His Resurrection and His Ascension are not only future hopes, but actual spiritual phenomena of our individual Christian life: God 'even when we were dead in sins, hath quickened us together in Christ (by whose grace you are saved). And hath raised us up together and hath made us sit together in the heavenly places, through Jesus Christ.'[2] It is the merit of Catholic exegesis to read phrases like these not only in the light of the world to come, but in the light of the present time; our supernatural estate, as we possess it here on earth, is a resurrection and an ascension. Our conflicts with the external powers of darkness are, on the whole, only a small sector of the great combat; few of us are destined to lay down our life for the Name of Christ, to share in Christ's testimony, to be martyrs; but we are all called to that high state of spiritual triumph, that mental illumination which it is so difficult to preserve in its untarnished brightness, the spontaneous and unquestioning acceptance of Christ's practical sovereignty over all flesh. So we make our own the wonderful doxology of Jude the Apostle: 'Now to Him who is able to preserve you without sin and to present you spotless before the presence of His glory with exceeding joy, in the coming of Our Lord Jesus Christ: to the only God our Saviour through Jesus Christ Our Lord, be glory and magnificence, empire and power, before all ages, and now, and for all ages of ages. Amen.'[3]

[1] Rom. vi. 8-11.   [2] Eph. ii. 5, 6.   [3] Jude 24, 25.

Epilogue

ON taking leave of my reader I must remind him once more of a truth which has been the undertone of all that has been said in the preceding chapters, that a victorious Christ, such as I have tried to describe, is the Church's supreme glory; Christians, in the diversities of their graces, either individually or as a society, are victorious only in the victory of Christ.

Our master in divinity, St. Thomas Aquinas, makes a statement which may seem astonishing, for it is so very original. 'Christ,' he says, 'is the total wealth of the Church; He with the other elect, is not greater than He Himself alone.'[1] In other words, what is of utmost importance for the Church is this, that her Christ should be what He is: He is the totality of her goodness, the saints do not add to Him, but receive from Him. So what really matters is our knowledge of what Our Lord has achieved; our achievements, big and small, are precontained in His mighty victory. No doubt many of us have to learn gradually this truly Christian method of appreciation; to do so we must fall back on traditional theological principles. Modern sentiment is all for human achievements, and it looks at times as if man gave himself the air of a conqueror without any reference to Him who gives all the means necessary for the deed; even our Christian life and our spiritual career might suffer at times from this intellectual presumption unless we remember always that Christ has won our battles for us long before we were born.

[1] Sent. IV, Dist. 49, Quest. iv., Art. 3, ad 4.

THE DIVINE MOTHERHOOD

In the classical theologies of the Incarnation Mariology forms the natural corollary of Christology. In this monograph on the Divine Maternity Abbot Vonier has not aimed at giving us a formal or exhaustive treatise; but he simply expresses the deep convictions on that sweet mystery, which have sprung as much from his childlike devotion to Mary, as from his intellectual grasp of Catholic dogma concerning the Mother of the Son of God.— Editor.

Cum opus, cui titulus *The Divine Motherhood*, a Revmo P. D. Anschario Vonier, O.S.B., Abbate Buckfastriensi, conscriptum, censor a Nobis deputatus rite examinaverit nihilque contra fidem vel mores in eodem deprehenderit, quantum ad Nos attinet, imprimi permittimus.

Sublaci, die 15 Decembris, 1920.

D. BENEDICTUS GARIADOR, O.S.B.
Abbas Generalis

D. VINCENTIUS M. J. GOOSEMANS, O.S.B.
a Secretis

Nihil obstat.

HENRICUS DAVIS, S.J.
Censor deputatus

Imprimatur.

Westmonasterii, die 13 Decembris, 1920
EDMUNDUS CAN. SURMONT.
Vic. Gen.

CHAPTER I

Mary's Personal Sanctity

IT is possible for us to make the distinction between Our Lady's personal sanctity and her divine motherhood. Her immaculate conception, her absolute sinlessness, her immense charity, may be considered as her personal sanctity. She was already endowed with this personal sanctity when the Archangel Gabriel approached her with his message of infinite import: 'Hail, full of grace, the Lord is with thee; blessed art thou among women.' Great as was Mary's sanctity at that moment, immediately preceding her divine motherhood, there is nothing that could compel us to say that such sanctity could not be granted by God to a human being quite irrespective of the mystery of the divine motherhood. God could grant the privileges of immaculate conception and of absolute sinlessness in soul and body to anyone born of Adam. The words of the heavenly spirit are a description of Mary's soul such as it was before the mystery of the Incarnation lifted it to an entirely new plane of sanctity and perfection. They have reference to Mary's actual state. The pure angel meets the spotless woman.

In a memorable passage of the Gospels we find this distinction between Mary's divine motherhood and her personal sanctity made use of by Christ Himself, in order to enhance the importance of personal sanctity. 'And it came to pass, as He spoke these things, a certain woman from the crowd, lifting up her voice, said to Him: Blessed is the womb that bore Thee, and the paps that gave Thee suck. But He said: Yea rather, blessed are they who hear the word of God and keep it.'[1] This contrasting of the divine motherhood and personal sanctity by the Son of God Himself is, no doubt, one of the most telling things in the sacred Gospels. The circumstance that we owe this passage to St. Luke is not without its significance; St. Luke is pre-eminently the Evangelist of the divine motherhood, and we have here the last of the three blessings on Mary's head enumerated

[1] Luke xi. 27, 28.

by him, the first being found in Gabriel's salutation, and the second in the greeting with which Elizabeth met her cousin. Nothing could give us a more exalted view of the value and nature of personal sanctity than the rejoinder of Our Lord to the woman's spontaneous praise of the divine motherhood. We were in need of this corrective, as nothing is more difficult to man than a practical love and appreciation of the things that constitute personal sanctity. The most exalted spiritual marvel is, by the very laws of the divine life, intimately connected with personal sanctity. On the other hand, nothing would be less justifiable than to read into Our Lord's words the least depreciation of the worth of the divine motherhood as such. He emphasizes the value of personal sanctity by means of the highest created term of comparison—the divine motherhood. It would be futile to ask ourselves the question whether in practice divine motherhood could be separated from personal sanctity; whether it would be possible for a creature to be the Mother of God, and yet be deprived of personal sanctity. No doubt such a thing implies a contradiction. Certainly Our Lord's words by no means suggest that He assumed such an hypothesis. He fully accepts the praise bestowed on the divine motherhood, but He commends it still more by extending it to personal sanctity.

The distinction we make between Our Lady's personal sanctity and her divine motherhood is justified on the ground that it would be possible, theoretically speaking, for a human being to have as much grace as Mary had independently of the divine motherhood. But the problem may be put in another form; we may ask ourselves whether divine motherhood is at all possible without personal sanctity, and that of a very high degree. We feel instinctively, of course, that the Mother of God ought to be a very holy being; but to what extent personal sanctity and divine maternity are inseparable is not so easy for us to decide. From the sacred Gospels and from Catholic theology we learn a vast amount as to the nature and the extent of the divine motherhood. We know a good deal, too, from faith and tradition, concerning Our Lady's personal sanctity; we know her to have been conceived immaculate, to have been absolutely sinless, to have been confirmed in grace. But to what extent these personal privileges were postulated by the divine motherhood we cannot say so readily. There is, however, one spiritual fact of absolute certainty: the divine motherhood is the primary, the central fact in Mary's election and predestination on the part of God. She is not just a saint upon whom divine motherhood was bestowed as an extra grace; she is the divine Mother to whom sanctity has been granted as a necessary spiritual complement. Divine motherhood is a grace, or rather a spiritual marvel so prodigious, so unique in its nature, that it must be considered as the paramount spiritual factor in the person who receives it. All other endowments of soul and body in that ever-blessed person could not be anything except a preparation for, and a consequence of, that great mystery of divine life. So while we may fail to see whether sanctity of the highest degree is united with divine motherhood through a necessary law of life, one thing we cannot fail to see is this priority of the divine motherhood in Mary's election; she is simply the Mother of God. Such is the appellation and definition of Mary.

Now if this little book is to have achieved anything, the reader ought not to lay it aside after perusing it, without having gained such a view of the excellence of the divine motherhood as to have made it a necessity for his mind to admit that Mary's personal sanctity was intrinsically connected with her maternity, through a law of supernatural life which God Himself could not have suspended.

CHAPTER II

The Motherhood of Elizabeth

JUST as the Person of the Son of God has its human and finite counterpart in the person of John the Baptist, the Precursor, so the divine motherhood of Mary stands in the Gospel of St. Luke intimately associated with another motherhood, that of Elizabeth. Elizabeth's motherhood played a wonderful rôle in the mystery of the Incarnation; it was to Mary the one external proof of the possibility of a divine and virginal motherhood, and Mary's mind had the human satisfaction of possessing a visible evidence in favour of an incomprehensible spiritual fact. Elizabeth's motherhood was the

Angel's argument to establish the veracity of his incredible message. He used no other, but used it with irresistible efficacy: 'And behold thy cousin Elizabeth, she also hath conceived a son in her old age; and this is the sixth month with her that is called barren, because no word shall be impossible with God.'[1] The act of faith by which Mary assented to the Angel's message was the greatest the supernatural world has ever produced; yet in this act of faith, as in every other, there was the working of the human mind, the *motivum credibilitatis*, the rational ground for assent. Elizabeth's motherhood, so unexpected, so entirely above ordinary human laws, was to Mary's sublime faith the *motivum credibilitatis*. Mary's mind worked intensely; the motherhood that was promised her was seemingly impossible on account both of her virginity and the nature of the Child to be born. The Archangel, most privileged spirit, entered into the workings of that mind and followed them step by step; for it was his office not only to deliver the message but also to make it appear credible, to obtain the intellectual acceptance of it by Mary. Elizabeth's motherhood, thus carefully narrated to Mary, turned the scales; and her mental acceptance of the mystery was complete and unreserved. That Mary's act of faith at that moment was an effort of heroic perfection we can conclude from the words of praise which the Holy Ghost put on the lips of Elizabeth when her cousin came to visit her: 'And blessed art thou that hast believed, because those things shall be accomplished that were spoken to thee by the Lord.'[2]

The motherhood of Elizabeth is the greatest and noblest instance of a purely human motherhood: 'Amen I say to you, there hath not risen among them that are born of women a greater than John the Baptist.'[3] This testimony of the Son of God to John's greatness would suffice to give to Elizabeth a unique place of honour among all the women who have the dignity of motherhood. But there is, besides the greatness of her offspring, the wonderful circumstance of that maternity. It is as supernatural, as much above the laws of human fertility, as it possibly could be. The priest Zachary, Elizabeth's husband, never doubted the presence of the Angel that appeared to him, standing on the right side of the altar of incense; he knew that he was conversing with the Angel of the Lord. Yet the promise of a son seemed so incredible, that by a strange contra-

[1] Luke i. 36, 37.   [2] Luke i. 45.   [3] Matt. xi. 11.

diction he actually doubted the possibility of such an occurrence. 'And Zachary said to the Angel: Whereby shall I know this? For I am an old man, and my wife is advanced in years.'[1] The doubts of the old man were such as to deserve the severe rebuke of the Angel, and the punishment of temporary dumbness: 'Because thou hast not believed my words, which shall be fulfilled in their time.'[2] The hesitancy of Zachary is, like the doubt of St. Thomas the Apostle, an indirect testimony: it brings out a supernatural fact, in this case the miraculous character of John's birth. With Elizabeth, of course, we are not in the presence of a miraculous phenomenon of such transcending glory as in the case of Mary's motherhood; Zachary is truly the father of John the Baptist. Yet it was at the same time so evident a sign of God's favour that Mary no longer hesitated in her mind as to the possibility of her own motherhood, the moment she heard the news from the Angel that Elizabeth was with child.

Elizabeth's motherhood may be considered as a term of comparison, to enable us the better to understand and measure the excellency of Mary's motherhood. The Gospel of St. Luke opens with a detailed description of the holiest and purest human motherhood that could possibly be imagined. The Evangelist takes pleasure in giving us a full description of the glories of that venerable mother. The narrative is artistically perfect, there is a glorious crescendo in this intertwining of the two motherhoods, that of Elizabeth and that of Mary. When we have read all about Elizabeth's motherhood, we ask ourselves whether it is possible for a woman to have God nearer to her in the joys of maternity, than she experienced in that wonderful proximity of heaven in the origin of John's life. But a greater thing is still to come, an event that will make a most dramatic appeal to the strongest faith. With Elizabeth's motherhood God's action and grace surround, as with an odour of heavenly life, the laws of created life. With Mary it will be all heavenly life. God's action is not merely the companion of created causality; it is supreme, exclusive, absolutely unconditioned by the created law of life.

On the other hand, this artistic intertwining of the two maternities on the part of the Evangelist is a guarantee to us that both were motherhoods in the full sense of the word. There will always be the

[1] Luke i. 18.   [2] Luke i. 20.

danger for some minds to place Mary's divine rôle in a totally un-
earthly sphere of things, to think of her motherhood as of something belonging to quite another world. Its very sublimity might
detract from its created reality. But with Mary's motherhood so
closely related to Elizabeth's, we ought to see at once that she is
truly a mother in the ordinary human, created mode of maternity.
When Elizabeth and Mary met for the first time after the Angel's
message we have two mothers meeting, one as truly and as really a
mother as the other: 'And whence is this to me, that the Mother of
my Lord should come to me?'[1] Elizabeth's exclamation of joy is also
a proclamation of the reality of Mary's motherhood; her own offspring, still hidden in her womb, had leaped for joy at the presence
of Him who could not have been there in person if Mary's were not
truly a mother's womb; 'Blessed is the Fruit of thy womb!' We
have to read this in conjunction with that other sentence, 'The
infant in my womb leaped for joy.' Elizabeth, in her tender love for
her cousin, keeps the great mystery for us children of earth, prevents
it from receding into a realm that is no longer human. Mary's
maternity is truly a divine maternity; but it has also the joys and the
essential characteristics of a human motherhood. It was the mission
of the Archangel Gabriel to reveal the secrets of the divine maternity; it was Elizabeth's mission to assure us that Mary is as truly a
human mother as she herself.

Chapter III

The Measure of the Divine Motherhood

THE message of the Archangel Gabriel to Zachary, the husband of Elizabeth, contains a full description of the character
and career of the child that would be born of her: 'For he
shall be great before the Lord, and shall drink no wine nor strong
drink; and he shall be filled with the Holy Ghost, even from his
mother's womb. And he shall convert many of the children of

[1] Luke i. 43.

Israel to the Lord their God. And he shall go before Him in the spirit and power of Elias: that he may turn the hearts of the fathers unto the children, and the incredulous to the wisdom of the just, to prepare unto the Lord a perfect people.'[1] The measure of the praise bestowed on the child to be born is also the measure of Elizabeth's motherhood: she is to be truly the mother of one so great that his greatness surpasses all that has gone before in the spiritual history of Israel; Elizabeth is the mother of the Precursor, and her maternity stretches as far as his whole career. The parents of John shall have joy and gladness in the greatness of their son: for this is a universal law of human parenthood that the career of any man, however great, is a true glory for his father and his mother; human parenthood embraces the whole mortal career of the offspring.

The heavenly messenger entrusted by God with the task of announcing the glories of the two maternities, that of Elizabeth and that of Mary, keeps the same order on both occasions: he begins with the praise of the promised offspring, in order to show to what an extent the parents, privileged by God, are honoured; he gives the measure of both motherhoods by describing the careers of the sons. So we have in the wonderful message to Mary the parallel of that other message delivered to John's father. 'Fear not, Mary, for thou hast found grace with God. Behold thou shalt conceive in thy womb and shalt bring forth a son; and thou shalt call His name Jesus. He shall be great and shall be called the Son of the Most High. And the Lord God shall give unto Him the throne of David His father; and He shall reign in the house of Jacob for ever. And of His kingdom there shall be no end.'[2]

Elizabeth's motherhood does Christian theology a most valuable service by giving it, by way of a comparison, the measure of Mary's motherhood. Mary is Mother to the full extent of Gabriel's description of her Son's career, just as Elizabeth's motherhood embraces the whole life of the Precursor. John's career, vast and exalted as it is, is of a definite character; Elizabeth is welcome to all its glories. The career of Jesus stretches beyond all temporal bounds, it embraces eternity: 'And of His kingdom there shall be no end', yet Mary's motherhood stretches as far, is co-extensive with it. In virtue of that sweet parallelism between Mary's motherhood and Elizabeth's

[1] Luke i. 15-17.   [2] Luke i. 30-33.

motherhood which God's wisdom has inserted into the very origin of Christianity, we take Gabriel's description of Christ's character and mission for a measure whereby to estimate the extent of Mary's maternity: Mary is from the very beginning the Mother of One whose kingdom is eternal. So the divine motherhood of Mary is eternal, not only temporal, in character. Gabriel's description of the Child to be born of Mary contains, as in an angelic summary, the whole greatness of Jesus: He is the Son of God; He is heir to all the promises of Israel; He is immortal. To all that immensity of glory and greatness Mary is welcome, as the true Mother; she may rejoice in it all, she may take pride in it all, it is all part of her motherhood. She is to be the Mother of One who is great: 'He shall be great', as Elizabeth was to be the mother of a great one. Both mothers have that privilege. But when the Angel proceeds to develop the respective greatness of John and Jesus, from the sphere of finite things in the case of John he soars to the infinite in the case of Jesus, and Mary's motherhood soars up with Him. Elizabeth's motherhood does not go beyond John's mortal career. The pure spirit of John, after the great prophet's martyrdom at the hands of Herod, is not the son of Elizabeth. But the risen Christ is the Son of Mary, and His Resurrection is part of Mary's motherhood, part of all that was promised her when she was told that her Son's kingdom would never have an end.

Mary's divine motherhood then differs from all other motherhoods, that of Elizabeth not excepted, in this important characteristic, that it bears relation to One who is eternal through the very principles of life that have their beginning in Mary's womb. As Jesus, through the very laws of His divine being, could never be made to see corruption, 'for neither was He left in hell, neither did His flesh see corruption,'[1] Mary is His Mother uninterruptedly, as long as there is identity and continuance of the body which He took from her. His death, in virtue of the divine being that was in Him, never meant the least interruption of His personal existence, never meant the least breaking up of the elements of that bodily organism that had first been framed in Mary's womb. No other mother can claim such continuance of the life she first gave and fostered. The death of Jesus on the Cross could be no interruption of that relation-

[1] Acts ii. 31.

ship of nature which existed between Mary and her divine Son from the hour of His conception by her. Our Lord's Resurrection is something more than the coming back to life of a dead man; it means this other marvel, that in virtue of the Hypostatic Union His personal existence had never been suspended: soul and body, though separated through death, were united in the one divine Person of the Word. So it would not be enough for us to say that the Resurrection gave back to Mary her Son; we ought to say that even in death Jesus was truly Mary's Son, for since He was also the Son of the Most High, His Sonship, with regard both to His heavenly Father and to His earthly Mother, could suffer no eclipse. The measure therefore of the divine motherhood is infinitude and eternity. Gabriel the messenger of God promised Mary a Son of infinite excellence, who would be called the Son of the Most High, and would have eternal duration of life; her motherhood then necessarily assumes these characteristics.

Chapter IV

'He shall be great'

BOTH in the case of John and of Jesus the first promise made by the Archangel Gabriel to the respective parents is the future greatness of the offspring. Of John the Angel says, 'he shall be great before the Lord'. With Jesus the announcement is much more categorical; there is foretold an absolute greatness of person, for He shall be called the Son of the Most High, a thing infinitely above being great before the Lord: 'He shall be great and shall be called the Son of the Most High'.[1] Mary's divine maternity embraces the whole great Christ whose name is above all other names.

When we read in the Acts of the Apostles that the disciples of Christ were assembled in the expectation of the Holy Ghost, with 'Mary the Mother of Jesus'[2], we may give the phrase its full literal meaning, Mary being then as truly the Mother of Jesus who had

[1] Luke i. 32.   [2] Acts i. 14.

ascended into heaven, and who was about to send His Spirit of Love, as she was the Mother of Jesus at the wedding-feast at Cana. She knew then that she was the Mother of One who was great beyond all comparison. But the quality first enunciated by the Angel Gabriel as being the essential feature of her Son, was the one to be revealed last. The divine motherhood appeals to us chiefly in connection with Christ's littleness. Whenever art has attempted the glorious subject of that divine motherhood, it has generally depicted it in its earliest stages, when the Son of Mary was not yet great, but little. But no artist has ever been capable of adequately portraying the peculiar look of love and hope with which the divine Mother gazed at her Infant Son, the message of Gabriel ringing in her ears: 'He shall be great'. Yet this message ought to permeate all Christian art in its treatment of the Mother and Child. Mary holds in her arms One who shall be great; nothing will ever prevent His becoming great; she is sure of that, though she may be in doubt as to many things that will constitute His final greatness. She holds up that sweet Child of hers, so helpless, so tiny, and she speaks to us the words of the heavenly messenger: 'He shall be great'. Nothing so stirs human motherhood as the hope of greatness for the helpless and inarticulate little child. But Mary's joy was complete; it was no mere hope, it was a divine assurance.

In all our meditations on the divine maternity we ought to keep constantly before our minds those words of Gabriel. Forgetfulness of that important announcement 'He shall be great' might lead to a certain naturalism in our devotion to the Mother and the Infant Jesus. Between Mary and her Child there is more than the sweet affection between a beautiful mother and her first-born. There is the faith, as vivid as the natural love of a mother can be, in the Child's incomparable greatness which is to be revealed some day. Artistic presentment of the Madonna which does not express that unique feature falls short of the true Christian view of the divine maternity. The Catholic love of the Mother of God is essentially a generous thing; her divine maternity is a masterpiece of God's wisdom, giving pleasure to the keenest intellect. It is a source of spiritual power; it is the foundation of an immense hope; it breeds a love strong as death. The whole of creation stands in awe before the overpowering glory of that blessed vision—the Mother with her

Child. Catholic art, in its purer and stronger phases, depicting Mary and her divine Infant, can afford to neglect the element of natural tenderness, in order to emphasise that faith that was in the Mother of Jesus, that her Child should be great, that He was already great even though still reposing on her breast.

CHAPTER V

The Terms of the Divine Motherhood

WHEN Zachary had heard the message that his wife Elizabeth would bear him a son of such supreme greatness and sanctity, instead of accepting these tidings loyally and gratefully, his mind was overpowered by a great doubt, a grave difficulty arising out of the natural and physical order of things: 'Whereby shall I know this? For I am an old man, and my wife is advanced in years'.[1] In Gabriel's interview with Mary there is at the same point of the interview a similar interruption on the part of the person addressed by the heavenly messenger. 'And Mary said to the Angel: How shall this be done, because I know not man?'[2] But here the parallelism between Zachary and Mary ceases. The two questions, though similar in nature, are vastly dissimilar in spirit and provoke answers infinitely different in purport. Mary's query is followed by the highest exposition of the mystery of the Incarnation ever uttered here on earth. What Gabriel replied is a statement of eternal beauty and incomparable profundity. Zachary, on the contrary, is sharply rebuked, the Angel showing indignation at the old man's hesitation, because he failed to recognize the character of the messenger that had come to him. 'And the Angel answering, said to him: 'I am Gabriel, who stand before God, and am sent to speak to thee and to bring thee these good tidings. And behold, thou shalt be dumb ... because thou hast not believed my words, which shall be fulfilled in their time.'[3] From this diversity of the Angel's conduct with regard to the two questioners we see at a glance what depth of

[1] Luke i. 18.   [2] Luke i. 34.   [3] Luke i. 19, 20.

wisdom and humility there must be in Mary's restrained interruption. We have here the terms that shape divine maternity into something so unexpected, so unforeseen, absolute virginity.

Mary's virginity is twofold: there is her own virginal integrity as a vessel of election, as one chosen for the highest form of spiritual life, it is a great grace, but not miraculous; the other is her virginity as Mother, a miraculous grace, not found elsewhere in the whole vast realm of God's creation. The first kind of virginity is a grace that is being shared by many, since Mary's Son died on the Cross. But of the second kind of virginity there never could be another instance. What we might call Our Lady's personal virginity is in itself a most sublime thing, because it was a thing without a precedent. The idea of consecrated virginity has become one of the most popular Christian ideas. Our Lady is the beginning of it all. Hers was to be virginity in wedlock, for no other kind of virginity could explain the Gospel. She was, in the words of the Evangelist, 'a virgin espoused to a man whose name was Joseph, of the house of David.'[1] On the other hand, her reply to the Angel's message is absolute and emphatic: 'How shall this be done, because I know not man?'[2] Virginity was Mary's irrevocable resolve. Such resolve had come to her not from her people's tradition, but from heaven.

But on this first, this personal virginity, there is grafted another kind—the virginity of the divine motherhood. It might be said in a general way that the early Christian generations were more captivated by the virginity of motherhood in Mary, whilst in our own times we think more of her personal virginity. Our Liturgy, which, of course, expresses the earlier Christian mind, is full of the virginity of the divine motherhood; it never tires of the great antithesis that Mary is at the same time Virgin and Mother: *Salve, sancta parens enixa puerpera regem. Virgo prius ac posterius, Gabrielis ab ore sumens illud Ave. Rubum, quem viderat Moyses incombustum, conservatam agnovimus tuam laudabilem virginitatem, Dei Genitrix.*[3] These are a few of the ways in which the older Christian generations expressed their faith in Mary's virginity. It is nearly always the virginity of the Mother that fills them with holy admiration.

[1] Luke i. 27.   [2] Luke i. 34.
[3] Hail, holy Mother, giving birth to the King. Thou Virgin, before and after receiving from the lips of Gabriel that Ave. In the bush, which Moses saw unconsumed by fire, we see the image of thy glorious virginity, O Mother of God.

Mary's virginity as the Mother of God is more than a mere preservation of her personal virginity. It is a virginity of a higher kind, a truly divine mystery. It is a supereminent virginity, a supernatural gift abiding in Mary's bodily frame, of such quality as is not found in the purest maiden here on earth. Mary's motherhood is Mary's virginity, she is the Virgin of virgins, *Virgo virginum*, in virtue of her divine motherhood, as such motherhood implies an action of the Holy Ghost in the very springs of Mary's life that raised her blood to the plane of divine incorruptibility. To say that Mary remained virgin in spite of her being Mother would not be an adequate rendering of her unique privilege. If we say merely that Mary's virginity was safeguarded in the higher grace of her motherhood, we admit, indeed, a marvellous thing, a miraculous operation on the part of God; but we seem to imply that the divine motherhood might have been a danger to her virginity, which was averted by that miraculous interposition. But in that case the virginity of Mary, though miraculously preserved, would still be the natural virginity of a human maiden. A glorious thing indeed it would be, and many a passage in the liturgical prayers of the Church speaks of the miraculous privilege in this more elementary way. But surely there is more in Mary's virginity. She is the virgin she is, not in spite of her motherhood, but because of her motherhood. The divine quality that has made Mary's flesh into the Mother she is, also made her into the Virgin she is; a virgin of no mere earthly integrity but of heavenly life. Her virginity is a positive, divine quality, not simply a preservation of the natural maiden state.

When Mary challenged for one moment Gabriel's astonishing message with the question that went to the very root of the matter: 'How shall this be done, because I know not man?' she asked for a solution of the double difficulty of the motherhood and the preservation of virginity. How can one who knows not man become a mother, and how can one who has resolved upon virginity possess the honour of maternity? The Archangel's answer unfolds the mystery of the new divine paternity, and in that act of God's paternity there is contained for Mary not only a motherhood such as there never was before, but also a virginity absolutely incomprehensible to man. The active principle in that begetting of a new life is the Holy Ghost: 'The Holy Ghost shall come down upon thee'. The divine action, 'the power of the Most High', which will be as the paternal origin of the One to be born, is far-reaching and all-transforming. The sanctity and the power of the active principle in Christ's temporal generation are the twofold solution of Mary's twofold difficulty. The Archangel assures Mary that she will enjoy not only her motherhood but also her virginity, a virginity far superior to the one she already experienced. The supereminent virginity of the Mother thus becomes, with the sanctity of the active principle, a contributory cause of the sanctity of the Offspring. 'And therefore also the Holy which shall be born of thee shall be called the Son of God.'[1]

'Holy and spotless virginity, with what praise I shall extol thee I know not, for thou didst enclose in thy womb Him whom the heavens cannot contain.' These words of the Roman Breviary well describe any writer's embarrassment when he tries to expatiate on Mary's virginity. Divine maternity is incompatible with the loss of virginity, and the mode in which the Son of God took blood from Mary's veins brought physical nature, brought created human life, into a relationship with the God of all sanctity such as no created intellect can understand. Mary's life and God's life were fused in one sublime spiritual result, the conception of the God Incarnate: *Qui conceptus est de Spiritu Sancto, natus ex Maria Virgine.* This article of the Creed must have been sweet music to the older generations of Christians, as to them the virginity of Mary's maternity was evidently a source of endless spiritual joy. Let us hasten back to that majestic concept of the Blessed Virgin; let us see in her great virginity one of God's masterpieces in the supernatural order. We ought to feel an instinctive sympathy for that spiritual marvel, since we are children of God of whom it is said that we are 'born, not of blood, nor of the will of flesh, nor of the will of man, but of God.'[2]

[1] Luke i. 35.   [2] John i. 13.

Chapter VI

'The Holy Thing which shall be born of thee'

NO one can fail to have his attention arrested by the unexpected turn of Gabriel's speech when he explains to Mary how she, the Virgin, is to become the Mother: 'And therefore also the Holy Thing which shall be born of thee shall be called the Son of God'.[1] It is beyond the shadow of a doubt that the Archangel used the neuter form of speech when speaking of the Offspring Mary was to expect. He did not say 'The Holy One who shall be born of thee shall be called the Son of God,' but 'The Holy Thing.' The original Greek has the neuter form, so has the Latin Vulgate, and the English Bible is an exact translation when it renders the sentence as quoted above.

There is wonderful emphasis and power in this angelic phrase. If Gabriel had said 'the Holy One who shall be born of thee shall be called the Son of God' it would have been a less efficacious way of bringing home to Mary, and through her to us, the fact that her Son would be more than man; she will be given a Child who will be something beyond all human possibilities, nay, something beyond all created personality. The Angel's choice of words calling the result of the Holy Ghost's action a 'Something', for such is virtually the meaning of his terminology, is infinitely subtle, and was bound to challenge Mary's attention, as it does ours. Gabriel's phrase makes it at once possible for us to throw aside all human limitations, all personal restrictions of a created order. Being a Holy Thing it may be a human or a divine being, a finite or an infinite being, but it is certainly a being of unusual perfection; it is a Holy Thing in virtue of the divine action on Mary. The alternative phrase 'The Holy One who shall be born of thee shall be called the Son of God' would contain a difficulty; for it would, in a way, limit the meaning of the subject of the proposition. A Holy One to be born of a woman would of necessity be a human being; a Holy Thing to be born may be something unspeakably wonderful. What will it be? The Angel

[1] Luke i. 35 (A.V.).

says it at once: It 'shall be called the Son of God'. Christian phraseology, following in this the *Verbum caro factum est* of St. John, prefers
the expression 'God was made man' to the expression 'man was
made God', as it renders more powerfully the truth that Mary's
Offspring was never anything but God; the infinitely mysterious
Thing in Mary's bosom, after the Angel's departure, was God.
St. John's phrase, then, 'The Word was made flesh' and Gabriel's
statement 'The Holy Thing that shall be born of thee shall be called
the Son of God', are kindred language; they indicate that at no
moment of time, however brief, could that adorable Thing which
was in Mary's bosom be called by any other name than the name of
God; the Archangel's subtle phrase makes it clear that Mary is
directly, and without any intermediary, the Mother of God.

We have seen in a previous chapter how Mary's motherhood has,
from its very nature, an infinite extension; as Mary is the Mother of
Jesus according to the totality of His career, according to His immortal nature and His everlasting kingdom; for there was promised
to Mary a Son whose rule over creation would never have an end.
There is another such infinitude implied in Mary's motherhood: she
is Mother according to the infinity of God's effective power. Her
motherhood was activated by the overshadowing of the Most High.
Nothing but an infinite Thing could be the result of such a motherhood. Nothing is impossible to God, in whom all inferior causalities
are contained as in the supreme and all-sufficient cause. It is in God's
power to cause man to be born of woman without the intervention
of a human father. But in such an hypothesis we should have a
maternity that would differ *toto coelo* from Mary's maternity. It
would be a miraculous, but not an infinite maternity. The man born
would be finite, mortal, merely human. But Mary's womb produced
an infinitely Holy, an eternal, a divine Thing, through the very laws
of the divine vitalities that were operative in her when she conceived by the Holy Ghost. It is the only instance in the whole realm
of the natural and supernatural world, outside the Eucharistic
mystery, where a finite thing, as was Mary's life-blood, becomes the
object of an act of God's omnipotence with an infinite result as the
term of such activity. The Holy Thing which was produced is what
It is in virtue of Mary's maternity as much as in virtue of the power
of the Holy Ghost. We must conclude, therefore, that Our Lady's

maternity itself was raised to a plane high enough to meet God's creative paternity, when the Word was made flesh. Let us always bear in mind the great truth that the Blessed Virgin's maternity was a most natural maternity in the sense that she fully responded to it, was not overwhelmed by it, that there was no separation between her and her Offspring; Christ came from her as her own dear Child, the Fruit of her own blessed womb. I am right, therefore, in asserting that Mary's maternal function in the conception of Christ was raised to an incredibly high plane of vitality so as to make her maternity not only an instrumental, but a natural maternity. If Mary's mission had been merely to minister the human element to the Word when He became flesh, her maternity would have been just instrumental; it would have existed only to serve a higher purpose. But Mary's rôle is more than that; she is permanently the Mother of God: her maternity is not a transient ministration, but an abiding dignity that makes her share with God the Father, in literal truth, the parenthood of Jesus Christ.

A threefold hypothesis may make this point clearer still. We can think of a woman being made a mother by the direct productive act of God, as already said; in that case the offspring of that mother would not be divine, but human. Then there can be the conception in a woman's womb of a divine Person, as happened in the Incarnation, but the woman being merely instrumental to the production of the body, in such a case it would be divine maternity in the most restricted physiological sense. Thirdly, there is the glorious possibility of perfect divine maternity with all the graces and privileges, with all the rights and splendours, of one who shares to the full, with God the Father, the parenthood of the God Incarnate. Such is Mary's maternity; such is the meaning of Elizabeth's salutation, or rather the salutation of the Holy Ghost through the mouth of Elizabeth, when full of the divine Spirit she cried with a loud voice: 'Blessed art thou among women, and blessed is the Fruit of thy womb. And whence is this to me, that the Mother of my Lord should come to me?'[1] Elizabeth was the first creature to call Mary 'the Mother of God'; she gave us the grandest title of Our Lady: 'Mother of God'. The Archangel, indeed, had said as much, but only by implication; Elizabeth, the happiest of human mothers, has the privilege of having

[1] Luke i. 42, 43.

spoken for the first time the words 'Mother of God'. When, moreover, in the same breath she calls blessed the Mother and the Fruit
of her womb, bestowing the same encomium on the two lives which
were not yet disjoined, she gives us an additional reason for saying
that Mary's maternity had been raised to the divine plane of dignity
and perfection, where one and the same blessedness holds Mother
and Offspring wrapt in a matchless sanctity.

We may elucidate still further the nature of Mary's share in the
dignity of parenthood with regard to the Son of God, by asking ourselves how it comes about that the Holy Ghost could never be called
the Father of Christ, though it was through the Holy Ghost's operation that His conception took place; whilst, on the other hand,
Mary is to be called the Mother of Christ in all accuracy of language.
Only one of the three Persons of the Trinity, the Eternal Father, is
truly the Father of Christ; and one other person only, Mary, is
truly the Mother of Christ. The answer which St. Thomas Aquinas
gives in his *Summa* to the query just formulated is eminently calculated to give us a deeper understanding of Mary's share in Christ's
parentage. 'Christ,' says the great Doctor, 'was conceived by Mary
the Virgin, who supplied the life-matter, in such wise as to produce
similarity of kind, and therefore He is called her Son. On the other
hand, Christ, in His human nature, was conceived of the Holy
Ghost, as from the active principle, but not in such wise as to
produce similarity of kind, as a son is born of his father; and therefore Christ is not said to be the Son of the Holy Ghost.'[1] The reason
why the Holy Ghost, by His operation in Mary's womb did not produce an offspring in similarity of kind, as does a human father, is
given by St. Thomas in the body of the Article in which the
question just quoted is raised. The Son of God, he says, though
becoming incarnate, existed before the Incarnation. In His divine
substance He had perfect similarity of nature and kind from the
Eternal Father, the first Person of the Trinity. Therefore He was
Son already, the Only-Begotten of the Father. Becoming incarnate
through the operation of the Holy Ghost could not make Him Son
of the Holy Ghost, as such a relation of parentage already belonged
to the Father. But it made Him truly the Son of Mary; because
Mary, and she alone, gave Him a true similarity of human nature, as

[1] *S. Th.* III, Quest. xxxii, Art. 3, ad 1.

the Eternal Father, and the Eternal Father alone, had given Him similarity of divine nature, through the eternal filiation of the Word. The Eternal Father and Mary are the true parents of Jesus Christ. I am here paraphrasing the words of St. Thomas, but his doctrine is unmistakable. Mary's motherhood will always be vaster than the concepts of the greatest thinker. We can only touch the fringe of an ever-widening circle of divine vitalities of the first order.

CHAPTER VII

The Tree of Jesse

THE Archangel Gabriel, when delivering the great message to Mary, speaks of the Child as being at the same time the Son of the Most High and the Son of David. 'He shall be great and shall be called the Son of the Most High. And the Lord God shall give unto Him the throne of David His father.'[1] Considering that Mary's virginity was the presupposed, the indispensable condition of her divine motherhood, we may at once take it for granted that between Mary and David there is the closest alliance in this ever-blessed mystery of the Incarnation; David could not be called Christ's father except through Mary, and nothing could be a more emphatic assertion of the fact that Mary is the true Mother of the Son of the Most High than the Angel's mode of speaking when he calls the future Offspring 'the Son of David', with a natural right of succession to the throne of David.

Christ succeeds to David through His own Mother. Christ came from heaven with immense greatness and power as the Son of the Most High, but He came also with full rights to an earthly throne; this throne belonged to Him in virtue of natural heredity, as much as the heavenly throne; being the Son of Mary He is truly the Son of David, and His eternal kingship over heaven and earth comes to Him by a double birth-right, the one based on His Father's glory, and the other based on His Mother's lineage, as she was the daughter

[1] Luke i. 32.

of David. No words could be more pregnant with the idea of direct, perfect, unlimited motherhood, than this phrase of the heavenly spirit; had he said to Mary that she was to be the Mother of God, he could not have said more than what he clearly implied. He who is to be called the Son of the Most High is the Son of David, with the right of an heir to the throne of His father; therefore Mary's maternity has not merely the physiological rôle of giving life to the human nature of the God Incarnate; it has the full juridical and ethical value of a mother who is the heiress to immense rights, and has full power to transmit these rights to the Son whom she bears. This value of Mary's motherhood as the only rightful possessor and transmitter of immense regal rights is a thing of wonderful beauty; it makes the whole genealogy of David culminate in Mary. When in their mighty cathedrals our forefathers used their artistic genius to depict the Tree of Jesse in stone or colour, they gave expression to their spiritual understanding of this juridical aspect of the divine motherhood.

St. Paul, in his Epistle to the Romans, gives us, as in a summary, the full spiritual significance of this Tree of Jesse: 'For I wished myself to be an anathema from Christ, for my brethren; who are my kinsmen according to the flesh; who are Israelites; to whom belongeth the adoption as of children and the glory and the testament and the giving of the law and the service of God and the promises: whose are the fathers and of whom is Christ, according to the flesh, who is over all things, God blessed for ever. Amen.'[1] Whole books might be written on the spiritual power of the promise made to Abraham and his seed. This promise is the one great supernatural factor of the world before the Incarnation took place. It is, I might almost say, the supernatural order in its juridical aspect, before it became a great living reality. 'For God making promise to Abraham, because He had no one greater by whom He might swear, swore by Himself, saying: Unless blessing I shall bless thee, and multiplying I shall multiply thee. And so patiently enduring he obtained the promise. For men swear by one greater than themselves: and an oath for confirmation is the end of all their controversy. Wherein God, meaning more abundantly to shew to the heirs of the promise the immutability of His counsel, interposed an oath.'[2]

---

[1] Rom. ix. 3-5.   [2] Heb. vi. 13-17.

Now this whole juridical order ultimately rests on Mary, as on the one surviving heiress of the great family whose destinies were essentially Messianic; if Mary were not the true Mother of Christ, with unlimited rights and powers to transmit to her Son great super-natural inheritance, the whole divine order of the promise, there would be a gap in that supernatural order, between what came before and what came after the Incarnation.

The juridical value of the great promise is entirely dependent on the factor which is so energetically described in the Scriptures as 'seed'. 'To Abraham were the promises made and to his seed. He saith not: And to his seeds, as of many. But as of one: And to thy seed, which is Christ.'[1] We see from this text of St. Paul that Christ Himself is to be considered as the One to whom the great promise is made, not only is Christ the fulfilment of that promise, but in His ultimate glory and triumph all that God ever promised will attain maturity and completion. I am correct, therefore, in saying that Christ inherited through His Mother the right to all the great things promised to the Patriarchs. Gabriel's words are unmistakable; something will be given to the Child from the Mother's side, the wondrous thing called the throne of David. The Angel completes the announcement about the great inheritance, with these words: 'And He shall reign in the house of Jacob for ever'.[2] The whole of St. Paul's Epistle to the Romans deserves to be pressed into service here, with its prodigious illuminations about the rejection and final reconciliation of Israel. We have not yet reached that fulness which will come when Israel will be converted to Christ. 'For I would not have you ignorant, brethren, of this mystery (lest you should be wise in your own conceits) that blindness in part has happened in Israel, until the fulness of the Gentiles should come in. And so all Israel should be saved, as it is written: There shall come out of Sion, He that shall deliver and shall turn away ungodliness from Jacob. And this is to them my covenant: when I shall take away their sins'.[3] I do not think that there is any temerity in saying that Mary's rôle in the world's salvation will be understood by man completely only when the Jewish race, fully converted to Christ, will own her as the one daughter of David through whom the whole economy of the supernatural order had to pass in virtue of her divine motherhood.

[1] Gal. iii. 16.   [2] Luke i. 32.   [3] Rom. xi. 25-27.

It has always been difficult for a certain class of minds to see in Mary more than the parent of the human nature of Christ, to give Mary more than a mere ministerial, instrumental rôle of supplying the *caro*, flesh, in the Christian mystery of the *Verbum caro factum*, the Word made flesh. The Catholic Church, on the contrary, has never hesitated in making Mary the true natural Mother of the whole Person of Christ, the Mother of God. The juridical transmission through Mary, in virtue of her full and true motherhood, of the great promise can be quoted as an evidence of the exactness of official Catholic thought. It is only a complete person, a person *sui iuris*, that can be considered as an heir. So Christ's whole divine Person was heir to the promise. The parent who transmits the promise to the last heir, is of necessity parent in the full sense to that person; so Mary had to be parent to the complete Person of the Son of God if the old order of the promise was to unite Abraham and Christ in one legal bond of supernatural predestination.

We may conclude these considerations on the juridical import- ance of Mary's motherhood in the eternal economy of the super- natural with a doctrine propounded by St. Thomas Aquinas with all the loving reverence of one who understood, as far as human intellect can understand it, that wonderful blending of motherhood and virginity. In common with many other writers on things divine, St. Thomas makes use of the expression *purissimi sanguines*, the most pure blood, to describe what were the human elements out of which the Holy Ghost fashioned the Body of the Son of God in the womb of Mary.[1] On the one hand, we must give to Mary the whole physio- logical rôle of maternity; on the other, we have in her case to dis- card every element, however remote, that depends for its fertilisa- tion and fructification on the intervention of sex-factors. Christian Doctors have thought that the expression *purissimi sanguines* meets this twofold requirement of maternity and virginity, that the *purissimi sanguines* are all that is required to make of Christ the great Seed, to whom promises were made in Abraham. If anything is abundantly clear in the Scriptures it is the rôle of natural parent- hood in the transmission of the great promise. 'For nowhere doth He take hold of the angels, but of the seed of Abraham he taketh hold.'[2] Mary's *purissimi sanguines* were the seed of Abraham, and in

[1] *S. Th.* III, Quest. xxxi, Art. 5.   [2] Heb. ii. 16.

them, as in most precious pearls, there was the virtue and the truth of the whole supernatural order of promise. But the very might of that promise, suspended, as it were, in the *purissimi sanguines* of the Virgin, makes it more imperative for us to conclude that in Mary's bosom not one of the developments that go to make natural maternity could ever have been absent. Mary did not do less for her Child than other mothers do for their offspring. It all points to a 'taking hold' of Mary's life-blood by the power of the Most High, in a way that is unsurpassed in the whole realm of nature and grace, with the exception of the Eucharistic Transubstantiation.

In the Eucharistic Transubstantiation it would seem at first sight that the whole physical order of the bodily substance had been suspended; yet the precise result of the words of Consecration is Christ's true physical Body, the Body born from Mary the Virgin. *Ave, verum corpus, natum ex Maria Virgine*; such are the words of the Church when the consecrated Host is worshipped. So, likewise, in the Incarnation, it would seem as if all the laws that govern man's descent had been put aside; but the reality is very different. The reality is a motherhood most perfect and true in every sense, a motherhood capable of the greatest human responsibilities as well as of relationships with God Himself such as no other creature possesses. This, then, seems to me the peculiar characteristic which both the Eucharist and the divine motherhood have in common, that in both instances the apparent over-ruling of natural laws by God's omnipotence produces results which are of the same kind as the realities thus suspended, though they be of an infinitely higher order; in one case you have Christ's Body and Blood instead of the natural substance of bread and wine; in the other you have divine maternity instead of human conception.

CHAPTER VIII

The Blessed Fruit of Mary's Womb

MARY'S visit to her cousin Elizabeth was the occasion of one of the greatest miracles in the purely spiritual realm: the sanctification of John the Baptist in his mother's womb. 'For behold as soon as the voice of thy salutation sounded in my ears, the infant in my womb leaped for joy.'[1] Christian tradition holds that the soul of John at that moment received sanctifying grace, Mary's sweet voice being like the sacramental instrument of the supernatural transformation. But the source of the grace that came to the soul of John was the ever blessed Fruit hidden in Mary's bosom. Mary brought into Elizabeth's house the personal fulness of all grace in the Blessed Thing that was still part of her own maiden life. It would be an inadequate treatment of our sublime subject, the divine motherhood, if we neglected to consider the teachings of Catholic theology concerning the bodily and spiritual conditions of the blessed Fruit of Mary's womb, of the Holy Thing that sanctified the soul of John, and made the infant leap for joy in the mother's womb. We could never understand fully the spirit of the *Magnificat* unless we remembered what was the Life that was throbbing within Mary's bosom when she spoke her immortal Canticle.

Here we may leave the text of St. Luke's Gospel and take for our guide St. Thomas Aquinas, the great theologian of the Incarnation. In the Third Part of his *Summa*, the 33rd and 34th Questions, the holy Doctor treats of the state of the *Proles*, the divine embryo in Mary's womb, and its perfections. There are two main principles which ought to govern our thoughts when so many times each day in reciting the 'Hail Mary', with Elizabeth we bless Mary in the Fruit of her womb. The first is this: there was not the minutest fraction of time in which the new Thing made of Mary's blood was not God. The second, which is a logical consequence of the first, is thus formulated by St. Thomas: 'The mystery of the Incarnation is considered as a condescension of the fulness of the Godhead into human nature, rather than the promotion of human nature, already existing,

[1] Luke i. 44.

as it were, to the Godhead.'[1] I do not say that these two principles stand at the head of the treatises mentioned; but an analysis of all our Doctor says makes it clear that they are really at the heart of all his doctrine on Our Lady's wonderful secret.

In virtue of the first principle, which is of strict Catholic faith, we have to admit that, whatever may be the generative process with other human beings, in the case of Christ's conception there never was anything but a clearly defined human embryo, with an immortal soul. It is against the very laws of the Incarnation to suppose that at any moment, however brief, the new Life that stirred within Mary's life was not the life of a bodily organism animated with a rational, immortal soul. The presence of the intellectual soul from the very start is indispensable to the Hypostatic Union; the divine Person of God the Son took flesh by means of that immortal human soul, not vice versa; for, says St. Thomas: 'The flesh would not have been assumable [in the Hypostatic Union], except by its relation to the rational soul, through which it becomes human flesh.'[2] This rational soul, again, had full intellectual activity, perfect use of all its specifically spiritual power; it had freedom of will, freedom of choice, a clear vision of all things intellectual. It was an intellect of full maturity and a will of perfect manhood. Here our second principle helps us to extend this subject still further. The blessed Fruit of Mary's womb had all the fulness of grace, the full power of meriting eternal life for those who were to be redeemed; beatific vision was as complete in that soul from the first moment, as it ever was after, even on the Resurrection morning. Christ was the perfect 'comprehensor', i.e. One who had the clear beatific vision of God in the very first instant of His being conceived.[3] If Heaven was ever encompassed within a creature, Mary was its abode during the nine months of her pregnancy.

In our days there is a distinct tendency among writers on the mystery of the Incarnation to make the Redeemer of mankind subject to that idolized theory of modern thinkers, the ascent from a lower life to a higher. Whatever may be the merits of such a philosophy, it is distinctly repugnant to those who grasp the mystery of the Incarnation more completely to associate this way of thinking

---

[1] *S. Th.* III, Quest. xxxiv, Art. 1, ad 1.   [2] *S. Th.* III, Quest. vi, Art. 1.
[3] *S. Th.* III, Quest. xxxiv, Art. 4.

with the Fruit of Mary's womb. There we have not a struggle heavenwards, but we have heaven opened, and the plenitude of grace coming out of it descending towards man. Therefore our theology starts with infinite fulness of grace, light and power, in the Holy Thing that rests in Mary's virginal bosom. Christian sanctity, in its vaster aspect, is not a struggle from poverty to possession; but it is an immense, infinite possession from the very start, from the womb of God's Mother, from the most indivisible point of inception; the second act in the drama of sanctity, the properly human act, is that 'of His fulness we all have received; and grace for grace.'[1] For a woman to bear in her bosom a Being of such spiritual magnitude is truly to be the Mother of God. The most inalienable of all motherly functions, that of giving of her own life-blood to build up the growing organism of the Man-Child within her, was indeed for Mary divine motherhood, because she was building up the Body of One who was God, not unconsciously, in a state of dormancy, as it were, but in the full splendour of the saints, *in splendoribus sanctorum.*

With regard to the strictly bodily condition of the blessed Fruit of Mary's womb, we have to admit, of course, that Christ's sense life was not developed until after His birth. Consequently such mental life as depended on a developed sense life had to await the natural maturity of time, as with all other human beings. What we have said about the completeness of the intellectual life of the soul of Christ in the womb of Mary in no wise does away with the reality of His embryonic state.

I must ask my readers not to exact more from me on this subject. The Church, in her Liturgy, has found the very words becoming such a mystery. She apostrophises Mary: 'O Virgin of virgins, how will this be, because no one was ever like thee before, and no one will ever be like thee again?' The divine Mother is made to reply: 'Daughters of Jerusalem, why do you wonder at me? The Thing you see is a divine mystery.' *O Virgo virginum, quomodo fiet istud, quia nec primam similem visa es nec habere sequentem? Filia Ierusalem, quid me admiramini? Divinum est mysterium hoc, quod cernitis.*[2]

---

[1] John i. 16.   [2] Officium Exspectationis Partus B. M. V.

CHAPTER IX

The Twofold Birth of the Son of God

BIRTH is the only event in Christ's career of which it can be said that it took place twice, once in eternity, and once in time. In all correctness of language we may say He was born twice over. Suppose a man were to run two races, with an interval of time between the two events; it would certainly not be true to say that it was only one race because it was the same person who ran twice. So it would be against all the laws of thought to say that Christ has only one birth, because the same Person, Christ, is born on both occasions. This comparison comes from St. Thomas himself.[1] The holy Doctor adds that there is much more reason for making one and the same Christ have two distinct births than for saying of one and the same man that he ran two races, when there was an interval of time between the two efforts; for in Christ's twofold birth there is the distinction between time and eternity, not only between one time and another as in the case of the two races. One of Christ's births is in eternity, and can only be in eternity; the other is in time, and can only be in finite duration. It is this radical distinction that makes birth with the Son of God a twofold event, a double splendour. We say very truly then that one and the same Person, Christ, is born in eternity from the Father, and in time from Mary.

The first birth of the Son of God is thus described in Psalm 109: 'With Thee is the principality in the day of Thy strength: in the brightness of the saints: from the womb before the day-star I begot Thee.' The narrative of the second birth has gladdened the hearts of all Christian generations; it is the earliest supernatural impression which the little Catholic child receives, and no scene has so captivated the imagination of millions as does Christ's crib, with its angels and its shepherds. The words of St. Luke that are the counterpart of David's marvellous vision in the psalm of the eternal birth are nearly as few and as succinct as in that oracle, though they be a narrative, not a prophecy: 'And she brought forth her firstborn Son, and wrapped Him up in swaddling clothes and laid Him in a

[1] S. Th. III, Quest. xxxv, Art. 2, ad 4.

manger.'[1] The contrast between the two births of one and the same Son of God has been the theme of the preachers of all times. As I am concerned exclusively with the theme of the divine motherhood, it is for me to point out, not the external contrasts in the circumstances of the two births, but the similarity which is established between Mary and the Eternal Father through the fact that Christ is born as truly from the one as from the other. All created perfection is a ray from God's own light; it is a resemblance of God. No higher metaphysical explanation can be given of the meaning of the universe than to say it is a resemblance of God, that its ultimate destiny is to represent Deity in a finite way. The eternal generation of the Word, the birth of the Son from the Father, would seem to belong too exclusively to God's inner life to be communicable to the created universe, to have any resemblance in the realm of nature and grace. Yet Mary is God's resemblance in this very thing, the birth of the Son, the second Person of the Trinity. When we meditate on the Incarnation there is a certain danger against which we have to be on our guard: we might too easily suppose that there is no life-development in the Incarnation, that it is all a series of miracles, and that therefore no biological conclusions could be deduced from it with any certainty. So we might exaggerate the miraculous side of Christ's birth from Mary, and thus unconsciously deprive Mary of the true glories of motherhood, making the blessed maternity into a mere instrument of God's omnipotence. But if Catholic theology insists on anything it is on this, that Mary is not a miraculous Mother to the Son of God, but a natural Mother. *Sic igitur ex parte Matris nativitas illa fuit naturalis, sed parte operationis Spiritus Sancti fuit miraculosa: unde Beata Virgo est vera et naturalis Mater Christi:* 'From the Mother's side Christ's birth was a natural birth, but from the side of the Holy Ghost's working it was a miraculous birth; therefore the Blessed Virgin is a true and natural Mother to Christ.'[2] I thought it worth quoting the Latin text of St. Thomas in the enunciation of this most important truth; the human birth of Our Lord was miraculous only from the side of the active principle, the Holy Ghost; but Mary's own motherhood, though begun miraculously, developed naturally. The initial miracle, great as it was, in no wise curtailed the life-functions which naturally belong to a

---

[1] Luke ii. 7.   [2] S. Th. III, Quest. xxxv, Art. 3, ad 2.

mother. It ought not to be difficult then to see how birth of one and the same Person, the divine Son, brings Mary near to God, gives her the most perfect resemblance to God's internal life. The second Person of the Trinity came forth naturally, through birth, from the Father. The birth of God takes Mary out of the ordinary plane of sanctity and gives her a place no other creature can share. It is as true to say that God is born of the Virgin as to say that God is born of God. We do say of course that Mary is Mother to the Son of God, not through the divine nature of that Person, but through His human nature; divinity was not formed from Mary's most pure blood, but only humanity. This distinction, however, in no wise does away with the greater truth that Mary is truly a God-bearer, not merely a man-bearer. Theologians give an illustration to enable us more easily to understand this. In each human being the soul comes directly from God, whilst the body owes its origin to the factors of parental generation; but who would ever say that a mother is mother, not to her boy, but merely to his body? She is mother to the whole person. So likewise in the Incarnation; of Mary a Child was born who is the Son of God, born of God from all eternity. Moreover, the sacred Humanity which owes its life to Mary's most pure blood is not a simple human nature; it is a deified Humanity, united hypostatically with the Eternal Word; just as the ordinary human body that is built up in a mother's womb is not merely an organism, but an organism penetrated through and through by the presence of an immortal spirit, the rational soul. As we saw in a previous chapter, Mary was giving of her life to an Organism in which there was the clear vision of God, in virtue of the very laws of life belonging intrinsically to It, because It lived and existed through divine existence, the existence of the divine Word. When shall we grasp the great truth that Christ's human nature was raised up to the plane of the infinite through Hypostatic Union? Even if we were to confine our attention exclusively to the human nature of Christ in Mary's childbirth, we should still be in presence of a Mother who bore an infinitely Holy Thing. But Mary is the Mother of the whole Person of Christ, and from the highest summits of heaven to the farthest ends of the universe the mystery of God's birth is found to exist only in two forms, in the Eternal Father and in Mary.

The solemn announcement of Christmas Day, in the Roman

Martyrology, may fitly be quoted here: *Anno imperii Octaviani Augusti quadragesimo secundo, toto orbe in pace composito, sexta mundi aetate, Iesus Christus aeternus Deus, aeternusque Patris Filius, mundum volens adventu suo piissimo consecrare, de Spiritu Sancto conceptus, novemque post conceptionem decursis mensibus in Bethlehem Iudae nascitur ex Maria Virgine factus Homo:* 'In the forty-second year of the rule of Octavianus Augustus, whilst the whole universe was enjoying peace, the sixth age of the world, Jesus Christ the Eternal God and Son of the Eternal Father, in order that He might sanctify the world through His merciful coming, having been conceived of the Holy Ghost, and nine months having passed since His conception, is born in Bethlehem of Juda from Mary the Virgin, being made Man.' Unless we give to Christ's second birth an infinite spiritual significance we shall never be able to understand this language of the Church. If the first birth, the eternal birth, is the source of all life, so is the second birth, the birth from Mary. *Hodie nobis de coelo pax vera descendit; hodie per totum mundum melliflui facti sunt coeli; hodie illuxit nobis dies redemptionis novae, reparationis antiquae, felicitatis aeternae:* 'To-day true peace came down to us from heaven; to-day over all the world the heavens distilled honey; to-day there shone for us the day of the new redemption, of the long-expected restoration, of the eternal happiness.' Such words as these make up the Christmas Liturgy, and show very clearly how, in the mind of the Catholic Church, Christ's second birth is an event of infinite splendour, of endless vitality; very often the words applicable to the first birth are applied to the second, as the two births, though such distinct events, have a common characteristic of spiritual immensity. But in the centre of all this glory is the Virgin Mother whose womb brought forth Him to whom the Eternal Father says: 'From the womb before the day-star I begot Thee.'[1]

We may conclude this chapter with the principal Collect of Christmas Day, with its clear enunciation as to the spiritual power contained in Christ's second birth, the birth from Mary: *Concede, quaesumus, omnipotens Deus: ut nos Unigeniti tui nova per carnem Nativitas liberet; quos sub peccati iugo vetusta servitus tenet.* 'Grant, we beseech Thee, almighty God, that the new birth of Thine only-begotten Son in the flesh may deliver us, who are held by the old bondage under the yoke of sin.'

[1] Psalm 109.

CHAPTER X

The Human Messenger of the Divine Motherhood

IN Gabriel's great message there is a complete absence of any allusion to Christ's human career with its terrible conclusion. The Angel speaks of the eternal, unchanging glories of the Child that will be born of Mary; of the sufferings and the death that were to be the condition of that glory there is not the remotest mention. It was the office of the heavenly messenger to announce to Mary the full, the eternal nature of her motherhood; the temporary, earthly eclipse of that great glory was not a necessary part of his message. It was reserved to a human being, to an old man, to complete the great gospel of the divine motherhood. Simeon, the just man, who is nearing the end of his own days, speaks the second portion of that evangel of love and tenderness, Mary's maternity. Gabriel the Archangel and Simeon the old man pour out from their minds what the Spirit of God had put there: the great secret of one who is at the same time Mother of God and Mother of the Man who is to die on the Cross like a criminal.

Gabriel's message is quite exclusive; it contains nothing except the idea of Sonship, divine and human. The Child whom Mary is to call Jesus is the Son of God and the Son of David, and the eternal kingship of the Child is the result of that double Sonship. The coming down of the Holy Ghost upon Mary, the overshadowing of her person by the power of the Most High, are explanations of that double Sonship, and they reconcile virginity and motherhood. The Angel is the messenger of the divine motherhood in its strictest acceptation; he departs after having spoken in human terms 'the mystery which hath been hidden from all eternity in God who created all things.'[1] Christ's work and mission is not told yet to Mary. Joseph, her spouse, is the first to hear something of that secondary mystery, the work of Redemption to be carried out by Mary's Son. The primary mystery, the divine Sonship itself, is Mary's personal secret. 'Joseph, son of David, fear not to take unto thee Mary thy wife, for that which is conceived in her, is of the

[1] Eph. iii. 9.

Holy Ghost. And she shall bring forth a Son: and thou shalt call His name Jesus. For He shall save His people from their sins.'[1] To Simeon further light is bestowed on the immense temporal mission of the Child, and he sings his moving *Nunc dimittis*, the glorious canticle of the rôle of Mary's Son here on earth. 'He also took Him into his arms, and blessed God and said: Now Thou dost dismiss Thy servant, O Lord, according to Thy word, in peace. Because my eyes have seen Thy salvation, which Thou hast prepared before the face of all peoples: a light to the revelation of the Gentiles and the glory of Thy people Israel.'[2] The Evangelist adds that the Child's 'father and mother were wondering at those things which were spoken concerning Him.' This confirms what has just been said about the restricted nature of the message delivered by Gabriel: Mary had heard nothing of Christ's temporal mission; Joseph had received the bare announcement of the redemption of the Jewish people from their sins; but Simeon in his ecstasies breaks down all the barriers: the whole world is to come under the powerful influence of the Child; all peoples, and, O! new message of grace! even the Gentiles will live in the light of the countenance of that little One.

From the Child Simeon turns to the Mother, and then he completes Gabriel's message in a most unexpected way. The holy man scans the features of the beautiful Child; there, in the light of God, he sees the lines of a terrible fate. Did he see the Cross? Most likely not; but he saw enough to make his noble heart go out to the sweetest of all creatures standing before him in the full joy of an incomparably pure maternity. 'And Simeon blessed them, and said to Mary His Mother: Behold this Child is set for the fall and for the resurrection of many in Israel and for a sign which shall be contradicted. And thy own soul a sword shall pierce, that, out of many hearts thoughts may be revealed.'[3] The meaning of the divine motherhood is now completely told. It implies greatest sorrow as well as greatest joy. No such message was given to Elizabeth, John's mother. Her son was destined to be put to death by the basest of human beings, the corrupt creatures of an infamous court. It was a grim destiny, though a noble ending to the Nazarene's austere life. But the Mother of God had a maternity which was inseparable from

[1] Matt. i. 20, 21.   [2] Luke ii. 28-32.   [3] Luke ii. 34, 35.

God's highest attribute, truth. She was to suffer from the opposition between truth and falsehood, between light and darkness: 'But now you seek to kill Me, a Man who have spoken the truth to you, which I have heard of God. This Abraham did not.'[1] This is the way Christ, in the fulness of His Manhood, addresses the Jewish rulers. He thus gives us the clearest commentary on the words of Simeon. To rule in the house of Jacob for ever was one of the essentials of the divine Sonship according to Gabriel's message. The bitter opposition of that house of Jacob was Mary's first great trial of soul, when she followed her Son in His public life. There must be something evil in the heart of her own people, something horribly dark which she had not suspected. Out of many hearts thoughts were being constantly revealed which ought not to belong to the family of Abraham: 'This Abraham did not.' The matchless power of truth that was in Jesus provoked the hatred of a class of so-called religious men who had falsified in their own conscience, and in the conscience of their fellow Jews, the very idea of God. 'It is My Father that glorifieth Me, of whom you say that He is your God. And you have not known Him, but I know Him. And if I shall say that I know Him not, I shall be like to you, a liar. But I do know Him, and do keep His word. Abraham your father rejoiced that he might see My day: he saw it, and was glad.'[2] These words, which are a sequel to the words just quoted, express better than anything else the radical conflict of ideals between Christ and the men who boasted of their descent from Abraham. Both in virtue of her own divine motherhood, as she was the Mother of the One who came 'full of grace and truth', and in virtue of her being the repository of all the promises made to Abraham and his seed, Mary's heart was to be pierced with a sword of sorrow, and her grief would be such as no woman has ever known.

Mary's motherhood never knew the physical pains that are the inseparable condition of all maternity since the Fall. She was entirely free from the law which God laid upon Eve: 'In sorrow shalt thou bring forth children.'[3] St. Thomas, speaking of Christ's birth, says that in that birth there was no kind of pain, as there was no diminution of virginal integrity; there was instead the greatest possible unadulterated joy because the Man God was born into the world: *Sed fuit ibi maxima iucunditas ex hoc quod homo Deus est natus in*

---

[1] John viii. 40.   [2] John viii. 54-56.   [3] Gen. iii. 16.

mundum.[1] Nor does it appeal to the theological mind to insinuate that perhaps such pains of childbirth, if they had been allowed to take place, might have contributed towards the fulness of Redemption; for why should not Christ be born in pain as He was to die in pain? Would it not add to the perfection of the Great Sacrifice to have the sorrow of His birth added to the sorrows of His death? But again: *Dolores parientis matris non pertinebant ad Christum, qui pro peccatis nostris satisfacere veniebat,* says St. Thomas.[2] The pains of His Mother in childbirth did not belong to Christ's mission, who came to make satisfaction for our sins. Such pains would have been entirely outside Himself; they have nothing to do with His own sacrifice.

But the sorrows predicted by Simeon were to be of a different nature; they depended completely on Christ's sorrows, they were an echo of those sorrows, and Mary's motherhood has been the most sorrowful of all motherhoods, because she was truly the Mother of the One whom the prophet calls the 'Man of sorrows.'[3] Just as Catholic thought instinctively recoils from the notion that there might have been pain in the birth of Christ, so is it full of the immense atoning value of Mary's sorrows in conjunction with her Son's rejection by His own people. I said in a previous chapter that Mary's maternity was more than an instrumental maternity; Mary shares to its full extent, with the Eternal Father, the parentage of the Incarnate Son of God; she has all the rights and privileges, as well as all the love and tenderness of a parent; as the Mother of the Son of God she was admitted into the secrets of the awful spiritual drama that led to the fall of many in Israel, that led even to the Cross. As a mother Mary did not suffer physically; but morally her sufferings went as far as the divine parenthood itself. It was not the body, but the soul of that parent that was to make the supreme sacrifice: 'And thy own soul a sword shall pierce.' Gabriel had spoken to Mary of her Child's right over the throne of David: 'The Lord shall give unto Him the throne of David His father.' Mary, in her own Canticle, the *Magnificat,* had sung with such enthusiasm Israel's privilege through the mystery that was in her: 'He hath received Israel His servant, being mindful of His mercy.' But Mary was also destined to hear Israel cry out, in a wild outburst of hatred

---

[1] *S. Th.* III, Quest. xxxv, Art. 6.   [2] *Ibidem.*   [3] Is. liii. 3.

against her Son: 'His blood be upon us and upon our children!' There is in Mary's sorrow something patriarchal, something that could only be felt by a soul in intimate contact with the immensities of God's judgments over mankind.

CHAPTER XI

Hope and Wonder in the Divine Motherhood

IT seems to be the general persuasion of the Church that the great mystery of the Incarnation took effect at the moment when the Angel left Mary, after she had said: 'Behold the handmaid of the Lord; be it done to me according to thy word!' The Angel then departed from her but not without having adored the God made flesh. It is true that Elizabeth, Mary's cousin, when the latter visited her, still speaks of things that will come in the future: 'Blessed art thou that hast believed, because those things shall be accomplished that were spoken to thee by the Lord.'[1] At the same time Elizabeth addresses Mary as one already blessed with the glories of motherhood: 'Blessed art thou among women, and blessed is the Fruit of thy womb.' So there is no room for doubt as to Mary's blessed pregnancy, when she went to visit Elizabeth. It is necessary therefore to connect Elizabeth's prophecy with Gabriel's words as to the future greatness of the Child to be born, the throne of David, and the eternal rule in the house of Jacob.

The mysterious Conception was an accomplished fact; the divine Birth was Mary's certain and joyful hope; but as to the future greatness of the Child much was still obscure to her. Elizabeth's spirit, moved by the Holy Ghost, had leaped forward into futurity, and had seen the accomplishment of the wonderful things predicted to Mary. Mary's faith as to the first portion of the angelic message was to be an assurance to her of the gradual accomplishment of the second part, the promissory part, of the same heavenly oracle. It is no doubt in connection with Christ's eternal mission, and its

[1] Luke i. 45.

gradual development, that there was at times wonder and astonishment in Mary's mind. The central fact of the divine Sonship of Jesus was as clear to her as the noontide light; but the way in which Christ's great domination would be accomplished was not yet revealed to her. She believed in it firmly, as she believed in the mystery which was already contained in her chaste bosom; the manner of it, however, had not been made so clear to her as the mode of the Incarnation itself. So it happened that Mary did not always understand when it was a question of Christ's external influence, open or secret; with Joseph she wondered as to the meaning of it all. 'And He said to them: How is it that you sought Me? Did you not know that I must be about My Father's business? And they understood not the word that He spoke unto them.'[1] It must be admitted that little has been revealed to us concerning the ways and the times of Christ's triumph and sovereignty; what we know about Christ's Person is very much more than what we know about His actual influence on mankind. The Mother of God herself seems to have received her lights in the same proportion: her knowledge as to Christ's Person was immense; her knowledge of the ways in which He would become the Ruler in the House of Jacob for ever seems to have been much less explicit. Here one may quote Christ's words to the group of disciples who went up with Him to Mount Olivet on the Ascension day. 'They therefore who were come together asked Him, saying: Lord, wilt Thou at this time restore again the kingdom to Israel? But He said to them: It is not for you to know the times or moments which the Father hath put in His own power; but you shall receive the power of the Holy Ghost coming upon you, and you shall be witnesses unto Me in Jerusalem, and in all Judea, and Samaria, and even to the uttermost part of the earth.'[2] There is given to the disciples a most explicit knowledge of Christ, of the Holy Ghost, of the specifically spiritual means that will save mankind; but the knowledge of God's external providence in shaping human events so as to make them subservient to the triumph of Christ's grace is not bestowed on them in the same measure. Our Lady is no exception to this dispensation, though we may admit in her case a much larger measure of vision of the future. Nothing compels us to believe that Christ's external career was manifested to her

---

[1] Luke ii. 49, 50.   [2] Acts i. 6-8.

at once, at an early stage; it unfolded itself but gradually to her eyes; she wondered and suffered; though she could never suffer scandal, and she soon came to comprehend the fact, hidden for so long from the disciples, that Christ 'ought to have suffered these things, and so to enter into His glory.'[1]

In her glorious Canticle of thanksgiving, the *Magnificat*, the Mother of God renders in her own words, with the exultation of a supremely pure human heart, the burden of the message delivered by Gabriel. The song contains no dark anticipations, any more than did Gabriel's announcement. Her own maternity, her people's joy in the new King whom Gabriel had announced, such is the double theme of that immortal outpouring of a maiden's spirit. The Lord had done great things to her, and all generations shall call her blessed; but the thought of her fathers, of Abraham, never leaves her; the seed of Abraham is in her own virginal bosom. One might almost call Mary's song a national anthem, the hymn of Israel, if one did not bear in mind the Messianic rôle of Abraham's race, and its privilege of making the Incarnate God a perfect participant of the human nature, by bestowing upon Him the blood that is common to all those that are descended from Adam. When Mary sings of her people, of Israel the servant of God, she does so not as all other Jewish singers had done, as Deborah and Anna had done; her song is the very heart of the incomparable new mystery, the Incarnation; the great things done in her by Him who is mighty, and whose name is holy, are the promises made to Abraham, passed on from generation to generation, and now come to their perfect fulfilment in the 'Seed', in the Holy Thing that is in her bosom; she, Mary, stands between the generations of the promise and the generations of the reality; and she, the heiress of the blessings bestowed upon the patriarchs, will be the blessed one for all ages to come. Never did maternity embrace a greater sphere, and never had it been so personally, so supremely triumphant. Mary then understood fully the Incarnation in what might be called its life aspect; she understood the nature of the new life that was in her, and how life would come from her; but it is impossible for us to tell whether at that moment she knew clearly the other aspect of the same mystery, the tragic and agonizing death. She knew then that all generations would

[1] Luke xxiv. 26.

call her blessed, that she had been made the Mother of the living; but the scene on Calvary, when her crucified Son gave her as Mother to redeemed man, in the person of John, was no doubt a mystery hidden from her eyes. St. John begins the narrative of Christ's Passion with the words: 'Jesus, therefore, knowing all things that should come upon Him, went forth and said to them: Whom seek ye?'[1] This clear foreknowledge of His own career seems to have been the exclusive property of Christ; He had such knowledge from His very infancy. Mary's initiation into the mystery of her Son's Passion and Death was gradual, and often she must have wondered what would be the next terrible thing she had to learn.

Chapter XII

The Sweetness of the Divine Motherhood

THERE could be no greater danger for Christian truth than to neglect its majestic, its lofty aspect for the sake of more sentimental elements. The dignified smile of Christian truth is that of a queen, not the bubbling laughter of a child. Nevertheless, it is a wonderful smile, and one that enraptures the intellect as well as the heart. The divine motherhood itself is a thing of wondrous majesty, an immense beacon of immaculate white light, penetrating like a two-edged sword into the intellect of man and angel. The divine motherhood is a glorious system of highest metaphysics well calculated to captivate the attention of the most searching and exacting mind. Is there anything, after the Hypostatic Union itself, more gratifying, more absorbing for the speculative mind than the doctrine of Christ's birth in time, with Christ's eternal birth going on in the unchangeable eternity of the Father? Yet this belongs to the very essence of the divine motherhood. But sweetness comes out of the mouth of the Strong One. If Christian theology has its smile, the divine motherhood is that smile. Outside the clear vision of God nothing can reveal so vividly as the divine motherhood that

[1] John xviii. 4.

aspect of God to the contemplation of which the psalmist invites us when he says: 'O, taste, and see that the Lord is sweet.'[1] So the attitude of the Catholic mind has always been this; it takes for granted that between Our Lord and His blessed Mother there was a love of sweetness and tenderness such as the world had never witnessed before, and will never witness again. We feel instinctively that Mary was the closest and most intimate friend Jesus had here on earth, and that between them there was such similarity of character as to make theirs a friendship stronger than death. All the passionate outpourings of love which make the Canticle of Canticles the highest expression of human sentiment we apply to Mary enamoured of her divine Son.

We call Mary the greatest of all the martyrs, because in her love she suffered more than any other human creature. The tenderness of the divine Mother for her divine Infant appeals to all men. But it is an attitude that is exclusively, I might almost say temperamentally, Catholic to see the same tenderness of love existing between Mary and her Son at all stages of His life, to consider that there is the same virginal spirit of tenderest affection in the Pietà which we naturally attribute to the Madonna. In their striking preference for the Pietà, the Mother of Dolours, our Catholic forefathers showed their Christian temperament; they knew instinctively that between Jesus and His Mother the sweetness of Bethlehem never ceased, that it rather grew in strength and intensity as the two wonderful lives reached maturity and revealed their unsearchable depths. Such Catholic sentiment is totally foreign to the Protestant. The Protestant has made capital out of Christ's words at the wedding feast of Cana: 'And Jesus saith to her: Woman, what is that to Me and to thee? My hour is not yet come.'[2] For him these words cloud the whole relationship between Mother and Son. It is certainly astonishing to see what an unfortunate rôle these words have played in our Mariology since the Mother of God has not been loved as a Mother by the whole of Christendom. A Catholicism that loves this Mother takes it for granted that the words are no rift in the profound harmony of love between Jesus and Mary; it knows that such words could come from Jesus, still a child at heart, loving His Mother then as He did when an Infant at Nazareth. The nature of

[1] Ps. xxxiii. 9.   [2] John ii. 4.

the emphasis we lay on that text, or others of a similar turn, depends entirely on our initial sentiment about the relation that existed between Christ and His Mother. I believe that no friendship ever existed that was like that of Jesus and Mary; even if there were some severity in Christ's phrase, I take it that it had no such effect on Mary's mind, and indeed it obviously had not, as appears from the sequel of the same Gospel narrative. There was, either in Christ's way of uttering them or in the deeper meaning of the words themselves, something that made them truly expressions of love and trust, a trust answered at once by Mary's complete confidence: 'His mother said to the waiters: Whatsoever He shall say to you, do ye.'[1] But your Protestant critic, starting with a very different attitude of mind, with a kind of jealousy of Mary's spiritual privilege, will read into the same words nothing less than a severe rebuke. His reading of this particular passage is coloured by a much darker mentality, the innate jealousies certain minds nourish against the excellency of that sweetest of all creatures, the ever-blessed Mother of God. But surely the Catholic attitude is the natural one; it is simply the outcome of the whole doctrine of the Incarnation. A sinless Mother, a virgin Mother, a Son who is God's Only-Begotten, everything that is holiest and highest; what could all this produce, asks the Catholic, except love, tenderness, sweetness of the most marvellous kind between the Mother and the Son? Why should there be anything but perfect love; what possible element is there that might prevent these two ever-blessed persons, Jesus and Mary, from tasting to the full the cup of created love?

So we take it for granted that the life at Nazareth was the happiest in the history of mankind. It is perhaps one of the most marvellous features of the Christian faith that it admits the immense life of the Incarnate Son of God could be contained within the limits of an ordinary human existence, the life of a carpenter of Nazareth: 'Is not this the carpenter, the Son of Mary?'[2] Contrary to all usual imaginings, we have in the Incarnation the element of the marvellous, of the superhuman in the highest degree, combined with the most absolute ordinariness of human conditions. We likewise admit, as an intuition of the heart as well as of the mind, that the immense love, the superhuman tenderness of the *Mater amabilis* had un-

[1] John ii. 5.   [2] Mark vi. 3.

restricted exercise in the daily contact of a model home. There was not, there could not be, the least incident, the least movement, which was not replete with divine sweetness of love during those many happy years. It is in that intercourse with the Son of God that Mary's absolute sinlessness becomes a positive, a living thing, as it means the power of communing with infinite sanctity without a blush, without a tremor, but, on the contrary, with the natural effusiveness of a beautiful mother.

Catholic love for the Mother of God reveals an artistic sense of restraint in its reluctance to ask for elaborate details of the life at Nazareth. We know that at Nazareth there dwells a life that is not of man's experience, hardly of man's comprehension. Is there anybody here on earth who knows what real love is, who could draw a picture of two lives of superhuman intensity finding, in their very intensity, a most complete blending of all their movements, affections, aspirations? Let me watch from the hill-top over Nazareth a woman going down to the well with the pitcher poised on her head, and a boy of fifteen at her side. I know that between the two there is a love such as is not found among the spirits that dwell before the throne of God. But I know, too, that I am not entitled to see more lest I die of wonderment. Our own too human intercourse is well described by St. Augustine in one of his sermons: 'Why do we all labour? Is it not because we are all mortal men, easily broken, weak, carrying earthen vessels which make strait room for each other?' Of such frailty we have the sad and constant experience. How the *Mater amabilis* dwelled with Him to whom the prophet gives the name of *Admirabilis* is to a great extent a mystery, a part of the vaster mystery of Christ's twofold birth.

It is evident that the Catholic view of the divine motherhood, as feebly portrayed in this chapter, must make a tremendous difference in our mental attitude towards the character of the Incarnation, nay, towards the character of God. The element of loving charm could never be excluded from a view of God and His dealings with men in minds that relish the sweetness of God's character. The Fatherhood of God is an idea far from exhaustive of God's nature. Alone it would isolate God from a vast part of our own nature. In the sweetness of the divine motherhood there is revealed to us something of God that is not directly contained in the idea of the divine Fatherhood; and nothing will ever replace in man's mind the wonderful influence of faith in Mary's love. Intellects devoid of that faith will never understand the true character of the God Incarnate; their Christianity will always be as the cold sun of a winter's day instead of the life-giving mellowness of the sun in Spring.

CHAPTER XIII

The Power of the Divine Motherhood

CATHOLIC theological thought is all in favour of the greatness of the creature; it starts with the metaphysical assumption that it is God's wonderful purpose to make the things He creates truly great and glorious. With the Psalmist the Catholic instinctively addresses God: 'Thou art the God that dost wonders.'[1] God is wonderful, not only in Himself, He is wonderful in His creatures; His creation, the thing that is outside Himself, is a source of endless wonderment to the truly Christian mind. Catholic theology has no jealousies for God's glory that are unwarranted; the greatness of the creature, far from throwing a dark shadow on God's glory, is on the contrary its brightest ray. The Catholic theologian, again, is far from any awkwardness of mind in assigning respectively God's greatness and the creature's greatness; the two are a wonderful blending of different perfections, the infinite and the finite. The two perfections are never opposed to each other, but are sweetly wedded together into an adorable harmony. God's interest is His creation, and the greater the creation, the happier the Catholic mind.

But Catholic theology goes one step further; it wants God's creative, productive, power to be communicated to the finite creation as far as is possible. Not only are we intensely happy to see God put outside Himself, into a separate mode of existence, things that so closely resemble Himself in splendour, but we know that God is not jealous of the very power that enables Him to do these

[1] Ps. lxxvi. 15.

marvels; He wants His creatures to share the same powers as far as their finiteness—the intrinsic condition of created things—allows. The only thing God does not give up is His glory of being the ultimate source of all perfection and power. But power, beyond measure and comprehension, power that stretches from end to end, He is willing to give. It is astonishing to read in our theology to what heights such productive power (whether in the spiritual or the natural order) can rise; the making of a thing from nothingness, *creatio ex nihilo*, seems to be the only clear case where created power is quite helpless. We love to see God surrounded by mighty creatures, by giants in mind and will. *Maior autem perfectio est, quod aliquid in se sit bonum, et etiam sit aliis causa bonitatis, quam si esset solummodo in se bonum. Et ideo sic Deus gubernat res, ut quasdam aliarum in gubernando causas instituat; sicut si aliquis magister discipulos suos non solum scientes faceret, sed etiam aliorum doctores:* 'It is a greater degree of excellency for a being to be good in itself, and at the same time a cause of perfection to other beings, than to be merely good in itself. God then so rules all things that He makes certain beings to be causative in their turn in the ruling of the universe; as a good teacher will do more than impart knowledge to his disciples, he will make them learned masters in their turn.'[1] It is a specifically Catholic attitude of mind to welcome created greatness and power in the beings endowed with reason and free will—angels and men. 'God is wonderful in His saints, the God of Israel is He who will give power and strength to His people.'[2] It is in this characteristic more than in any other that the Catholic mind differs so radically from the Protestant. It seems to us quite natural to find our saints and angels doing the mighty works of God, through their wonderful activities keeping the world from sinking into moral and physical chaos. Nor do we limit the powers of God's friends to any special activity; their power of prayer, for instance, is only one of the many potencies that are in them. They are powerful in most direct and efficacious ways, though these may be hidden from our mortal gaze.

These reflections of a general theological nature are not inappropriate at the end of my little treatise on the divine motherhood. Conscious or unconscious assimilation of the thoughts just

[1] S. *Th.* I, Quest. ciii, Art. 6.   [2] Ps. lxvii. 36.

enunciated constitutes Catholic devotion to the Mother of God, the *Virgo potens*. Divine motherhood is an immense power in the world of grace; the greatest, after the redemptive power of Christ. 'Thou art beautiful, O my love, sweet and comely as Jerusalem, terrible as an army set in array.'[1] These words, expressing at the same time greatest human endearment and an overwhelming sense of irresistible warlike strength, have always been applied to the blessed Mother of God by the Christian Liturgy. The idea of immense power in connection with divine motherhood is a most distinctively Catholic frame of mind. The very fact of the divine motherhood, of the second birth of the Son of God, is congenial to the Catholic mind in virtue of that intellectual blend which I have just described. One might say that the divine motherhood is a particular application of the more universal law that God communicates power and life to His creatures *ad infinitum*. Nothing comes more naturally to us than to address the Mother of God by those very titles which we give to God our Redeemer: *Salve, Regina, Mater misericordiae, vita, dulcedo et spes nostra*. We call her the Mother of mercy, we call her life, we call her sweetness, we call her our hope without any limitation of meaning, because we cannot see any limits to her greatness and power, though we know that there must be limits somewhere; but, wherever they may be, those limits will never be reached by another creature exploring, as it were, Mary's spiritual potency. In theory we know that Christ is the Author of mercy, He is our Life, Sweetness and Hope, in an infinitely higher way than is Mary; but this distinction need never enter into our practical devotion, because the height of Mary's spiritual stature will never be measured by man or angel. Adoration is due to God exclusively for this one reason that He is the Ultimate Source of all things. Whatever is not the First Cause of all things cannot be adored. In practice, then, we Catholics make this the only reservation with regard to the Mother of God. If there be limits to her greatness, those limits are beyond our purview. Christ's Redemption, being the act of God, is the ultimate cause and source of all grace; like creation itself it is a title to adoration. Mary's powerful rôle in the supernatural order of Redemption has again this one limitation: she is not the ultimate source and cause of the redemptive grace.

[1] Cant. of Cant. vi. 3.

There is another consideration which may help us better to understand the nature of the effective influence which the divine motherhood must for ever exert in the spiritual world. We too easily speak of the natural and the supernatural orders as of abstractions. The two orders are essentially two categories of rational beings; or, anyhow, a set of rational beings endowed with two different kinds of mental qualities. The supernatural order, to confine our attention to that for the moment, is anything but an abstract ideal, a mere theory, or even a series of phenomena. The supernatural order is essentially a class of rational beings in whom the higher life, a participation in God's life, is realized, and as it were personified. Christ, the Son of God made Man, is the central figure of that supernatural order, being, in His own Person, grace and truth. The supernatural order consists of the living, rational, creatures who with Christ share in the life of God. With a view to making the supernatural order glorious and wonderful, the jewel and crown of His whole creation, God makes great in grace those living creatures in whom that sublime gift, the divine Life, flows and throbs. So we need not be surprised to find individual, rational, creatures raised up so high through their participation in the divine Life. Divine motherhood is precisely this, that a rational creature, even a human creature, has been admitted to the greatest possible participation of the divine Life, after the Hypostatic Union itself. Mary in fact is a great and powerful, supernatural person, and to set any limits to the possibilities of her effective influence in the world of spirits is too arbitrarily to restrict what God has made greater than we can conceive. We know where the created differs from the Uncreated; but we do not know what are the limits to the spiritual powers of one who shares in divine Life to the extent of being the Mother of God. I might say that if we want to find limits to Mary's spiritual powers the burden of beating the bounds rests with us. God has put before our eyes in the divine motherhood a creature not of limits, but of grace beyond man's comprehension; limits, with Mary's spiritual estate, are very much after-thoughts; they are not suggested by what we know of her grace. We Catholics are satisfied with the radical difference between a creature and the Creator. But as for setting boundaries to the spiritual powers of the Mother of God, nothing in our mentality invites us to do so. The real distinction between the created and Uncreated does not lie directly in the fact that one is finite and the other is infinite; in higher metaphysics and theology distinction between the finite and the Infinite is less radical than the deeper distinction, that a being has all it has either from itself, or from another; it is either Absolute or contingent being. To have its being from Itself, and to be the cause and source of all other beings, is the exclusive property of the Uncreated; it is infinite therefore in every sense, as a result of this radical self-sufficiency. But in theology we do not necessarily begrudge the creature a certain infinitude, if that infinitude be compatible with the fact that it comes from Another, from the First Cause of all things. So we admit that there may be true infinitude in a creature, at least in a given direction, though it could never be an infinitude in every respect. In this sense then we generally say that the divine motherhood is an infinite dignity, a privilege that has no limits in excellence of relationship with God. We do not say that Mary is a being that is infinite, but we say that in Mary there is something which is truly infinite: her dignity as the Mother of God. The master of Thomas Aquinas, St. Albert the Great, has the following delightful phrase in a commentary on the text of the Gospel which narrates the Annunciation: *Filius infinitat matris bonitatem, infinita bonitas in fructu infinitam quandam adhuc ostendit in arbore bonitatem.* Rendered freely this means that Mary's Son gives infinitude to His Mother's excellence, there being in the tree which produces the fruit some of that infinite perfection which properly belongs to the fruit itself.

In practice the Catholic Church looks upon the Mother of God as being an unbounded power in the realm of grace; she is considered as the Mother of the redeemed on account of the universality of her grace; in virtue of her divine motherhood Mary is simply the greatest, the most effective, the most universal supernatural power in heaven and on earth, outside the Three Divine Persons.

CHAPTER XIV

An Invocation

TRUE civilisation is easily tested by its attitude towards motherhood. There can be no real refinement of human feeling where man's heart is not full of delicacies for the dignity of motherhood; therefore there can be no true civilisation where motherhood is either shunned or degraded. If there is anything that belongs to the health of nations, it is a loving reverence for the burdens of human motherhood. The very size of such a need ought to make it seem a supremely reasonable thing that God has given to mankind divine motherhood. Great as this gift is, it is not too great for human need; the dangers and servitudes that beset human motherhood in this corrupt world are so terrible that there is a kind of just proportion in this omnipotent act of God.

Christianity is the religion of birth. It starts with the eternal birth of its Head and Redeemer; it comes from the highest heavens to our earth through the birth from Mary the Virgin. It sums up its whole spiritual power in the word 'birth': 'Jesus answered and said to him: Amen, amen, I say to thee, unless a man be born again, he cannot see the kingdom of God. Nicodemus saith to Him: How can a man be born when he is old? Can he enter a second time into his mother's womb, and be born again? Jesus answered: Amen, amen, I say to thee, unless a man be born again of water and the Holy Ghost, he cannot enter into the kingdom of God. That which is born of the flesh is flesh; and that which is born of the Spirit is spirit. Wonder not that I said to thee: You must be born again.'[1] Christianity's moral power, Christianity's social contribution to the life of mankind is the sanctity and obligatoriness of the laws that govern the birth of man.

In Rome there is a shrine to the *Madonna del Parto*, the Madonna of the Child-birth. Rome's instinct and language are always true; they reveal a comprehension of divine things which has the characteristic of universality. The direct simplicity of such a title proves that in it the Christian man and woman have come very near to the

[1] John iii. 3-7.

Fountains of Life. For me the *Madonna del Parto* is a portion of that ever-blessed realm of thought whose outlines are sketched in the beginning of St. John's Gospel: 'In the beginning was the Word; and the Word was with God; and the Word was God. The same was in the beginning with God. All things were made by Him; and without Him was made nothing that was made. In Him was life; and the life was the light of men.'[1]

Ever blessed Mother of God, thy maternity fills my mind with raptures. Thou art the greatest mystery of life after the Triune God. Whence is this to me that the Mother of my Lord should be loved by me? But how could I fail to love this marvel of life? The Birth of the Word is eternal, unchanging; it was, it is, it always will be. The birth of the Child which is thine, O blessed Mother of God, I gaze upon as I should upon an immense lake on an island which the boundless sea holds encompassed on all sides: it is the Birth of God surrounded by a more immense Birth of God. Thou, O blessed Lady, art the island containing the one and contained by the other. From thee, as from a point of vantage, I hope to contemplate for ever the two Lives in which lies the happiness of all created intellects; the Life that is born in eternity and the Life that was born in time. There was a time when the world's evil frightened my soul, when I looked upon it with scared eyes and an anguished heart, as if it were something mighty with power and substance in it. But from the day when I began to understand thy motherhood more clearly, and to love it more ardently, my soul has ever made merry over the idle efforts of the princes of darkness to cow man's spirit, their vain attempts to establish a mendacious sovereignty of gloom. The Creator of the starry skies smiles sweetly at thee, O fairest of all women, and thou returnest His smile in triumphant peace; I know that with God smiling at His sweet Mother the grim powers of evil are already defeated.

[1] John i. 1-4.